RENEWALS 458-4574

DATE

MAR 2 5 2009

D0787907

WITHDRAWN
UTSA LIBRARIES

SELF-INJURY IN YOUTH

SELF-INJURY IN YOUTH

The Essential Guide to Assessment and Intervention

Mary K. Nixon ■ Nancy L. Heath

Routledge
Taylor & Francis Group
New York   London

Library
University of Texas
at San Antonio

Routledge
Taylor & Francis Group
270 Madison Avenue
New York, NY 10016

Routledge
Taylor & Francis Group
2 Park Square
Milton Park, Abingdon
Oxon OX14 4RN

© 2009 by Taylor & Francis Group, LLC
Routledge is an imprint of Taylor & Francis Group, an Informa business

Printed in the United States of America on acid-free paper
10 9 8 7 6 5 4 3 2 1

International Standard Book Number-13: 978-0-415-95725-0 (Hardcover)

Except as permitted under U.S. Copyright Law, no part of this book may be reprinted, reproduced, transmitted, or utilized in any form by any electronic, mechanical, or other means, now known or hereafter invented, including photocopying, microfilming, and recording, or in any information storage or retrieval system, without written permission from the publishers.

Trademark Notice: Product or corporate names may be trademarks or registered trademarks, and are used only for identification and explanation without intent to infringe.

Library of Congress Cataloging-in-Publication Data

Self-injury in youth : the essential guide to assessment and intervention / [edited by]
Mary K. Nixon and Nancy L. Heath.
    p. ; cm.
Includes bibliographical references and index.
ISBN 978-0-415-95725-0 (hardbound : alk. paper)
    1. Self-injurious behavior. 2. Self-mutilation. 3. Adolescent psychotherapy. I. Nixon,
Mary K. (Mary Kay) II. Heath, Nancy L.
    [DNLM: 1. Self-Injurious Behavior--diagnosis. 2. Adolescent. 3.
Psychotherapy--methods. 4. Self-Injurious Behavior--prevention & control. WM 165
S4655 2008]

RJ506.S44S45 2008
616.85'82--dc22   2008025831

Visit the Taylor & Francis Web site at
http://www.taylorandfrancis.com

and the Routledge Web site at
http://www.routledge.com

Dedication

In memory of my father, whose generosity taught me much;
and to Kathleen and Colin, who have ensured that
my "formation" continues.

– MKN

With love to (Alexander) Scott and Sophia Rose,
you are my greatest accomplishments.

For Rose Seguin whose strength in the darkest of times
is inspirational.

– NLH

Contents

Preface by Mary K. Nixon   *xiii*

Preface by Nancy L. Heath   *xv*

Acknowledgments   *xvii*

About the Editors   *xix*

Contributors   *xxi*

1   *Introduction to Nonsuicidal Self-Injury*
    in Adolescents   *1*
    Mary K. Nixon and Nancy L. Heath

SECTION I
BACKGROUND INFORMATION: WHO SELF-INJURES AND WHY?   7

2   *Self-Injury Today: Review of Population and*
    Clinical Studies in Adolescents   *9*
    Nancy L. Heath, Kristin Schaub, Shareen Holly, and
    Mary K. Nixon

3   *Functions of Adolescent Nonsuicidal Self-Injury*   *29*
    Elizabeth E. Lloyd-Richardson, Matthew K. Nock, and
    Mitchell J. Prinstein

SECTION II
ETIOLOGY OF SELF-INJURY   43

4   *Psychosocial Risk and Protective Factors*   *45*
    E. David Klonsky and Catherine R. Glenn

5   *Nonsuicidal Self-Injury and Co-Occurrence*   59
     Nicholas Lofthouse, Jennifer J. Muehlenkamp, and Robyn Adler

6   *Neurobiological Perspectives on Self-Injury*   79
     Elizabeth A. Osuch and Geoffrey W. Payne

SECTION III
EFFECTIVE PRACTICE FOR SELF-INJURY IN YOUTH   111

SECTION IIIA
ASSESSMENT OF NONSUICIDAL SELF-INJURY   113

7   *Measurement of Nonsuicidal Self-Injury in
     Adolescents*   115
     Paula Cloutier and Lauren Humphreys

8   *Assessment of Nonsuicidal Self-Injury in Youth*   143
     Nancy L. Heath and Mary K. Nixon

SECTION IIIB
INTERVENTION AND PREVENTION ISSUES   171

9   *Intervention and Prevention in the Community*   173
     Janis Whitlock and Kerry L. Knox

10   *Nonsuicidal Self-Injury in the Schools: Prevention
     and Intervention*   195
     Richard A. Lieberman, Jessica R. Toste, and Nancy L. Heath

11   *Psychosocial Interventions for Adolescents*   217
     Mary K. Nixon, Harjit Aulakh, Laurel Townsend, and
     Meghan Atherton

12   *Working with Families and Adolescents with NSSI*   237
     Heather Vale, Mary K. Nixon, and Anna Kucharski

13   *Adolescent Nonsuicidal Self-Injury in an Inpatient
     Setting*   257
     Nicholas Lofthouse and Laurence Katz

14   *Use of Medication in the Treatment of Nonsuicidal
     Self-Injury in Youth*   275
     Paul L. Plener, Gerhard Libal, and Mary K. Nixon

15 *Resource Guide for Working with Youth* **309**
Jessica R. Toste, Shareen Holly, and Kristin Schaub

16 *Concluding Comments from the Editors* **317**
Nancy L. Heath and Mary K. Nixon

Index **319**

A nice deep gash
To change my pain.
My heart hurts no more,
Solid as rock

Scars lining my skin
To forget my emotions
My pain inside
Shows on the outside

No tears in my eyes
Blood drops streak my skin
Those trusty scissors
Make me alive again

—Anonymous

Preface
by Mary K. Nixon

During the period of editing and writing this book, friends and non-mental health professional colleagues would ask me, "What is the book about?" In certain cases, I was met with no comment after telling them that the book was a guide for professionals who work with youth who purposefully self-injure. It is a topic that is not always a "conversation maker." In talking with others, though, it seemed there was a curiosity, a need for them to understand why this occurred and what might contribute to it. Several talked about youth they knew who self-injured or someone in their family. At times, it would develop into an interesting exchange of thoughts and ideas that they themselves had. Many wondered why young people would willingly do this to their bodies.

I became interested as a child and adolescent psychiatrist and clinician-researcher in examining this area from a research perspective because of two particular situations: Adolescents in the partial hospitalization program that I directed over 15 years ago continually told me that self-injuring was the "only thing that worked" in terms of coping with difficult and distressing feelings, certainly better than any therapy and medication I might have or considered using and better than any other coping strategy that we had gone over repeatedly. Many wanted to stop but found this reinforcement difficult to overcome. As part of a treatment team, we spent much time discussing how best to intervene and assist these youth, always with a nonjudgmental approach and every attempt to understand their behavior from their perspective. When I attempted to seek out more information at that time, I was stunned by the lack of evidence, both from the perspective of better understanding this behavior and what may be effective treatment for self-injury in this age group.

This became the beginning of an incredibly rewarding and at times challenging journey of researching and treating youth who self-injure and their families. I have been privileged to be able to continue my clinical and research work that originated at the Children's Hospital of

Eastern Ontario in Ottawa, now in Victoria, British Columbia, with a range of similarly dedicated colleagues. I have also been keenly aware that the many stories of self-injuring youths, although unique each on their own, share commonalities such as guilt and shame and feeling misunderstood regarding their self-injury as well as their courage in sharing their stories with me. The following is a composite story for the purposes of illustrating what might be disclosed in my office by a young woman, aged 16 years, who was to be assessed regarding her history of repeated self-injury:

> My parents divorced when I was nine. My father is an alcoholic who has never admitted he has a problem. My mother and I have had a tense relationship since I can't remember when. She might be depressed herself too. Things got so bad between us, my mother kicked me out two years ago. I lived with my aunt, then with my father, and finally moved back in with my mother last summer. We still fight over just about anything. I had a terrible school year last year and that's why I changed schools this year. I started hurting myself last year just to numb myself and get away from the things and feelings that were upsetting me. I would use a cigarette to burn my hand. I did this about five times, then stopped because the kids at school noticed my scars and started saying things about me. Since then, I have been feeling more depressed. This is the first time that I have accepted to get some professional help beyond talking with my school counselor and mother.

Teamwork and sharing and exchanging knowledge and ideas among disciplines has inevitably aided me with my work with youth. With a similar experience, it has been my pleasure to collaborate with my colleague Dr. Nancy Heath in the Department of Educational and Counseling Psychology at McGill University in Montreal. When we finally met in person, it was particularly exciting and memorable moment, as very few researchers in Canada were working in the area of self-injury and we both shared concerns regarding the need for more evidence-based research on this subject. I am delighted that our collaboration has expanded to co-editing this book and that we have taken an interdisciplinary approach to the writing and range of contributors to this book.

Preface
by Nancy L. Heath

For almost 20 years I have worked as a researcher in the area of educational psychology or school psychology. My research has always centered on the adaptive functioning of youth at risk. I am interested in how students who struggle with learning, social, and behavioral problems in school avoid depression and maintain their self-esteem. My research program in this area has been continually funded by educational, psychological, and medical agencies and resulted in numerous presentations and publications. However, a new direction was given to my work about a decade ago. In the mid-1990s a doctoral student of mine, Shana Ross, was completing a school psychology internship in a high school and noticed how many of her students were telling her about cutting and burning themselves "to feel better." When we examined the literature to find answers, we were amazed that there was nothing on this type of self-injury in the schools. This led us to conduct one the first-ever studies of nonsuicidal self-injury (NSSI) in high school students, and the only one to this day that involved both survey screening and interviews. The overwhelming interest in that initial study by researchers, clinicians, parents, and individuals who self-injure led me to redirect a significant portion of my research program to the study of NSSI in schools and community settings.

Since that time, we have learned a great deal about NSSI, and we have developed a much more complex understanding of the behavior as the field has continued to develop. Unfortunately, what becomes immediately apparent to me in my workshops for professionals in the community and in the hospital settings is how little of this growing body of knowledge is being communicated to those on the front lines. This book attempts to bridge the gap between researchers and practitioners—all practitioners who are encountering this frightening behavior.

This book is unique in the area, being specifically designed for use by professionals across numerous disciplines and settings (school psychologists, counselors, social workers, case workers, physicians, nurses, community health workers, family therapists, and psychiatrists). To truly achieve this, we needed to have an interdisciplinary collaboration in producing this book. For me, as a researcher and professional in the area of school psychology and counseling, the opportunity to collaborate on this book with Dr. Mary K. Nixon, an experienced researcher and clinician in adolescent psychiatry, was extraordinary. We both contributed our own perspectives, expertise, and contacts to the project, resulting in a final product that truly represents a broad range of professionals. Our contributors include world leaders in NSSI from community health, school psychology, psychology, and child and adolescent psychiatry.

It is our hope that this book will be useful in both informing practitioners about current research on NSSI and providing direction in prevention, assessment, and intervention with youth who engage in NSSI. With these goals in mind, the book is organized into four sections. In Section I, "Background Information," Chapters 2 and 3 provide important information on prevalence and theory of the functions of the behavior. In Section II, "Etiology of Self-Injury," Chapters 4 through 6 cover the risk and protective factors, the co-occurrence of psychopathology, and the neurobiology of the self-injury. Section III, "Effective Practice," is divided into a subsection on assessment of NSSI (Chapters 7 and 8) and a subsection on prevention and intervention across settings and disciplines (Chapters 9 to 14).

We are thankful to all those who contributed to the writing of this book, who shared our common goal of a much needed evidence-based interdisciplinary text on this topic.

REFERENCE

Ross, S., & Heath, N. L. (2002). A study of the frequency of self-mutilation in a community sample of adolescents. *Journal of Youth and Adolescence, 31,* 67–77

Acknowledgments

We would like to thank Dana Bliss, George Zimmar, Fred Copper-smith, and Robert Sims of Routledge for their interest and support in this project. We are indebted to Jessica Toste, a hugely talented graduate student, who worked intensively with us to pull this manuscript together. Her organizational skills are without parallel! We would also like to thank Anna Kucharsky, Meghan Atherton, and Kate Creedon, who have all assisted us at various times and displayed a keen interest and diligent approach to their work. The authors who have contributed their time and expertise to the success of this interdisciplinary project are to be congratulated on their contributions to the literature in this field. We would also like to acknowledge Adil Virani and Elizabeth Osuch, who assisted in reviewing certain contents. In addition, we must acknowledge and offer our thanks to the youth, their families, and our dedicated clinical colleagues, all of whom continue to inspire us in our work and research.

And finally ...

To my family and friends, who have offered much support, understanding, and encouragement through the years. — MKN

To Ted, Scott, and Sophia, I offer my deepest thanks for their support in my work. They are always interested, encouraging, and loving. Their humor enlivens my days. — NLH

About the Editors

Mary K. Nixon, M.D., FRCPC, is a child and adolescent psychiatrist practicing in Victoria, British Columbia. She previously worked at the Children's Hospital of Eastern Ontario in Ottawa, where she was director of psychiatry research and head of the Mood and Anxiety Clinic. She is the founding editor of the *Journal of the Canadian Academy of Child and Adolescent Psychiatry* and a member of the board of the CACAP for the past seven years. She is a research associate at the Center for Youth and Society at the University of Victoria, affiliate associate professor in the Division of Medical Sciences, University of Victoria, and clinical associate professor in the Department of Psychiatry, University of British Columbia. Her current research interests include population-based surveys of nonsuicidal self-harm in youth, assessment of self-injury in youth, and the evaluation of group-based treatments for youth who self-injure and their families.

Nancy L. Heath, Ph.D., is a Professor in the Department of Educational and Counselling Psychology at McGill University. She is a professor in the School/Applied Child Psychology program and the Director of programs in Human Development, General Educational Psychology, and Inclusive Education. Her research program explores resilience and adaptive functioning in youth at-risk; with her most recent work focusing on the understanding of occurrence and response to non-suicidal self-injury in the schools. She has published and presented internationally in the area of NSSI in youth and young adults, and is a founding member of the International Society for the Study of Self-Injury (ISSS). In 2001, she was elected as a Fellow in the International Academy of Research on Learning Disabilities. In 2004, she was awarded the William Dawson Scholar Award (Internal Canada Research Chair-II) at McGill for outstanding research and contributions to the field.

Contributors

Robyn Adler, BA, is a child and adolescent psychometrist at the Ohio State University Medical Center's Neuroscience Facility. She is a National Yoga Alliance certified teacher in Columbus, Ohio. Her main interest is in the area of the mind–body connection to achieve overall mental health and well being.

Meghan Atherton, BA, is a recent graduate in Psychology from the University of Victoria. She is currently working as a research assistant for the Centre for Youth and Society at the University of Victoria. Ms. Atherton is interested in adolescents and the relationship among their health choices, self-esteem, and self-image. Specific areas of interest include dating relationships, drug and alcohol use, physical health (nutrition and exercise), and peer relationships.

Harjit Aulakh, MA, is a doctoral student at McGill University and currently works as a clinician with Saanich Child and Youth Mental Health Centre (British Columbia Ministry of Children and Family Development), providing therapeutic services for youth of all ages. She is a cofacilitator of a treatment group for youth who self-injure, and her research interests include evidence-based therapeutic strategies with youth who engage in NSSI, risk and resilience factors associated with youth engaging in high-risk behaviors, as well as the neurological underpinnings of addiction and impulse control problems.

Paula Cloutier, MA, is a research associate at the Mental Health Patient Service Unit at the Children's Hospital of Eastern Ontario. She serves as a research consultant for the Patient Service Unit and is a member of the Children's Hospital of Eastern Ontario's Research Institute. She has over 15 years of research experience in the area of mental health. Her research interests include assessment of NSSI in adolescents and pediatric emergency mental health service delivery and utilization. Her expertise also lies in the area of research design and statistical analysis.

Catherine R. Glenn, BA, graduated with a degree in psychology from the University of Virginia in 2004 and is currently a clinical psychology doctoral student at Stony Brook University. She has authored a number of articles on self-injury and conducts research on social and cognitive mechanisms that cause and maintain the behavior.

Shareen Holly, MA, is doctoral student in the School/Applied Child Psychology program in the Department of Educational and Counselling Psychology at McGill University. Her research focuses on aspects related to the social contagion of NSSI, as well as the functions associated with NSSI among university students.

Lauren Humphreys, PhD, CPsych, is a clinical psychologist at the Mental Health Patient Service Unit at the Children's Hospital of Eastern Ontario (CHEO) and a member of the CHEO Research Institute. She provides outpatient assessment and treatment for children and youth with mood and anxiety disorders. She has a number of publications based on her past research pertaining to psychosocial aspects of genetic testing. Her current research interests lie in the areas of adolescent NSSI and outcome evaluation for mental health services.

Laurence Y. Katz, MD, FRCPC, is a child and adolescent psychiatrist at the PsycHealth Centre in Winnipeg, as well as an associate professor of psychiatry at University of Manitoba. He was the psychiatrist for an acute care child and adolescent psychiatry inpatient unit at the Health Sciences Centre in Winnipeg, a teaching and research hospital, for eight years. He is a trainer in dialectical behavior therapy for Behavioral Tech, LLC in Seattle and established and researched the modification of dialectical behavior therapy for suicidal adolescent inpatients.

E. David Klonsky, PhD, received his degree in clinical psychology from the University of Virginia and is currently assistant professor of psychology at Stony Brook University. Dr. Klonsky has published numerous articles as well as an edited volume on the topic of self-injury. Along with many others who authored chapters in this book, he is a founding member of the International Society for the Study of Self-injury (ISSS).

Kerry L. Knox, PhD, MS, is an interdisciplinary trained scientist in the fields of epidemiology, behavioral science, anthropology, neurobiology, and physiology. She is an associate professor at the University of Rochester School of Medicine. The focus of her work is public health approaches to suicide prevention, in particular, in veterans and military populations.

Anna Kucharski, MA, is a youth worker who has worked in various capacities including child life, street outreach, residential settings, and providing supportive housing to young mothers. She is currently the assistant coordinator of the Interdisciplinary National Self-Injury in Youth Network of Canada (INSYNC).

Gerhard Libal, MD, MPH, is a senior consultant in the Department of Child and Adolescent Psychiatry, University of Basel. He was trained as a child and adolescent psychiatrist and a psychotherapist at the Innsbruck University Hospital (Austria) and the University Hospital of Ulm (Germany), and received his MPH from John Hopkins University. His research focuses on liaison psychiatry in residential homes and working with aggressive and self-injuring adolescents. Dr. Libal coordinates a specialized psychopharmacology clinic designed to support clinicians when using medication in children and adolescents with difficult to treat conditions, with particular emphasis on patient education and therapeutic drug monitoring.

Richard A. Lieberman, MA, NCSP, is a lecturer in the Graduate School of Education at Loyola Marymount University and currently coordinates the Suicide Prevention Unit for the Los Angeles Unified School District. He has authored numerous book chapters, articles, curricula, and videos on the topics of youth suicide prevention, self-injury, and school crisis intervention.

Elizabeth E. Lloyd-Richardson, PhD, is an assistant professor of psychiatry and human behavior at the Warren Alpert Medical School of Brown University and a staff psychologist at the Miriam Hospital in Providence, Rhode Island. She is a clinical psychologist, specializing in child and adolescent psychopathology, particularly as it relates to medical conditions and health behaviors. Her research focuses primarily on prevention and early intervention of health risk behaviors among adolescents and young adults, with a particular emphasis on smoking cessation and weight management treatments.

Nicholas Lofthouse, PhD, is a licensed clinical psychologist, training supervisor, and researcher who provides evidence-based assessments and treatments for children, adolescents, and families in an inpatient and outpatient medical center setting. He is a clinical assistant professor at the Ohio State University Medical Center. He has published in the areas of childhood comorbidity, adolescent NSSI, school problems, sleep difficulties, and psychosocial interventions associated with childhood bipolar disorder. Dr. Lofthouse's current research interests include adolescent NSSI, neurofeedback treatment for children with ADHD, sleep problems associated with childhood bipolar disorder, and parents' and children's knowledge about mental health difficulties and treatment.

Jennifer J. Muehlenkamp, PhD, is an assistant professor of psychology at the University of North Dakota and a licensed, practicing psychologist. Her research focuses on identifying risk and protective factors of self-injurious behaviors in youth, as well as understanding the interrelationship between self-injury and suicide. Clinically, she treats both adolescents and young adults struggling to overcome self-injury and related disorders. Dr. Muehlenkamp is an active member of numerous professional organizations in psychology and is currently serving as chair of the Research Division for the American Association of Suicidology, as well as treasurer for Division 12 of the American Psychological Association.

Matthew K. Nock, PhD, is the John L. Loeb associate professor of the social sciences and director of the Laboratory for Clinical and Developmental Research in the Department of Psychology at Harvard University. His research focuses on the etiology, assessment, and treatment of self-injurious and aggressive behaviors.

Elizabeth A. Osuch, MD, is an associate professor and Rea chair of Affective and Anxiety Disorders at the University of Western Ontario and the London Health Sciences Centre. Dr. Osuch trained in the United States at Michigan State University for medical school and then Sheppard Pratt Hospital for psychiatry residency. She completed a fellowship in clinical research at the Biological Psychiatry Branch of the National Institute of Mental Health. Her clinical and research work in London, Ontario, focuses on depression and anxiety in youth over the age of 16. She is utilizing fMRI to investigate the brain circuitry of healthy and pathological conditions, especially as related to the neuronal processing of reward.

Geoffrey W. Payne, PhD, was one of the founding members of the Northern Medical Program at the University of Northern British Columbia, where he is currently an assistant professor of physiology. Dr. Payne received a MSc in neuroscience and pharmacology and a PhD in cardiovascular and renal physiology from Memorial University of Newfoundland. He went on to Yale University, where he completed a postdoctoral fellowship in the field of microcirculation and impact of diseases.

Paul L. Plener, MD, works as a resident at the Department of Child and Adolescent Psychiatry and Psychotherapy, University of Ulm, Germany. He received training in cognitive behavioral therapy and dialectical behavior therapy and was awarded a Donald J. Cohen fellowship by the IACAPAP. His main fields of research for the past years have been the epidemiology and psychopharmacological treatment of adolescent NSSI. He is currently studying the emotional processing in NSSI.

Mitchell J. Prinstein, PhD, is an associate professor and director of clinical psychology at the University of North Carolina at Chapel Hill. He received his PhD from the University of Miami and completed his internship and postdoctoral fellowship at the Brown University Clinical Psychology Training Consortium. Dr. Prinstein's research examines interpersonal models of internalizing symptoms and health risk behaviors among adolescents, with a specific focus on the unique role of peer relationships in the developmental psychopathology of depression, self-injury, and suicidality. He currently serves as an associate editor for the *Journal of Consulting and Clinical Psychology*; a member of the NIH Study Section on Psychosocial Development, Risk, and Prevention; and a member of the editorial boards of several developmental psychopathology journals.

Kristin Schaub, MA, is a PhD student in School/Applied Child Psychology at McGill University. Her research interests include NSSI in youth, specifically the risk factors and addictive aspects of this behavior. She completed her master's thesis in this area and is continuing to examine NSSI in her doctoral studies.

Jessica R. Toste, BEd, MA, is a doctoral student in educational psychology at McGill University. Her research interests focus on resilient functioning and educational outcomes of youth at risk. Ms. Toste is a learning disabilities specialist with the Learning Associates of Montreal and has years of experience working in community-based educational programs with students with special needs and youth at risk.

Laurel A. Townsend, PhD, RPsych, obtained her degree in clinical psychology, with a specialization in neuropsychology, from the University of Victoria in 1996. Following completion of her degree, she held a position in adult outpatient psychiatry at the London Health Sciences Centre prior to moving into community-based mental health with youth. She now works as a psychologist at the Saanich Child and Youth Mental Health Services, British Columbia Ministry of Children and Family Development.

Heather Vale, MA, RCC, is a psychotherapist in private practice in Victoria, British Columbia, where she also works for Child and Youth Mental Health. She specializes in working with couples and families, trauma, and resiliency.

Janis Whitlock, PhD, MPH, is a lecturer and research scientist at the Family Life Development Center at Cornell University. She is also director of the Cornell Research Program on Self-Injurious Behavior in Adolescents and Young Adults. Dr. Whitlock specializes in human development, with an emphasis on social and emotional development, adolescent and young adult mental health, epidemiology, and program development and evaluation. Her research focuses on NSSI, school and community contexts for development, and measurement of well-being in adolescents and young adults.

1

Introduction to Nonsuicidal Self-Injury in Adolescents

MARY K. NIXON AND NANCY L. HEATH

B.J., a 15-year-old young man, presented to emergency at his local hospital for the third time in the past two months. The first occasion was when he was seen at school with multiple scratches on his forearms and sent to the local mental health emergency service, as he refused to speak to the school counselor and appeared distressed. B.J. was angry about the need to be assessed, indicating to the emergency mental health clinician that, although he had scratched himself purposefully, it meant nothing to him other than a "test to see how it felt." He gave no history, nor did his parents, of any precipitating or contributing events and reluctantly agreed to see his school counselor "to touch base." The second encounter occurred the day after his girlfriend broke up with him. He took liquor from his parents' cupboard, became intoxicated, and did not realize until after he became sober that he had sliced his forearm many times with an old pocket knife in his room. His mother, unaware of the breakup and his drinking, checked in on him later that evening and noticed blood stains on his clothing and the smell of liquor. Both parents sat with B.J. that evening to attempt to understand what was going on. It was agreed that B.J. would see his family doctor, whom he had known for many years, and take the next day off school. Both parents were quite distressed by this event, as they had not had any sense that B.J. was having such difficulty. B.J assured his parents that it was not a suicide attempt and revealed the recent breakup as a major stress.

The next day, his doctor interviewed B.J. alone, and he revealed that he was feeling angry and upset over the breakup with his girlfriend (they had been dating for seven months and had been arguing recently, as she disapproved of his recent episodes of alcohol abuse and his increasing moodiness). The doctor assessed that there were adjustment issues related to the breakup and that B.J. should seek some counseling regarding stress management and coping. A referral was made to the local community mental health center and, although he agreed to see his school counselor, he did not show for his appointment, and the counselor had to seek him out. On his third presentation, a month later, this time to emergency, the emergency physician had to steri-strip two cuts on his forearm that he had inflicted several hours before with a woodcarving knife. He was found in the bathroom by his sister, who became concerned when she saw blood in the sink and his forearm covered in towels and called her parents.

Working with youth who self-injure often means that clinicians, mental health professionals, school counselors, teachers, and youth workers alike are faced with the challenge of how best to understand the behavior and intervene. The case of B.J. illustrates that these youth can be difficult to engage and that contact and potential interventions may take place at a number of levels. Studies have shown that many professionals who work with youth who self-injure find it one of the most challenging behaviors to contend with. Teachers indicate that self-injury is increasing in the schools, that it provokes strong and negative reactions, and that they are often ill equipped to know what to do when encountering the behavior and often feel a sense of horror (Heath, Toste, & Beettam, 2006). High school counselors also identified an overwhelming need for more information and practice guidelines to deal with self-injury in the schools (Heath, Toste, & White Kress, 2007; McAllister, 2003). Mental health and medical professionals state that nonsuicidal self-injury (NSSI) is one of the most difficult behaviors to encounter in a client (Rayner & Warner, 2003).

HISTORICAL AND SOCIAL–CULTURAL CONSIDERATIONS OF SELF-INJURY

The act of self-injury has been documented from the beginning of recorded history, with the earliest reports found in ancient Hebrew, Greek, Roman, and Japanese texts (Bennum, 1984). Favazza (1989, 1998), in his cross-historical and cross-cultural examination of self-mutilative behavior, described "body modification" rituals that occurred in ancient Aztecs, Mayans, and Olmecs religions. Certain passages in the Bible invoke sinners to remove offending eyes or limbs to purify themselves (Favazza, 1989). In the 21st century, forms of self-injury continue to be performed as a rite of passage or a form of spiritual healing. Armando Favazza's classic text (first published in 1987 and with a second edition in 1998), *Bodies Under Siege: Self Mutilation and Body Modification in Culture and Psychiatry*, remains an excellent comprehensive review and discussion of the full range of self-mutilative practices and behaviors over time and across cultures. The second edition

contains an epilogue written by Fakir Musafar, a leader of modern prim-
itivism, who describes the practice of "body play" including body tattooing, scarification, and piercing, practices that appears to be gaining
more popularity in Western culture.

Favazza defined self-mutilation as "the deliberate destruction or
alteration of one's body tissue without conscious suicidal intent." He
then distinguished culturally sanctioned self-mutilation, such as rituals
(e.g., facial or body scarification in certain tribal cultures to mark initiation and passage into manhood) and practices (e.g., self-flagellation as
a religious act of penitence during the Middle Ages) from deviant self-
mutilation, where the behavior is "a product of a mental disorder and
anguish." This distinction between "socially sanctioned" self-injury or
mutilation and nonsocially sanctioned self-injury has been an important
concept in working toward a more specific understanding of the range
and classification of self-injuring behaviors.

The conceptualization of nonsocially sanctioned self-injury has
changed by the era. Himber (1994) observed that the earliest writers
described self-injury as acting out castration fears and as an expression of a repressed death wish. However, as psychodynamic influence
grew, individuals who engaged in self-injury were viewed as struggling
with separation-individuation and dependency issues. In the 1960s,
new attention was given to a particular subtype of self-injurers, designated the "wrist-cutter syndrome" (Favazza, 1998). The case of a young
unmarried woman was described, who suffered from problems with
sexuality, addiction, and interpersonal interactions and repeatedly and
superficially cut her wrist.

Ross and McKay, in their 1979 book, *Self Mutilation*, represented
some of only a few authors to write on this subject in the postmodern
era, followed shortly by Pattison and Kahan's (1983) frequently cited
article on "deliberate self harm." The latter paper offered a profile of
repetitive self-injurers who had onset of this behavior during adolescence that was of low lethality types (excluding self-poisoning) and
without conscious suicidal intent. They suggested that persons engaging in self-injury presented with psychological symptoms such as anxiety, anger, despair, and cognitive constriction, with possible associated
depression or psychosis. The combined efforts of Ross and McKay, as
well as Pattison and Kahan, set the stage for the beginning of more
intensive study of this behavior.

DEFINITIONS AND SELF-INJURY

Over the years, the concept of the wrist-cutter syndrome and terms
such as self-mutilation have lost favor, both to find less suggestive terminology as well as the need to clearly distinguish types of self-injuring
behaviors, in particular, differentiating those related to suicide intent
versus those that not associated with suicidal intent. The lack of stan-

dardized definitions has led to difficulties in terms of comparisons of prevalence rates for self-injury, understanding specific correlates and predictors as well as planning and evaluating effective interventions. Additional terms such as *self-injurious behavior, parasuicide, deliberate self-harm, self-carving*, and *self-cutting* have all been used to describe all or some aspects of self-injury. Favazza and Rosenthal (1993) and Favazza and Simeon (1995) made several preliminary distinctions regarding how nonculturally sanctioned self-injury may present by differentiating major (e.g., castration, eye nucleation) from superficial to moderate self-injury (such as scratching or cutting). Minor to moderate forms could be impulsive or compulsive (responding to ego dystonic urges) and episodic or repetitive in nature, with the mild to moderate impulsive type identified as providing a form of release or relief from tension that could then be reinforcing of the behavior.

Certain standard terminology has been used among researchers in the study of self-injury. Deliberate self-harm includes a broad range of self-harm behaviors (e.g., self-injury, self-poisoning, and the deliberate abuse of substances and alcohol to harm oneself) and does not distinguish whether suicidal intent is present or not (Hawton, Haw, Houston, & Townsend, 2002). An act of deliberate self-harm, by definition, can therefore include a serious suicide attempt such as hanging or jumping from a height or superficial wrist cutting with no suicidal intent. Whereas a broader definition ensures that all behaviors are considered, for example, from the assessment perspective, it is limiting in that one cannot directly infer that all deliberate self-harm behaviors are similar regarding motivation and that a specific approach to assessment or treatment would be effective for all types.

NSSI exists within the range of deliberate self-harming behaviors. It can be defined as purposely inflicting injury that results in immediate tissue damage, done without suicidal intent and not socially sanctioned within one's culture nor for display. It therefore excludes extreme tattooing or body piercing, body modification, and culturally sanctioned ritualistic injury or mutilation. NSSI includes, but is not limited to, cutting, pin-scratching, carving, burning, and self-hitting. The most common types are cutting and scratching, most typically done on the inner aspect of the forearm, although not necessarily restricted to that location (Laye-Gindhu & Schonert-Reichl, 2005; Nixon, Cloutier, & Aggarwal, 2002). It is perhaps most closely related to the original distinction of the superficial to moderate form of "impulsive" self-injury to which previous authors referred. Self-injury can occur in individuals with cognitive impairment and pervasive developmental disorders such as autism and is typically termed "self-injurious behavior" (SIB) and will be used in this book, for example, when discussing neurobiology studies and psychopharmacologic treatments, where the literature examining self-injurious behavior among individuals with developmental delays is discussed.

The focus of this text remains on NSSI as it presents in noncognitively impaired youth. Whereas the aim is to specifically address the assessment and treatment of NSSI in youth, this does not in any way suggest that other self-harming behaviors may not co-occur. Therefore, screening for other self-harming behaviors is one aspect of assessment, which is further discussed in Chapters 7 and 8 on measurement and assessment, respectively.

NSSI IN ADOLESCENTS

The need to provide a comprehensive text that specifically focuses on a youth-centered approach to NSSI is important for a number of reasons. Practitioners often fail in their understanding and interventions with youth when a "top-down" adult-oriented approach is taken. This is often because limited evidence exists regarding effective interventions in this age group, and most of the studies are on adult populations. The age of onset of NSSI is typically during the adolescent period (Lloyd Richardson, Perrine, Dierker, & Kelley, 2007; Nixon, Cloutier, & Jansson, 2008). As will be discussed in Chapter 9, "Community Interventions and Prevention," this period is marked with tasks and challenges associated with this important phase of development. Youth and families must work through issues related to such tasks as separation and individuation while the adolescent brain and its neuronal networks continue to develop and mature. Although some risk taking during this period may be considered within normal limits, it is important that those who work closely with youth examine what is socially or culturally accepted and what constitutes behavior that goes beyond this framework.

Practitioners are encountering and attempting to deal with this behavior in youth, with little or no training or evidence-based information. Misinformation may also hinder professionals from responding appropriately. This book is the first to provide a practical guide for a range of practitioners in a variety of settings who are encountering youth with NSSI, for example, for the teacher who is unsure what to say when it is apparent that a student is self-injuring, for the social worker in the community clinic who needs to decide how and whether to make a referral, for the therapist in private practice who needs to know when and how best to intervene, for the family doctor who has limited time and requires information that targets how best to use his or her skills and training, and for the child and adolescent psychiatrist and psychologist who is looking for an evidence-based-oriented text that provides a comprehensive review of NSSI. We hope the information offered in this book will assist a range of professionals, all with important roles in working with youth, in having a set of tools and a guide to the various steps associated with assessing and intervening in the care of youth who present with NSSI. There has been considerable need for an evidence-based text that synthesizes such information, albeit limited at this time, with the intention to guide best practice, with youth and their families being the ultimate beneficiaries.

REFERENCES

Bennum, I. (1984). Psychological models of self-mutilation. *Suicide and Life Threatening Behavior, 14,* 166–186.

Favazza, A. R. (1989). Why patients mutilate themselves. *Hospital and Community Psychiatry, 40*(2), 137–145.

Favazza, A. R., & Rosenthal, R. J. (1993). Diagnostic issues in self-mutilation. *Hospital and Community Psychiatry, 44*(2), 134–140.

Favazza, A., & Simeon, D. (1995). Self-mutilation. In E. Hollander & E. J. Stein (Eds.), *Impulsivity and aggression* (pp. 185–200). Chichester, UK: John Wiley and Sons.

Favazza, A. R. (1998). The coming age of self-mutilation. *Journal of Nervous & Mental Disease, 186*(5), 259–268.

Favazza, A. R. (1987). *Bodies under siege: Self-mutilation and body modification in culture and psychiatry* (2nd ed.). London: John Hopkins University Press.

Hawton, K., Haw, C., Houston, K., & Townsend, E. (2002). Family history of suicidal behaviour: Prevalence and significance in deliberate self-harm patients. *Acta Psychiatrica Scandinavica, 106,* 387–393.

Heath, N. L., Toste, J. R., & Beettam, E. (2006). "I am not well-equipped": High school teachers' perceptions of self-injury. *Canadian Journal of School Psychology, 21*(1), 73–92.

Heath, N. L., Toste, J. R., & White Kress, V. (2007). [School counselors' experiences with non-suicidal self-injury]. Unpublished raw data.

Himber, J. (1994). Blood rituals: Self-cutting in female psychiatric patients. *Psychotherapy, 31,* 620–631.

Laye-Gindhu, A., & Schonert-Reichl, K. A. (2005). Nonsuicidal self-harm among community adolescents: Understanding the "whats" and "whys" of self-harm. *Journal of Youth and Adolescence, 34,* 445–457.

Lloyd-Richardson, E. E., Perrine, N., Dierker, L., & Kelley, M. L. (2007). Characteristics and functions of non-suicidal self-injury in a community sample of adolescents. *Psychological Medicine, 37*(8), 1183–1192.

McAllister, M. (2003). Multiple meanings of self-harm: A critical review. *International Journal of Mental Health Nursing, 12,* 177–185.

Nixon, M. K., Cloutier, P. F., & Aggarwal, S. (2002). Affect regulation and addictive aspects of repetitive self-injury in hospitalized adolescents. *Journal of the American Academy of Child & Adolescent Psychiatry, 41*(11), 1333–1341.

Nixon, M. K., Cloutier, P., & Jansson, S. M. (2008). Nonsuicidal self-harm in youth: A population-based survey. *Canadian Medical Association Journal, 178,* 306–312.

Pattison, E. M., & Kahan, J. (1983). The deliberate self-harm syndrome. *American Journal of Psychiatry, 140*(7), 867–872.

Rayner, G. A., & Warner, S. (2003). Self-harming behavior: From lay perceptions to clinical practice. *Counselling Psychology Quarterly, 16,* 305–329.

Ross, R. R., & McKay, H. B. (1979). *Self-Mutilation.* Lexington, MA: Lexington Books.

BACKGROUND INFORMATION: WHO SELF-INJURES AND WHY?

2

Self-Injury Today

Review of Population and Clinical Studies in Adolescents

NANCY L. HEATH, KRISTIN SCHAUB,
SHAREEN HOLLY, AND MARY K. NIXON

In this chapter, the practitioner will gain an understanding of:

- How prevalence differs across settings
- Whether NSSI is increasing
- The most common age of onset for NSSI
- Myths and facts about gender differences, and who is at risk for NSSI

This chapter explores the prevalence of nonsuicidal self-injury (NSSI) in adolescents and young adults. Although it is an apparently straightforward task, many complicating factors need to be considered. Common queries posed by the practitioner when confronted with an adolescent who engages in NSSI include How prevalent is this behavior? When does it start? Is it increasing? Is this predominately a female behavior? and Is this behavior more common in certain groups of youth? Over the past 10 years, studies on youth have attempted to address these essential questions. In the following pages we will review the research that may answer some of these questions, summarize the factors to be examined when critically evaluating prevalence literature, and conclude with a discussion of the implications of the current findings for practice.

HOW PREVALENT IS NSSI?

A number of articles provide prevalence data on self-injury. However, the undiscerning reader may be more confused than enlightened following perusal of this literature. Various articles report a prevalence rate as low as 4% (Briere & Gil, 1998) and as high as 46.5% (Lloyd-Richardson, Perrine, Dierker, & Kelley, 2007) in community samples and even higher in clinical samples (Nock & Prinstein, 2004) with a range of examples in between. What contributes to this remarkable variability? Essentially, because the study of NSSI is a newly emerging field, there is little consistency concerning methodology in the study of self-injury. In critically reviewing the literature, a number of methodological variations need to be considered in the interpretation of the results. These include definitional and measurement issues, sample selection, and composition. Below, we will discuss these issues and interpret the literature with reference to these important features.

WHAT? DEFINITION AND MEASUREMENT ISSUES

Three major differences occur in the definition and measurement of self-injury:

- Does the self-injury definition exclude suicide attempts and suicide intent? What does it include and exclude?
- Is the self-injury assessment done by a standardized assessment tool or open-ended question? By anonymous survey or interview?
- What is the time frame for the presence of self-injury?

Many studies employ a definition of self-injury that includes any form of deliberate self-inflicted injury including self-poisoning, jumping from heights, and drug overdose (De Leo & Heller, 2004; Haavisto et al., 2005; Hawton, Fagg, Simkin, Bale, & Bond, 2000; Hawton et al., 2003). Reflecting this broad definition of self-injury, the Child and Adolescent Self-harm in Europe (CASE) group defines self-harm as

> an act with a non-fatal outcome in which an individual deliberately did one or more of the following: Initiated behavior (for example, self-cutting, jumping from a height), which they intended to cause self-harm; Ingested a substance in excess of the prescribed or generally recognized therapeutic dose; Ingested a recreational or illicit drug that was an act that the person regarded as self-harm; Ingested a non-ingestible substance or object. (Hawton, Rodham, Evans, & Weatherall, 2002)

Whereas this includes self-cutting or burning, it goes beyond the construct of NSSI and therefore results in very different prevalence and gender findings. Related to this issue is the need to evaluate the specific behaviors included in the definition. For example, a recent study found a surprisingly high last-12-month prevalence of 46.5 % (Lloyd-Richardson et al., 2007) in a community sample of adolescents, despite excluding suicide attempts. Close examination of the behaviors included revealed that picking at an area of the skin until it bleeds was included as a form of self-injury. When the behavior was limited to cutting/carving, burning, self-tattooing, scraping, and erasing skin (i.e., using an eraser to rub skin to the point of burning and bleeding), the 12-month prevalence was recalculated as 27.7% (Lloyd-Richardson et al., 2007). In contrast, other studies may limit the behavior to only "cutting," failing to include burning, self-hitting, and other behaviors that may be more common in males. How self-injury is operationalized in these studies leads to substantial difficulties in cross-study comparison. Although the definitional issues concerning self-injury have been outlined in the introduction, the importance of determining the operational definition used when assessing the prevalence literature will become apparent in the review below.

Once definitional issues have been considered, the next aspect to evaluate is how the self-injury was measured. Self-injury "checklists" suggest to participants an array of possible self-injurious behaviors that they may have engaged in, whereas a more open-ended "have you ever hurt yourself on purpose" relies on the individual's interpretation of what should or shouldn't be included. Furthermore, when assessed by anonymous survey rather than interview, different results are obtained. An example of this is Ross and Heath (2002), who began with a survey question to 440 high school students embedded in a "coping questionnaire" that asked if they had ever hurt themselves on purpose. In the response to this open-ended question, 21.2% responded they had hurt themselves on purpose at least once, but in follow-up interview only 13.9% were found to correspond to the definition. The others (a) stated that they meant they had hurt themselves emotionally; (b) stated that they had engaged in food restriction; or (c) denied that they had meant the response. Thus, an interview format can result in lower prevalence partly due to better accuracy and partly due to refusal to self-disclose.

Finally, the last factor to consider in interpreting prevalence studies is the time frame and frequency variables that are used for criteria. Most common is lifetime prevalence and single occurrence, that is, has the individual ever engaged in self-injury in their lifetime even once. However, some studies use a time frame of "the past year," "past six months," or "currently engaging in self-injury." Similarly, for repetition, some studies use more than 10 times for self-injury, more than 3 times, or the term *repetitive self-injury*. Occasionally, these disparate measurements are equated as "a prevalence of NSSI."

WHERE? SETTING ISSUES

In evaluating prevalence studies of self-injury, a critical difference is whether the participants were drawn from a community or clinical setting. Although clinical settings can vary significantly from inpatient, outpatient, and emergency room presentations and clinics, they share more commonalities than differences relative to the community settings that include schools, colleges, and general population studies. A second consideration for setting is the geographical location in terms of country, as well as urban versus rural settings.

WHO? SAMPLE SELECTION

A final determining element of the prevalence findings is the sample selection used in the study. Different prevalence rates are found for samples that are younger adolescents (12–16) than with wider age spans or even young adults. There are a number of studies of self-injury in young adults in clinical settings, a few of young adults in community settings, a limited number of studies of adolescents in clinical settings, and only a handful of studies of self-injury in adolescents in community settings. Therefore, some authors rely on the young adult studies to draw conclusions about prevalence in adolescence. A second aspect of sample selection is the proportion of females to males. The majority of studies in clinical settings have a larger number of females than males, leading to conclusions about the frequency, type, and function of self-injury that is largely a female perspective on self-injury. Only very recently have there been some studies that have shed light on the nature of self-injury in males (e.g., Muehlenkamp & Gutierrez, 2007; Whitlock, Eckenrode, et al., 2006). These last two sample selection issues are limited largely to community studies. In a number of community studies of young adults, college students have been used, and due to ethics requirements, the participants have responded to recruitment ads for a study of self-injury (e.g., Gratz, Conrad, & Roemer, 2002). The use of college students precludes the generalization of those results to a more diverse community sample, although it remains unclear if self-injury is more or less prevalent in high-functioning college samples relative to general samples.

PREVALENCE STUDIES: THE FINDINGS

In summary, critical analysis of prevalence reports in research need to compare and evaluate on the following indices: use of common definition and measurement, clinical or community samples, and sample selection and composition. Prevalence studies are reviewed with reference to these methodological variables with the goal of making some general conclusions concerning the basic questions first raised. Tables 2.1 and 2.2 provide a summary of the reviewed studies with the key information. Table 2.1 reviews the community studies, and Table 2.2 reviews the clinical setting studies. Only studies that excluded suicide attempts and intent were included in the tables.

To summarize the findings illustrated in Tables 2.1 and 2.2, there are a few obvious differences. First, it is apparent that, not surprisingly, the clinical settings consistently have a much higher prevalence of NSSI than do the community settings when compared for definition, time frame, and sample selection. Briere and Gil's (1998) study of adults provides one of the only direct comparisons between prevalence of self-injury (over the past six months) in a community (4%) versus a clinical (21%) sample, concluding that self-injury is higher in the clinical sample. Furthermore, depending on the severity of the setting, inpatient versus outpatient, the prevalence reflects the difference.

In general, lifetime prevalence rates for adolescents in the community center around 15–20%. Where notably discrepant results are found (e.g., Gratz 2006; Gratz et al., 2002; Lloyd, 1997; Lloyd-Richardson et al., 2007) with much higher prevalence results, checklists of all possible self-injurious behaviors have been presented to the participants, resulting in participants endorsing every behavior that they have engaged in, which consistently leads to higher incidence reporting. Furthermore, when providing a list of many possible forms of tissue damage (e.g., biting; sticking pins, needles, and staples into skin; scraping skin), you effectively broaden the definition and are relying on the participants' understanding of the construct. Ideally, a follow-up interview would assist in clarifying whether their understanding of "sticking needles" corresponded to self-injury or drug use.

A second observation is that there is more likely to be significant gender differences in clinical samples versus community samples (e.g., Jacobsen, Muehlenkamp, & Miller, 2006; Nixon, Cloutier, & Aggarwal, 2002). This is probably because (a) females are more prone to seek help than males; and (b) many of the clinical setting studies include overdose or inappropriate ingestion of medication without suicidal intent, which has been found to be a largely female behavior (Briere & Gil, 1998; Rodham, Hawton, & Evans, 2004). Indeed, when we examine the presence or absence of the gender difference in the community samples of adolescents, it appears as if the inclusion of overdose and pill abuse may be a factor in the observed gender differences. Studies of self-injury in the community that find a gender difference (Laye-Gindhu & Schonert-Reichl, 2005; Nixon, Cloutier, & Jansson, 2008; Patton et al., 1997) include overdose or medication abuse without suicide intent, whereas every investigation that limits itself to cutting, burning, self-hitting to bruise, or other forms of tissue damage fails to find a gender difference (Lloyd-Richardson et al., 2007; Muehlenkamp & Gutierrez, 2004, 2007; Izutsu et al., 2006; Zoroglu et al., 2003). This pattern holds in the young adult literature, with

TABLE 2.1 Prevalence of Non-suicidal Self-Injury with Clinical Settings

Study	Time Frame	Design	Sample (Age)	Location	Recruitment	Gender Distribution	Ethnic Distribution	Prevalence	Gender Differences	Ethnicity Differences	NSSI Definition
						Adolescent Studies					
Nixon et al., 2002	Not specified	Screening was done by staff for SI	M = 15.7 (1.5)	Ontario, Ottawa, Canada	Study on SI	14% male 86% female	97.6% C	38%	Significantly more females than males self-injuring	Unavailable	Physically harming oneself without conscious suicidal intent
Guertin, Lloyd-Richardson, Spirito, Donaldson, & Boergers, 2001	1 year	Forced choice with the option of providing other SI behaviors	M = 15.1 Range = 12–18	General hospital emergency department (ED)	Study on Suicide	16% male 84% female	71% C	55%	Unavailable	SI group was more likely to be C	Cutting, burning, hitting, pulling hair, biting, inserting objects under skin, picking; not suicide attempts

Study	Time frame	Method	Age	Location	Study type	Gender	Ethnicity	Prevalence	Gender differences	Ethnic differences	Definition
Jacobsen et al., 2006	Lifetime	Semi-structured interview	M = 15.08 Range = 12–19	New York	Study on SI and suicide	34% male 66% female	68.8% HIS 20.5% AA 4.7% C 4.3% Other	12% SI only 17% SI and suicide attempt	Females are three times more likely than males to be in one of the three self-harm groups (SI, SI with suicide, and suicide) than the no self-harm group; no difference in gender distribution across the three self-harm groups	None found	Cutting, burning, overdosing, jumping from high place, ingesting poison, done without suicidal intent
Walsh & Rosen, 1985	1 year	Gathered from daily written reports by direct care staff	M = 16.1	Worcester, Mass.	Study on SI	64% male 36% female	Unavailable	40%	Unavailable	Unavailable	No specific definition provided
Nock & Prinstein, 2004	1 year	Forced choice with the option of providing other SI behaviors	M = 14.8 Range = 12–17	New England	Study on SI	30% male 70% female	72.2% C 1.2% LAT 4.6% AA 2.1% Other	82.4%	No gender differences found for frequency, method, or age of onset	No ethnic differences found for frequency, method, or age of onset	Cutting, burning, hitting, pulling hair, biting, inserting objects under skin, picking; not suicide attempts
Adult Studies											
Briere & Gil, 1998	6 months	Forced choice, one item	M = 36 Range = 18–58	United States	Taken from a larger study on trauma	22% male 78% female	81% C 6% AA 12% A 5% A	21%	No gender differences	Unavailable	Intentionally hurting oneself without suicidal intent

TABLE 2.1 Prevalence of Non-suicidal Self-Injury with Clinical Settings (continued)

Study	Time Frame	Design	Sample (Age)	Location	Recruitment	Gender Distribution	Ethnic Distribution	Prevalence	Gender Differences	Ethnicity Differences	NSSI Definition
Claes, Vandereycken, & Vertommen, 2005	1 year	Forced choice	M = 24.33 (7.4) N = 101	Specialized inpatient unit for eating disordered patients	Study on piercing, tattooing, and SI	All female	Unavailable	64.9%	N/A	Unavailable	Scratching, cutting, burning, biting
Deiter, Nicholls, & Pearlman, 2000	Lifetime	Checklist forced choice	M = 38 Range = 18–77 N = 233	Partial hospital-treatment center and outpatient psychotherapy clinic	Study on SI	25% male 75% female	Unavailable	58%	Unavailable	Unavailable	Cutting, burning, hitting, biting, scratching, head-banging; suicide attempts included
Evren, Kural, & Cakmak, 2006	Not specified	Semi-structured interview	N = 112	Istanbul, Turkey	Study on SI	All male	Unavailable	33%	N/A	Unavailable	Cutting, burning, hitting, pulling hair, biting, inserting objects under skin, picking; not suicide attempts
Fliege, Kocalevent, Walter, Beck, & Gratz, 2006	Lifetime	Two measures, both forced choice	M = 41.9 (14.9) Range = 17–77	Germany	Study on SI	67% female 33% male	Unavailable	30% & 20%	No gender differences	Unavailable	Physically harming oneself without conscious suicidal intent
Pattison & Kahan, 1983	Varying	Case studies	M = 23 Range= 6–75	Various clinical settings	Clinical literature review for published case studies of SI	48% male 52% female	Unavailable	N/A	No gender differences	Unavailable	Cases chosen based on deliberate self-harm of low lethality; no overdoses, no indirect self-harm, no very young children

Abbreviations: SI = self-injury, C = Caucasian, AA = African American, H= Hispanic, A = Asian, NA = Native American, LAT = Latin American the exception of Whitlock, Eckenrode, et al., (2006), who reported only a very small gender difference. Of note, one robust gender difference in adolescents and young adults in community settings that is just emerging is that males and females engage in different types of self-injury. Specifically, males are more likely to self-hit, and females are more likely to cut (Heath, Toste, Nedecheva, & Charlebois, 2008; Izutsu et al., 2006; Laye-Gindhu & Schonert-Reichl, 2005; Whitlock, Eckenrode, et al., 2006). Thus, self-injury is not necessarily a predominately female behavior, and the types of self-injury appear to differ by gender.

Interestingly, with regard to location, there appears to be little variation in the behavior of adolescents across urban and suburban settings or countries. Ross and Heath (2002) compared an urban to a suburban high school setting and found no differences. Other researchers with a variety of school samples have found similar prevalence rates (e.g., Laye-Gindhu & Schonert-Reichl, 2005; Muehlenkamp & Gutierrez, 2004). At this time there are too few studies in non-Western countries to make any generalized assumptions regarding self-injury in adolescents across cultures. However, Izutsu et al., (2006) De Leo and Heller (2004), and Zoroglu et al., (2003) in Japan, Australia, and Turkey, respectively, report similar lifetime prevalence rates of self-injury as defined in this chapter, ranging from approximately 10–20%. This may indicate that the occurrence of self-injury crosses at least some cultures. Studies of self-injury are lacking in less-developed countries where anecdotally, clinicians report not seeing the behavior except in conjunction with personality disorders (Heath, Toste, & Zinck, 2008).

Another interesting finding in community sample studies is that there appears to be a racial difference, with Caucasian youth being more likely to engage in NSSI such as cutting, burning, and self-hitting than African-American and African-Canadian youth (Lloyd-Richardson et al., 2007; Muehlenkamp & Gutierrez, 2004, 2007; Ross & Heath, 2002; Whitlock, Eckenrode, et al., 2006). Clinically, this has been reported for a number of years, but only recently has there been empirical support for this observation. A final, more tentative finding in some of the young adult community studies is that NSSI may occur more frequently in individuals who are gay, lesbian, or conflicted about their sexual orientation (e.g., Gratz, 2006; Whitlock, Eckenrode, et al., 2006). However, this preliminary finding requires further study.

Critical analysis of prevalence studies with reference to definitional and methodological variations provides the reader with a clearer picture of the occurrence of NSSI in youth. It is important to emphasize that the exclusion in this review of suicide attempts, intent, or behaviors resulted in the exclusion of a number of substantial bodies of work that employ the CASE definition of self-harm. Specifically, the work of Hawton and colleagues in the U.K., (e.g., Hawton et al., 2000; Hawton et. al., 2002; Hawton et al., 2003; Hawton, Harriss, & Zahl, 2006) and De Leo and Heller's large-scale study of high school students in Aus-

TABLE 2.2 Prevalence of NSSI within Community Settings

Study	Time Frame	Design	Sample (Age)	Location	Recruitment	Gender Distribution	Ethnic Distribution	Prevalence	Gender Differences	Ethnicity Differences	NSSI Definition
						Adolescent Studies					
Laye-Gindhu & Schonert-Reichl, 2005	Lifetime	Open-ended, forced choice	High school students M = 15.34 Range = 13–18	Public high school in Canada	Study on health behaviors	44% male 56% female	70% C 13% AS 7% mixed 10% other	13.2%	Yes (16.9% females, 8.5% males)	None	SI leading to immediate visible injury
Izutsu et al., 2006	Current	Forced choice	High school students M = 14	Japan	Study on SI	50% male 50% female	N/A	24.50%	Yes, (30.40% males, 18.6% females)	N/A	Substance abuse
Muehlenkamp & Gutierrez, 2004	Lifetime	Open-ended, forced choice	High school students M = 16.27	Midwests	Ongoing larger study	55.5% male 45.5% female	62.2% C 15.2% AA 7.7% H 14.9% other	15.9% (42% doing it currently, 24% past year)	No (45.2% SIers female)	C more likely to SI	Hanging, jumping from high places, overdoses
Muehlenkamp & Gutierrez, 2007	Lifetime	Forced choice rating scales	M = 15.53	Midwest	Ongoing suicide screening	62.3% female 7.7% male	43.8% C 28.4% AA 8.1 H 11.8% multi-ethnic 2.0% A 1.4% unknown	16.1%	None for NSSI group	C more likely to SI	Scratching
Nixon et al., 2008	Lifetime	Interview and self-report	M = 17.8 Range = 14–20	British Columbia, Canada	Prevalence and mental health issues	46% male 54% female	N/A	16.9%	Yes (22.9% male, 77.1% female)	N/A	Deliberate self-harm
Patton et al., 1997	Past 12 months	Open ended	Community M = 15.9	Victoria, Australia	Study on health issues	37.5% male 65% female	N/A	5.1%	Yes (6.4% females, 4.0% males)	N/A	Self-poisoning, recklessness

Study	Time frame	Method	Sample	Location	Study type	Gender	Ethnicity	Prevalence	Gender differences	Ethnicity differences	Type of SI
Rodham et al., 2004	Past 12 months	Open ended and forced choice	High school students Range = 15–16	England	Study on lifestyle and coping skills	22% male 78% female	N/A	3.65%	Yes (differences in intent)	N/A	Self-cutting only
Ross & Heath, 2002	Lifetime	Forced choice, interview	High school	Canada	Study on coping	50% male 50% female	77% C 5% AA 6.5% A 3.3% H 8.2% other	13.9%	No, based on gender distribution	N/A	Scratching, picking at wounds, inserting objects under skin or nails
Lloyd, Kelley, & Hope, 1997	Past 12 months	Forced choice checklist	M = 15.37 Range = 12–19	Baton Rouge, Louisiana	Study on SI	44% male 56% female	63% C 29% AA 1% A 1% LAT	39%	No gender differences	C more likely to SI than AA	Cutting, self-hitting, pinching, scratching, biting, burning
Lloyd-Richardson et al., 2007	Past 12 months	Forced choice checklist	High school students M = 15.5	United States	Study on difficulties faced by teens	43% male 57% female	50.9% AA 43.7% C 1.8% A 1.3% LAT 2.4% other	46.5% total; 27.7% moderate or severe	None (mild SI 43.7% male, moderate and severe SI 46% male)	C + AA more likely to SI moderately or severely	Scratching, picking at wounds, inserting objects under skin or nails
Zoroglu et al., 2003	Lifetime	Forced choice	High school students M = 15.9	Istanbul, Turkey	Study on life experiences	38.9% male 61.1% female	N/A	21.4%	None (21.5% Female, 21.3% Male)	N/A	Slashing, pulling hair
Adult Studies											
Briere & Gil, 1998	Past 6 months	Forced choice	M = 46 Range = 18–90	United States	Study on trauma	50% male 50% female	75% C 11% AA 7% H 3% A 2% NA 2% other	4%	No (4.12% female, 3.0% male)	N/A	Scratching

TABLE 2.2 Prevalence of NSSI within Community Settings (continued)

Study	Time Frame	Design	Sample (Age)	Location	Recruitment	Gender Distribution	Ethnic Distribution	Prevalence	Gender Differences	Ethnicity Differences	NSSI Definition
Boudewyn & Liem, 1995	Lifetime	Forced choice	College students M = 24.87 Range = 16–65	USA	Study of mental health	39% male 61% female	66% C 44% other	Approx. 13.53%	Approx. 9.57% males, 15.55% females	N/A	N/A
Gratz et al., 2002	Lifetime	Forced choice checklist	College students M = 22.73	United States	Study of SI	33% male 67% female	62% C 18% A 10% AA 5% H 5% other	38%	No (36% female, 41% male)	None	Based on DSHI (biting, bone breaking)
Gratz, 2006	Lifetime	Forced choice checklist	M = 23.29 Range = 18–55	United States	Study of SI	All female (males excluded)	66% C 16% A 8% AA 5% H 5% other	37%	N/A	C + other more likely to SI	Based on DSHI (biting, bone breaking)
Heath et al., 2007	Lifetime	Forced choice	College students M = 20.64 Range = 18–55	Canada	Study of coping	22% male 78% female	N/A	11.68%	None	N/A	Scratching, picking at wound, inserting objects under skin or nails
Klonsky, Oltmanns, & Turkheimer, 2003	Lifetime	Forced choice or two items	M = 20	United States	Study on personality and pathology	62% male 38% female	65% C 17% AA 4% H 3% A 1% NA 10% other	4%	None (item 1 = 2.5% males, 2.4% females, item 2 = 2.5% males, 1.7% females)	N/A	Based on two items from schedule for nonadaptive and adaptive personality

Nada-Raja, Skegg, Langley, Morrison, & Sowerby, 2003	Past 12 months	Interview	Community M = 26	Dunedin	Study on SI	51% male 49% female	N/A	15%	N/A (9.12% males, 5.80% females)	N/A	ICD definition + biting, withholding food, excessive exercise, intoxication
Whitlock, Eckenrode, & Silverman, 2006	Lifetime	Forced choice	College students M = N/A Range = 18–24	United States	Study on mental health	47.3% male 56.3% female	64.7% C 3.7% AA 4.3% H 17.1% A 10.2% other	17%	Yes (% N/A)	A least likely to SI	Scratching, pinching, interfering with wound healing, rubbing glass, hair pulling

Abbreviations: SI = self-injury, C = Caucasian, AA = African American, H = Hispanic, A = Asian, NA = Native American, LAT = Latin American tralia (2004) were not included. The contribution of the research from the CASE group must be acknowledged, as it has specific implications for the study of NSSI. Consistent with broader definitions of self-injury, researchers employing the CASE definition find reliable gender differences. In a large study of past-year deliberate self-harm in adolescents, Hawton and colleagues reported 6.9% prevalence, with significantly more females than males (Hawton et al., 2002). De Leo and Heller's study of 3,767 high school students in Australia reported a lifetime deliberate self-harm prevalence of 12.4%, with approximately 60% reporting cutting and 30% reporting overdoses, and a significant gender difference. The importance of determining the presence or absence of suicide intent in estimates of self-harm for purposes of clarity across the field has been acknowledged (e.g., Silverman, Berman, Sanddal, O'Carroll, & Joiner, 2007).

Close scrutiny is needed in evaluating prevalence studies. The clinician as critical consumer of this material needs to be cognizant of the numerous variables that can influence the final results.

WHEN DOES IT START? AGE OF ONSET

Although there is substantial variation in definitions of self-injury, measurement issues, and sample selection, with regards to findings of age of onset, there is general agreement. Researchers around the world regardless of definition or measurement approach concur that the majority of youth who engage in self-injury begin between the ages of 13 and 15 (e.g., Muehlenkamp & Gutierrez, 2007; Ross & Heath, 2002; Sourander et al., 2006). However, although the majority begin at this time, there is some evidence that a significant proportion of youth begin earlier. For example, Ross and Heath (2002) in their study of high school students found that 25% of their sample indicated they first engaged in self-injury before age 12.

IS IT INCREASING?

Although the media largely states that self-injury is increasing, documenting this is more difficult. Whereas many researchers and clinicians agree that self-injurious behaviors are increasing among adolescents (e.g., Derouin & Bravender, 2004; Plener & Muehlenkamp, 2007; Walsh, 2006; White Kress, 2003), very little empirical evidence exists to support this claim. Most commonly, the support for the statement that self-injury is increasing is derived from studies of trends in "self-harm" in the United Kingdom (e.g., Hawton et al., 2003; Olfson, Gameroff, Marcus, Greenberg, & Shaffer, 2005), all of which employ a much broader definition that includes all nonfatal self-inflicted harm (e.g., overdoses, suicide attempts). Evaluating prevalence estimates in the literature over the past 15 years would be misleading because, in clinical settings, this behavior was often subsumed under personality disorders and not reported separately. In addition, a very limited number of community studies were conducted, and, without the current level of cultural awareness of the behavior, self-reports may have been minimized due to social desirability. Consistent with the idea that youth today are more comfortable seeking help for self-injury, Whitlock, Eells, Cummings, and Purington (2008) found that the majority of mental health providers from college and university counseling centers in their study reported both increases in overall prevalence of mental health disorders among youth and specific increases in help seeking for self-injuring behaviors over the past five years. Furthermore, the frequency of the topic of self-injury in the media has increased in the past 15 years, which may influence reports and identifications of self-injury.

SUMMARY

Prevalence varies across community and clinical settings depending on numerous definitional and methodological variations in the studies. Current evidence suggests that (a) approximately 15% to 20% of adolescents in the community admit to engaging in self-injury at least once; (b) in clinical settings, more females engage in NSSI, whereas in the community it appears that there is no gender difference in prevalence but the type of the self-injury differs; (c) NSSI may be more common in Caucasian youth and gay and lesbian youth or youth who are conflicted about their sexuality; (d) for the majority, self-injury begins between the ages of 13 and 15, although a minority do begin earlier; and (e) the cultural awareness and study of self-injury is increasing, but it remains unclear if self-injury itself is on the rise in youth.

IMPLICATIONS FOR PRACTITIONERS

Whether self-injurious behaviors are increasing or not, it is clear that the phenomenon is prevalent among adolescents and young adults within both community and clinical populations. Practitioners must be prepared to work with youth who self-injure or to refer, if need be. Given that cultural awareness about self-injury is growing, youth are increasingly comfortable talking about it with each other; however, they may remain apprehensive about discussing NSSI with a clinician and other professionals, for fear of being labeled or judged.

Prevalence rates differ based on whether or not youth are in a community or clinical setting, but evidence shows that rates also differ depending on the type of youth within the community. For instance, in a high-functioning group in the community, males and females typically show similar rates of NSSI engagement. However, among the general public, rates show that females are more likely to engage in NSSI, or at least are more likely to seek help for their self-injuring. Additionally, practitioners should be aware that males and females differ in the methods used for self-injury, with females more likely to cut or overdose without suicidal intent, and males tending to hit themselves.

Typically, self-injury begins in early- to mid-adolescence; therefore, practitioners should be cognizant of this trend when working with youth aged 13–15. Practitioners should also be aware that rates of NSSI are higher in Caucasian youth, as well as in nonheterosexual youth or youth struggling with their sexuality. Finally, it is important to consider the benefits and disadvantages of using a checklist or rating scale to track behaviors as opposed to an interview format to assess self-injury. Practitioners should be aware of the typical profile of self-injurers reported in the literature but also be aware of the high level of secrecy and deception surrounding NSSI. Self-injury is prevalent among adolescents and young adults, and practitioners should be prepared to deal with the behaviors when working with youth in clinical and community settings.

CONCLUSION

The number of adolescents and young adults who engage in self-injury depends on a variety of factors, including the nature of the setting. For instance, are they in a clinical or psychiatric facility or group, or perhaps are they in a school setting or the wider community? The different settings can inform us about the prevalence of NSSI, the severity, and even the functions of the behavior, in addition to telling us something about the gender distribution we are likely to see among the self-injurers. Self-injury is often initiated in mid-adolescence; however, with heightened awareness about the behavior among youth, and the popular media, there is a risk of this behavior starting earlier.

REFERENCES

Boudewyn, A. C., & Liem, J. H. (1995). Psychological, interpersonal, and behavioral correlates of chronic self-destructiveness: An exploratory study. *Psychological Reports, 77,* 1283–1297.

Briere, J., & Gil, E. (1998). Self-mutilation in clinical and general population samples: Prevalence, correlates, and functions. *American Journal of Orthopsychiatry, 64,* 609–620.

Claes, L., Vandereycken, W., & Vertommen, H. (2005). Self-care versus self-harm: Piercing, tattooing, and self-injuring in eating disorders. *European Eating Disorders Review, 13,* 11–18.

Deiter, P. J., Nicholls, S. S., & Pearlman, L. A. (2000). Self-injury and self capacities: Assisting an individual in crisis. *Journal of Clinical Psychology, 56,* 1173–1191.

De Leo, D., & Heller, T. S. (2004). Who are the kids who self-harm? An Australian self-report school survey. *Medical Journal of Australia, 181,* 140–144.

Derouin, A., & Bravender, T. (2004). Living on the edge: The current phenomenon of self-mutilation in adolescents. *American Journal of Maternal/Child Nursing, 29,* 12–18.

Evren, C., Kural, S., & Cakmak, D. (2006). Clinical correlates of self-mutilation in Turkish male substance-dependent inpatients. *Psychopathology, 39,* 248–254.

Fliege, H., Kocalevent, R. D., Walter, O. B., Beck, S., & Gratz, K. L. (2006). Three assessment tools for deliberate self-harm and suicide behavior: Evaluation and psychopathological correlates. *Journal of Psychosomatic Research, 61,* 113–121.

Gratz, K. L. (2006). Risk factors for deliberate self-harm among female college students: The role and interaction of childhood maltreatment, emotional inexpressivity, and affect intensity/reactivity. *American Journal of Orthopsychiatry, 76,* 238–250.

Gratz, K., Conrad, S. D., & Roemer, L. (2002). Risk factors for deliberate self-harm among college students. *American Journal of Orthopsychiatry, 72,* 128–140.

Guertin, T., Lloyd-Richardson, E., Spirito, A., Donaldson, D., & Boergers, J. (2001). Self-mutilative behavior in adolescents who attempt suicide by overdose. *Journal of the American Academy of Child and Adolescent Psychiatry, 40,* 1062–1069.

Haavisto, A., Sourander, A., Multimaki, P., Parkkola, K., Santalahti, P., Helenius, H., et al. (2005). Factors associated with ideation and acts of deliberate self-harm among 18-year-old boys. A prospective 10-year follow up study. *Social Psychiatry and Psychiatric Epidemiology, 40,* 912–921.

Hawton, K., Fagg, J., Simkin, S., Bale, E., & Bond, A. (2000). Deliberate self-harm in adolescents in Oxford, 1985–1995. *Journal of Adolescence, 23,* 47–55.

Hawton, K., Hall, S., Simkin, S., Bale, L., Bond, A., Codd, S., et al. (2003). Deliberate self-harm in adolescents: A study of characteristics and trends in Oxford, 1990–2000. *Journal of Child Psychology and Psychiatry, 44*(8), 1191–1198.

Hawton, K., Harriss, L., & Zahl, D. (2006). Deaths from all causes in a long-term follow up study of 11583 deliberate self-harm patients. *Psychological Medicine, 36,* 397–405.

Hawton, K., Rodham, K., Evans, E., & Weatherall, R. (2002). Deliberate self harm in adolescents: Self report survey in schools in England. *British Medical Journal, 325,* 1207–1211.

Heath, N. L., Toste, J. R., Nedecheva, T., & Charlebois, A. (2008). An examination of non-suicidal self-injury among college students. *Journal of Mental Health Counselling, 30*(2), 1–20.

Heath, N. L., Toste, J., & Zinck, L. C. (2008). Understanding adolescent self-injury from a resilience perspective: A model for international interpretation. In L. Liebenberg & M. Ungar (Eds.), *Resilience in action: Working with youth across cultures and contexts.* University of Toronto Press.

Izutsu, T., Shimotsu, S., Matsumoto, T., Okada, T., Kikuchi, A., Kojimoto, M., et al. (2006). Deliberate self-harm and childhood hyperactivity in junior high school students. *European Child and Adolescent Psychiatry, 14,* 1–5.

Jacobsen, C. M., Muehlenkamp, J. J., & Miller A. L. (2006). Psychiatric impairment among adolescents engaging in different types of deliberate self-harm. Manuscript submitted for publication.

Klonsky, E. D., Oltmanns, T. F., & Turkheimer, E. (2003). Deliberate self-harm in a nonclinical population: Prevalence and psychological correlates. *American Journal of Psychiatry, 160,* 1501–1508.

Laye-Gindhu, A., & Schonert-Reichl, K. A. (2005). Nonsuicidal self-harm among community adoelscents: Understanding the "whats" and "whys" of self-harm. *Journal of Youth and Adolescence, 34,* 445–457.

Lloyd, E. E. (1997). Self-mutilation in a community sample of adolescents. *Dissertation Abstracts International: Section B: The Sciences & Engineering,* 58(9-B), 5127.

Lloyd, E. E., Kelley, M. L., & Hope, T. (1997). *Self-mutilation in a community sample of adolescents: Descriptive characteristics and provisional prevalence rates.* Society for Behavioral Medicine annual meeting. New Orleans, LA.

Lloyd-Richardson, E. E., Perrine, N., Dierker, L., & Kelley, M. L. (2007). Characteristics and functions of non-suicidal self-injury in a community sample of adolescents. *Psychological Medicine, 37*(8), 1183–1192.

Muehlenkamp, J. J., & Gutierrez, P. M. (2004). An investigation of differences between self-injurious behavior and suicide attempts in a sample of adolescents. *Suicide and Life-Threatening Behavior, 34,* 12–23.

Muehlenkamp, J. J., & Gutierrez, P. M. (2007). Risk for suicide attempts among adolescents who engage in non-suicide self-injury. *Archives of Suicide Research, 11,* 69–82

Nada-Raja, S., Skegg, K., Langley, J., Morrison, D., & Sowerby, P. (2004). Self-harmful behaviors in a population-based sample of young adults. *Suicide and Life-Threatening Behavior, 34,* 177–186.

Nixon, M. K., Cloutier, P. F., & Aggarwal, S. (2002). Affect regulation and addictive aspects of repetitive self-injury in hospitalized adolescents. *Journal of the American Academy of Child & Adolescent Psychiatry, 41,* 1333–1341.

Nixon, M. K., Cloutier, P., & Jansson, S. M. (2008). Nonsuicidal self-harm in youth: A population-based survey. *Canadian Medical Association Journal, 178,* 306–312.

Nock, M. K., & Prinstein, M. J. (2004). A functional approach to the assessment of self-mutilative behavior. *Journal of Consulting and Clinical Psychology, 72,* 885–890.

Olfson, M., Gameroff, M. J., Marcu, S. C., Greenberg, T., & Shaffer, D. (2005). Emergency treatment of young people following deliberate self-harm. *Archives of General Psychiatry, 62,* 1122–1128.

Pattison, E. M., & Kahan, J. (1983). The deliberate self-harm syndrome. *American Journal of Psychiatry, 140,* 867–872.

Patton, G. C., Harris, R., Carlin, J. B., Hibbert, M. E., Coffey, C., Schwartz, M., et al. (1997). Adolescent suicidal behaviors: A population-based study of risk. *Psychological Medicine, 27,* 715–724.

Plener, P. L., & Muehlenkamp, J. (2007). Correspondence: Letter to the editor. *Psychological Medicine, 37,* 1.

Rodham, K., Hawton, K., & Evans, E. (2004). Reasons for deliberate self-harm: Comparison of self-poisoners and self-cutters in a community sample of adolescents. *Journal of the American Academy of Child and Adolescent Psychiatry, 43*, 80–87.

Ross, S., & Heath, N. L. (2002). A study of the frequency of self-mutilation in a community sample of adolescents. *Journal of Youth and Adolescence, 31*, 67–77.

Silverman, M. M., Berman, A. L., Sanddal, N. D., O'Carroll, P. W., & Joiner, T. E. (2007). Rebuilding the Tower of Babel: A revised nomenclature for the study of suicide and suicide behaviours. Part 2: Suicide-related ideations, communications, and behaviors. *Suicide and Life-Threatening Behavior, 37*, 264–277.

Sourander, A., Aromaa, A., Pihlakoski, L., Haavisto, A., Rautava, P., Helenius, H., et al. (2006). Early predictors of deliberate self-harm among adolescents. A prospective follow-up study from age 3 to age 15. *Journal of Affective Disorders, 93*, 87–96.

Walsh, B. W. (2006). *Treating self-injury: A practical guide*. New York: Guilford Press.

Walsh, B. W., & Rosen, P. (1985). Self-mutilation and contagion: An empirical test. *The American Journal of Psychiatry, 142*, 119–120.

White Kress, V. E. (2003). Self-injurious behaviors: Assessment and diagnosis. *Journal of Counseling and Development, 81*, 490–496.

Whitlock, J., Eckenrode, J., & Silverman, D. (2006). Self-injurious behaviors in a college. *Pediatrics, 117*, 1939–1948.

Whitlock, J., Eells, G., Cummings, N., & Purington, A. (2008). Nonsuicidal self-injury in college populations: Mental health provider assessment of prevalence and need. Manuscript submitted for publication.

Zoroglu, S. S., Tuzun, U., Sar, V., Tutkun, H., Savas, H. A., Ozturk, M., et al. (2003). Suicide attempt and self-mutilation among Turkish high school students in relation with abuse, neglect and dissociation. *Psychiatry & Clinical Neurosciences, 57*, 119–126.

3

Functions of Adolescent Nonsuicidal Self-Injury

ELIZABETH E. LLOYD-RICHARDSON, MATTHEW K. NOCK, AND MITCHELL J. PRINSTEIN

In this chapter, the practitioner will gain an understanding of:

- The array of possible functions of NSSI for youth
- How these functions are expressed by youth
- A popular cognitive behavioral model of NSSI functions

Nonsuicidal self-injury (NSSI) consists of a broad class of behaviors defined by direct, deliberate, socially unacceptable destruction of one's own body tissue without intent to die (Favazza, 1989). Whereas NSSI has been described in the clinical literature for nearly a century (Menninger, 1938), allowing for ample descriptive information of the phenomenon and its psychosocial correlates, we have little understanding of what precipitates NSSI and the functions it serves for individuals. Several theoretical models have been proposed to organize clinical descriptions (Favazza, 1998; Messer & Fremouw, 2007; Suyemoto, 1998), although almost none have been empirically evaluated in self-injurers.

The general consensus is that NSSI is most commonly initiated in adolescence (Favazza & Conterio, 1988), with prevalence from 5.1% to over 40% of adolescent and young adult populations, and it has been suggested that these rates may be increasing (see Chapter 2 for review). Yet, despite the prevalence of this behavior, improving our understanding of NSSI has been difficult given continued struggles with several key issues, such as the use of multiple disparate terms to describe the behavior (e.g., self-injurious behavior, self-mutilation, deliberate self-harm, NSSI), a lack of a clear definition of what is included within this definition, and whether NSSI behaviors should be considered distinct from suicide attempts. These issues are addressed in detail in other chapters in this book, and they directly impact the progress that has been made investigating the functions that NSSI serves, particularly among adolescents.

The purpose of this chapter is to review the existing literature pertaining to the many functions NSSI serves in adolescence. A cursory review of the self-injury literature will find numerous case reports documenting clinical descriptions of NSSI and its various motives. This chapter, however, will draw from the limited empirical studies conducted to date that have investigated the functions of NSSI in youth, also referencing adult studies when appropriate. Furthermore, we intend to present an overarching theoretical framework in which to consider and organize the existing literature of the functions of NSSI. We begin our discussion by presenting three brief clinical vignettes that illustrate the many functions served by NSSI from the perspective of the adolescent. These will be referred to for illustration of concepts throughout this chapter.

CLINICAL VIGNETTES

Samantha: 14 years old (ninth grade); 2-year history of NSSI.

The reasons I cut are to deal with my own insecurities about my looks and about who I am. I look in the mirror and I do not like my body. For the past three years, I have been keeping a log of the calories and the food that I eat. I look at my mother and see how perfect she is. I cut myself when I feel bad about my body. I wear long sleeves even in the summer to hide the scars, but I know my family has seen them. They do not say anything. Recently over Christmas break, my brother made fun of me about my body in front of a guy that I like and then my brother tried to touch me against my will. I didn't know what to do. I was so hurt that I cut again. I only talk to my best friend at school, and she knows everything about me including the cutting. She threatened to tell her parents but I made her promise that she wouldn't. When things are going well for me, I do not cut myself, but when I start to feel worried about my body I want to punish myself for how I look. Sometimes my insecurities get the best of me, and cutting is the only thing that brings relief from feeling so bad. I know that cutting is not a good thing to do, but it's my only escape.

Jack: 17 years old (11th grade); 2-year history of NSSI.

I don't understand why I feel so stressed all the time. I've felt this way ever since I can remember. Sometimes I wish there could be something that happened to me to explain why I feel this way. I wish I could say it was because I didn't have enough to eat or a caring family, but I can't put into words why I feel the way I do. Very few people know that I have these feelings. Most people just see what I allow them to see. Hurting myself is the easiest way I know to help with dealing with all of the hurt, anger, and pain of life. It's not so much the big things, but the little stresses that are so hard to handle. But, I worry that I'm needing to do it more and more, because the relief I'm getting from it just doesn't last as long as it used to. Sometimes I feel numb, and inflicting pain is the only way I truly feel something. It's beginning to feel like less of a choice to cut myself. Now I can't imagine not having it as a way to cope.

Karen: 20 years old (currently enrolled in college); 6-year history of NSSI.

I have always had boyfriends since I was in junior high, but last year I started to date someone seriously. I would cut myself infrequently—maybe twice a year—but in the past 8 months I have begun to do it more frequently. My boyfriend will make comments about my looks, which makes me feel like I'm not good enough. I want him to love me for who I am—scars and all. We spend a lot of our time together drinking [alcohol] and listening to music. I think that drinking—kind of like cutting—is a way to show your pain to others. It's a way to tell the world that you're hurting inside. Just like some of my friends that starve themselves. And even though I know that cutting is a reflection of the pain I feel, it's impossible for me to imagine not doing it. If you take it away, I'd be like everyone else.

A FUNCTIONAL MODEL OF NSSI

Although many clinicians and authors have proposed explanations of why people engage in NSSI, relatively little systematic research has addressed this question. Most theoretical and empirical work on the functions of NSSI has focused on the negatively reinforcing properties of NSSI (e.g., Chapman, Gratz, & Brown, 2006; Haines, Williams, Brain, & Wilson, 1995; Klonsky, 2006). Several authors have proposed other functions of NSSI, including antidissociation, antisuicide, boundary definition, self-punishment, and sexual conflict (Favazza, 1989; Klonsky, 2006, 2007; Messer & Fremouw, 2007; Suyemoto, 1998).

Before reviewing and synthesizing the theoretical literature on the functions of NSSI, there are several important factors worth consideration. First, NSSI is contextually complex, meaning that an individual is inextricably tied to his environment. As Suyemoto (1998) ascribes in her review of functional models of NSSI, "One of the most difficult tasks in attempting to understand any pathological behavior is discerning why this *particular* behavior, at this *particular* time, serves this *particular* function, for this *particular* patient." Thus, an individual portrait of a self-injurer may embody many reasons for NSSI that vary over time and context. It is also likely that changes may take place in an individual along the course of their experimentation with self-injury, altering the functions served by the behavior.

Similarly, a second consideration is that NSSI is likely an overdetermined behavior, meaning it may serve multiple functions simultaneously for an individual. Research done by Brown and colleagues (2002) evaluated motivations for both suicide attempts and NSSI in a sample of 75 women diagnosed with borderline personality disorder. Overall reasons for NSSI differed from those for suicide attempts, with participants endorsing an average of 10 reasons for their latest NSSI episode, most frequently described as intending to express anger, punishing oneself, generating normal feelings, and distracting oneself. While recent reviews outline the empirical support for various functions of NSSI, the theoretical and empirical relationships between these various functions remains unclear (Klonsky, 2007). From a clinical perspective, it is immensely challengng to tease apart the specific functions of NSSI for an individual. However, our understanding of these functions is critical to success in altering future behaviors and improving the lives of these patients.

A third issue involves the lack of understanding we have of NSSI among youth. Models of NSSI proposed in the adult literature have only recently been evaluated in adolescent populations. A recent article by Messer and Fremouw (2007) reviews data supportive of seven explanatory models of NSSI in adolescents based on historical literature. While the authors critique the methodological limitations to existing research, they document empirical support for a behavioral and environmental model of NSSI and emphasize the complex nature of adolescent NSSI. It remains unclear how these functional models may be relevant to various populations of youth and under what circumstances they may deviate from those based on adult samples.

Lastly, at least two factors have limited research on the functions of NSSI. First, many authors use the term *function* in different ways. This is not merely an academic issue, but one that can lead to confusion across researchers and clinicians and in explaining NSSI to clients and the public. A long and rich literature on learning theory and behavior therapy has taken a functional approach to understanding, predicting, and treating behavior. From this perspective, the study of the function of a behavior refers to an analysis of the effects or events that cause or determine a given behavior. The goal of the clinician is to examine the antecedents and consequences of a behavior to understand and treat it. It is from this tradition that *functional analyses* or *behavioral analyses*, which are used in several different forms of behavioral therapies, were derived. Much of the prior work on NSSI has used the term *function* more loosely to simply mean the reason for or purpose of a behavior. For instance, the suggestion that NSSI serves an antisuicide or boundary definition function says little about the antecedents or consequences of NSSI.

A second limitation is that, although multiple functions have been proposed, few attempts have been made to integrate these into a cohesive theoretical model that can inform research and practice in this area. Chapman and colleagues (2006) proposed an experiential avoidance model of NSSI, arguing that the leading theories of NSSI (e.g., affect regulation model, dissociation model, and boundaries model) can be unified by the notion that NSSI allows the individual to escape or otherwise manage their emotions. NSSI is a self-punishment that is negatively reinforced through the reduction of unwanted internal emotional experiences. The authors argue that experiential avoidance allows for the integration of various pieces of the puzzle of NSSI, with support from research documenting common patient reports of emotional relief or regulation following NSSI (Brown, Comtois, & Linehan, 2002) and corroborating findings from psychophysiological studies (Haines et al., 1995). Indeed, among hospitalized adolescent self-injurers, affect regulation ("to cope with feelings of depression"; "to release unbearable tension") was the most frequently endorsed reason for NSSI (Nixon, Cloutier, & Aggarwal, 2002). Although this proposed theoretical framework is promising, evaluation of the experiential avoidance model and its proposed pathways is warranted. Furthermore, while emphasizing the negatively reinforcing properties of NSSI, it is likely that NSSI serves more than this single function.

In an attempt to address the limitations denoted above, we recently proposed and evaluated a comprehensive, four-function model of NSSI among adolescents that is consistent with and draws from prior work on learning theory and behavior therapy (see Nock & Prinstein, 2004, 2005), as well as research on the functions of NSSI among samples of individuals with developmental disabilities (e.g., Iwata et al., 1994) and adult women diagnosed with borderline personality disorder (Brown et al., 2002). Specifically, we proposed a theoretical model in which the functions of NSSI differ along two dichotomous dimensions: reinforcement for the behavior that is either negative (i.e., followed by the removal of an aversive stimulus or event) or positive (i.e., followed by the presentation of a favorable stimulus or event), and consequences that are either automatic (i.e., intrapersonal) or social (i.e., interpersonal) in nature (see Figure 3.1).

Automatic-negative reinforcement refers to an adolescents' use of NSSI to remove or stop some undesirable cognitive or emotional state, such as to release tension or to distract from disturbing thoughts. Automatic functions serve to regulate one's own *internal* states. As mentioned above, this is the function most often stated by theoretical and empirical reports, frequently described as negative affect regulation. Studies of both community adolescent self-injurers (Lloyd-Richardson, Perrine, Dierker, & Kelley, 2007; Rodham, Hawton, & Evans, 2004; Ross & Heath, 2003), as well as hospitalized adolescent self-injurers (Nixon et al., 2002), lend strong support for an automatic-negative reinforcement model of NSSI, with commonly endorsed reasons for NSSI including "to get out my frustrations," "to reduce emotional pain," to express my anger toward others," and "to reduce tension." The clinical vignette descriptions of both Samantha and Jack highlight some of the negative internal states these teens work to regulate, including reduction in stress, feelings of guilt and anger, and physical insecurities and feelings of imperfection. Indeed, among hospitalized youth, automatic-negative reinforcement is the function reported most often (Nixon et al., 2002; Nock & Prinstein, 2004) and is the only one of the four functions to be

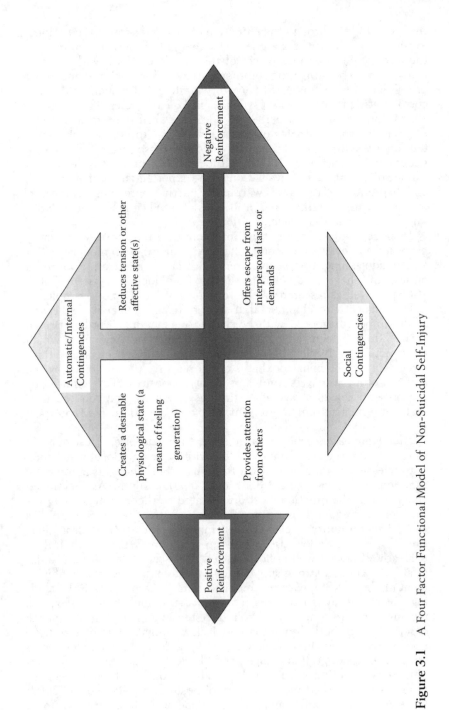

Figure 3.1   A Four Factor Functional Model of Non-Suicidal Self-Injury

significantly related to the presence of suicide attempts (Nock & Prinstein, 2005).

In contrast, *automatic-positive reinforcement* refers to the use of NSSI to generate some desired internal state. For instance, many clients report engaging in NSSI to "just feel something." Among a clinical adolescent sample, this is the second most endorsed function in this model, and endorsement of this function is strongest in the presence of symptoms of posttraumatic stress disorder and depression (Nock & Prinstein, 2005). This is not surprising, as these disorders are characterized by symptoms of depressed mood, anhedonia, and numbness. Jack's writing describes his use of NSSI to escape feeling numb and "feel something," even if it is pain. His clinical vignette also suggests a developmental progression in his NSSI from initial automatic-negative reinforcement functions to more frequent self-injury, serving an automatic-positive reinforcement role.

In contrast to the automatic functions, the social functions serve to regulate one's external environment. *Social positive reinforcement* (SPR) refers to the use of NSSI to gain attention from others or to access some social resource. For instance, adolescents' reports of engaging in NSSI "to let others know how I am feeling" and "to get my clinician to (react in a certain way)" are consistent with a social positive reinforcement function. Among a sample of community adolescents, self-injurers endorsed social-reinforcement motives nearly as frequently as automatic-reinforcement motives (Lloyd-Richardson et al., 2007). Thus, community adolescents reported engaging in NSSI to influence the behaviors of others, as well as to regulate their own emotional states. In the vignette about Karen, she used NSSI as a dysfunctional way of communicating with her boyfriend and peers. Self-injury served several purposes by allowing her to express her displeasure at her boyfriend's comments on her appearance, allowing her to express in a nonverbal way the extreme pain she felt inside, and providing her with a way to feel different and stand apart from her peers. In the vignette about Samantha, we notice that, whereas she describes wearing long-sleeved clothing, she observes that her family is well aware of the hidden scars and appears to be beckoning her family to notice and pay attention to her scars and, thus, her internal pain. Although not always initiating NSSI for social-positive reinforcement motives, many teens may learn that allowing their parents or caregivers to discover their wounds may grant them access to the care they need and desire.

Social-negative reinforcement refers to the use of NSSI to escape from some interpersonal demands or tasks. Adolescents' reports of engaging in NSSI "to get out of going to school," "to get other people to leave me alone," or to "get my parents to stop fighting" are all consistent with a social-negative reinforcement function of NSSI. In the case of Karen, she describes a withdrawal from her college peer group, with the exception of her boyfriend. NSSI and alcohol abuse offer escape from the increasing demands of college life. The social functions of NSSI have been hypothesized by clinicians and families for many years, but until recently have not been examined directly. Our data suggest that, whereas hospitalized adolescents may report social functions for NSSI less frequently than automatic functions, they do endorse these functions with some regularity. Among community samples, social functions were endorsed on average as frequently as automatic functions. Endorsement of social functions is associated with the report of other social concerns by adolescents and with symptoms of depression, highlighting the fact that, just because adolescents are engaging in NSSI for social purposes, it does not mean that they are asymptomatic.

FUNCTIONS OF NSSI ACROSS VARIOUS POPULATIONS

It is important to not generalize functions of NSSI across all populations. No prior studies have examined either the psychiatric–psychosocial correlates or the functions of NSSI across developmental levels or across different referral populations (e.g., community samples, clinical outpatients, inpatients, or individuals with a specific disorder, i.e., borderline personality disorder). Moreover, no longitudinal research is available to examine whether functions of NSSI change over the course of the behavior (i.e., onset, maintenance, etc.) or as individuals gain additional experience with NSSI. Each of these gaps represents high-priority aims for future research.

A review of findings across investigations offers some preliminary evidence that functions of NSSI may change across development. Among adults, the most commonly reported function of NSSI pertains to emotion regulation (Gratz, 2003). Within community-based samples of adults (Briere & Gil, 1998; Gratz 2000; Klonsky, 2006), clinically referred samples of adults with borderline personality disorder (Brown et al., 2002), or prior sexual abuse (Briere & Gil, 1998), and even case reports (e.g., Anderson & Sansone, 2003), the relief of negative emotions (i.e., anger, anxiety, stress, sadness, guilt, or loneliness) is most commonly cited as a function served by NSSI (i.e., automatic reinforcement function). A qualitative investigation of adult self-injurers and nursing care providers for self-injurers describes both groups as explaining NSSI as a means of communicating distress by using the body as a tool, using NSSI "to express the inexpressible at that time in this way" (Reece, 2005).

Some research, predominantly on clinically referred samples of adults, also has supported an automatic-positive reinforcement function of NSSI, including the generation of feelings of vitality (e.g., Haas & Popp, 2006) or to inflict feelings of self-punishment. Recent work assessing emotional states immediately prior to, and following NSSI among community-based adolescents and young adults (Nock & Prinstein, 2006) as well as adult inmates (Chapman, 2004) is consistent with the automatic-negative reinforcement function of NSSI; individuals report high levels of emotional distress prior to, but not following, NSSI, as well as high levels of relief following engagement in this behavior. Similarly, Haines et al., (1995) investigated psychophysiological and subjective responding during situations of imagined NSSI scenarios presented to self-injuring prison inmates, noninjuring prison controls, and nonprison controls. Results found that self-injurers experienced a decrease in psychophysiological arousal and subjective response when presented with NSSI imagery scripts, lending support to an automatic-negative reinforcement model of NSSI (Haines et al., 1995). The vast majority of this prior work on functions of NSSI among adults has examined females exclusively, and few have included samples with sufficient ethnic diversity to examine potential cultural differences in NSSI functions.

Among adolescent samples, as described earlier, initial research suggests the automatic-negative reinforcement function of NSSI to be the most commonly reported function (e.g., to stop bad feelings) among clinically referred samples (Nock & Prinstein, 2004; Kumar, Pepe, & Steer, 2004), as well as incarcerated samples (Penn, Esposito, Schaeffer, Fritz, & Spirito, 2003). Nevertheless, social-negative reinforcement functions are also commonly reported among these groups, and among a community sample of adolescents, social-reinforcement items were, on average, endorsed as frequently as intrapersonal, automatic-reinforcement items (Lloyd-Richardson et al., 2007). It is reasonable to suspect that, among youth, social reinforcement functions of NSSI may be particularly salient. Both theoretical and empirical evidence support this idea. Developmental theories suggest that youths' behavior may be especially susceptible to interpersonal influence at the transition to adolescence (Steinberg & Silverberg, 1986), as well as the transition to emerging adulthood and the college years (Klonsky, 2006). Adolescents (and adolescent females in particular) are especially reactive to interpersonally themed stressors (Rudolph, 2002) and are most likely to use interpersonal models (e.g., peers) as a basis for social comparison and identity development (Harter, Stocker, & Robinson, 1996). In support of this, Hilt and colleagues (in press) found improvements in parent–child relationships among preadolescents following at least one episode of NSSI but no similar increases among their peers who did not engage in NSSI. Thus, coping with the heightened distress accompanying interpersonal stressors at this developmental stage and exposure to admired others who engage in risk-taking behaviors, such as NSSI, substance abuse, or eating disorders, each may serve as unique risk factors for the onset of this behavior.

The notion that NSSI may be prompted by emulation of admired peers, or contagion among youth, also is supported by recent preliminary findings. Nock and Prinstein (2005) reported that among adolescent psychiatric inpatients who engaged in NSSI, over 82% reported a close friend who also engaged in similar behaviors. Recent research also has documented a variety of online Internet discussions regarding NSSI predominantly populated by youth (Whitlock, Powers, & Eckenrode, 2006).

Common themes on these Internet forums include the discussion of specific strategies and techniques for engaging in NSSI, as well as discussions regarding disclosure to others and support (Whitlock et al., 2006). The perceived attractiveness or normalization of NSSI behaviors undoubtedly can be enhanced through unsupervised Internet-based discussions.

CLINICAL IMPLICATIONS AND CONCLUSIONS

Clinical Assessment

As discussed in Chapter 8, and supported in this review, detailed and thorough assessment of the functions that NSSI serves for a particular individual is a necessary element to the broader clinical assessment and treatment process. It can aid in early detection of NSSI behaviors and early intervention efforts, assist in broader case conceptualization and thus allow for enhanced functional analysis of the antecedents and consequences of NSSI, as well as internal–external risk and protective factors, and aid in the continued monitoring of NSSI behaviors and changes that may occur over time in frequency, type, or function. As described elsewhere in this book, more attention has been paid recently to the development of various assessment tools for NSSI and the functions it serves (see Chapter 7). Moving from early efforts to assess NSSI via clinical interview to the use of more detailed, structured questionnaires that outline multiple NSSI behaviors and functions has allowed for a more thorough discussion of the behaviors being engaged in, their contributing factors, and the resulting outcomes for a particular adolescent.

Treatment Planning

Interventions can be developed that are designed for a particular individual and the functions served by their NSSI. Indeed, in support of the assessment model outlined in Chapter 8, we would argue that a thorough functional, or behavioral, analysis of NSSI is *necessary* for determining the treatment path. This analysis then allows for discussion of the cognitive, emotional, and environmental events that lead up to and are a consequence of the self-injury. In addition, treatment progress can then be monitored over time through periodic reevaluation of the frequency, severity, and functions of NSSI.

   In essence, it is important to have a functionally guided treatment approach for NSSI among adolescents, although further evaluation of the efficacy of functionally guided treatment approaches is needed. Although some functions of NSSI appear to be more clearly indicated in the research literature, empirical evidence supports the need for treatment approaches that distinguish NSSI by functional dimensions of automatic versus social reinforcement and positive versus negative reinforcement. Additional research is clearly needed distinguishing these described functions on various dimensions of NSSI such as developmental course, type of NSSI engaged in (minor versus moderate or severe NSSI), and length of NSSI history, as these variables may inform additional aspects of NSSI intervention.

REFERENCES

Anderson, M., & Sansone, R. (2003). Tattooing as a means of acute affect regulation. *Clinical Psychology & Psychotherapy, 10*(5), 316–318.

Briere, J., & Gil, E. (1998). Self-mutilation in clinical and general population samples: Prevalence, correlates, and functions. *American Journal of Orthopsychiatry, 68*(4), 609–620.

Brown, M. Z., Comtois, K. A., & Linehan, M. M. (2002). Reasons for suicide attempts and non-suicidal self-injury in women with borderline personality disorder. *Journal Abnormal Psychology, 111*(1), 198–202.

Chapman, A. L. (2004). *Exploring the function of deliberate self-harm: Experiential avoidance and borderline personality disorder (BPD)*. In Emotional Responding and Emotion Regulation in Self-Harm. Symposium presented at the 38th annual meeting of the Association for the Advancement of Behavior Therapy (AABT), New Orleans, LA.

Chapman, A. L., Gratz, K. L., & Brown, M. Z. (2006). Solving the puzzle of deliberate self-harm: The experiential avoidance model. *Behavior Research and Therapy, 44*(3), 371–394.

Favazza, A. R. (1998). The coming of age of self-mutilation. *Journal of Nervous and Mental Disease, 186*, 259–268.

Favazza, A. R. (1989). Why patients mutilate themselves. *Hospital and Community Psychiatry, 40*, 137–145.

Favazza, A. R., & Conterio, K. (1988). The plight of chronic self-mutilators. *Community Mental Health, 24*, 22–30.

Gratz, K. L. (2000). *The measurement, functions, and etiology of deliberate self-harm*. Unpublished master's thesis, University of Massachusetts, Boston.

Gratz, K. L. (2003). Risk factors for and functions of deliberate self-harm: An empirical and conceptual review. *Clinical Psychology: Science & Practice, 10*, 192–205.

Haas, B., & Popp, F. (2006). Why do people injure themselves? *Psychopathology, 39*(1), 10–18.

Haines, J., Williams, C. L., Brain, K. L., & Wilson, G. V. (1995). The psychophysiology of self-mutilation. *Journal of Abnormal Psychology, 104*, 471–489.

Harter, S., Stocker, C., & Robinson, N. S. (1996). The perceived directionality of the link between approval and self-worth: The liabilities of a looking glad self-orientation among young adolescents. *Journal of Research on Adolescence, 6*(3), 285–308.

Hilt, L. M., Nock, M. K., Lloyd-Richardson, E. E., & Prinstein, M. J. (in press). Longitudinal study of non-suicidal self-injury among young adolescents: Rates, correlats, and preliminary test of an interpersonal model. *Journal of Early Adolescence.*

Iwata, B. A., Pace, G. M., Dorsey, M. F., Zarcone J. R., Vollmer, T. R., Smith, R. G., et al. (1994). The functions of self-injurious behavior: An experimental-epidemiological analysis. *Journal of Applied Behavior Analysis, 27*(2), 215–240.

Klonsky, E. D. (2006). *The functions of deliberate self-harm in college students.* Unpublished dissertation, University of Virginia, Richmond.

Klonsky, E. D. (2007). The functions of deliberate self-injury: A review of the evidence. *Clinical Psychology Review, 27*, 226–239.

Kumar, G., Pepe, D., Steer, R. A. (2004). Adolescent psychiatric inpatients' self-reported reasons for cutting themselves. *Journal of Nervous and Mental Disease, 192*(12), 830–836.

Lloyd-Richardson, E. E., Perrine, N., Dierker, L., & Kelley, M. L. (2007). Characteristics and functions of non-suicidal self-injury in a community sample of adolescents. *Psychological Medicine, 37*(8), 1183–1192.

Menninger, K. (1938). *Man against himself.* New York: Harcourt Brace World.

Messer, J. M., & Fremouw, W. J. (2007). A critical review of explanatory models for self-mutilating behaviors in adolescents. *Clinical Psychology Review,* doi:10.1016/j.cpr.2007.04.006.

Nixon, M. K., Cloutier, P. F., & Aggarwal, S. (2002). Affect regulation and addictive aspects of repetitive self-injury in hospitalized adolescents. *Journal of the American Academy of Child and Adolescent Psychiatry, 41*(11), 1333–1341.

Nock, M. K., & Prinstein, M. J. (2004). A functional approach to the assessment of self-mutilative behavior. *Journal of Consulting and Clinical Psychology, 72*(5), 885–890.

Nock, M. K., & Prinstein, M. J. (2005). Contextual features and behavioral functions of self-mutilation among adolescents. *Journal of Abnormal Psychology, 114*(1), 140–146.

Nock, M. K., & Prinstein, M. J. (2006). *Real-time measurement of self-injurious thoughts and behaviors using electronic diaries.* Paper presented at the annual convention of the Association for Behavioral and Cognitive Therapies, Chicago, IL.

Penn, J., Esposito, C., Schaeffer, L., Fritz, G., & Spirito, A. (2003). Suicide attempts and self-mutilative behavior in a juvenile correctional facility. *Journal of the American Academy of Child & Adolescent Psychiatry, 42*(7), 762–769.

Reece, J. (2005). The language of cutting: Initial reflections on a study of the experiences of self-injury in a group of women and nurses. *Issues in Mental Health Nursing, 26*, 561–574.

Rodham, K., Hawton, K., & Evans, E. (2004). Reasons for deliberate self-harm: Comparison of self-poisoners and self-cutters in a community sample of adolescents. *Journal of the American Academy of Child & Adolescent Psychiatry, 43*(1), 80–87.

Ross, S., & Heath, N. L. (2003). Two models of adolescent self-mutilation. *Suicide and Life-Threatening Behavior, 33*(3), 277–287.

Rudolph, K. D. (2002). Gender differences in emotional responses to interpersonal stress during adolescence. *Journal of Adolescent Health, 30*(4, suppl), 3–13.

Steinberg, L., & Silverberg, S. B. (1986). The vicissitudes of autonomy in early adolescence. *Child Development, 57*(4), 841–851.

Suyemoto, K. L. (1998). The functions of self-mutilation. *Clinical Psychology Review, 18,* 531–554.
Whitlock, J., Powers, J., & Eckenrode, J. (2006). The virtual cutting edge: The Internet and adolescent self-injury. *Developmental Psychology, 42*(3), 407–417.

ETIOLOGY OF SELF-INJURY

4

Psychosocial Risk and Protective Factors

E. DAVID KLONSKY AND CATHERINE R. GLENN

In this chapter, the practitioner will gain an understanding of:

- The nature of risk and protective factors
- Identified risk and protective factors for NSSI
- How knowing risk and protective factors may influence clinical practice

This chapter examines psychosocial risk and protective factors for non-suicidal self-injury (NSSI). We begin by addressing the meaning and significance of risk and protective factors. Understanding the etiology, or causes, of a disorder helps researchers develop treatments. For example, once doctors learned that a particular strain of bacteria was responsible for strep throat, they could successfully treat the condition with antibiotics. Unfortunately, the origins of psychiatric problems are usually more complicated. Most psychiatric problems result from complex interactions of genetic dispositions and environmental events or stressors, and rarely are there one-to-one relationships between causes and mental disorders.

A first step toward determining the causes of a psychiatric problem is determining risk and protective factors. A risk factor is a variable that, when present, indicates an increased probability that a disorder will occur. For example, people with anxiety disorders are three times more likely to attempt suicide than individuals without anxiety disorders (Kessler et al., 1999). Risk factors may be formally defined as "events or circumstances that are correlated with an increased likelihood or risk of a disorder and potentially contribute to a disorder...mental disorders appear to be produced by the combination of many different biological, psychological, and social risk factors" (Oltmanns & Emery, 1995). It is important to note that risk factors do not necessarily cause a disorder. Although someone with an anxiety disorder has a statistically increased chance of attempting suicide, we would stop short of concluding that anxiety causes attempted suicide. After all, many people have significant anxiety problems and never attempt suicide.

Protective factors, conversely, lower the probability that a disorder will be present. For example, adolescents who feel more connected to their parents and families are less likely to attempt suicide. Protective factors are thought to confer resilience and the ability to "bounce back" from adversity (Butcher, Mineka, & Hooley, 2004). Recent evidence suggests that resilience is common in children and adolescents and a part of normal human adaptation (Masten, 2001). Thus, protective factors may be viewed as variables that increase resilience in the face of environmental stressors and risk factors that increase the probability of undesirable outcomes.

A variety of family, social, environmental, and psychological variables have the potential to increase or decrease risk for psychiatric problems. The remainder of this chapter is devoted to psychosocial variables that increase or decrease risk for NSSI.

The following case of a 19-year-old college student with a 6-year history of episodic NSSI illustrates how misunderstanding concerning the underlying factors of NSSI may adversely affect the therapeutic relationship.

Cindy remembered being a relatively happy child. She did well in school but tended to spend a lot of time on her own. Her parents had divorced when she was 6 years old, and her father had subsequently moved across the country. She lived with her mother and two younger brothers. Her mother was always busy at work or out with a new boyfriend, and Cindy did not have a great relationship with her brothers. Cindy remembered starting to feel stressed out shortly after she started middle school. She was overwhelmed with school and felt like she had few people to talk to about her problems. Cindy was not doing as well in school and did not have many friends. Around this time, Cindy began drinking whenever she started to feel out of control or upset and often drank until she passed out. Later, she experimented with marijuana to relieve her bad moods and negative feelings about herself. During one binge drinking episode, she accidentally cut herself with a pair of scissors. She was amazed at the great relief she felt afterwards and soon began cutting on a regular basis.

No one knew about her cutting behavior all through middle school and high school. Cindy would restrict her cutting to her inner thighs and surrounding areas where it was not visible. Although the cuts were superficial and caused minimal tissue damage, they sometimes left scars. When she went to college, Cindy felt overwhelmed by her courses and the new environment. Her cutting increased substantially, and she decided to go see the campus counselor to discuss her concerns. After a few sessions, Cindy felt that she had a good relationship with the counselor and revealed her history of NSSI. The counselor responded with a series of questions about suicidal thoughts and plans and asked Cindy to contract for safety. Cindy tried to explain that she had no intention of killing herself; her NSSI had nothing to do with suicide. However, the counselor seemed unaware that NSSI often differs from attempted suicide in terms of intent and medical severity. The counselor continued to ask about suicide and, when Cindy seemed hesitant to acknowledge her attempts and contract for safety, suggested that Cindy admit herself to an inpatient facility at the university hospital to keep herself safe. Although Cindy agreed to sign the no-suicide contract, she stopped seeing the counselor and became reluctant to trust or disclose her NSSI to mental health professionals in the future.

RISK FACTORS

Childhood Environment and Adversities

Regarding risk factors, we will focus on the roles of childhood environment and adversities, emotion dysregulation, self-derogation, and psychiatric status. Marsha Linehan (1993) presents one of the most established and well-known theories about the development of NSSI. Linehan suggests that early invalidating environments lead individuals to develop poor interpersonal and emotion-regulation skills, which in turn lead to maladaptive coping behaviors such as NSSI. According to Linehan, an invalidating environment can take many forms, such as neglect, the stifling of emotional expression, or emotional, physical, or sexual abuse.

Research is generally consistent with Linehan's theory. Individuals who self-injure more often report histories of early separation from parents, family violence, and poor parental relationships (Carroll, Schaffer, Spensley, & Abramowitz, 1980; Gratz, Conrad, & Roemer, 2002; Tulloch, Blizzard, & Pinkus, 1997). Studies have also found that individuals who self-injure are more likely to have experienced emotional or physical neglect (Dubo, Zanarini, Lewis, & Williams, 1997; van der Kolk, Perry, & Herman, 1991). Other studies, however, have reported inconsistent findings. NSSI was unrelated to emotional neglect by a parent in both men and women with borderline personality disorder (BPD; Zweig-Frank, Paris, & Guzder, 1994a, 1994b). In a study of college students, emotional neglect by a parent was related to NSSI for females but not males (Gratz et al., 2002). Recently, Heath and colleagues (Heath, Schaub, & Toste, 2007; Heath, Toste, Nedecheva, & Charlebois, 2008), in studies of college students, found that NSSI may or may not be related to attachment difficulties but was reliably found not to be related to childhood trauma or abuse. However, taken as a whole, research suggests that self-injurers report a lower quality of family environment compared to non-self-injurers; at the same time, not all self-injurers are distinguished by a poor family environment, and there is no evidence that family variables play a causal role in the development of NSSI.

Of all family variables that might relate to NSSI, child physical and sexual abuse have received the most attention. Many mental health professionals take for granted that child abuse plays a primary role in the development of NSSI. For example, both van der Kolk et al. (1991) and Yates (2004) hypothesize that childhood trauma such as physical and sexual abuse creates the need for NSSI as a maladaptive coping mechanism. Noll, Horowitz, Bonanno, Trickett, & Putnam (2003) propose that sexually abused individuals who self-injure "may be reenacting the abuse perpetrated on them" (p. 1467). Cavanaugh (2002) describes NSSI as a "manifestation of sexual abuse" (pp. 97, 99). It is noteworthy, therefore, that systematic research has yielded mixed results.

Studies of both community samples (Paivio & McCulloch, 2004) and psychiatric patients (Ystgaard, Hestetun, & Loeb, 2004) have reported increased histories of child sexual abuse in those who self-injure. Other studies of community samples (Heath et al., 2007; Heath et al., 2008; Rodriguez-Srednicki, 2001) and psychiatric patients (Bierer, Yehuda, & Schmeidler, 2003; Schwartz, Cohen, Hoffman, & Meeks, 1999) have found negligible relationships between child sexual abuse and NSSI. In a recent large-scale study, self-injurers were slightly more likely to report a history of child sexual abuse (Whitlock, Eckenrode, & Silverman, 2006). To accurately determine the relationship between child sexual abuse and NSSI, it is necessary to take into account all relevant studies, including those finding a small or no relationship. A recent review examining results from 43 studies found that the relationship between child sexual abuse and NSSI was relatively small (Klonsky & Moyer, 2008). This review also concluded that child sexual abuse could be conceptualized as a proxy risk factor (see Kraemer, Stice, & Kazdin, 2001) for NSSI. In other words, child sexual abuse and NSSI may be associated because they are correlated with the same psychiatric risk factors, as opposed to there being a unique or causal link between child sexual abuse and NSSI.

Interestingly, physical abuse may relate to NSSI to a greater extent than child sexual abuse. Green (1978) found that physically abused children were more than twice as likely to engage in NSSI compared to physically neglected children and approximately six times as likely compared to "normal" children. In two other studies, histories of child physical abuse were more strongly and uniquely associated with NSSI than histories of child sexual abuse (Evren & Evren, 2005; Zoroglu et al., 2003). One exception is a study by Zweig-Frank et al. (1994a), which found no difference in rates of child physical abuse between women with and without histories of NSSI.

Emotion Dysregulation

In addition to family environment variables, certain characteristics of the individual represent risk factors for NSSI. One such variable is emotion dysregulation. As noted earlier, Linehan (1993) views NSSI as a maladaptive emotion regulation strategy. This perspective suggests that individuals who have difficulty regulating negative emotions are at increased risk for NSSI. Research on the psychological correlates and functions of NSSI supports this contention.

Regarding functions (refer to Chapter 3 for a more detailed discussion of functions), self-injurers consistently report that a primary motivation for NSSI is to experience relief from overwhelming negative emotions such as anger, fear, and loneliness (Briere & Gil, 1998; Favazza & Conterio, 1989). Haines, Williams, Brain, & Wilson (1995) provided evidence that NSSI occurs in response to heightened physiological arousal and serves to efficiently reduce arousal. A recent, comprehensive review of research on NSSI motivations found strong evidence that (a) negative emotions precede NSSI, (b) decreased negative emotion coupled with increases in relief and calm occur after NSSI, and (c) most self-injurers cite the desire to alleviate negative emotions as a primary reason for NSSI (Klonsky, 2007). Thus, it appears clear that difficulty regulating emotions increases risk for NSSI.

Consistent with these findings, research has documented a variety of emotion problems in individuals who self-injure. For example, two studies found that self-injurers are more likely to experience periods of dissociation, during which the experience of emotion is impaired (Gratz et al., 2002; Zlotnick et al., 1996). People often describe feeling nothing or feeling unreal during dissociative episodes. In addition, self-injurers appear more likely to exhibit alexithymia; that is, they have greater difficulty in identifying or understanding their feelings compared to non-self-injurers (Zlotnick et al., 1996). Self-injurers also appear to be less aware (i.e., mindful) of their emotions (Lundh, Karim, & Quilisch, 2007). Deficiencies are not limited to emotional experience and awareness in NSSI. Research has also found that self-injurers more often struggle to express their emotions relative to non-self-injurers (Gratz, 2006).

Two studies directly assessed emotion dysregulation in individuals with and without histories of NSSI. Although both utilized college student samples, the results are informative. In Gratz and Roemer (2004), self-injurers were characterized by significantly more emotion dysregulation as measured by the Difficulties in Emotion Regulation Scale (DERS). Heath and colleagues (Heath et al., 2007; Heath et al., in press) found similar results using the DERS. In their college studies, self-injurers were distinguished from non-self-injurers by high scores on the DERS, with consistently high scores across almost all subscales. Taken as a whole, robust evidence suggests that emotion dysregulation is a significant risk factor for the development of NSSI.

Self-Derogation

There is also reason to believe that individuals high in self-derogation are at increased risk for NSSI. Self-punishment and self-directed anger are frequently cited as motivations for NSSI (Klonsky, 2007). Other studies suggest that individuals high in self-derogation are disproportionately likely to self-injure (Herpertz, Sass, & Favazza, 1997; Klonsky, Oltmanns, & Turkheimer, 2003; Soloff, Lis, Kelly, Cornelius, & Ulrich, 1994). Recently, Lundh et al. (2007) found that self-injurers were characterized by low self-esteem. In our opinion, individuals high in *both* emotion dysregulation and self-derogation are at particular risk for NSSI, although research has not yet explicitly addressed the combination of these characteristics in relation to NSSI risk.

Psychiatric Status

As described in Chapter 5, a variety of psychiatric disorders are known to co-occur with NSSI. Whereas Chapter 5 provides a detailed review of associations between NSSI and various psychiatric conditions, for the purposes of this chapter, we will focus on select disorders that appear to confer heightened risk for the development of NSSI. It is important to note, however, that in many cases NSSI is at least as likely to precede as follow the development of psychiatric disorders. Therefore, it would not be inappropriate to characterize NSSI as a risk factor for the disorders we will discuss, even though we will speak of these disorders as risk factors for NSSI.

Of all disorders, BPD may confer the strongest risk for NSSI. NSSI is considered a symptom of BPD in the psychiatric nosology (American Psychiatric Association, 2000), and numerous studies confirm a robust relationship between NSSI and BPD (Andover, Pepper, Ryabchenko, Orrico, & Gibb, 2005; Briere & Gil, 1998; Klonsky et al., 2003; Stanley, Gameroff, Michalsen, & Mann, 2001; van der Kolk et al, 1991; Zlotnick, Mattia, & Zimmerman, 1999). Because emotion dysregulation is considered a core feature of BPD (Linehan, 1993), it is not surprising that BPD increases risk for NSSI. As noted previously, emotion dysregulation is also present in individuals who self-injure, and NSSI is typically utilized as a way to cope with overwhelming emotions. Thus, the presence of BPD signifies the presence of what may be the primary cause of NSSI: emotion dysregulation. It is not definitively known, however, whether NSSI typically develops before, after, or together with other BPD symptoms. Longitudinal studies are necessary to address this issue.

Other psychiatric problems also increase risk of NSSI, perhaps for similar reasons as BPD. For example, symptoms of both depression and anxiety are associated with NSSI (Andover et al., 2005; Hawton, Rodham, Evans, & Weatherall, 2002; Nixon, Cloutier, & Aggarawal, 2002; Klonsky et al., 2003; Ross & Heath, 2002). Emotion dysregulation may be present in both of these disorders (Gross & Munoz, 1995; Mennin et al., 2005), which may explain why their presence increases the probability of NSSI. A direct comparison suggests that anxiety exhibits a stronger relationship to NSSI than depression (Klonsky et al., 2003), perhaps because anxiety is more closely related to the emotional arousal that often prompts NSSI (Klonsky, 2007).

There is also reason to believe that eating disorders such as bulimia and anorexia increase risk for NSSI. Some evidence suggests that disordered eating behaviors such as purging may relieve acute negative emotions and serve similar functions as NSSI (Jeppson, Richards, Hardman, & Granley, 2003; Mizes & Arbitell, 1991). Not surprisingly, a recent large-scale study of college students found that eating disorder features were significantly more common in self-injurers (Whitlock et al., 2006). It is worth noting, however, that not all studies confirm a link between eating disorder symptoms and NSSI (Zlotnick et al., 1999).

Finally, substance disorders may increase risk for NSSI. Conceptually, NSSI and substance abuse may be viewed as similar in that both involve causing harm to the body physically or physiologically. For example, individuals who inject themselves with needles or ingest harmful substances may be capable of harming themselves through other means such as skin-cutting or burning. Joiner (2005) theorizes that substance use helps individuals habituate to self-inflicted violence. Although there is not direct evidence for this conceptual explanation, there is evidence that individuals with substance disorders are more likely to self-injure than nonsubstance users (Langbehn & Pfohl, 1993).

PROTECTIVE FACTORS

Considerably less research exists on protective factors for NSSI as compared to risk factors. Most of what we know comes from studies that focused on suicidal behavior or self-injurious behaviors regardless of suicidal intent.

Effective Management of Negative Emotions

Some suggest that more effective management and expression of negative emotions is a protective factor for NSSI (Skegg, 2005), a reasonable hypothesis in light of the evidence for emotion dysregulation in NSSI. There is clear evidence that rates of NSSI are lower in people who experience negative emotions less intensely and less often (Klonsky et al., 2003). Interestingly, experiencing positive emotions more intensely or more often does not appear to lower risk of NSSI (Klonsky et al., 2003).

Family and Social Support

A few studies have examined sources of family and social support as protective factors for NSSI. In a study of high school students, family intactness and cohesion was associated with lower risk for self-injurious behaviors (Rubenstein, Halton, Kasten, Rubin, & Stechler, 1998). Family cohesion was most powerful as a protective factor in families that were not intact (e.g., due to divorce). In a study of psychiatric patients, self-reports of familial responsibility and concern for social disapproval were both associated with a lower risk of attempted suicide. Evidence also exists that increased religious affiliation lowers risk for suicidal behavior (Dervic et al., 2004; Malone et al., 2000). Unfortunately, parallel research has not been conducted on religious affiliation as a potential protective factor for NSSI.

RISK AND PROTECTIVE FACTORS FOR DIFFERENT MANIFESTATIONS OF NSSI

There is considerable diversity in the manifestation of NSSI. For example, NSSI can vary in terms of method (e.g., cutting, burning, scratching), location (e.g., arms, legs, torso), and severity (e.g., superficial, significant tissue damage, highly lethal). It is possible that some of these features have different risk or protective factors. This possibility is most evident in studies examining the relationship between gender and aspects of NSSI. Recent research suggests that females are more likely to cut themselves, whereas males are more likely to perform other self-injurious behaviors such as self-hitting, banging, or burning (Claes, Vandereycken, & Vertommen, 2007; Holly, Heath, Toste, & Schaub, 2007; Laye-Gindhu & Schonert-Reichl, 2005; Whitlock et al., 2006). It also appears that females are more likely to injure their wrists or thighs, whereas males are more likely to injure their hands (Whitlock et al., 2006).

It could be particularly useful to identify risk and protective factors for more severe forms of NSSI. Some researchers conceptualize self-injurious behaviors along a continuum of severity, with methods causing severe tissue damage on one end (e.g., cutting, burning) and methods causing little or no tissue damage on the other end (e.g., interfering with wound healing, pinching) (Skegg, 2005). Not surprisingly, self-injurers from treatment samples appear to be at greater risk for more severe behaviors than self-injurers drawn from community samples. For example, studies of psychiatric patients find that skin-cutting is the most common form of NSSI (Briere & Gil, 1998; Herpertz, 1995; Langbehn & Pfohl, 1993). In contrast, scratching was the most common form in a large sample of college students (Whitlock et al., 2006). Very little is known about clinical variables in relation to NSSI severity. One study provides partial evidence that anxiety confers greater risk for skin-cutting than other forms of NSSI (Andover et al.,

TABLE 4.1   Summary of Risk and Protective Factors for NSSI

Risk factors	*Emotion dysregulation:*
	Negative emotionality
	Dissociative experiences
	Alexithymia
	Self-derogation
	Psychiatric disorder:
	Borderline personality disorder
	Anxiety
	Depression
	Eating disorders
	Substance disorders
	Childhood environment and adversities:
	Familial neglect
	Child abuse (physical, emotional, sexual)
	Attachment difficulties
Protective factors	Effective management of negative emotions
	Family and social support

2005). Because NSSI severity may be associated with suicidal intent and behavior (Skegg, 2005), it is important that research continue to identify risk and protective factors for more severe forms of NSSI. See Table 4.1 for a summary of risk and protective factors.

CLINICAL IMPLICATIONS

Melissa, a 15-year-old high school sophomore, has a 1-year history of NSSI. This case illustrates how misinformation concerning risk and correlates of NSSI may contribute to a poor treatment trajectory.

Melissa was a straight A student and a "perfect child" in her parents' eyes from the time she was little. She was very social and had many friends growing up. Melissa was always striving to be better and was often very hard on herself when she failed to meet her own standards. After entering high school, Melissa felt like she could not keep up with her peers and was very upset by her inferior academic performance. Her parents were also unhappy with her grades and told her that she had "better shape up if you want to get into a good college." Melissa became despondent, feeling as though she had lost her identity as the model student and daughter. She began to care about very few things and gradually ceased to feel anything at all. Toward the end of the first semester of freshman year, she cut her forearm for the first time with her father's razor blade that she found in the bathroom. She liked feeling something, even if it was pain, and the cutting also seemed to temporarily help her feel better. Her cutting behavior continued through the winter with little notice from her parents.

Her mother first became suspicious when Melissa continued to wear long sleeves into the spring and summer. She eventually noticed Melissa's scars and took Melissa to a psychologist. Upon hearing that Melissa was engaging in NSSI, the psychologist suspected a diagnosis of BPD. Melissa's feelings of emptiness and arguments with her mother were regarded as further evidence for BPD. In reality, Melissa was typically a very compliant and respectful daughter. The family arguments were prompted by her mother's discovery of the NSSI. In addition, the feelings of emptiness were indicative of depression rather than BPD.

Unfortunately, the premature diagnosis of BPD was used to inform case conceptualization and treatment planning. Because the psychologist worked from the premise that Melissa had BPD, his assessment overlooked key variables underlying Melissa's depression and NSSI, such as her perfectionism and intense sense of failure. In addition, he tended to see Melissa's NSSI as a form of manipulation characteristic of some patients with BPD. As a result, Melissa felt misunderstood, rapport was damaged, and the case formulation and treatment plan did not meet Melissa's needs.

Knowledge of psychosocial variables that increase and decrease risk for NSSI has several clinical applications. This knowledge is particularly useful for clinical assessments. Many individuals are secretive about and unlikely to reveal their NSSI unless directly asked about it. (Of course, some might withhold information even when asked about NSSI.) The presence of risk factors can help indicate when specific assessment of NSSI is appropriate.

It is also important to obtain information about risk factors once an individual's NSSI has been revealed. Some risk factors may contribute to the initiation and maintenance of NSSI. For example, determining that a patient who self-injures is frequently emotionally dysregulated may help the therapist determine motivations for NSSI (e.g., perhaps to alleviate overwhelming negative emotions) and points of intervention. Similarly, assessing protective factors can also be helpful for treatment planning. Protective factors such as effective management of emotions and strong family and social support may lessen the need for NSSI. Treatment can target these variables when they are found to be impaired in self-injurers. For example, therapists can help patients develop effective emotion regulation strategies and mobilize support from friends and family members. Dialectical behavior therapy, which was designed in part to improve emotion regulation and interpersonal effectiveness skills, has shown promise for reducing NSSI (Linehan, 1993).

Understanding risk and protective factors can also help clinicians avoid misconceptions that can harm rapport and case conceptualization. For example, many health professionals believe NSSI is usually associated with a history of childhood sexual abuse (Cavanaugh, 2002; Noll et al., 2003; Yates, 2004). We know of one case in which a young woman was repeatedly asked whether she was sure she had never been abused by her father after revealing her NSSI to her therapist. In this instance, the therapist had no other reason to suspect abuse other than the presence of NSSI. In reality, the association between child sexual abuse and NSSI is modest, and probably not central to the development of NSSI (Klonsky & Moyer, 2008). Had the therapist in our example known this, he or she could have avoided a line of questioning that was likely distressing and painful and instead focused on issues relevant for the young woman's treatment. For both clinicians and researchers, developing effective interventions starts with the accurate identification of factors that increase and decrease the behavior.

It is also important to keep in mind that the presence of risk factors does not necessarily imply the presence of NSSI. For example, emotionally dysregulated individuals may find adaptive (e.g., seeking social support) or nonadaptive (e.g., substance use) ways to cope that do not involve NSSI. Even when all risk factors are present, NSSI may not be viable due to blood phobia, high pain sensitivity, general squeamishness, or because the idea of self-injuring simply never occurred to the person. In the end, individuals should be treated on a case by case basis in a manner informed but not dictated by knowledge of risk and protective factors.

REFERENCES

American Psychiatric Association. (2000). *Diagnostic and Statistical Manual of Mental Disorders* (4th ed., text revision). Author: Washington, DC.

Andover, M. S., Pepper, C. M., Ryabchenko, K. A., Orrico, E. G., & Gibb, B. E. (2005). Self-mutilation and symptoms of depression, anxiety, and borderline personality disorder. *Suicide and Life-Threatening Behavior, 35,* 581–591.

Bierer, L. M., Yehuda, R., & Schmeidler, J. (2003). Abuse and neglect in childhood: Relationship to personality disorder diagnoses. *CNS Spectrums, 8,* 737–730, 749–754.

Briere, J., & Gil, E. (1998). Self-mutilation in clinical and general population samples: Prevalence, correlates, and functions. *American Journal of Orthopsychiatry, 68,* 609–620.

Butcher, J. N., Mineka, S., & Hooley, J. M. (2004). *Abnormal Psychology.* Boston: Pearson Education.

Carroll, J., Schaffer, C., Spensley, J., & Abramowitz, S. I. (1980). Family experiences of self-mutilating patients. *American Journal of Psychiatry, 137,* 852–853.

Cavanaugh, R. M. (2002). Self-mutilation as a manifestation of sexual abuse in adolescent girls. *Journal of Pediatric Adolescent Gynecology, 15,* 97–100.

Claes, L., Vandereycken, W., & Vertommen, H. (2007). Self-injury in female versus male psychiatric patients: A comparison of characteristics, psychopathology and aggression regulation. *Personality and Individual Differences, 42*(4), 611–621.

Dervic, K., Oquendo, M. A., Grunebaum, M. F., Ellis, S., Burke, A. K., & Mann, J. J. (2004). Religious affiliation and suicide attempt. *American Journal of Psychiatry, 161,* 2303–2308.

Dubo, E. D., Zanarini, M. C., Lewis, R. E., & Williams, A. A. (1997). Childhood antecedents of self-destructiveness in borderline personality disorder. *Canadian Journal of Psychiatry, 42,* 63–69.

Evren, C., & Evren, B. (2005). Self-mutilation in substance-dependent patients and relationship with childhood abuse and neglect, alexithymia, and temperament and character dimensions of personality. *Drug and Alcohol Dependence, 80,* 15–22.

Favazza, A. R., & Conterio, K. (1989). Female habitual self-mutilators. *Acta Psychiatrica Scandinavica, 79,* 283–289.

Gratz, K. L. (2006). Risk factors for deliberate self-harm among female college students: The role and interaction of childhood maltreatment, emotional inexpressivity, and affect intensity/reactivity. *American Journal of Orthopsychiatry, 76,* 238–250.

Gratz, K. L., Conrad, S. D., & Roemer, L. (2002). Risk factors for deliberate self-harm among college students. *American Journal of Orthopsychiatry, 72,* 128–140.

Gratz, K. L., & Roemer, L. (2004). Multidimensional assessment of emotion regulation and dysregulation: Development, factor structure, and initial validation of the difficulties in emotion regulation scale. *Journal of Psychopathology and Behavioral Assessment, 26,* 41–54.

Green, A. H. (1978). Self-destructive behavior in battered children. *American Journal of Psychiatry, 135,* 579–582.

Gross, J. J., & Munoz, R. F. (1995). Emotion regulation and mental health. *Clinical Psychology: Science and Practice, 2,* 151–164.

Haines, J., Williams, C. L., Brain, K. L., & Wilson, G. V. (1995). The psychophysiology of self-mutilation. *Journal of Abnormal Psychology, 104,* 471–489.

Hawton, K., Rodham, K., Evans, E., & Weatherall, R. (2002). Deliberate self harm in adolescents: Self report survey in schools in England. *British Medical Journal, 325,* 1207–1211.

Heath, N. L., Schaub, K., & Toste, J. R. (2007). *Childhood trauma, attachment, and emotion regulation in college students who engage in non-suicidal self-injury.* Unpublished master's thesis. McGill University, Montreal.

Heath, N. L., Toste, J. R., Nedecheva, T., & Charlebois, A. (2008). An examination of non-suicidal self-injury among college students *Journal of Mental Health Counseling.* 30(2), 1–20.

Herpertz, S. (1995). Self-injurious behavior: Psychopathological and nosological characteristics in subtypes of self-injurers. *Acta Psychiatrica Scandinavica, 91,* 57–68.

Herpertz, S., Sass, H., & Favazza, A. (1997). Impulsivity in self-mutilative behavior: Psychometric and biological findings. *Journal of Psychiatric Research, 31,* 451–465.

Holly, S., Heath, N. L., Toste, J. R., & Schaub, K. (2007). *Social influence and functions of non-suicidal self-injury in a sample of university students.* Unpublished master's thesis. McGill University, Montreal.

Jeppson, J. E., Richards, P. S., Hardman, R. K., & Granley, H. M. (2003). Binge and purge processes in bulimia nervosa: A qualitative investigation. *Eating Disorders, 11,* 115–128.

Joiner, T. (2005). *Why People Die By Suicide.* Cambridge, MA: Harvard University Press.

Kessler, R. C., Borges, G., & Walters, E. E. (1999). Prevalence of and risk factors for lifetime suicide attempts in the National Comorbidity Survey. *Archives of General Psychiatry, 56,* 617–626.

Klonsky, E. D. (2007). The functions of deliberate self-injury: A review of the evidence. *Clinical Psychology Review, 27,* 226–239.

Klonsky, E. D., & Moyer, A. (2008). Childhood sexual abuse and non-suicidal self-injury: A meta-analysis. *British Journal of Psychiatry, 192,* 166–170.

Klonsky, E. D., Oltmanns, T. F., & Turkheimer, E. (2003). Deliberate self-harm in a nonclinical population: Prevalence and psychological correlates. *American Journal of Psychiatry, 160,* 1501–1508.

Kraemer, H. C., Stice, E., Kazdin, A., et al. (2001). How do risk factors work together? Mediators, moderators, and independent, overlapping, and proxy risk factors. *American Journal of Psychiatry, 158,* 848–856.

Langbehn, D. R., & Pfohl, B. (1993). Clinical correlates of self-mutilation among psychiatric inpatients. *Annals of Clinical Psychiatry, 5,* 45–51.

Laye-Gindhu, A., & Schonert-Reichl, K. A. (2005). Nonsuicidal self-harm among community adolescents: Understanding the "whats" and "whys" of self-harm. *Journal of Youth and Adolescence, 34,* 447–457.

Linehan, M. (1993). *Cognitive-behavioral therapy for borderline personality disorder.* New York: Guilford Press.

Lundh, L.-G., Karim, J., & Quilisch, E. (2007). Deliberate self-harm in 15-year-old adolescents: A pilot study with a modified version of the Deliberate Self-Harm Inventory. *Scandinavian Journal of Psychology, 48,* 33–41.

Malone, K. M., Oquendo, M. A., Haas, G. L., Ellis, S. P., Li, S., & Mann, J. J. (2000). Protective factors against suicidal acts in major depression: Reasons for living. *American Journal of Psychiatry, 157,* 1084–1088.

Masten, A. S. (2001). Ordinary magic: Resilience processes in development. *American Psychologist, 56,* 227–238.

Mennin, D. S., Heimberg, R. G., Turk, C. L., & Fresco, D. M. (2005). Preliminary evidence for an emotion dysregulation model of generalized anxiety disorder. *Behaviour Research and Therapy, 43,* 1281–1310.

Mizes, J. S., & Arbitell, M. R. (1991). Bulimics' perceptions of emotional responding during binge-purge episodes. *Psychological Reports, 69,* 527–532.

Nixon, M. K., Cloutier, P. F., & Aggarwal, S. (2002). Affect regulation and addictive aspects of repetitive self-injury in hospitalized adolescents. *Journal of the American Academy of Child & Adolescent Psychiatry, 41,* 1333–1341.

Noll, J. G., Horowitz, L. A., Bonanno, G. A., Trickett, P. K., & Putnam, F. W. (2003). Revictimization and self-harm in females who experienced childhood sexual abuse. *Journal of Interpersonal Violence, 18,* 1452–1471.

Oltmanns, T. F., & Emery, R. E. (1995). *Abnormal psychology.* Englewood Cliffs, NJ: Prentice Hall.

Paivio, S. C., & McCulloch, C. R. (2004). Alexithymia as a mediator between childhood trauma and self-injurious behaviors. *Child Abuse and Neglect, 28,* 339–354.

Rodriguez-Srednicki, O. (2001). Childhood sexual abuse, dissociation, and adult self-destructive behavior. *Journal of Child Sexual Abuse, 10,* 75–90.

Ross, S., & Heath, N. (2002). A study of the frequency of self-mutilation in a community sample of adolescents. *Journal of Youth and Adolescence, 31,* 67–77.

Rubenstein, J. L., Halton, A., Kasten, L., Rubin, C., & Stechler, G. (1998). Suicidal behavior in adolescents: Stress and protection in different family contexts. *American Journal of Orthopsychiatry, 68,* 274–284.

Schwartz, R. H., Cohen, P., Hoffman, N. G., & Meeks, J. A. (1989). Self-harm behaviors (carving). *Clinical Pediatrics, 28,* 340–346.

Soloff, P. H., Lis, J. A., Kelly, T., Cornelius, J., & Ulrich, R. (1994). Self-mutilation and suicidal behavior in borderline personality disorder. *Journal of Personality Disorders, 8,* 257–267.

Skegg, K. (2005). Self harm. *Lancet, 366,* 1471–1483.

Stanley, B., Gameroff, M. J., Michalsen, V., & Mann, J. J. (2001). Are suicide attempters who self-mutilate a unique population? *American Journal of Psychiatry, 158,* 427–432.

Tulloch, A. L., Blizzard, L., & Pinkus, Z. (1997). Adolescent-parent communication in self-harm. *Journal of Adolescent Health, 21,* 267–275.

van der Kolk, B. A., Perry, J. C., & Herman, J. L. (1991). Childhood origins of self-destructive behavior. *American Journal of Psychiatry, 148,* 1665–1671.

Whitlock, J., Eckenrode, J., & Silverman, D. (2006). Self-injurious behaviors in a college population. *Pediatrics, 117,* 1939–1948.

Yates, T. M. (2004). The developmental psychopathology of self-injurious behavior: Compensatory regulation in posttraumatic adaptation. *Clinical Psychology Review, 24,* 35–74.

Ystgaard, M., Hestetun, I., Loeb, M., & Mehlum, L. (2004). Is there a specific relationship between childhood sexual and physical abuse and repeated suicidal behavior? *Child Abuse and Neglect, 28,* 863–875.

Zlotnick, C., Mattia, J. I., & Zimmerman, M. (1999). Clinical correlates of self-mutilation in a sample of general psychiatric patients. *Journal of Nervous and Mental Disease, 187,* 296–301.

Zlotnick, C., Shea, M. T., Pearlstein, T., Simpson, E., Costello, E., & Begin, A. (1996). The relationship between dissociative symptoms, alexithymia, impulsivity, sexual abuse, and self-mutilation. *Comprehensive Psychiatry, 37,* 12–16.

Zoroglu, S. S., Tuzun, U., Sar, V., Tutkun, H., Savas, H. A., Ozturk, M., et al. (2003). Suicide attempt and self-mutilation among Turkish high school students in relation with abuse, neglect, and dissociation. *Psychiatry and Clinical Neurosciences, 57,* 119–126.

Zweig-Frank, H., Paris, J., & Guzder, J. (1994a). Psychological risk factors for dissociation and self-mutilation in female patients with borderline personality disorder. *Canadian Journal of Psychiatry, 39,* 259–264.

Zweig-Frank, H., Paris, J., & Guzder, J. (1994b). Psychological risk factors and self-mutilation in male patients with BPD. *Canadian Journal of Psychiatry, 39,* 266–268.

CHAPTER 5

Nonsuicidal Self-Injury and Co-Occurrence

NICHOLAS LOFTHOUSE,
JENNIFER J. MUEHLENKAMP, AND ROBYN ADLER

In this chapter, the practitioner will gain an understanding of:

- What is meant by co-occurring disorders in youth with NSSI
- How suicidal behavior and NSSI may or may not co-occur
- The range of co-occurring disorders in youth with NSSI
- The standardized assessment of co-occurring disorders

Comorbidity is the co-existence of two or more distinct diseases or disorders in the same individual at the same time (Achenbach, 1991; Caron & Rutter, 1991). Research on this clinical phenomenon is extremely important to our field because of its implications for past, current, and future classification systems, etiological theories, treatment outcomes, treatment recommendations, and developmental course (Keiley, Lofthouse, Bates, Dodge, & Pettit, 2003). However, the term, like *self-injury*, has repeatedly been used in inaccurate and inconsistent ways in research and clinical work. One central issue in this area relates to the fundamental distinction between what Caron and Rutter (1991) call "apparent comorbidity" and "true comorbidity." The former refers to the coexistence of multiple conditions being produced artifactually by one or more confounds such as chance occurrence, referral and detection biases, nosological confusion, multiformity, developmental transience, and measurement variance (Caron & Rutter, 1991; Hinden, Compas, Howell, & Achenbach, 1997; Klein & Riso, 1993; Lilienfeld, Waldman,

& Israel, 1994). In contrast, true comorbidity is reserved for cases where these artifacts have been empirically ruled-out as explanations for joint occurrence. Unfortunately, many researchers have not separated artifactual from true comorbidity but have instead accepted comorbidity as a factual rather than hypothetical entity.

Another major issue in this area is that the terms *co-occurrence, comorbidity*, and *covariance* have been used interchangeably when, in actuality, they are three separate phenomena (Hinden et al., 1997; Lilienfeld et al., 1994). The most general of the three, co-occurrence, refers to the identification of two or more simultaneously occurring psychiatric conditions (diagnoses, syndromes, or symptoms), regardless of whether they exist for valid or artifactual reasons. In contrast, comorbidity is the valid coexistence of two or more distinct categorical disorders, as used in the *Diagnostic and Statistical Manual*, fourth edition (*DSM-IV*; American Psychiatric Association [APA], 1994). Finally, covariation refers to the valid coexistence of two or more distinct dimensional syndromes, such as those employed by Achenbach's empirically derived taxonomy (Achenbach & McConaughy, 2003). Unfortunately, the term *comorbidity* has generally been applied to describe any association of psychiatric conditions, whether distinct or dimensional, valid or artifactual. These distinctions are more than just semantic nitpicking. As Lilienfeld and colleagues (1994) contend, "the use of imprecise language may lead to correspondingly imprecise thinking" (p.79). It is therefore essential that we not only use the same terminology but also use it accurately and consistently to effectively communicate and develop our understanding of psychopathology. Applying these criteria to the area of self-injury among youth, research to date has yet to control for the various artifacts that would allow use of the terms *comorbidity* and *covariance*. Instead, our current "level of understanding" (Kazdin, 1983) suggests we should use the term *co-occurrence* when referring to the simultaneous presence of self-injury and other psychiatric conditions in the same individual at the same time.

With these concerns in mind, in this chapter, we intend to discuss why we think a study of self-injury and co-occurrence in adolescents is important, discuss the differences between and of nonsuicidal self-injury (NSSI) and suicidal self-injury, review the current literature on NSSI and co-occurrence, and present clinical recommendations for its assessment and treatment.

THE IMPORTANCE OF CO-OCCURRENCE
FOR THE STUDY OF ADOLESCENT NSSI

As a psychiatric condition must first occur in its own right before being able to co-occur with another condition, the topic of co-occurrence is of particular importance to NSSI, which has yet to attain the status of a separate psychiatric condition. One of Feighner et al.'s (1972) criteria for obtaining diagnostic validity for a psychiatric phenomenon involves its delineation from other disorders. Therefore, a primary reason for studying co-occurrence and NSSI is to examine the psychiatric conditions with which it is and is not associated. Currently, NSSI is only listed under one *DSM-IV* diagnosis, that of borderline personality disorder (BDP). This is problematic for several reasons. Diagnosing an adolescent with any personality disorder is a controversial issue in the field, not least due to the lack of research. However, the current edition of the *DSM* notes that a personality disorder can be diagnosed in patients under 18 years of age when "maladaptive personality traits appear to be pervasive, persistent, and unlikely to be limited to a particular developmental stage or an episode of an Axis I disorder" (APA, 1994, p. 631). Demonstrating that a personality disorder is "unlikely to be limited to particular developmental stage" is challenging, as few longitudinal studies of the stability of personality disorders from adolescence to adulthood exist, and those that are available reveal mixed results for continuity. Likewise, demonstrating that a personality disorder is "unlikely to be limited to "an episode of an Axis I disorder" is also a thorny issue because no research has examined the separation or "true" comorbidity of Axis I and II disorders in adolescence. Furthermore, in a clinic setting, to demonstrate that a patient's Axis II disorder is unlikely due to an Axis I disorder, first you would have to remediate the Axis I disorder and then reassess for Axis II psychopathology.

Even if a solid empirical base for diagnosing adolescents with personality disorders existed, to-date only one study has investigated NSSI and BPD in adolescence. Nock, Joiner, Gordon, Lloyd-Richardson, and Prinstein (2006) used structured psychiatric interviews to examine the relationship of NSSI and various Axis I and II disorders in a sample of 12–17-year-old inpatients and found that 51.7% met criteria for BPD. However, as they pointed out, this figure may be an overestimate because they were unable to examine the rate of BPD without parceling out the symptom of NSSI. In research with adult samples, Herpetz, Sass, and Favazza (1997) found that if self-injurious behavior was statistically controlled, only 29% actually met the diagnostic criteria for BPD. In addition, Favazza and Rosenthal (1990) reported that once self-injurious behavior stops, many individuals no longer meet diagnostic criteria for BPD.

A second major reason for studying psychiatric conditions co-occurring with adolescent NSSI is that multiple disorders tend to lead to worse developmental outcomes than single-form disorders (see review by Nottelman & Jensen, 1995). In that sense, a co-occurring condition can be viewed as a risk factor, which, in itself may be a developmental cause, consequence, or concomitant of NSSI. Although no longitudinal studies of adolescent NSSI currently exist, one particular negative outcome Joiner (2005), amongst others, has suggested is that individuals who engage in NSSI are at increased risk of later dying by suicide. Thus, to offset their rather insidious impact on development, co-occurring conditions necessitate greater clinical attention and further etiological and treatment research.

Third, research on co-occurrence is crucial for knowing how to assess and treat adolescents with NSSI. We need to be aware of which psychiatric conditions tend to occur with NSSI and how to effectively assess and monitor them. In terms of treatment, disregarding the occurrence of another condition may have significant implications for treatment recommendations, treatment outcomes, and the interpretation of results from previous treatment efficacy studies and future intervention research. Indeed, Stahl and Clarizio (1999) wondered if comorbidity may partly explain why "it has been difficult for clinicians to achieve outcome results as good as those reported in randomized clinical trials, which often exclude patients with certain comorbid disorders" (p. 48).

Finally, due to past studies not separating NSSI from suicidal self-injury and the tendency for the field to merge results from adolescent and adult studies into discussions about NSSI, little is known about co-occurrence and NSSI in adolescence alone. Due to the developmental and environmental differences between adolescents and adults, merging results from these groups into our conceptualization of adolescent NSSI may actually diminish our ability to comprehend NSSI in this population. Thus, research specifically on NSSI and co-occurring psychiatric conditions in adolescent-only samples would increase our understanding of this phenomenon. Accordingly, to impart more clarity on this subject, the remainder of our chapter will focus on the presentation, assessment, and treatment of NSSI and co-occurring psychiatric conditions among 12–18 year-olds.

NSSI AND THE IMPORTANCE OF INTENT

Just as with comorbidity, to avoid the use of imprecise language and subsequent imprecise thinking about NSSI and instead effectively communicate about and develop valid theories and treatments for this severe and destructive phenomenon, it is essential that we consistently use the same precise terminology. For many, acts of self-injury have been seen as suicide attempts or suicidal "cries for help," and at times, suicide attempts are viewed as attention-seeking acts of self-injury. Confusion regarding whether or not a self-damaging act is a suicide attempt has been perpetuated by a history of terms that failed to differentiate the behaviors. Professionals within the field are approaching a consensus about the types of behaviors representing suicide attempts and those representing NSSI. The key defining feature is the intent or purpose underlying the behavior. As defined by Silverman and colleagues (Silverman, Berman, Sanddal, O'Carroll, & Joiner 2007), suicide attempts are behaviors that may or may not result in injury for which there is either implicit or explicit intent to die. In contrast, NSSI is a behavior in which immediate tissue damage is present (e.g., bruising, breaking of skin) for which there is *no* implicit or explicit intent to die but instead a desire to alleviate emotional distress. As Walsh (2006) so perceptively notes, "The key point regarding intent is that the suicidal person wants to eliminate consciousness permanently; the self-injurer wants to modify consciousness, to reduce distress, in order to live another day" (p. 8).

In addition to the intent underlying these behaviors, research and clinical experience have identified other characteristics that distinguish NSSI from suicide attempts (see Table 5.1). Although most of this research has been on adults, more recent work by Muehlenkamp and Gutierrez (2004, 2007) has found differences between NSSI and suicidal behavior among adolescents. In 2004, using nonclinical samples of adolescents, they found that adolescents who engaged in NSSI were less repulsed by life than were suicidal adolescents. More recently, in 2007, using a community sample of 540 adolescents, they found that adolescents with NSSI who had also attempted suicide at another time in their lives were more likely to report high levels of suicidal ideation and fewer reasons for living than were adolescents with NSSI who had never attempted suicide. This difference suggests that individuals who turn to NSSI may not have had as many perceived negative experiences with which they were unable to cope as those who attempt suicide, and, therefore, they do not have as negative an attitude toward life. Having fewer negative experiences and a more positive attitude toward life may prevent adolescents with NSSI from attempting suicide.

TABLE 5.1   Characteristic Differences Between Suicide and NSSI

Characteristic	Suicide	NSSI
Demographics	Males > females	Females > males (not always)
Intent	To die	To alleviate emotional distress
Lethality	High, needs medical treatment	Low, rarely needs medical treatment
Repetition	Infrequent	High, chronic in nature
Methods	Often one chosen method	Multiple methods
Prevalence	Low	High, up to 70% in patients
Hopelessness	Commonly present	Infrequent, less likely
Psych consequences	Exacerbation of psychological pain	Relief of psychological pain

Thus, it appears that an intent to die is an important characteristic differentiating suicide attempts from NSSI and should be a key component in any assessment of self-injurious acts.

RESEARCH ON NSSI AND CO-OCCURRENCE

We conducted a review of the literature on adolescent (ages 12-to-18 years) NSSI and co-occurring psychiatric conditions via two methods: (a) a PsychInfo (1872 to October 2007) and Medline (1950 to October 2007) abstract search,* and (b) examining citations in articles on adolescent NSSI. This approach yielded over 100 peer-reviewed publications, the majority of which did not examine co-occurring psychiatric conditions. Unfortunately, most of the articles examining co-occurrence failed to differentiate NSSI from suicidal self-injury, leaving only 15 published studies that specifically examined NSSI and co-occurring psychiatric conditions in adolescent samples (excluding those with mental retardation, developmental delays, or schizophrenia). Because of its relevance to this area, we also report on one of our in-press studies (Jacobson, Muehlenkamp, & Miller, in press). Due to possible differences in co-occurrence across different populations, we organized the review by inpatient, outpatient, and community samples (see Table 5.2). To the authors' knowledge, this is the first detailed review of studies specifically examining NSSI with co-occurring psychopathology in adolescent-only samples.

As can be seen in Table 5.2, much of the research in this area has been conducted in North America (United States or Canada), mostly with female Caucasian participants. Taking into consideration the limitations of all the reviewed studies noted in the Research Limitations and Future Directions section, within inpatient samples, NSSI most frequently co-occurred with depression, followed by suicidal behavior, anxiety and substance use, and then problems with eating and hostility and anger. In outpatient samples, the most common forms of co-occurrence were suicidal behavior followed by depression, anxiety, and substance use. Finally, in community samples, NSSI was most frequently associated with suicidal behavior, followed by depression and substance use, hostility and anger, and then anxiety. A synthesis of the 16 studies' main findings suggests that NSSI occurs with a wide variety of additional psychiatric conditions during the lifetime of the adolescents sampled. However, the most frequently reported conditions were depression and suicidal behavior, followed by substance use, then anxiety and hostility and anger. Although substance use was prevalent, two studies (Nock & Prinstein, 2005; Schwartz, Cohen, Hoffmann, & Meeks, 1989) reported

---

* Using the search terms "self-injury" or "self-injurious" or "self-mutilation" or "self-mutilate" or "self-harm" or "cutting" and "child" or "children" or "adolescent" or "adolescence" or "youth" or "juvenile."

that most adolescents do not use alcohol or drugs during acts of NSSI. However, a more recent study by Lloyd-Richardson, Perrine, Dierker, & Kelley (2007) found that community adolescents who engaged in moderate or severe NSSI were more likely to use alcohol or drugs during NSSI (27%) than those who engaged in minor NSSI (3%). Several studies reported disorders of eating and conduct. Finally, only one study (Nock et al., 2006) assessed personality disorders, but those seemed to be relatively prevalent, especially BPD (52%).

CO-OCCURRENCE OF NSSI AND SUICIDALITY AMONG ADOLESCENTS

Despite the characteristics in Table 5.1 differentiating adolescent NSSI and suicidal behaviors, there still appears a great deal of overlap between the two. As can be seen in Table 5.2, within inpatient samples, Darche (1990) found that 48% of adolescents with NSSI recalled suicidal acts at some point in their lives. Nixon, Cloutier, & Aggarwal, (2002) noted that 74% of adolescents reported a suicide attempt and 64% almost daily suicidal ideation during the 6 months before admission, and 74% were admitted for suicidal ideation. Similarly, Nock et al. (2006) discovered that 70% of his sample reported at least one and 55% two or more suicide attempts during their lifetime.

In outpatient samples, Schwartz et al. (1989) found that 59% recalled a prior suicide attempt and 27% recalled three or more previous suicide attempts. Crowell et al. (2005) noted that 87% reported a self-harm act with the intent to die at some point in their lives. Jacobson et al. (in press) identified 70 adolescents with NSSI, of which 40 (57%) had also made suicide attempts at some point in their lives.

Within community samples, in Laye-Gindhu and Schonert-Reichl's (2005) study of adolescents with NSSI, 83% reported suicidal ideation, 40% reported suicide plans, and 26% reported suicide attempts. More recently, Muehlenkamp and Gutierrez (2007) reported that 30% of adolescents with NSSI also made suicide attempts at some point in their lives. Lloyd-Richardson et al. (2007) found that 21% of their NSSI sample had a history of suicide attempts, whereas 9% had a suicide attempt in the past year. In their sample, NSSI adolescents who had a suicide attempt in the past year were more likely to have a history of psychiatric in- and outpatient treatment, greater current suicide ideation, more moderate-to-severe NSSI, more types of NSSI and to endorse more reasons and functions for NSSI. Using a German adolescent community sample, Brunner et al. (2007) found that 63% reported suicidal ideations, 38% reported suicide plans, and 41% reported suicide attempts sometime during their lives. They also noted that compared to occasional NSSI, repetitive NSSI was related to increased suicidal behavior.

Unfortunately, we cannot definitely conclude that NSSI and suicide attempts co-occur because all but one study (Nixon et al., 2002) failed to

TABLE 5.2   Studies of NSSI and Co-occurrence

NSSI relative to comparison group, significantly > higher or < lower

Sample	Study	Demographics[a]	Comparison Group	Symptoms/Disorders Co-occurring with NSSI[b]
INPATIENT				
U.S.	Darche (1990)	N = 48 13–17 years old 100% female Ethnicity not noted	Non-NSSI inpatient controls	DSM-III-R diagnoses: sleep (83%), eating (60%), affective (40%) Hallucinations (29%) * > Suicidal acts (48%) * > BDI depression scores * > SCL-90: depression, anxiety, somatization, hostility, global scores * > MAPI body comfort and < MAPI confidence scores
U.S.	Kumar, Pepe, & Steer, (2004)	N = 50 13–17 years old 62% female 64% Caucasian	None	DSM-IV-TR diagnoses: unipolar (58%), major depressive disorder (24%), bipolar disorders (24%), "other" disorders (18%) Additional Axis I diagnoses: 1 (36%), 2 (38%), 3 (26%) Additional Axis I diagnoses: anxiety (22%), alcohol and substance abuse (22%), disruptive (28%) BDI mean depression scores = moderate range BHS mean hopelessness scores = moderate range

Canadian	Nixon et al. (2002)	N = 42 12–18 years old 86% female Ethnicity not noted	None	74% had suicide attempt and 64% had almost daily suicidal ideation 6 months before admission 74% admitted for suicidal ideation and 33% for depression Self-reported eating (50%) and drug or alcohol abuse (43%) problems BDI depression severe range (78.6%) STAXI anger scores elevated: Total (52.4%), state (59.5%), internalized (52.4%), externalized (52.4%)
Finnish	Makikyro et al. (2004)	N = 84 12–17 years old 67% female 98% Caucasian	Inpatients: With suicidal ideation With attempted suicide Without suicidal ideation Without attempted suicide	* Female tobacco users NSSI (52%) > non–tobacco users NSSI (35%) *Depression doubles risk for NSSI
U.S.	Nock & Prinstein (2005)	N = 89 12–17 years old 74% female 76% Caucasian	None	FASM automatic negative reinforcement function significantly correlated with HSC total hopelessness score and DISC recent suicide attempts FASM automatic positive reinforcement function significantly correlated with DISC major depressive and posttraumatic stress symptoms FASM social positive and negative reinforcement functions significantly correlated with CAPS total perfectionism score and DISC depression

TABLE 5.2 Studies of NSSI and Co-occurrence (continued)

Sample	Study	Demographics[a]	Comparison Group	Symptoms/Disorders Co-occurring with NSSI[b]
U.S.	Nock et al. (2006)	N = 89 12–17 years old 74% female 76% Caucasian	None	70% had at least one and 55% ≥2 lifetime suicide attempts 88% had at least one DSM-IV DISC diagnosis (M = 3, range 0–8): 63% had externalizing disorders: 49% conduct disorder, 45% oppositional defiant disorder 52% had internalizing disorders: 42% major depressive disorder, 24% posttraumatic stress disorder, 16% generalized anxiety disorder 60% had substance disorders: 39% nicotine dependency, 30% marijuana dependency, 18% alcohol abuse, 17% alcohol dependency, 13% marijuana abuse 67% had DIPD diagnoses: 52% borderline, 31% avoidant, 21% paranoid
OUTPATIENT				
U.S.	Schwartz et al. (1989)	N = 41 14–18 years old 100% female 100% Caucasian	None	59% had prior suicide attempt 27% had three or more previous suicide attempts

| U.S. | Crowell et al. 2005 | N = 23
12–18 years old
100% female
74% Caucasian | Non-NSSI clinical controls | 87% had lifetime suicidal act
* > scores on 10/10 CBCL narrow and broadband syndrome scale scores
* > scores on 9/10 YSR narrow and broadband syndrome scale scores
* > scores on 9/10 TRF narrow and broadband syndrome scale scores
* > scores on 10/10 YI-4 scale scores
* > scores on 5/10 ASI-4:P scale scores
ASI-4:P or YI-4 symptom criteria met for dysthymia (64%), major depression (64%), generalized anxiety (50%), anorexia (36%), social phobia (36%), panic attacks (32%)
* > CDI depression scores
* > PANAS trait negative affectivity score
* < PANAS trait positive affectivity score
* > SRSUQ rates on all substances except heroin: alcohol (65%), tobacco (44%), marijuana (52%), cocaine/crack (30%), amphetamines (22%), hallucinogens (22%), inhalants (26%) |

TABLE 5.2 Studies of NSSI and Co-Occurrence (continued)

Sample	Study	Demographics[a]	Comparison Group	Symptoms/Disorders Co-occurring with NSSI[b]
U.S.	Jacobson et al. (in press)	N = 30 (NSSI only) 13–17 years old 83% female 83% Hispanic	Outpatient: History of suicide without NSSI History of suicide and NSSI (n = 40) No history of NSSI or suicide	Suicide attempt and NSSI = 57% of entire sample K-SADS diagnoses: major depressive disorder (46%), dysthymia (28%), any anxiety disorder (32%), any disruptive disorder (33%), any substance use disorder (14%) SCID-II-BDP: 27% features of BPD * < suicide-NSSI group on BDI-II depression * < suicide-NSSI group on SIQ suicidal ideation * < suicide-without NSSI group on SIQ suicidal ideation
COMMUNITY				
Canadian	Ross & Heath (2002)	N = 61 13–17 years old 64% female 77% Caucasian	Non-NSSI community controls	* > BDI depression scores * > BAI anxiety scores
Canadian	Ross & Heath (2003)	N = 61 13–17 years old 64% female 77% Caucasian	Non-NSSI community controls	* > HDHQ: acting-out hostility, criticism of others, guilt, paranoid hostility, self-criticism, extrapunitive, intropunitive, and total scores
U.S.	Muehlenkamp & Gutierrez (2004)	N = 62 15–16 years old 55% male 74% Caucasian	Community: History of suicide without NSSI No history of NSSI or suicide	*NSSI and suicide-NSSI groups > controls on RADS depression, SIQ suicidal ideation, and MAST negative attitudes to life scores *NSSI < suicide-NSSI group on MAST repulsion by life score

Canadian	Laye-Gindhu & Schoner-Reichl (2005)	N = 64 13–18 years old 53% female Mostly Caucasian	Non-NSSI community controls	83% had suicidal ideation, 40% had suicidal plans, 26% had suicide attempts * > 5/5 RAASI psychological adjustment difficulties scale scores * > ADS total anger score * > SHS risky behaviors * > SHS smoking (girls only)
German	Brunner et al. (2007)	N = 859 14–15 year olds 50% female Ethnicity not noted	Non-NSSI Occasional NSSI Repetitive NSSI	Compared to non-NSSI, occasional, and repetitive NSSI had: * > Smoking for females * > Illicit drugs * > Suicidal ideation * > Suicidal attempts * > Suicide plan (repetitive-NSSI only) * > Body-image problems, too thin or fat (repetitive-NSSI only) * > Dieting (occasional-NSSI only) * > YSR anxious or depressed * > YSR delinquent behavior * > YSR aggressive behavior (occasional-NSSI only)
U.S.	Lloyd-Richardson et al. (2007)	N = 293 14–16 years old 65% female 49% Caucasian	Non-NSSI Minor NSSI Moderate or severe NSSI	9% had suicide attempt in past year Alcohol or drug use during NSSI: moderate or severe NSSI (27%) > minor NSSI (3%) History of suicide attempt: moderate or severe NSSI (28%) > minor NSSI (10%) > non-NSSI (2%) Suicide Ideation Questionnaire: moderate or severe NSSI > minor NSSI > non-NSSI

TABLE 5.2 Studies of NSSI and Co-occurrence

Sample	Study	Demographics[a]	Comparison Group	Symptoms/Disorders Co-occurring with NSSI[b]
U.S.	Muehlenkamp & Gutierrez (2007)	N = 87 (NSSI only) 15–16 years old 60% female 57% Caucasian	Community: History of suicide without NSSI History of suicide and NSSI - No history of NSSI/suicide	Suicide attempt and NSSI = 30% of entire sample * < Suicide-NSSI group on RADS anhedonia and negative self-evaluation * < Suicide-NSSI group on SIQ suicidal ideation * > Suicide-NSSI group on 4/5 RFL-A reasons for living *NSSI and suicide-NSSI groups > controls on RADS depression and SIQ suicidal ideation & fewer RFL-A reasons for living

[a]N = NSSI group number

[b]*Study Measures*: ADS = Anger Discomfort Scale, ASI-4-P = Adolescent Symptom Inventory: Version 4 – Parent (*DSM-IV* screen), BAI = Beck Anxiety Inventory, BDI (II) = Beck Depression Inventory (second edition), BHS = Beck Hopelessness Scale, CAPS = Child and Adolescent Perfectionism Scale, CBCL = Child Behavior Checklist, CDI = Child Depression Inventory, DISC = Diagnostic Interview Schedule for Children, DIPD = Diagnostic Interview for DSM-IV Personality Disorders, FASM = Functional Assessment of Self-Mutilation Questionnaire, HDHQ = Hostility and Direction of Hostility Questionnaire, HSC = Hopelessness Scale for Children, K-SADS = Schedule for Affective Disorders & Schizophrenia for School Age Children, MAPI = Millon Adolescent Personality Inventory, MAST = Multi-Attitude Suicide Tendency Scale, PANAS = Positive and Negative Affect Schedule, RFL-A = Reasons for Living Inventory for Adolescents, RAASI = Reynolds Adolescent Adjustment Screening Inventory, RADS = Reynolds Adolescent Depression Scale, SCID-II-BDP = Structured Clinical Interview for DSM-IV Personality Disorder Questionnaire-Borderline Personality Disorder Module, SCL-90 = Symptom Checklist-90, SHS = Self-Harm Survey, SIQ = Suicidal Ideation Questionnaire, SRSUQ = Self-Report Substance Use Questionnaire, STAXI = State-Trait Anger Inventory, TRF = Teacher Report Form, YI-4 = Youth Inventory (DSM-IV screen), YSR = Youth Self Report

measure or document whether both NSSI and suicidal behaviors were present at the same time. We can only conclude that most individuals engage in NSSI and acts of suicide at some point in their lives. However, this pattern should still increase concern and can complicate treatment, which makes careful assessment of each type of self-injury critical.

RESEARCH LIMITATIONS AND FUTURE DIRECTIONS

We were only able to identify 16 studies on adolescent NSSI because the intent of the adolescents' behavior has rarely been explicitly assessed in studies of self-harm. With future research, we need to ask and clearly document participants' intent. Another fundamental research limitation is that many studies did not measure or document whether both NSSI and other psychiatric conditions were present during the same time period and thus co-occurring. Therefore, we can merely conclude that NSSI appears to be related, in some developmental fashion, to a variety of additional psychiatric conditions. Even for those few studies that did measure NSSI and additional psychopathology at the same time, we cannot conclude that true comorbidity or true covariance exists because the artifacts mentioned at the beginning of the chapter have not been empirically ruled out as explanations for joint occurrence. In future efforts, we need to measure and record the onset and duration of NSSI and additional psychiatric conditions and attempt to rule out as many confounds as possible.

Existing research is also restricted by the employment of convenient and cross sectional samples. Research utilizing longitudinal designs of nationally representative community samples would improve the generalizability of findings, as would large-scale studies of inpatient and outpatient samples. Additionally, research needs to isolate the unique biopsychosocial components contributing to NSSI so that developmental trajectories of the behavior, as well as processes leading to suicide, within this group can be explored. Finally, even though a study of adolescent NSSI and true comorbidity and covariance has many benefits (as noted earlier in this chapter), there may be a limit to what this research can offer us in understanding the specific reasons why an adolescent engages in NSSI. Therefore, in future research, we need to examine why some adolescents initially chose to engage in NSSI whereas others do not and why some continue whereas others stop performing NSSI.

CLINICAL RECOMMENDATIONS

As the assessment and treatment of NSSI is covered in greater detail in Chapters 7, 8, and 13, we offer general recommendations for assessing and treating co-occurrence. First, to obtain a comprehensive and detailed account of a patient's co-occurring psychopathology, we suggest that clinicians thoroughly evaluate all *DSM-IV* Axis I and Axis II symptoms and their time of occurrence. A practical method of screening for *DSM-IV* Axis I conditions, involves Gadow and Sprafkin's self- (1999), parent- (1997), and teacher-rated (1997) adolescent symptom inventories can be used with follow-up clinical interviews to obtain additional information on *DSM-IV* diagnostic criteria. Alternatively, a structured clinical interview, such as the Children's Interview for Psychiatric Syndromes-Child and Parent Forms (Weller, Weller, Rooney, & Fristad, 1999a,b) can be used to evaluate Axis I conditions. For Axis II diagnoses, we recommend the Diagnostic Interview for *DSM-IV* Personality Disorders (Zanarini, Frankenburg, Sickel, & Yong 1996). With research consistently documenting the high prevalence of suicide attempts among adolescents who engage in NSSI, clinicians referred adolescents who self-injure need to routinely assess for suicidal intent and, if it is present, conduct a meticulous history of suicidality (for specific recommendations see Chapter 7, 8, and 13; American Academy of Child and Adolescent Psychiatry, 2001; Nock, Wedig, Janis, & Deliberto, in press).

To guide treatment planning and course, due to the added clinical complexity that co-occurring conditions can create, we strongly suggest an initial and ongoing thorough case conceptualization (see Chapter 2 in Friedberg & McClure, 2002, for a general case conceptualization framework for adolescents). If suicidal intent or behaviors are present, treatment should focus on the suicidal behavior first. Interventions that address the primary concerns fueling the adolescent's suicidal wishes combined with the development of an empathic, collaborative, and therapeutic relationship; structured problem-solving; skills training and relapse prevention will likely lead to a successful reduction of suicidality. Once the suicidal behavior has remediated, it is recommended that treatment move on to addressing the biopsychological factors underlying the NSSI. Of course, it is also possible to integrate treatment of suicidality into the ongoing treatment of NSSI. This would involve adopting crisis management interventions for the suicidal behavior as it arises that compliment the standard treatment being used to address the NSSI.

To treat the myriad combinations of diagnoses and symptoms that to co-occur with NSSI, we recommend examining evidence-based practices (EBP) for each condition and then using a modular "common-elements" approach (Chorpita, Daleiden, & Weisz, 2005) guided by your case conceptualization to apply specific EBP's techniques and procedures to specific symptom clusters. Currently, the most practical method for clinicians to learn about EBPs for a wide variety of conditions is via one of the following four books: *Child and Adolescent Therapy: Science and Art* (Shapiro, Friedberg, & Bardenstein, 2006), *Evidence-Based Psychotherapies for Children and Adolescents* (Kazdin & Weisz, 2003), *Psychosocial Treatments for Child and Adolescent Disorders: Empirically Based Strategies for Clinical Practice* (Hibbs & Jensen, 2005), and *Treatment of Childhood Disorders* (Mash & Barkley, 2006). In addition, the most user-friendly way for clinicians to keep up to date about EBP's is via the Evidence Based Services webpage of the Child and Adolescent Mental Health Division of the Hawaii State Department of Heath (http://www.hawaii.gov/health/mental-health/camhd/library/webs/ebs/ebs-index.html). This website offers free information, practice profiles, and biennial EBP reviews by the Evidence-Based Services Committee (chair: Bruce Chorpita, Ph.D.), for youth with anxious-avoidant, attention-hyperactivity, depressive-withdrawn, or disruptive-oppositional problems.

In terms of prioritizing which co-occurring conditions to treat, we suggest collecting additional data by asking patients about their main concerns, determining which conditions are the most severe and impairing in the patient's life, and using your case conceptualization to identify conditions that may be elevating a patient's risk for current and future NSSI.

CONCLUSION

Research on comorbidity and covariance and research on NSSI among adolescents have both suffered from the lack of an accurate and consistent application of an operationalized definition. Due to the failure of most researchers to differentiate NSSI from suicidal self-injury and true from artifactual comorbidity and covariance, we were only able to review 16 relevant studies that specifically examined NSSI and co-occurring psychiatric conditions in adolescent samples. Regrettably, as most studies did not document the NSSI and additional psychopathology being present during the same time period (i.e., co-occurring), we can only conclude that NSSI appears to be related, at some time point in adolescence, with a wide variety of additional psychiatric conditions, especially depression, suicidal behavior, substance use, anxiety, and hostility and anger. In future, our studies on adolescent NSSI and co-occurrence need to be more specific in terms of differentiating NSSI from suicidal self-harm, document the onset and duration of NSSI and all psychiatric conditions, and attempt to rule out as many artifacts of co-occurrence as possible.

Due to the additional conditions that accompany NSSI, clinicians first need to conduct a comprehensive and detailed assessment of all *DSM-IV* Axis I and Axis II symptoms. A subsequent case conceptualization will then drive treatment planning and prioritization of interventions. Finally, the application of EBP's via a modular approach may be most beneficial for treating the complex presentation of psychopathology that occurs with NSSI in adolescence.

REFERENCES

Achenbach, T. M. (1991). "Comorbidity" in child and adolescent psychiatry: Categorical and quantitative perspectives. *Journal of Child and Adolescent Psychopharmacology, 1*, 1–8.

Achenbach, T.M., & McConaughy, S. H. (2003). *The Achenbach system of empirically based assessment.* In C. R. Reynolds & R. W. Kamphaus (Eds.), *Handbook of psychological and educational assessment of children: Personality, behavior and context* (2nd ed.). New York: Guilford Press.

American Academy of Child and Adolescent Psychiatry. (2001). Practice parameter for the assessment and treatment of children and adolescents with suicidal behavior. *Journal of the American Academy of Child and Adolescent Psychiatry, 40*, 24S–51S.

American Psychiatric Association. (1994). *Diagnostic and statistical manual of mental disorders* (4th ed.). Washington, DC: Author.

Brunner, R., Parzer, P., Haffner, J., Rainer, S., Roos, J., Klett, M., et al. (2007). Prevalence and psychological correlates of occasional and repetitive deliberate self-harm in adolescents. *Archives of Pediatrics and Adolescent Medicine, 161*, 641–649.

Caron, C., & Rutter, M. (1991). Comorbidity in child psychopathology: Concepts, issues, and research strategies. *Journal of Child Psychology and Psychiatry, 32*, 1063–1080.

Chorpita, B. F., Daleiden, E. L., & Weisz, J. R. (2005). Identifying and selecting the common elements of evidence-based interventions: A distillation and matching model. *Mental Health Services Research, 7*, 5–20.

Crowell, S. E., Beauchaine, T. P., McCauley, E., Smith, C. J., Stevens, A. L., & Sylvers, P. (2005). Psychological, autonomic, and serotonergic correlates of parasuicide among adolescent girls. *Development and Psychopathology 17*, 1091–1104.

Darche, M. A. (1990). Psychological factors differentiating self-mutilating and non-self-mutilating adolescent inpatient females. *Psychiatric Hospital, 21*, 31–35.

Feighner, J. P., Robins, E., Guze, S. B., Woodruff, R. A., Winokur, G., & Munoz, R. (1972). Diagnostic criteria for use in psychiatric research. *Archives of General Psychiatry, 26*, 57–63.

Friedberg, R. D., & McClure, J. M. (2002). *Clinical practice of cognitive therapy with children and adolescents.* New York: Guilford.

Gadow, K. D., & Sprafkin, J. (1997). *Adolescent Symptom Inventory-4 screening manual.* Stony Brook, NY: Checkmate Plus.

Gadow, K. D., & Sprafkin, J. (1999), *Youth's Inventory-4 manual.* Stony Brook, NY: Checkmate Plus.

Favazza, A., & Rosenthal, R. J., (1990). Varieties of pathological self-mutilation. *Behavioral Neurology, 3*, 77–85.

Herpetz, S., Sass, H., & Favazza, A. (1997). Impulsivity in self-mutilative behavior: Psychometric and biological findings. *Journal of Psychiatric Research, 31.* 451–465.

Hibbs, E. D., & Jensen, P. S.(2005). *Psychosocial treatments for child and adolescent disorders: Empirically based strategies for clinical practice* (2nd ed.) Washington, DC: American Psychological Association.

Hinden, B. R., Compas, B. E., Howell, D. C., & Achenbach, T. M. (1997). Covariation of the anxious-depressed syndrome during adolescence: Separating fact from artifact. *Journal of Consulting and Clinical Psychology,* 65, 6–14.

Jacobson, C. M., Muehlenkamp, J. J., & Miller, A. L. (in press). Psychiatric impairment and self-harm behaviors in a clinical sample of adolescents. *Journal of Clinical Child and Adolescent Psychology.*

Kazdin, A. E. (1983). Psychiatric diagnosis, dimensions of dysfunction, and child behavior therapy. *Behavior Therapy, 14,* 73–99.

Kazdin, A. E., & Weisz, J. R. (2003). *Evidence-based psychotherapies for children and adolescents.* New York: Guilford Press.

Keiley, M. K., Lofthouse, N., Bates, J. E., Dodge, K. A., & Pettit, G. S. (2003). Differential risks of covarying and pure components in mother and teacher reports of externalizing and internalizing behavior across ages 5 to 14. *Journal of Abnormal Child Psychology, 31,* 267–283.

Klein, D. N., & Riso L. P. (1993). Psychiatric disorders: Problems of boundaries and comorbidity. In. C. G. Costello (Ed.), *Basic issues in psychopathology.* New York: Guilford Press.

Kumar, G., Pepe, D., & Steer, R. A. (2004). Adolescent psychiatric inpatients' self-reported reasons for cutting themselves. *Journal of Nervous and Mental Disease, 192,* 830–836.

Laye-Gindhu, A., & Schonert-Reichl, K. A. (2005). Self-harm among community adolescents: Understanding the "whats" and "whys" of self-harm. *Journal of Youth and Adolescence, 34,* 447–457.

Lilienfeld, S. O., Waldman, I. D., & Israel, A. C. (1994). A critical examination of the use of the term and concept of comorbidity in psychopathology research. *Clinical Psychology: Science and Practice, 1,* 71–83.

Lloyd-Richardson, E. E., Perrine, N., Dierker, L., & Kelley, M. L. (2007). Characteristics and functions of non-suicidal self-injury in a community sample of adolescents. *Psychological Medicine, 37,* 1183–1192.

Makikyro, T. H., Hakko, H. H., Timonen, M. J., Lappalainen, J. A. S., Ilomaki, R. S., Marttunen, M. J., et al. (2004). Smoking and suicidality among adolescent psychiatric patients. *Journal of Adolescent Health, 34,* 250–253.

Mash, E. J., & Barkley, R. A. (2006). *Treatment of childhood disorders* (3rd ed.). New York: Guilford Press.

Muehlenkamp, J. J., & Gutierrez, P. M. (2004). An investigation of differences between self-injurious behavior and suicide attempts in a sample of adolescents. *Suicide and Life-Threatening Behavior, 34*(1), 12–23.

Muehlenkamp, J. J., & Gutierrez, P. M. (2007). Risk for suicide attempts among adolescents who engage in non-suicidal self-injury. *Archives of Suicide Research, 11,* 69–82.

Nixon, M. K., Cloutier, P. F., & Aggarwal, S. (2002). Affect regulation and addictive aspects of repetitive self-injury in hospitalized adolescents. *Journal of the American Academy of Child and Adolescent Psychiatry, 41,* 1333–1341.

Nock, M. K., Joiner, T. E., Gordon, K. H., Lloyd-Richardson, E., & Prinstein, M. J. (2006). Non-suicidal self-injury among adolescents: Diagnostic correlates and relation to suicide attempts. *Psychiatry Research, 144,* 65–72.

Nock, M. K., & Prinstein, M. J. (2005). Clinical features and behavioral functions of adolescent self-mutilation. *Journal of Abnormal Psychology, 114,* 140–146.

Nock, M. K., Wedig, M. W., Janis, I. B., & Deliberto, T. L. (in-press). *Evidence-based assessment of self-injurious thoughts and behaviors*. In J. Hunsley & E. J. Mash (Eds.), *A guide to assessments that work*. New York: Oxford University Press.

Nottelman, E. D., & Jensen, P. S. (1995). *Comorbidity of disorders in children and adolescents: Developmental perspectives*. In T. H. Ollendick & R. J. Prinz (Eds.), *Advances in clinical child psychology*, (Vol. 17, pp. 109–155). New York: Plenum.

Ross, S., & Heath, N. L. (2002). A study of the frequency of self-mutilation in a community sample of adolescents. *Journal of Youth and Adolescence, 31*(1) 67–77.

Ross, S., & Heath, N. L. (2003). Two models of adolescent self-mutilation. *Suicide and Life-Threatening Behavior, 33*(3), 277–287.

Schwartz, R. H., Cohen, P., Hoffmann, N. G., & Meeks, J. E. (1989). Self-harm behaviors (carving) in female adolescent drug abusers. *Clinical Pediatrics, 28*(8), 340–346.

Shapiro, J. P., Friedberg, R. D., & Bardenstein, K. K. (2006). *Child and adolescent therapy: Science and art*. New York: John Wiley & Sons.

Silverman, M. M., Berman, A. L., Sanddal, N. D., O'Carroll, P. W., & Joiner, T. E. (2007). Rebuilding the Tower of Babel: A revised nomenclature for the study of suicide and suicidal behaviors. Part 2: Suicide-related ideations, communications, and behaviors. *Suicide and Life-Threatening Behavior, 37*(3), 264–277.

Stahl, N. D., & Clarizio, H. F. (1999). Conduct disorder and comorbidity. *Psychology in the Schools, 36*(1), 41–50.

Walsh, B. W. (2006). *Treating self-injury: A practical guide*. New York: Guilford Press.

Weller, E. B., Weller, R., Rooney, M. T., & Fristad, M. A. (1999a). *Children's Interview for Psychiatric Syndromes (ChIPS)*. Washington, DC: American Psychiatric Association.

Weller, E. B., Weller, R., Rooney, M. T., & Fristad, M. A. (1999b). *Children's Interview for Psychiatric Syndromes-Parent's Version (P—ChIPS)*. Washington, DC: American Psychiatric Association.

Zanarini, M. C., Frankenburg, F. R., Sickel, A. E., & Yong, L. (1996). *The Diagnostic Interview for DSM-IV Personality Disorders*. Boston: McLean Hospital.

6

Neurobiological Perspectives on Self-Injury

ELIZABETH A. OSUCH AND GEOFFREY W. PAYNE

In this chapter, the practitioner will gain an understanding of:

- The key aspects of the neurobiological mechanisms associated with NSSI including implicated neurotransmitters and neuronal pathways
- Nonprimate and primate animal models used to understand the neurobiological underpinnings of repetitive NSSI
- Theoretical models that consider the brain and behavior from the neurobiological perspective (e.g., learning and memory, the role of sensory perception, the role of reinforcement by brain reward mechanisms, and state regulation)
- Current research that has contributed to the development of these models

Our understanding of the neurobiological etiology of nonsuicidal self-injury (NSSI) is in its extreme infancy. Although numerous researchers have investigated the social, behavioral, and psychological aspects of NSSI in human populations, there is a very small extant literature on the neurobiology of NSSI. This puts the field at a severe disadvantage with regard to developing preventions and treatments for this behavior when it is highly repetitive. In an era when NSSI seems to be increasing in both clinical and nonclinical populations in youth, this is an unsatisfactory state of affairs. Much more research into the neuroscience of NSSI is required.

Perhaps the most daunting challenge for such research is the complexity of the phenomenon of self-injury, which exists in both the developmentally delayed and nondevelopmentally delayed populations. There appear to be many motivations for NSSI, many predetermining variables for any individual act of NSSI, several seemingly very different diagnostic populations at risk for NSSI, and multiple complex intrapsychic explanations for the behavior in the extant literature. This behavior occurs in the developmentally disabled, the cognitively intact, the sexually abused, in children and adolescents, in the incarcerated, and in the psychotic. It can involve mild to severe forms of cutting of skin, self-burning, head banging, or hitting to necessarily severe forms such as breaking of one's bones, eating glass, eye enucleation, and self-castration. Thus, understanding the neurobiological etiology of NSSI in general and repetitive NSSI specifically requires the initiation of research involving the integration of knowledge from many areas of study utilizing subjects from several clinical populations.

This chapter give a brief review of the basic neuroscience involved in understanding the neurobiology of NSSI, including an overview of the neurotransmitter systems implicated in several psychiatric conditions and in NSSI. This will be followed by a discussion of the neuroscience of learning and habit formation and a discussion of neurodynamics as it relates to emotional state regulation. The second goal of this chapter is to illustrate a number of animal models of NSSI, which can be utilized to gain insight into how and why repetitive NSSI occurs. The third and final section of this chapter is devoted to a discussion of the neurobiology of the human phenomenon of NSSI.

Toward this end we will explore the existing literature in human populations with the highest prevalence of self-injury: individuals with developmental disabilities and those with borderline personality disorder. This latter group will also be understood in light of the frequent findings of childhood abuse in association with NSSI. The success of various treatment modalities will be reviewed as a way to shed light on some of the neurobiological systems and processes involved. After this background literature review, we will propose four neurobiological frameworks from which to understand and further research the phenomena of repetitive NSSI. These frameworks, or schemata, have at their foundation some of the basic principals of neuroscientific understanding, some of which were presented in the first section of this chapter. The schemata are not intended to be mutually exclusive interpretations of NSSI, because NSSI is not expected to be a unitary process with one determining cause. Rather, they are presented as potentially co-occurring neurobiological forces underlying an individual act of NSSI. It is hoped that the four schemata presented here will form the basis of further clinical research studies, including studies into the prevention and treatment of recurrent NSSI in clinical populations.

BASIC NEUROSCIENCE OF BRAIN AND BEHAVIOR: NEUROTRANSMITTERS AND SELF-INJURY

Brain chemistry is complex, and it is not the focus of this chapter to discuss all aspects of brain chemistry. When looking at key features of NSSI and the evaluation of associated neurotransmitters, specific aspects of NSSI are likely associated with certain neurotransmitters. These aspects include impulsivity, (self-) aggression, mood symptoms, and addiction. By understanding how neurotransmitter systems may be associated with these features, we can begin to build a neurobiological framework from which to investigate and understand the neurobiological underpinnings of repetitive NSSI.

Neurotransmitters allow the movement of information from one neuron to the next (see Figure 6.1). The release of neurotransmitters from one neuron, across the synaptic cleft, and the recognition of these chemicals by a specific receptor site on the adjacent neuron causes an electrical signal within the recipient cell facilitating the release of another particular neurotransmitter within this recipient cell, often

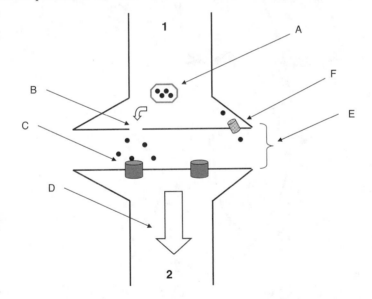

Figure 6.1   Schematic of 2 neurons (1 & 2) engaged in neurotransmission. Communication occurs when packaged synaptic vesicles containing neurotransmitter (A) in neuron 1 are released into the synaptic cleft (E) via exocytosis (B). The released neurotransmitter binds to receptors located on neuron 2 specific for it (C). This binding evokes a signal that promotes a response consistent with the specific neurotransmitter (D). The remaining neurotransmitter does not bind to its receptor and it taken back up into the neuron (F) to be repackaged and utilized again.

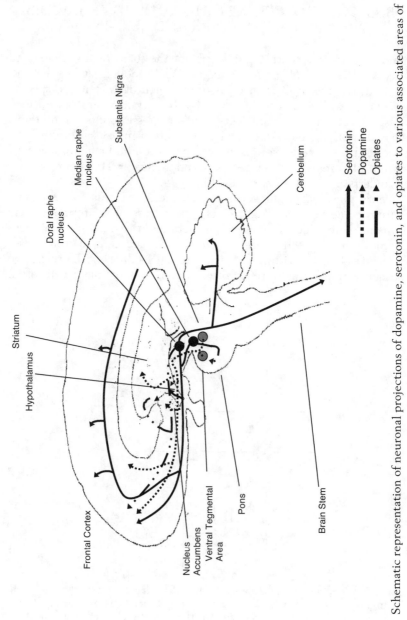

Figure 6.2 Schematic representation of neuronal projections of dopamine, serotonin, and opiates to various associated areas of the brain.

some distance from the initial neurotransmitter release. This is how signals are transmitted within the brain and from the brain to nerves, muscles, and glands throughout the body. The processes within the brain that lead to signals to distant sites such as muscles are far from simple, involving many processes within numerous modular neural networks. These actions are also influenced by previous learning, memory, emotional state, and genetic brain chemistry, some of which will be considered below. When acts of self-aggression, impulsivity, and addictive behavior are considered, the complexity of brain function is beyond allowing a direct, causal model. However, our current understanding of neurotransmitter function has greatly advanced our knowledge of the steps involved in translating brain signals into actions of all types, permitting a better understanding of brain function and effective treatments for disorders that affect neurotransmission.

Our current understanding of psychiatric symptoms of impulsivity, (self-) aggression, mood dysregulation, and addictions is that the key neurotransmitters and associated pathways involve serotonin, dopamine, and opioids. Figure 6.2 outlines the major pathways for these neurotransmitters. As can be seen, the complexity of neurons and projections for each of the neurotransmitters open questions as to where the difficulty is. For example, is the problem with the interactions between them or within one system? How much "abnormality" within a neurotransmitter system is required to promote the onset of NSSI in any given individual? The following section will provide a very brief overview of the three main neurotransmitter systems thought to be involved. Concentration on these three systems is not meant to suggest that they are the only neurotransmitters relevant to NSSI. Rather, they are the best understood systems at this time that have relevance to NSSI.

Serotonin

Serotonin (5-hydroxytryptamine [5-HT]) is derived from the amino acid tryptophan. Tryptophan is converted to serotonin by 5-hydroxytryptophan hydroxylase. Once released by serotonergic neurons in the brain, much of the 5-HT is inactivated by monoamine oxidase that coverts 5-HT to 5-hydroxyindoleacetic acid (5-HIAA). It is this major metabolite of 5-HT that can be used as an indicator of 5-HT release to investigate if serotonin function is deviated from normal levels. Serotonergic neurons originate in a series of nuclei known as the raphe nuclei. These neuron clusters may be allocated, on the basis of their distribution and main projections, into two groups: the *rostral group*, confined to the mesencephalon and rostral pons, with major projections to the forebrain, and the *caudal group*, extending from the caudal pons to the caudal portion of the medulla oblongata, with major projections to the caudal brainstem and to the spinal cord (Hornung, 2003) The behavior associated with lower than average levels of 5-HT are varied but include such important behaviors as attempted suicide. There is reason to believe that there is a link between this type of auto-aggression and NSSI. The aggressiveness of a depressed individual's behavior has been inversely linked to cerebrospinal fluid (CSF) levels of 5-HIAA (Asberg, Traskman, & Thoren, 1976) Also, CSF levels of 5-HIAA have been reported to be lower in violent offenders in comparison to nonviolent offenders (Linnoila et al., 1983). In a study of 21 patients with major depression; 5 exhibited "self-aggressive behaviors," and those 5 patients had significantly lower levels of 5-HIAA in comparison to patients not exhibiting aggressive behavior (Lopez-Ibor, Saiz-Ruiz, & Perez de los Cobos, 1985).

Neuroendocrine challenge studies have also substantiated the serotonin hypothesis of increased self-aggression. The prolactin response to a serotoninergic challenge such as fenfluramine is indicative of central serotonin function. In repeated fenfluarmine challenges in individuals diagnosed with personality disorder, reduced prolactin responses were observed in all patients in comparison to controls (Coccaro et al., 1987). This impaired prolactin response is positively correlated with increased self-aggression (i.e., suicide attempts) and indicative of decreased presynaptic serotonin activity. Although these studies were undertaken in individuals with personality disorders, it may elucidate a role for serotonin in the onset of "auto-aggression more generally."

Dopamine

Dopamine is derived from the conversion of dopa to dopamine by dopa decarboxylase. The major dopamine systems located in the brain include one that originates in the hypothalamus and one from a group of cells located in the ventral midbrain adjacent to the cerebral peduncles (substantia nigra and ventral tegmental area [VTA]; Figure 6.2). The system of importance for this review is the system of dopaminergic projections from the substantia nigra and VTA to many areas of the cortex (mesocortical) limbic areas (mesolimbic) and striatum. Currently, there are five known types of dopamine receptors (D1–D5), with the two most relevant being D1 and D2. Most data supporting a role of alterations in cerebral dopamine come from observing self-injurious behavior (SIB) in individuals with developmental delays such as those afflicted with Lesch-Nyhan syndrome LNS; (Lloyd et al., 1981). The theory that modulation in dopamine function plays a role in promoting the onset of self-injury stems from two hypotheses that include alterations in dopaminergic signaling or increased sensitivity of dopamine receptors (D1 or D2 in particular). Furthermore, animal data implicates these two receptor subtypes as important targets in the etiology of SIB.

Goldstein and colleagues attempted to prove the hypothesis that lower levels of dopamine or its metabolites and decreased numbers of striatal dopamine transporter sites were associated with SIB by conducting animal studies. In the first study, using rats, chemical disruption of the dopaminergic neurons that project to various regions of the brain promoted self-biting behavior following the administration of dopamine agonists. This behavior was inhibited when receptor antagonists for both D1 and D2 receptors were given. In a second study, monkeys that had their nigrostriatral dopamine neurons denervated also exhibited SIB when given L-dopa (a dopamine agonist). However, the application of D2 receptor antagonist had no effect on inhibiting the behavior, whereas a mixed D1-D2 receptor antagonist was just as effective in inhibiting the behavior as previously observed in the rodent model. These two studies allowed Goldstein and his colleagues to conclude that, in both rodent and primate models, sub-aggresion was potentially mediated through activation of the D1 receptor or in combination with D2 receptors, but not the D2 receptor pathway alone (Goldstein, 1989). The addictive nature of SIB may represent a behavior linking SIB with associated with alterations in the dopaminergic signaling pathway (Winchel & Stanley, 1991).

Opiate

The opioid signaling pathway and associated receptors are more complex than the serotonin and dopamine systems just described. We are currently aware of three opioid receptor subtypes (κ, μ, and δ) dispersed throughout the brain. The search for naturally occurring substances in the body that bind to these receptors led to the discovery of enkephalins, endorphins, and dynorphins, among other naturally occurring peptides that activate these receptors. Their physiological effects depend on which receptor is activated. Typically, endorphins bind to μ receptors, whereas the others (enkephalins and dynorphins) can bind to multiple receptor subtypes (see below for relevance). Brain locations of opiate receptors are determined by observing the neuronal bodies or axon terminals for enkephalins, endorphins, or dynorphins. Results show that enkephalins and dynorphins are found in the periaqeductal gray, rostral medulla, and dorsal horn of the spinal cord. Endorphins are found in the hypothalamus and send projections to the periaqeductal gray region. All projections are involved in the sensation of pain. It has been suggested that increased brain opiate activity may promote SIB behavior (Sandman, Hetrik, Taylor, & Chicz-DeMet, 1997; Winchel & Stanley, 1991). The two hypotheses involving alterations in opioid signaling to the developmentally delayed SIB population include the addiction to endogenous opioids and increased tolerance to painful stimuli (Sandman et al., 1997). The addiction hypothesis suggests that these individuals who engage in SIB have normal brain opioid signaling. However, due to extensive stimulation of this pathway and release of opiates during SIB, the individual goes through a "withdrawal" and needs to engage in SIB to activate the opioid pathway (Coid, Allolio, & Rees, 1983).

The other hypothesis involves alteration in pain perception. This stems from the notion that there is an increased activation of the opioid pathway that leads to increased "opiate tone," and by inference decreased pain perception. Sandman and colleagues observed that plasma levels of β-endorphin were significantly elevated relative to Adrenocorticotropic Hormone (ACTH) immediately following an SIB episode in developmentally delayed individuals. Additionally, the level of β-endorphin was predictive of treatment response (decreases in SIB) when faced with opioid antagonism with naltrexone (Sandman, Touchette, Lenjavi, Marion, & Chicz-DeMet, 2003). Coid and colleagues measured plasma concentrations of met-enkephalin, N-lipotropin and β-endorphin in patients who had been admitted to hospitals following onset of SIB. In these individuals, it was observed that the more extensive or prevalent the SIB was, the higher were the levels of met-enkephalin reported. This is correlational at best but does indicate the involvement or alterations in the opioid signaling pathway (Coid et al., 1983).

Summary of Brain Neurotransmitters

This summary of postulated neurotransmitters thought to be involved in NSSI must reiterate the extensive overlap in the projections of these systems as depicted in Figure 6.2. It is likely to be a complex combination of neurotransmitter systems and interactions that predisposes and promotes NSSI. This perspective is supported by the wide array of psychological and neurological conditions associated with self-injury, as outlined in the following section on human self-injury.

ANIMAL MODELS OF SELF-INJURY

There are four main animal models of self-injury. These four models have been fundamental in improving our understanding of the neurobiology of this behavior, but they do have limitations. Two are based on dopamine models (6-hydroxydopamine and pemoline). One is based on a recent model evaluating the role of calcium channel agonists. The final model looks at a primate model (versus rodent) of self-injury and explores variables associated with SIB at the level of individual animal.

6-Hydroxydopamine Neonate Model of SIB

This model was developed by Breese and colleagues in 1984 and served as the basis for subsequent studies establishing the model (Breese, Baumeister, Napier, Frye, & Mueller, 1985; Breese et al., 1984) to establish a link between Lesch-Nyhan Syndrome (LNS) and dopamine dysregulation. To investigate this hypothesis, the researchers lesioned brain dopaminergic neurons (see Figure 6.2 for review) in both neonatal and adult rats with 6-hydroxydopamine (6-OHDA). This was an attempt to show that the age at which the alterations occur is integral to promoting the onset of SIB. Results demonstrated that neonatally lesioned rats had learning deficits and elevated levels of serotonin in the striatum–characteristics observed in LNS. SIB was initiated with the application of selective dopamine agonists, indicating that increasing dopamine activity could result in the onset of SIB. This result was dependent upon activation of D1 receptors, as the selective activation of D2 receptors had no effect on initiating the SIB. Interestingly, concomitant application of a mixed D1-D2 receptor agonist was successful in promoting SIB. Of note, rats lesioned as adults were not susceptible to SIB when the dopamine system was stimulated. The elevated susceptibility of neonatally lesioned rats for SIB was demonstrated further by the enhanced occurrence of SIB when other neurotransmitter systems were stimulated. This model proposed a signaling mechanism (i.e., activation of dopaminergic neurotransmission) for promoting the onset of SIB, with D1 as the predominant receptor being implicated. The researchers proposed that early disruption in dopamine signaling facilitates an "increased sensitivity" so that normal levels of dopamine could promote an exaggerated response that manifests as SIB.

Pemoline-Induced SIB

The pemoline model of SIB was developed in the early 1980s (Mueller, Hollingsworth, & Pettit, 1986; Mueller & Nyhan, 1982). Pemoline (2-amino-5-phenyl-4-oxazolidinone), a chemical compound administered experimentally, exerts its action primarily through modulation of dopamine pathways but also has indirect serotonin (Zaczek, Battaglia, Contrera, Culp, & De Souza, 1989) and opioid activity (King, Au, & Poland, 1995). When pemoline is given in high doses to rats, it results in a sequence of behaviors that ends with self-biting (King, 1993; Sivam, 1995). The time course of the behavior is such that following application, the rat displays an increase in locomotor (movement) behavior. There is also an increase in "nervous" behaviors such as sniffing, head bobbing, and digging. About 24 hours following application of pemoline, the rats engage in self-biting behavior. This behavior subsides about 48 hours after the initial dose. This model substantiates those alterations in dopamine and perhaps serotonin neurotransmission as a potential site promoting the onset of SIB.

Calcium Channel Agonists and SIB

A recent study evaluating self-injury in animals focused on the role of calcium (Ca) channel agonists. One such channel is the L-type voltage-gated Ca channel that is found throughout the brain, in particular in areas of the striatum and cortex, and has important roles in cerebral neurotransmission for multiple neurotransmitters (Kasim et al., 2006; Kasim, Egami, & Jinnah, 2002). Jinnah et al. (1999) observed that when given a specific calcium channel agonist, mice demonstrated SIB. Increasing doses showed increasing severity and frequency in SIB in both young and adult mice. Younger mice exhibited an increased susceptibility to the onset of SIB (e.g., biting areas such as their feet and abdomen) in comparison to older animals. This behavior began within 10 minutes of drug application, peaking within 30 minutes and disappearing at 120 minutes. The animals also appeared more aggressive, suggesting a possible link to the serotonin system (Jinnah et al., 1999).

This group has done some follow-up studies evaluating other neurotransmitters and has found that depletion of serotonin stores prior to Ca channel agonist administration showed a "supersensitivity" to the drug and increased rates of biting with onset of SIB. This model appears to be one of the most promising animal models for SIB, because L-type calcium channel activation is involved with all three major neurotransmitters postulated to be involved in the onset of SIB (Kasim et al., 2006; Kasim et al., 2002).

Primate Model of Self-Injury

Most of the research on primates and self-injury has used psychosocial models with monkeys in captivity. Items of interest include age and social contact. Monkeys that were deprived of maternal and social interaction exhibited self-injury. Studies by Lichstein and Sackett in the 1970s showed key features in evaluating self-injury in macaque monkeys, including the following: (a) Species variation affects the likelihood that the monkey would develop self-injury, suggesting that genetics play a role. (b) Males are more likely to develop self-injury than females, implicating a role for gender. (c) Social isolation early in life, in comparison to social rearing, facilitates self-injury, implicating issues related to attachment. (d) Age is a major determinant of promoting the onset of the behavior, as monkeys that are postpubescent are more likely to develop self-injury than younger monkeys (Lichstein & Sackett, 1971). In summary, a number of potential causal factors at the level of the individual animal are associated with self-injury in the monkey model.

Limitations of Animal Models of Self-Injury

Although other animal studies evaluate self-injury, these four appear to be the most prominent. The main limitation of these studies is that not all examined potential neurotransmitters (e.g., serotonin, dopamine, and opiate) in the same model. Finally, in the rodent studies, there was no investiation of the impact of gender, mood, or stressors and how they impacted the onset of self-injury. All of these variables need to be addressed to develop a fully characterized and dependable animal model of NSSI.

MODELS FOR UNDERSTANDING NSSI IN HUMANS

Learning and Memory

The process of learning may play an important role in promoting NSSI behavior. One of the key features of the mammalian, and especially the primate, brain is the ability for stimuli and response sequences to be learned and remembered so that a desired effect can be elicited time and again. This feature of the brain of acquiring information from the environment and being able to store it to evoke behavior is remarkable. The theory, first proposed by Hebb in the late 1940s, was that memory storage was a result of changes in synaptic strength. Hebb suggested that excitatory synapses linking two cells could be strengthened if both cells were activated at the same time. This strengthening has been described as long-term potentiation. Briefly, during the activation and release of neurotransmitters, the transmission of a neuronal message may occur. Modifications in the neurotransmission can occur to increase the probability of a response to this message. NSSI can be considered a learned behavior that may be strengthened through the mechanisms of long-term potentiation. Furthermore, modifications in the neurotransmitters described above may be important in facilitating the learning and repetition of the NSSI. Examples of this will be described below.

Neurodynamics

To understand affect regulation, which likely plays a major role in NSSI, in neurobiological terms we will refer to concepts utilized in discussions of neurodynamics. This is a relatively recent construct of neuroscience (Freeman, 2000; Grigsby & Stevens, 2000, 2002; Le Van Quyen, 2003; Sarbadhikari & Chakrabarty, 2001) that provides an elegant and heuristic approach to relate neuronal activity to behavior using nonlinear dynamics. Toward this end, consider first the concept of "state." Quoting from one neuroscientist, the "state" of a complex organism, or the "instantaneous physiological state," as it is more descriptively called, is "the synthetic emergent property of a number of different systems influencing arousal, activity level, mood, short-term emotional status, motivational status, sleep-wake cycle, and other psychological phenomena." That is, at any moment, the state of a person is the result of multiple variables that encompass physiology and therefore brain chemistry and function—and, thus, affective and emotional status. An important aspect of state to understand here is that it probabilistically determines behavior. Specifically, "states are important in determining the likelihood that one will have certain thoughts, feelings, perceptions, memories, and inclinations toward behavior at any given moment" (Grigsby & Stevens, 2000, p. 165).

It is important to be aware of several underlying assumptions in this description. The most important is the assumption that the subjective experience of feelings, moods, and actions result from underlying neurobiology. The suggestion that they are, in fact, emergent properties of neurophysiological circumstances. It is important to note that, in this model, neurobiology "determines" behavior in a probabilistic fashion. Thus, while neurobiology does not determine behavior in an absolute way, it determines probabilities that any given neural network will be activated at any given time. In addition, while neurobiological state determines behavior, this behavior thereafter modifies state. That is, while state probabilistically determines action, any action alters the state of the organism to the extent that that action alters physiological variables.

The interplay between state and behavior is most evident when considering biologically imperative behaviors. When in a state of hunger, the probabilities for behaviors that involve seeking and eating food increase. Subsequently, the act of eating modifies the state to such an extent that the probability of seeking food and eating diminishes for the time being. The same interplay exists for the somewhat more subtle states that characterize affect and emotion.

As an example, consider when a mammal is in a state that is characterized by a subjective sense of fear. Certain physiological characteristics exist at such times, from which the feeling of fear emerges. These include increases in sympathetic nervous system tone with higher levels of circulating stress hormones such as epinephrine and cortisol. The state of fear results from a multitude of neurobiological processes in the brain and body that affect the probability that the animal (including humans) will behave in certain ways. These behaviors include fleeing the situation or behaving defensively (verbally or otherwise) if fleeing is not possible. The probability that certain other behaviors will occur is decreased in the state characterized by fear. These other behaviors include falling asleep, seeking or enjoying food, and initiating a sexual interaction. It is, of course, previous learning as well as temperament (how the neural networks are interconnected) that influence the precise behaviors that undergo increased and decreased probabilities in various states. Matters of the neurodynamics of state changes may be crucial to understanding the ways in which NSSI is used in the animal and human and will be discussed further in the section below on schemata for understanding NSSI.

SELF-INJURY IN HUMANS

Self-injury is part of the diagnostic criteria for borderline personality disorder (BPD) and occurs in 70–80% of such patients. There is also a strong association between suicidal and nonsuicidal self-injury and childhood traumatic exposure such as childhood sexual and physical abuse. Because of these associations, it is worthwhile to look at these populations as well as what has been helpful for them, to increase our neurobiological understanding of NSSI.

Etiological Studies

Borderline Personality Disorder

Most of the biological investigations of NSSI in humans without developmental disabilities are focused on borderline personality disorder patients, because that is the psychiatric diagnosis most closely associated with NSSI. Whereas there are obvious empirically verifiable abnormalities in the neurobiological and neurocognitive functioning within patients with developmentally delays, these are more subtle and difficult to identify in BPD. It is probable that NSSI in nondevelopmentally delayed humans is related to, but more complex than, SIB in developmentally delayed humans. Relatively less research has been conducted on the neurobiology of NSSI in nondevelopmentally delayed humans. One consistent finding, however, is abnormal sense perception in patients with BPD who engage in NSSI, particularly those who experience analgesia during self-injury. This involves a higher pain threshold as well as other characteristics (Bohus et al., 2000; Kemperman et al., 1997; Schmahl et al., 2004). Decrease in pain sensitivity is found in patients who attempt suicide as well (Orbach, Mikulincer, King, Cohen, & Stein, 1997; Orbach et al., 1996). The diminished pain sensitivity in BPD has been found to be associated with differences in brain activity in the dorsolateral prefrontal cortex, posterior parietal cortex, anterior cingulated cortex, and amygdala (Schmahl et al., 2006).

Childhood Abuse

The correlation between suicidal and NSSI and childhood trauma, especially childhood sexual abuse (with or without BPD) has been demonstrated repeatedly in studies (Bergen, Martin, Richardson, Allison, & Roeger, 2003; Curtis, 2006; Cyr, McDuff, Wright, Theriault, & Cinq-Mars, 2005; Evren & Evren, 2005; Gratz, Conrad, & Roemer, 2002; Matsumoto et al., 2004; Santa Mina et al., 2006; Weaver, Chard, Mechanic, & Etzel, 2004; Ystgaard, Hestetun, Loeb, & Mehlum, 2004). Many of these studies find high rates of self-injury in populations that report childhood sexual abuse and high rates of childhood sexual abuse in survivors of suicide attempts. Individuals who engage in NSSI have no intent for suicide, and yet repeated NSSI is a risk factor for suicide attempts. No research, to date, has demonstrated a neurological mechanism by which childhood sexual abuse leads to attempts at self-harm, either suicidal or otherwise, yet one group has made an advance in this area. At the genetic level of investigation, one team of researchers of NSSI in depressed, nondevelopmentally delayed youth found an association between the T allele of the G protein beta-3, NSSI, and childhood sexual abuse (Joyce et al., 2006). The cascade of molecular events that results from this allelic variation, combined with this environmental stressor and depressed mood, and how these predispose to NSSI in youth remains to be fully elucidated.

Treatment Studies

Clues to the neurobiological etiology of NSSI are also gleaned from psychopharmacology and nonpharmacological treatment successes and failures. Clinically, many classes of drugs have been tried for the treatment of self-injury in developmentally delayed patients as well as with cognitively intact individuals. Included are the antidepressants, stimulants, mood stabilizers, anxiolytics, beta-blockers, opioid antagonists, and antipsychotics. Positive effects seem to be commonly associated with antidepressants, opioid antagonists, and antipsychotics, whereas less success as occurred with the others (Antochi, Stavrakaki, & Emery, 2003; Garcia & Smith, 1999; Hammock, Schroeder, & Levine, 1995; Sandman et al., 2003; Symons, Thompson, & Rodriguez, 2004; Zarcone et al., 2001). A good review of the research on multiple types of self-injury, including suicide, and associated symptoms in the cognitively intact population is offered by Grossman and Siver (2001), and Chapters 4 and 5 of this text review issues of comorbidity, suicide, and psychosocial risk and protective factors.

Nonpharmacological approaches (behavioral and psychotherapeutic) have been studied in both developmentally delayed and nondevelopmentally delayed subjects and represent attempts to address the components of the behavior related to attention seeking, communication of stress and distress, efforts at self-regulation of affective and sensory states with self-stimulation, and the like (Bohus et al., 2004; Evans et al., 1999; Frey, Szalda-Petree, Traci, & Seekins, 2001; Hanley, Piazza, Fisher, & Maglieri, 2005; Lerman, Iwata, Zarcone, & Ringdahl, 1994; Lindberg, Iwata, & Kahng, 1999). One of the more successful therapies for the NSSI of BPD appears to be dialectical behavioral therapy (Bohus et al., 2004). There is, thus, some empirical ground for the use of both pharmacological agents and these behavioral approaches to help in decreasing self-injury in both the developmentally and nondevelopmentally delayed populations.

As is evident from this brief review of the literature, the precise manner in which BPD or childhood abuse lead to repetitive NSSI is incompletely understood. Uncovering these mechanisms remains a central goal for the study of NSSI. Evidence exists that the hypothalamic-pituitary-adrenal (HPA) axis, the endogenous opiate system including the pain perception system, the dopamine system, substance P, one allelic variant of the G protein beta 3, a history of childhood sexual abuse, and the basic sensory input and processing networks are all associated with NSSI in some populations. There is empirical support for the use of both pharmacological and behavioral approaches to decreasing NSSI, all of which contribute to the understanding of the etiology of the behavior, but no treatment has been found to work in all individuals. Indeed, many NSSI patients remain treatment refractory in spite of treatments that may temporarily or partially decrease the behavior. As researchers continue to investigate various levels in the cascade of an NSSI event and the points at which to successfully intervene—from perception, sensation and the decision to self-injure, to the act and resultant consequences—the greater will be our ability to benefit those who suffer from this behavior.

Neurobiological Schemata for Understanding the Etiology of NSSI

Numerous articles discuss the functions or purposes of NSSI, including Chapter 3 of this volume. However, many explanations of the function of NSSI are based not on neurobiological concepts but on intrapsychic and psychodynamic constructs. A few studies describe the functions of NSSI based on empirical data collected from patients themselves (Osuch, Noll, & Putnam, 1999) or review clinician observations and describe intrapsychic and interpersonal functions of NSSI (Suyemoto, 1998). Such perspectives are informative and important but are not as unbiased a foundation to research the behavior as neurobiologically based constructs can be. Because intrapsychic and interpersonal paradigms involve abstract concepts such as drives, meaning, intention and the self, they are more difficult to measure and less translatable from one individual to the next. Neurobiologically based constructs can be easier to objectively verify, which may make them a more solid basis for empirical research. Although not completely free from bias, they are somewhat more likely to withstand changes in study population, culture, scientific viewpoint, societal circumstances, and the like. In addition, they attempt to clarify the cascade of events that lead from molecular changes to behavioral outcome.

In formulating neurobiological schemata to study NSSI, we start with the basic assumption that it is a behavior that results from such a cascade of endogenous neurobiological events in response to preceding internal or external events or stimuli. The exact origins and the detailed molecular sequence leading to NSSI remains to be delineated. Four schemata through which to guide our understanding of NSSI at the level of the central nervous system as a whole are described here and can form the basis for further empirical study. These schemata are founded on understood principals of neuroscience and are not intended to be the only possible schemata from which to investigate the behavior. Table 6.1 outlines the four schemata and the associated assumptions. Each of these will be discussed in turn, with the intent that this will provide a broad foundation upon which to develop further approaches to studying the

TABLE 6.1   Schemata for Investigating the Neurobiology of NSSI and
Associated Assumptions

Neurobiological Schemata	Assumption
Behavioral reinforcement-learning–exogenous reward	The rewarding quality of the reinforcer is great enough to overcome the aversive quality of the NSSI, and/or, contrarily, the negative quality of the NSSI is less extreme than that of the negative reinforcer that is stopped by the behavior.
Endogenous reward–addiction	When NSSI is repeated by an individual, it can be assumed to activate the endogenous reward (e. g., opiate or dopamine) neurocircuitry.
Disordered sensory experiences	Tactile or other sensory abnormalities, such as decreased pain perception or feelings of dissociation, may contribute to NSSI.
State regulation	Unpleasant states (e.g., fear, loneliness, emptiness, anger, dissociation) are characterized by a high probability of the individual acting to try to alter the state, sometimes very effectively with NSSI.

fundamental biological processes underlying NSSI across populations, including cognitively intact humans. Although it is not unambiguous how these principals of neuroscience specifically explain individual acts of NSSI in humans from the molecular level to the behavioral level, it is hoped that this discussion will promote neurobiologically based studies of investigating and understanding the behavior.

Behavioral Reinforcement or Exogenous Reward

Any behavior that is reinforced—or rewarded—will likely be repeated, provided that repeating it is possible and provided that the reinforcement is sufficiently powerful to override any aversive attributes of the behavior. This includes behaviors that are socially desirable and healthy as well as behaviors that are socially undesirable and detrimental. This schema is relevant for behaviors that are not fundamentally—or endogenously—rewarding, which will be discussed in the next section.

Learning and behavioral reinforcement (training) is a process most pertinent to behaviors that are adverse, at least to some extent. Thus, getting the family dog to sit and wait for food until it receives a signal from its master involves a delay in gratification that is not pleasant, easy, or instinctual for the dog, yet it is a simple behavior to train in most dogs. As a behavior becomes more adverse, the significance and the probability (and awareness of certainty) of the exogenous reward must also increase for the training to take hold. For example, the dog must be trained in stages, first learning to wait a few seconds for the signal to eat, but after more repetitions (increased awareness of certainty of reward) is able to tolerate longer waits for the food reward. This delay in gratification would not occur without the intervention that training and learning involves. Learning can, of course, involve both positive and negative reinforcement as well as positive and negative punishment, but we will focus on reinforcement for this discussion, because only reinforcement relates to increasing the probability of a behavior.

Humans learn to do many things that are initially adverse but for which there is a subsequent reward. In the very young, the degree of aversion and the delay until gratification (reward) must be small. With age, cognitively intact humans learn to delay reward quite well and to undergo significant aversion, as long as the promised reward (and the awareness of the certainty of reward) is great. Examples include everything from teaching manners to young children to far more complex processes such at studying for exams and working toward retirement. Humans, in fact, are exquisite learners and have a greater capacity for learning than other species, as far as we understand. This capacity can contribute to NSSI in some individuals.

Within human NSSI populations of all types, there are many observations of the use of NSSI to gain exogenous rewards, including creating effects in others. Examples are NSSI that leads to directing attention and affection toward the individual, being relieved of demands placed upon the individual by others, or in more subtle cases, attempting to create a condition such as guilt or shame in someone in relationship with the individual. These all represent positive or negative reinforcement for the behavior of NSSI. Leaning and behavioral reinforcement are recognized as contributors to NSSI in developmentally delayed populations, and addressing the behavior from this perspective has been successful in various treatment interventions (Hanley et al., 2005; Lerman et al., 1994; Lindberg et al., 1999; Mace, Blum, Sierp, Delaney, & Mauk, 2001) (some of which also utilize punishment as an adjunct to manipulating reinforcements and rewards). NSSI in BPD is often assumed to be manipulative of those in relationship to the patient because these others often do feel manipulated, whether this perception is accurate or not, and they may inadvertently reinforce the behavior by unknowingly providing a reward for it, such as by providing closer or more thoughtful attention to someone for engaging in NSSI than at other times. The use of NSSI to avoid emotional arousal, which may constitute a negative reinforcer, has been used by one group to explain the role of learning in NSSI in cognitively intact individuals (Chapman, Gratz, & Brown, 2006).

For the behavioral reinforcement schema to be valid, one must assume that the rewarding quality of the reinforcer is great enough to overcome the aversive quality of the NSSI, or, contrarily, that the negative quality of the NSSI is less extreme than that of the negative reinforcer that is stopped by the behavior. It is not clear that getting a family member, romantic partner, or health care provider's attention, for example, would be sufficiently rewarding to overcome the pain of cutting one's arm, yet in some individuals with a biological vulnerability, perhaps reinforced by early life experiences such as abandonment, this may be the case. Considering the use of NSSI as a way to truncate momentary feelings of abandonment in this case may make the NSSI solution seem more reasonable, although it is distinctly short term.

Utilizing the schema of behavioral reinforcement and learning, NSSI in adults and adolescents with childhood sexual abuse may be easier to conceptualize. NSSI in abuse survivors may be understood, in the intrapsychic paradigm, as "repetition compulsion" but may be equally or better understood through the neuroscientific lens of associative learning. If affection and attention were associated with physical pain and potential tissue damage as through the recurrence of childhood sexual abuse by someone close to the child, it may be a learned association that is replicated through complex neurobiological mechanisms leading to NSSI. If a child is given special and valued attention when being hurt, then that child may quickly learn to associate much needed interpersonal attention with injury. Thus, an individual with such early life experiences may learn that the best and fastest (or perhaps the only) way to obtain the reward of attention and affection is through injury, which the individual can initiate at any time though NSSI. The process whereby early life events lead the individual to act in a way that replicates this association can be investigated utilizing our understanding of the neurobiology of learning.

As mentioned above in the section on basic neuroscience, the mechanisms by which learning is currently understood include synaptic and neuronal plasticity and long-term potentiation (Marrone, 2005; Schouenborg, 2004; Wolpaw & Carp, 2006). The more frequently particular neurons and synaptic connections are activated, the more probable it is that those neurons and synaptic connections will be active in the future, and the less cellular energy is needed to activate those neurons and synapses. It is by this repetition that some neural networks develop higher probabilities of activation while others become less probable candidates for activation. The dopamine neurocircuitry of reward is fundamentally involved here, because all exogenous rewards must involve activation of endogenous reward neurocircuitry. This suggests the inseparable nature of this schema and the schema of endogenous reward, as discussed below. However, it may be informative to maintain a distinction between rewards that include a reinforcing external act or event in response to an act of NSSI as compared with NSSI that involves primarily an endogenous reward with no such external reinforcer.

Addiction or Endogenous Reward

The dopamine or endogenous reward system of the brain has been nicely delineated in animals and in functional brain imaging paradigms in live humans. Again, this circuitry involves dopamine neurons in the ventral tegmental area that project to the nucleus accumbens (the mesolimbic pathway) and then to the limbic-cortical-striatal-thalamic circuit. Relevant brain regions include the orbital and medial frontal cortices, the amygdala and extended amygdala, and the hippocampus, among others (Chau, Roth, & Green, 2004). Stimuli of many kinds, including cocaine (Risinger et al., 2005), opiates (Becerra, Harter, Gonzalez, & Borsook, 2006), viewing attractive faces (Aharon et al., 2001; O'Doherty et al., 2003), playing a game for monetary reward (Delgado, Nystrom, Fissell, Noll, & Fiez, 2000), and listening to music (Menon & Levitin, 2005; Zatorre, 2003) activate the endogenous circuitry of reward processing. It is straightforward to make the case that any behavior that is voluntarily repeated engages the endogenous reward neurocircuitry. By this logic, when an individual repeats NSSI, it can be assumed to activate the endogenous reward processing neurocircuitry as well.

Addiction involves activation of the endogenous reward neurocircuitry of reward processing. It is likely that the difference between an ordinary pleasurable activity and an activity to which one is addicted is a matter of the nature of the alteration that occurs at the level of the neuron and synapse in the reward circuitry following administration of the stimulus (Jones & Bonci, 2005). Behaviorally, an addiction involves the willingness to endure considerable adverse consequences to obtain the reward—a reward that is often mostly or solely endogenous. This is not the case with ordinary pleasurable experiences, where there is significantly less willingness to undergo hardship to engage in the behavior and a willingness to postpone the behavior until it involves less aversion. This illustrates the difference between endogenous reward that is balanced with regard to cost (energy output and tolerance of aversive consequences) and endogenous reward in its most extreme form, which is addiction.

The activation of reward processing neurocircuitry in addiction is evident not only in cocaine and morphine use, as in the studies mentioned above, but also in cigarette smoking (McClernon, Hiott, Huettel, & Rose, 2005; Rose et al., 2003) alcohol use (Heinz et al., 2004; Tapert et al., 2003) and pathological gambling (Reuter et al., 2005). Thus, a multitude of substances and activities that are addictive have been demonstrated to activate the reward circuitry of the brain. It is possible that NSSI is another such activity in some individuals.

There is ample reason to believe that NSSI can be an addictive behavior for some. This is most obvious from the fact that individuals are willing to undergo the adverse experience of the self-injury itself to carry it out. This adversity can come in the form of pain, bodily deformation, and negative social repercussions. It is important to remember that not all people who engage in NSSI report pain during the act, even though they may experience other aversive qualities of NSSI. People suffering from recurrent NSSI repeat the behavior, and some endorse experiencing cravings for the act, as well as a need to increase the "dose" of NSSI. Many find it very difficult to stop the behavior (Nixon, Cloutier, & Aggarwal, 2002).

Therapeutic trials also lend credence to the fact that NSSI is an endogenously rewarding or addictive process in some individuals. Studies show that the opiate antagonist naltrexone is of help for reducing NSSI in some patients with developmental disability (Garcia & Smith, 1999; Symons et al., 2004). One meta-analysis of studies using naltrexone for NSSI in this population found that 80% responded positively to this agent, with 47% of subjects improving by at least 50% from baseline (Symons et al., 2004). Naltrexone has been helpful in some NSSI patients with BPD as well (Roth, Ostroff, & Hoffman, 1996; Sonne, Rubey, Brady, Malcolm, & Morris, 1996). Unlike the well-recognized addictions referenced above, no studies to date have investigated the reward neurocircuitry of NSSI in a functional brain imaging scanner, but one such a study is underway by the author (EAO). The result of this study will help uncover the role of endogenous reward and addiction during acts of NSSI in individuals who engage in it regularly.

Disordered Sensory Experiences

When mammals experience abnormal sensory experiences, they may engage in NSSI. This is common in house pets such as dogs and cats, for example, when they have the unusual sensation of a bandage or other foreign object on their fur or skin or when suffering from a topical injury. They often lick, scratch, or bite at the area in question, even to the extent of damaging their fur or skin. Infants and children also react with picking, scratching, hitting, and so on, areas of their body that are experiencing unusual sensations as a result of injury, bandaging, casting, or the like. This is confirmed in developmentally disabled persons, who have been found in several studies to have abnormal pain perception (Symons & Danov, 2005; Theodoulou, Harriss, Hawton, & Bass, 2005; Zafeiriou, Vargiami, Economou, & Gombakis, 2004). As described above, deficits in pain sensation have been associated with NSSI in BPD either at baseline or during acts of NSSI (Bohus et al., 2000; Kemperman et al., 1997; Russ, Campbell, Kakuma, Harrison, & Zanine, 1999; Russ et al., 1996; Schmahl et al., 2006; Schmahl et al., 2004). Decreased pain perception is also found in Prader-Willi syndrome (Brandt & Rosen, 1998) and may be involved in NSSI in that population. Thus, consideration of tactile sensory abnormalities may lead to advancements in our understanding of NSSI.

In addition to disorders of sense perception within the tactile modality, the idea of too much or too little sensory stimulation overall may come into play as a cause of NSSI. This includes conditions such as sensory deprivation in several forms, including those related to social deprivation or neglect in animals (Dellinger-Ness & Handler, 2006) and humans (especially powerful in infants and children), (Gratz et al., 2002) as well as boredom (Favazza, 1998; Singh et al., 2004). Research on individuals with developmental disabilities shows that the intro-duction of novel objects or time in a high stimulus "Snoezelen room" decreases the incidence of NSSI in these subjects (Lerman et al., 1994; Lindauer et al., 1999; Singh et al., 2004), though sometimes only when NSSI itself is specifically restricted (Lindberg et al., 1999). In addition, decreases on a measure of early visual information processing have been associated with BPD and, specifically, impulsivity (Keilp et al., 2006), which is thought to be related to NSSI.

At the other extreme, susceptible individuals may engage in NSSI when they are overwhelmed with sensory input either from exogenous stimuli or endogenously induced increases in sensitivity to stimuli. This may be why psychotic, autistic, and otherwise agitated individuals engage in such behaviors as head banging or hitting and animals given stimulants have an increase in NSSI. When some animals and humans are exposed to stressful or traumatic situations, there is an increased tendency to engage in NSSI (Briere & Gil, 1998; Novak, 2003; Pow-ers & McArdle, 2003). It can be easily construed that stress represents a decrease in the occurrence of restful states and a concomitant tem-porary, but overwhelming, increase in sensory stimuli. Events such as motor vehicle accidents, domestic abuse, criminal victimization, and the like all have the potential to overwhelm the sensory processing of the individual. This may be an early component of a cascade that leads some individuals—especially children, with their limited repertoire of coping—to a predisposition to engage in NSSI.

Related to disordered sensory experience is another less obvious sce-nario, that is, disordered perception or sensation of the self. Although considerably more abstract than sensory perception, per se, it may be that this involves disordered sensory experiences that contribute to NSSI in some subjects. For example, dissociation has been found to be associated with self-injury in numerous studies (Osuch et al., 1999; Russ et al., 1996; Yates, 2004; Zlotnick, Mattia, & Zimmerman, 1999). It is possible that the dissociated state is one in which there is a disor-dered sense perception of the body and the self, which may initiate a similar cascade of endogenous events as other forms of disordered sense perception. Dissociation can be explained using other schemata as well, as discussed below.

Because both increases and decreases in sensory experience can lead to NSSI, it is apparent that there may be an ideal range in which any individual at any given time has an optimal amount of stimuli. The size of this range likely varies from person to person at any point in time, with individuals who engage in repeated NSSI having a particularly narrow range and little capacity for adapting to or modifying incom-ing stimuli. This may be why individuals with neurocognitive deficits and previous experiences with overwhelming sensory stimuli may be at particular risk for NSSI. Thus, disordered sense perceptions may play a significant role in NSSI in several populations. As stated, this may include overwhelming stimuli from childhood sexual abuse or, alternatively, significant sensory deprivation as in early childhood neglect.

State Regulation

By far the most frequently endorsed motivation for engaging in NSSI in one empirical study of an inpatient psychiatric population was affect regulation (Osuch et al., 1999). This affect (or emotion) regulation appears to involve attempts to decrease unpleasant-feeling states in general and includes a desire to decrease feelings such as fear, loneliness, emptiness, anger, numbness or dissociation, guilt, shame, and sexual arousal. An association exists between the use of NSSI to regulate such states and the report of feelings of relief with this behavior (Osuch et al., 1999). Reference to our earlier discussion of neurodynamics is useful for understanding state regulation. Unpleasant states are characterized by a high probability of acting in a way to try to alter the state to the extent that this is possible. This is one definition of a state that is subjectively undesirable or unpleasant. States that represent brain physiology subjectively experienced as fear, sadness, guilt, shame, worthlessness, and so on are generally considered undesirable. Healthy individuals in such states have a high probability of engaging in acts to alter those states. They are experienced as unpleasant, and any behavior that, in turn, rapidly and effectively changes the state will likely become positively reinforced, and the probability that such a behavior will be repeated in similar stateswill increase.

Behaviors that alter states are those that change brain physiology. Such behaviors can include socially desirable as well as undesirable activities such as listening to music, talking with a close friend, taking physical exercise, writing a poem, eating, engaging in sexual activity, drinking alcohol, taking drugs, gambling, getting into a fight, and many others. It can be more difficult for some individuals to modify some states than others. This is particularly obvious in people who have psychiatric disorders such as depression or anxiety, which effectively increase the probability that undesirable states occur and decrease the probability of other, more pleasant states occurring. These conditions also decrease the probability that any given action will alter undesirable affective states. The activation of neural networks underlying undesirable states begins to act as "basins of attractions" (Grigsby & Stevens, 2000) that are difficult to modify.

When considering self-injury, it seems safe to assume that such an act has a fairly rapid and profound effect on state because both pain and physical injury have a profound effect on physiology. For example, stress hormones are excreted, endogenous opioids are released, and inflammatory and immune processes are activated if tissue is damaged. These chemical events affect the brain. Thus, NSSI is a highly effective way to alter state very quickly. As such, acts of NSSI may become dramatic modifiers of subjectively unpleasant states. Put another way, brain physiology is more likely to be dramatically altered quickly by an act of NSSI than it is by listening to music, taking a walk, or talking with a friend. This perspective presupposes that the NSSI or post-NSSI state is less undesirable than the previous unpleasant state. This may be particularly true in individuals with decreased pain perception, such that NSSI is not that unpleasant, and those for whom unpleasant states are especially intolerable. That is, where unpleasant states represent a greater neurobiological drive to alter those states and a lower probability of being able to tolerate them without acting to change them. When such conditions hold, it is easy to see how NSSI becomes an act with a high probability of repetition in such people once it is utilized. It is also noteworthy that studies demonstrate an association between alexithymia and NSSI (Evren & Evren, 2005; Paivio & McCulloch, 2004), suggesting that it is more common in people who are unable to utilize other means to alter state, such as verbal expression.

This schema is also helpful to understand obsessive–compulsive behavior, which may be relevant to NSSI in some individuals. In disorders characterized by obsessive–compulsive behaviors, a highly dysphoric state of anxiety exists. This state is characterized by a high probability of action that leads to its modification. The action itself changes the state to one of less dysphoria that has a lower drive to action. The duration of this more comfortable state is, unfortunately, short lived, and the original dysphoric state returns relatively quickly. The dysphoric state of anxiety apparently has a low energy of activation and thus a high probability of return. The comfortable state that exists after the compulsive act is completed has a lower probability of persistence. Thus, the cycle is repeated. NSSI may, in some individuals, have this pattern. A dysphoric state of anxiety may exist, and the act of NSSI may be highly efficient at truncating this state, even though the resultant relief is temporary. Such a pattern can quickly become reinforcing.

In this schema, at least four conditions can increase the probability that an individual will use NSSI as a way to modulate an undesirable state. These circumstances also illustrate the way in which the four schemata presented here may each be related by the drive to state regulation. These are any conditions that:

1. Increase the undesirability of certain states with the resultant inability to tolerate them, thereby increasing the drive to modify some states. This would include states characterized by sensory excesses or deficits as well as numerous other dysphoriac emotional states.
2. Decrease the modifiability of undesirable states, thereby increasing the probability for such undesirable states or increasing the energy

input required to change them. These include depression, anxiety (including obsessive-compulsive disorder), cognitive deficits, or other disorders that probabilistically limit activity of some neural networks. In such circumstances, more suitable means of state alteration (listening to music, talking with a friend, physical exercise) are ineffective at producing the necessary state change.

3. Decrease the probability for socially acceptable means of modifying undesirable states such as by previous learning, lack of healthy outlets, inefficacy of healthy outlets due to unique characteristics of neural activity in the individual (e.g., alexithymia).

4. Increase the probability of using NSSI to alter such states, as would occur through previous learning (exogenous reward) or endogenous reward.

Thus, this last schema can help unify the ways in which the previously described neurobiological schemata can be integrated with the ultimate goal of state regulation for the organism. As mentioned, affect or state regulation is the most commonly mentioned use of NSSI in the cognitively intact population.

SUMMARY

In this chapter we first reviewed several of the basic mechanisms of neuroscience that are needed to help understand self-injury in animals and humans. We then discussed several neurotransmitter systems that are likely involved in this behavior. Studies of treatment efficacy are useful for understanding any medical condition, and this is true of NSSI as well. The scientific data so far have led to several clues about the mechanisms of NSSI, including neurotransmitter systems such as dopamine and serotonin, yet there is a deficit in overarching neurobiological frameworks from which to understand it.

We have proposed four schemata to further guide the neuroscientific investigation of NSSI. These schemata are behavioral reinforcement–learning–exogenous reward, endogenous reward–addiction, disordered sensory experiences, and state regulation. The measure of the value of these frameworks is the degree to which they are useful in explaining observable phenomena. This chapter has given examples of how that might proceed, though it has not been inclusive of all phenomena related to NSSI. It should also be reiterated that these schemata are not intended to be mutually exclusive constructs, as they are each tools for assisting in representing the reality that is the functioning of the human brain. When we truly understand the processes of the brain, the schema through which we understand behavior will change, and some will become obsolete. In the meantime, it is hoped that the use of these neurobiologically based frameworks will assist the field in moving forward to understand and thereby prevent and treat the distressing acts that constitute NSSI.

REFERENCES

Aharon, I., Etcoff, N., Ariely, D., Chabris, C. F., O'Connor, E., & Breiter, H. C. (2001). Beautiful faces have variable reward value: FMRI and behavioral evidence. *Neuron, 32*(3), 537–551.

Antochi, R., Stavrakaki, C., & Emery, P. C. (2003). Psychopharmacological treatments in persons with dual diagnosis of psychiatric disorders and developmental disabilities. *Postgraduate Medical Journal, 79*(929), 139–146.

Asberg, M., Traskman, L., & Thoren, P. (1976). 5-HIAA in the cerebrospinal fluid biochemical suicide predictor? *Archives of General Psychiatry, 33*(10), 1193–1197.

Becerra, L., Harter, K., Gonzalez, R. G., & Borsook, D. (2006). Functional magnetic resonance imaging measures of the effects of morphine on central nervous system circuitry in opioid-naive healthy volunteers. *Anesthesia & Analgesia, 103*(1), 208–216.

Bergen, H. A., Martin, G., Richardson, A. S., Allison, S., & Roeger, L. (2003). Sexual abuse and suicidal behavior: A model constructed from a large community sample of adolescents. *Journal of the American Academy of Child & Adolescent Psychiatry, 42*(11), 1301–1309.

Bohus, M., Haaf, B., Simms, T., Limberger, M. F., Schmahl, C., Unckel, C., et al. (2004). Effectiveness of inpatient dialectical behavioral therapy for borderline personality disorder: A controlled trial. *Behavior Research and Therapy, 42*(5), 487–499.

Bohus, M., Limberger, M., Ebner, U., Glocker, F. X., Schwarz, B., Wernz, M., et al. (2000). Pain perception during self-reported distress and calmness in patients with borderline personality disorder and self-mutilating behavior. *Psychiatry Research, 95*(3), 251–260.

Brandt, B. R., & Rosen, I. (1998). Impaired peripheral somatosensory function in children with Prader-Willi syndrome. *Neuropediatrics, 29*(3), 124–126.

Breese, G. R., Baumeister, A. A., McCown, T. J., Emerick, S. G., Frye, G. D., & Mueller, R. A. (1984). Neonatal-6-hydroxydopamine treatment: Model of susceptibility for self-mutilation in the Lesch-Nyhan syndrome. *Pharmacology Biochemistry and Behavior, 21*(3), 459–461.

Breese, G. R., Baumeister, A., Napier, T. C., Frye, G. D., & Mueller, R. A. (1985). Evidence that D-1 dopamine receptors contribute to the supersensitive behavioral responses induced by l-dihydroxyphenylalanine in rats treated neonatally with 6-hydroxydopamine. *Journal of Pharmacology and Experimental Therapeutics, 235*(2), 287–295.

Briere, J., & Gil, E. (1998). Self-mutilation in clinical and general population samples: Prevalence, correlates, and functions. *American Journal of Orthopsychiatry, 68*(4), 609–620.

Chapman, A. L., Gratz, K. L., & Brown, M. Z. (2006). Solving the puzzle of deliberate self-harm: The experiential avoidance model. *Behavior Research and Therapy, 44*(3), 371–394.

Chau, D. T., Roth, R. M., & Green, A. I. (2004). The neural circuitry of reward and its relevance to psychiatric disorders. *Current Psychiatry Reports,* 6(5), 391–399.

Coccaro, E. F., Siever, L. J., Klar, H., Rubenstein, K., Benjamin, E., & Davis, K. L. (1987). Diminished prolactin responses to repeated fenfluramine challenge in man. *Psychiatry Research,* 22(3), 257-259.

Coid, J., Allolio, B., & Rees, L. H. (1983). Raised plasma metenkephalin in patients who habitually mutilate themselves. *Lancet,* 2(8349), 545–546.

Curtis, C. (2006). Sexual abuse and subsequent suicidal behavior: Exacerbating factors and implications for recovery. *Journal of Child Sexual Abuse,* 15(2), 1–21.

Cyr, M., McDuff, P., Wright, J., Theriault, C., & Cinq-Mars, C. (2005). Clinical correlates and repetition of self-harming behaviors among female adolescent victims of sexual abuse. *Journal of Child Sexual Abuse,* 14(2), 49–68.

Delgado, M. R., Nystrom, L. E., Fissell, C., Noll, D. C., & Fiez, J. A. (2000). Tracking the hemodynamic responses to reward and punishment in the striatum. *Journal of Neurophysiology,* 84(6), 3072–3077.

Dellinger-Ness, L. A., & Handler, L. (2006). Self-injurious behavior in human and non-human primates. *Clinical Psychology Review,* 26(5), 503–514.

Evans, K., Tyrer, P., Catalan, J., Schmidt, U., Davidson, K., Dent, J., et al. (1999). Manual-assisted cognitive-behavior therapy (MACT): A randomized controlled trial of a brief intervention with bibliotherapy in the treatment of recurrent deliberate self-harm. *Psychological Medicine,* 29(1), 19–25.

Evren, C., & Evren, B. (2005). Self-mutilation in substance-dependent patients and relationship with childhood abuse and neglect, alexithymia and temperament and character dimensions of personality. *Drug and Alcohol Dependence,* 80(1), 15–22.

Favazza, A. R. (1998). The coming of age of self-mutilation. *Journal of Nervous and Mental Disease,* 186(5), 259–268.

Freeman, W. J. (2000). Mesoscopic neurodynamics: From neuron to brain. *Journal of Physiology-Paris,* 94(5–6), 303–322.

Frey, L., Szalda-Petree, A., Traci, M. A., & Seekins, T. (2001). Prevention of secondary health conditions in adults with developmental disabilities: A review of the literature. *Disability and Rehabilitation,* 23(9), 361–369.

Garcia, D., & Smith, R. G. (1999). Using analog baselines to assess the effects of naltrexone on self-injurious behavior. *Research in Developmental Disabilities,* 20(1), 1–21.

Goldstein, M. (1989). Dopaminergic mechanisms in self-inflicting biting behavior. *Psychopharmacology Bulletin,* 25(3), 349–352.

Gratz, K. L., Conrad, S. D., & Roemer, L. (2002). Risk factors for deliberate self-harm among college students. *American Journal of Orthopsychiatry,* 72(1), 128–140.

Grigsby, J., & Stevens, D. (2000). *Neurodynamics of personality.* New York: Guilford Press.

Grigsby, J., & Stevens, D. (2002). Memory, neurodynamics, and human relationships. *Psychiatry,* 65(1), 13–34.

Grossman, R., & Siver, L. (2001). Impulsive self-injurious behavior: Neurobiology and psychopharmacology. In D. Simeon & E. Hollander (Eds.), *Self-injurious behavior: Assessment and treatment.* Washington, DC: American Psychiatric Press.

Hammock, R. G., Schroeder, S. R., & Levine, W. R. (1995). The effect of clozapine on self-injurious behavior. *Journal of Autism and Developmental Disorders, 25*(6), 611–626.

Hanley, G. P., Piazza, C. C., Fisher, W. W., & Maglieri, K. A. (2005). On the effectiveness of and preference for punishment and extinction components of function-based interventions. *Journal of Applied Behavior Analysis, 38*(1), 51–65.

Heinz, A., Siessmeier, T., Wrase, J., Hermann, D., Klein, S., Grusser, S. M., et al. (2004). Correlation between dopamine d(2) receptors in the ventral striatum and central processing of alcohol cues and craving. *American Journal of Psychiatry, 161*(10), 1783–1789.

Hornung, J. P. (2003). The human raphe nuclei and the serotonergic system. *Journal of Chemical Neuroanatomy, 26*(4), 331–343.

Jinnah, H. A., Yitta, S., Drew, T., Kim, B. S., Visser, J. E., & Rothstein, J. D. (1999). Calcium channel activation and self-biting in mice. *Proceeding of the National Academy of Sciences USA, 96*(26), 15228–15232.

Jones, S., & Bonci, A. (2005). Synaptic plasticity and drug addiction. *Current Opinions in Pharmacology, 5*(1), 20–25.

Joyce, P. R., McKenzie, J. M., Mulder, R. T., Luty, S. E., Sullivan, P. F., Miller, A. L., et al. (2006). Genetic, developmental and personality correlates of self-mutilation in depressed patients. *Australian and New Zealand Journal of Psychiatry, 40*(3), 225–229.

Kasim, S., Blake, B. L., Fan, X., Chartoff, E., Egami, K., Breese, G. R., et al. (2006). The role of dopamine receptors in the neurobehavioral syndrome provoked by activation of l-type calcium channels in rodents. *Developmental Neuroscience, 28*(6), 505–517.

Kasim, S., Egami, K., & Jinnah, H. A. (2002). Self-biting induced by activation of l-type calcium channels in mice: Serotonergic influences. *Developmental Neuroscience, 24*(4), 322–327.

Keilp, J. G., Gorlyn, M., Oquendo, M. A., Brodsky, B., Ellis, S. P., Stanley, B., et al. (2006). Aggressiveness, not impulsiveness or hostility, distinguishes suicide attempters with major depression. *Psychological Medicine, 36*(12), 1779–1788..

Kemperman, I., Russ, M. J., Clark, W. C., Kakuma, T., Zanine, E., & Harrison, K. (1997). Pain assessment in self-injurious patients with borderline personality disorder using signal detection theory. *Psychiatry Research, 70*(3), 175–183.

King, B. H. (1993). Self-injury by people with mental retardation: A compulsive behavior hypothesis. *American Journal of Mental Retardation, 98*(1), 93–112.

King, B. H., Au, D., & Poland, R. E. (1995). Pretreatment with mk-801 inhibits pemoline-induced self-biting behavior in prepubertal rats. *Developmental Neuroscience, 17*(1), 47–52.

Le Van Quyen, M. (2003). Disentangling the dynamic core: A research program for a neurodynamics at the large-scale. *Biological Research, 36*(1), 67–88.

Lerman, D. C., Iwata, B. A., Zarcone, J. R., & Ringdahl, J. (1994). Assessment of stereotypic and self-injurious behavior as adjunctive responses. *Journal of Applied Behavior Analysis, 27*(4), 715–728.

Lichstein, L., & Sackett, G. P. (1971). Reactions by differentially raised rhesus monkeys to noxious stimulation. *Developmental Psychobiology, 4*(4), 339–352.

Lindauer, S. E., DeLeon, I. G., & Fisher, W. W. (1999). Decreasing signs of negative affect and correlated self-injury in an individual with mental retardation and mood disturbances. *Journal of Applied Behavior Analysis, 32*(1), 103–106.

Lindberg, J. S., Iwata, B. A., & Kahng, S. W. (1999). On the relation between object manipulation and stereotypic self-injurious behavior. *Journal of Applied Behavior Analysis, 32*(1), 51–62.

Linnoila, M., Virkkunen, M., Scheinin, M., Nuutila, A., Rimon, R., & Goodwin, F. K. (1983). Low cerebrospinal fluid 5-hydroxyindoleacetic acid concentration differentiates impulsive from nonimpulsive violent behavior. *Life Sciences, 33*(26), 2609–2614.

Lloyd, K. G., Hornykiewicz, O., Davidson, L., Shannak, K., Farley, I., Goldstein, M., et al. (1981). Biochemical evidence of dysfunction of brain neurotransmitters in the Lesch-Nyhan syndrome. *New England Journal of Medicine, 305*(19), 1106–1111.

Lopez-Ibor, J. J., Jr., Saiz-Ruiz, J., & Perez de los Cobos, J. C. (1985). Biological correlations of suicide and aggressivity in major depressions (with melancholia): 5-hydroxyindoleacetic acid and cortisol in cerebral spinal fluid, dexamethasone suppression test and therapeutic response to 5-hydroxytryptophan. *Neuropsychobiology, 14*(2), 67–74.

Mace, F. C., Blum, N. J., Sierp, B. J., Delaney, B. A., & Mauk, J. E. (2001). Differential response of operant self-injury to pharmacologic versus behavioral treatment. *Journal of Developmental and Behavioral Pediatrics, 22*(2), 85–91.

Marrone, D. F. (2005). The morphology of bi-directional experience-dependent cortical plasticity: A meta-analysis. *Brain Research Brain Research Reviews, 50*(1), 100–113.

Matsumoto, T., Yamaguchi, A., Chiba, Y., Asami, T., Iseki, E., & Hirayasu, Y. (2004). Patterns of self-cutting: A preliminary study on differences in clinical implications between wrist- and arm-cutting using a Japanese juvenile detention center sample. *Psychiatry and Clinical Neuroscience, 58*(4), 377–382.

McClernon, F. J., Hiott, F. B., Huettel, S. A., & Rose, J. E. (2005). Abstinence-induced changes in self-report craving correlate with event-related FMRI responses to smoking cues. *Neuropsychopharmacology, 30*(10), 1940–1947.

Menon, V., & Levitin, D. J. (2005). The rewards of music listening: Response and physiological connectivity of the mesolimbic system. *Neuroimage, 28*(1), 175–184.

Mueller, K., Hollingsworth, E., & Pettit, H. (1986). Repeated pemoline produces self-injurious behavior in adult and weanling rats. *Pharmacology Biochemistry and Behavior, 25*(5), 933–938.

Mueller, K., & Nyhan, W. L. (1982). Pharmacologic control of pemoline induced self-injurious behavior in rats. *Pharmacology Biochemistry and Behavior, 16*(6), 957–963.

Nixon, M. K., Cloutier, P. F., & Aggarwal, S. (2002). Affect regulation and addictive aspects of repetitive self-injury in hospitalized adolescents. *Journal of the American Academy of Child and Adolescent Psychiatry, 41*(11), 1333–1341.

Novak, M. A. (2003). Self-injurious behavior in rhesus monkeys: New insights into its etiology, physiology, and treatment. *American Journal of Primatology, 59*(1), 3–19.

O'Doherty, J., Winston, J., Critchley, H., Perrett, D., Burt, D. M., & Dolan, R. J. (2003). Beauty in a smile: The role of medial orbitofrontal cortex in facial attractiveness. *Neuropsychologia, 41*(2), 147–155.

Orbach, I., Mikulincer, M., King, R., Cohen, D., & Stein, D. (1997). Thresholds and tolerance of physical pain in suicidal and nonsuicidal adolescents. *Journal of Consulting and Clinical Psychology, 65*(4), 646–652.

Orbach, I., Stein, D., Palgi, Y., Asherov, J., Har-Even, D., & Elizur, A. (1996). Perception of physical pain in accident and suicide attempt patients: Self-preservation vs self-destruction. *Journal of Psychiatric Research, 30*(4), 307–320.

Osuch, E. A., Noll, J. G., & Putnam, F. W. (1999). The motivations for self-injury in psychiatric inpatients. *Psychiatry, 62*(4), 334–346.

Paivio, S. C., & McCulloch, C. R. (2004). Alexithymia as a mediator between childhood trauma and self-injurious behaviors. *Child Abuse and Neglect, 28*(3), 339–354.

Powers, S. I., & McArdle, E. T. (2003). Coping strategies moderate the relation of hypothalamus-pituitary-adrenal axis reactivity to self-injurious behavior. *Annals of the New York Academy of Science, 1008*, 285–288.

Reuter, J., Raedler, T., Rose, M., Hand, I., Glascher, J., & Buchel, C. (2005). Pathological gambling is linked to reduced activation of the mesolimbic reward system. *Nature Neuroscience, 8*(2), 147–148.

Risinger, R. C., Salmeron, B. J., Ross, T. J., Amen, S. L., Sanfilipo, M., Hoffmann, R. G., et al. (2005). Neural correlates of high and craving during cocaine self-administration using bold FMRI. *Neuroimage, 26*(4), 1097–1108.

Rose, J. E., Behm, F. M., Westman, E. C., Mathew, R. J., London, E. D., Hawk, T. C., et al. (2003). PET studies of the influences of nicotine on neural systems in cigarette smokers. *American Journal of Psychiatry, 160*(2), 323–333.

Roth, A. S., Ostroff, R. B., & Hoffman, R. E. (1996). Naltrexone as a treatment for repetitive self-injurious behavior: An open-label trial. *Journal of Clinical Psychiatry, 57*(6), 233–237.

Russ, M. J., Campbell, S. S., Kakuma, T., Harrison, K., & Zanine, E. (1999). EEG theta activity and pain insensitivity in self-injurious borderline patients. *Psychiatry Research, 89*(3), 201–214.

Russ, M. J., Clark, W. C., Cross, L. W., Kemperman, I., Kakuma, T., & Harrison, K. (1996). Pain and self-injury in borderline patients: Sensory decision theory, coping strategies, and locus of control. *Psychiatry Research, 63*(1), 57–65.

Sandman, C. A., Hetrick, W., Taylor, D. V., & Chicz-DeMet, A. (1997). Dissociation of POMC peptides after self-injury predicts responses to centrally acting opiate blockers. *American Journal of Mental Retardation, 102*(2), 182–199.

Sandman, C. A., Touchette, P., Lenjavi, M., Marion, S., & Chicz-DeMet, A. (2003). Beta-endorphin and ACTH are dissociated after self-injury in adults with developmental disabilities. *American Journal of Mental Retardation, 108*(6), 414–424.

Santa Mina, E. E., Gallop, R., Links, P., Heslegrave, R., Pringle, D., Wekerle, C., et al. (2006). The self-injury questionnaire: Evaluation of the psychometric properties in a clinical population. *Journal of Psychiatric and Mental Health Nursing, 13*(2), 221–227.

Sarbadhikari, S. N., & Chakrabarty, K. (2001). Chaos in the brain: A short review alluding to epilepsy, depression, exercise and lateralization. *Medical Engineering and Physics, 23*(7), 445–455.

Schmahl, C., Bohus, M., Esposito, F., Treede, R. D., Di Salle, F., Greffrath, W., et al. (2006). Neural correlates of antinociception in borderline personality disorder. *Archives of General Psychiatry, 63*(6), 659–667.

Schmahl, C., Greffrath, W., Baumgartner, U., Schlereth, T., Magerl, W., Philipsen, A., et al. (2004). Differential nociceptive deficits in patients with borderline personality disorder and self-injurious behavior: Laser-evoked potentials, spatial discrimination of noxious stimuli, and pain ratings. *Pain, 110*(1–2), 470–479.

Schouenborg, J. (2004). Learning in sensorimotor circuits. *Current Opinion in Neurobiology, 14*(6), 693–697.

Singh, N. N., Lancioni, G. E., Winton, A. S., Molina, E. J., Sage, M., Brown, S., et al. (2004). Effects of snoezelen room, activities of daily living skills training, and vocational skills training on aggression and self-injury by adults with mental retardation and mental illness. *Research in Developmental Disabilities, 25*(3), 285–293.

Sivam, S. P. (1995). Gbr-12909-induced self-injurious behavior: Role of dopamine. *Brain Research, 690*(2), 259–263.

Sonne, S., Rubey, R., Brady, K., Malcolm, R., & Morris, T. (1996). Naltrexone treatment of self-injurious thoughts and behaviors. *Journal of Nervous and Mental Disease, 184*(3), 192–195.

Suyemoto, K. L. (1998). The functions of self-mutilation. *Clinical Psychology Review, 18*(5), 531–554.

Symons, F. J., & Danov, S. E. (2005). A prospective clinical analysis of pain behavior and self-injurious behavior. *Pain, 117*(3), 473–477.

Symons, F. J., Thompson, A., & Rodriguez, M. C. (2004). Self-injurious behavior and the efficacy of naltrexone treatment: A quantitative synthesis. *Mental Retardation and Developmental Disabilities Research Review, 10*(3), 193–200.

Tapert, S. F., Cheung, E. H., Brown, G. G., Frank, L. R., Paulus, M. P., Schweinsburg, A. D., et al. (2003). Neural response to alcohol stimuli in adolescents with alcohol use disorder. *Archives of General Psychiatry, 60*(7), 727–735.

Theodoulou, M., Harriss, L., Hawton, K., & Bass, C. (2005). Pain and deliberate self-harm: An important association. *Journal of Psychosomatic Research, 58*(4), 317–320.

Weaver, T. L., Chard, K. M., Mechanic, M. B., & Etzel, J. C. (2004). Self-injurious behaviors, PTSD arousal, and general health complaints within a treatment-seeking sample of sexually abused women. *Journal of Interpersonal Violence, 19*(5), 558–575.

Winchel, R. M., & Stanley, M. (1991). Self-injurious behavior: A review of the behavior and biology of self-mutilation. *American Journal of Psychiatry, 148*(3), 306–317.

Wolpaw, J. R., & Carp, J. S. (2006). Plasticity from muscle to brain. *Progress in Neurobiology, 78*(3-5), 233–263.

Yates, T. M. (2004). The developmental psychopathology of self-injurious behavior: Compensatory regulation in posttraumatic adaptation. *Clinical Psychology Review, 24*(1), 35–74.

Ystgaard, M., Hestetun, I., Loeb, M., & Mehlum, L. (2004). Is there a specific relationship between childhood sexual and physical abuse and repeated suicidal behavior? *Child Abuse and Neglect, 28*(8), 863–875.

Zaczek, R., Battaglia, G., Contrera, J. F., Culp, S., & De Souza, E. B. (1989). Methylphenidate and pemoline do not cause depletion of rat brain monoamine markers similar to that observed with methamphetamine. *Toxicology and Applied Pharmacology, 100*(2), 227–233.

Zafeiriou, D. I., Vargiami, E., Economou, M., & Gombakis, N. (2004). Self-mutilation and mental retardation: Clues to congenital insensitivity to pain with anhidrosis. *Journal of Pediatrics, 144*(2), 284.

Zarcone, J. R., Hellings, J. A., Crandall, K., Reese, R. M., Marquis, J., Fleming, K., et al. (2001). Effects of risperidone on aberrant behavior of persons with developmental disabilities: I. A double-blind crossover study using multiple measures. *American Journal of Mental Retardation, 106*(6), 525–538.

Zatorre, R. J. (2003). Music and the brain. *Annals of the New York Academy of Science, 999*, 4–14.

Zlotnick, C., Mattia, J. I., & Zimmerman, M. (1999). Clinical correlates of self-mutilation in a sample of general psychiatric patients. *Journal of Nervous and Mental Disease, 187*(5), 296-301.

GLOSSARY

6-hydroxydopamine: A neurotoxin used by neurobiologists to selectively kill dopaminergic and noradrenergic neurons.

Agonist: A drug or other chemical that can combine with a receptor on a cell to produce a physiologic reaction typical of a naturally occurring substance. Opposite of antagonist.

Andrenocorticotropic Hormone (ACTH): A hormone produced by the anterior lobe of the pituitary gland that stimulates the secretion of cortisone and other hormones by the adrenal cortex.

Decarboxylase: Any of various enzymes that hydrolize the carboxyl radical.

Denervate: To cut or otherwise interrupt the nerves.

Dopa: An amino acid, $C_9H_{11}NO_4$, formed in the liver from tyrosine and converted to dopamine in the brain.

Dynorphins: A family of endogenous opioid peptides.

Enkephalins: Olypeptides that serve as neurotransmitters and short-acting pain relievers. Enkephalins also influence a person's perception of painful sensations.

Exocytosis: A process of cellular secretion or excretion in which substances contained in vesicles are discharged from the cell.

HPA: Hypothalamic-pituitary-adrenal axis.

Neuron: The functional unit of the nervous system.

Neurotransmitters: Chemicals that allow the movement of information between cells.

Pemoline: A white crystalline synthetic compound, $C_9H_8N_2O_2$, used as a mild stimulant of the central nervous system, usually for treating hyperkinetic disorders in children.

Prolactin: A pituitary hormone that stimulates and maintains the secretion of milk.

Receptor: A specialized cell or group of nerve endings that responds to sensory stimuli.

Substance P: A neurotransmitter, especially in the transmission of pain impulses from peripheral receptors to the central nervous system.

Synapse: The junction across which a nerve impulse passes from an axon terminal to an adjacent neuron.

Synaptic cleft: The space between the cell membrane of an axon terminal and that of the target cell with which it synapses.

EFFECTIVE PRACTICE FOR SELF-INJURY IN YOUTH

Assessment of
Nonsuicidal Self-Injury

7

Measurement of Nonsuicidal Self-Injury in Adolescents

PAULA CLOUTIER AND LAUREN HUMPHREYS

In this chapter, the practitioner will gain an understanding of:

- The integration of standardized measures in the assessment of NSSI
- The potential role of standardized measures in treatment planning and practice
- The key components of a "gold standard" measurement tool
- The range and type and differences between standardized measures currently available
- The current evidence available on certain measures regarding reliability and validity
- How to contact those who have developed these measures of NSSI

With recent advances in the definition and understanding of the phenomenon of nonsuicidal self-injury (NSSI) in adolescents, new opportunities have emerged for assessing and monitoring adolescent NSSI in a systematic fashion. The use of well-designed measures has many potential benefits. For example, it is a systematic, objective, time efficient, often cost-effective, and sometimes norm-referenced means of gathering a considerable amount of relevant information about an individual. Although self-report measures do bring the risk of response biases (e.g., social desirability), such biases might be reduced with the use of structured interviews, which also hold the advantage of being systematic and objective modes of gathering information. There are various reasons why mental health professionals might want to measure adolescent NSSI.

Clinical Assessment. Measurement of NSSI in adolescents can be a valuable aspect of the clinical assessment process in mental health agencies. It can aid in early detection, which can facilitate early intervention, a significant benefit given findings suggesting that NSSI in adolescents can quickly evolve from a few isolated incidents to a repetitive behavior with an addictive quality (Nixon, Cloutier, & Aggarwal, 2002). Depending on the type of instrument used, the measurement of NSSI can also aid in case conceptualization. For example, recently developed measures of NSSI have focused on the different functions of NSSI, which may yield valuable information about the factors that precipitate and maintain the behavior in particular individuals. Adolescents may not have a clear understanding of the functions of their NSSI if asked generally during a clinical interview; however, a structured questionnaire with multiple options may help bring to the surface the underlying inter- and intrapersonal dynamics associated with the youth's self-injury.

Treatment planning and monitoring. On the basis of the clinical assessment, interventions can be developed that are geared toward particular individuals and the functions that NSSI serves for them. For example, tolerance of negative affect may constitute a key focus of treatment in an adolescent for whom NSSI is found to primarily serve an affect regulation function. Interpersonal therapy may be indicated in cases where social factors play a key role in the onset and maintenance of NSSI. Treatment progress can then be monitored over time by way of periodic reevaluation of the frequency, severity, and functions of NSSI. It has been demonstrated that in clients at risk of treatment failure, providing information about client progress to their therapists at various points during the course of treatment results in improved outcomes at termination of treatment and fewer cases of deteriorating functioning during the course of treatment (Lambert & Hawkins, 2004).

Research. To further advance current understanding of NSSI and associated mental health issues in adolescents, valid and reliable measures of NSSI are required for use in research protocols. Measurement of adolescent NSSI in the context of well-designed research projects will help elucidate various aspects of the behavior, including the prevalence, frequency, severity, and functions of NSSI.

Evidence-Based Practice. Improved understanding of NSSI, through carefully designed research, will lead to improved services to treat adolescents who engage in the behavior. Increasingly, publicly funded clinical agencies are being held accountable to show the effectiveness of the services they provide, in order to justify their continued existence. Program evaluation and clinical outcomes management are becoming more widespread and valued at all levels, from individual private practitioners to specific programs, agencies, and sources of funding. Valid and reliable measures of NSSI will form an important part of outcomes measurement in adolescent mental health.

REVIEW OF EXISTING MEASURES

Our original search was restricted to English-language measures and published literature. Search engines used included SCOPUS®, MED-LINE®, PsycINFO® , Health and Psychosocial Instruments (HaPI), and Mental Measurements Yearbook (MMYB). Given the growing interest and research in NSSI, we expanded the search to include unpublished literature to capture any promising measures that have been developed and are in the early stages of validation. We did not include screening questionnaires (e.g., How I Deal With Stress; Ross & Heath, 2002), surveys that were developed for research with no formal evaluation of the survey being reported (e.g., Favazza & Conterio, 1988; Hawton, Rodham, Evans, & Weatherall, 2002), or measures for which the primary focus was something other than NSSI (e.g., assessment tools related to eating disorders; see Sansone & Sansone, 2002, for a list of assessment tools for self-injury among those with eating disorders). Our search also excluded measures targeting self-injurious behaviors in individuals with intellectual disabilities or other developmental disabilities including autistic disorder. A recent detailed review of these measures can be found in Claes, Vandereycken, and Vertommen (2005).

The National Institute of Mental Health (NIMH) has published guidelines for the development, selection, and use of instruments for treatment planning and outcomes assessment (Ciarlo, Brown, Edwards, Kiresuk, & Newman, 1986; Newman, Rugh, & Ciarlo, 2004). These guidelines stipulate that a measure should be relevant to the target group being assessed, and it should be relatively straightforward to administer, with readily available training materials; where possible, objective referents should be used, so that scores have clear meanings that are consistent across clients. It is preferred that the measure provides information about the processes by which treatments may produce positive effects (e.g., adherence to a treatment technique). The use of multiple respondents is encouraged, and at a minimum, self-report is recommended. Cost and utility considerations are also highlighted. For example, materials and procedures for administration of the measure should be relatively inexpensive; the content and results of the measure should be readily understood and interpreted by nonprofessional audiences (including availability of norms for appropriate pretreatment and posttreatment groups); a measure should be useful in clinical services such as diagnosis, treatment planning, and case review; and it should be compatible with clinical theories and practices.

Finally, a measure should meet minimal criteria for psychometric adequacy, including reliability, validity, sensitivity to treatment-related change; freedom from response bias; and nonreactivity to extraneous situational factors such as physical settings, client expectation, and staff behavior (Ciarlo et al., 1986; Newman et al., 2004). Reliability has to do with measure quality: specifically, the consistency, stability, and repeatability of a measure across a wide variety of conditions. Validity refers to whether the instrument leads to valid conclusions or how well it measures what it claims to measure. There are several types of reliability (i.e., test-retest, internal consistency, inter-rater agreement) and validity (e.g., content, construct, concurrent), and the interested reader is referred to the classic text *Psychometric Theory*, by Nunnally and Bernstein (1994), as these concepts are important in assessing the quality of a measure.

The above guidelines might be considered a "gold standard" to which clinicians and researchers should aspire. The authors of these guidelines have noted that it is likely unrealistic to expect a measure to meet every one of these guidelines and that the key characteristics may differ depending on the particular measure or target population (Ciarlo et al., 1986; Newman et al., 2004). The measurement of NSSI is in its relatively early stages of development. As such, few of the measures reviewed here would be considered to meet the majority of the NIMH guidelines. Nevertheless, many show promise as useful tools to aid in answering specific questions about NSSI.

Table 7.1 presents an overview of measures that meet criteria for review in this chapter. It is designed to be brief and concise to provide an overview of the type of measure, type of self-injury being measured, details of what is measured, as well as summary information with respect to reliability and validity. Many measures include indices of both suicidal and nonsuicidal self-injury. Cicchetti's (1994) guidelines for evaluating the psychometric properties of assessment instruments present specific criteria for dimensions of test reliability. These criteria were used in the development of Table 7.1. More detailed information about each measure is included in text.

SELF-REPORT MEASURES

It should be noted that the labels and definitions of self-injury vary among the measures. In the following descriptions of the measures, we have attempted to be consistent in using the term *self-injury*, but when describing labels for subscales and factors, we have retained the terminology used by the authors.

TABLE 7.1 Overview of Measures of Self-Injury

SELF-REPORTS

Measure	Developed for adolescents	Has been used with adolescents	Self-injurious behavior measured	Characteristics of self-injury	Reliability[a]	Validity[b]
Self-Injury Inventory (Zlotnick et al., 1997)	No	Yes	Self-destructive and impulsive acts Self-mutilative acts without intent to die	Frequency Duration Types of self-injury	Internal consistency: good for "self-mutilative" subscale	None
Functional Assessment of Self-Mutilation (Lloyd, Kelley, & Hope, 1997)	Yes	Yes	Self-harm (with or without suicidal intent)	Method Frequency Reasons Context	Internal consistency: unacceptable to good	Content Construct Concurrent
Self-Harm Inventory (Sansone, Wiederman, & Sansone, 1998)	No	No	Suicidal behavior Indirect self-injury Direct self-injury	Total number of different self-injurious behaviors in respondent's history	Internal consistency: Good	Predictive Construct

TABLE 7.1 Overview of Measures of Self-Injury (continued)

Measure	Developed for adolescents	Has been used with adolescents	Self-injurious behavior measured	Characteristics of self-injury	Reliability[a]	Validity[b]
Self-Injury Motivation Scale II (Osuch, Noll, & Putnam, 1999)	No	Yes	Self-harm (with or without suicidal ntent)	Reasons	Internal consistency: excellent (total score), good to excellent (subscales in adults), poor to good (subscales in adolescents) Test-retest reliability: good (original SIMS)	Content Construct Concurrent Convergent
Self-Injury Questionnaire (Alexander, 1999)	No	No	Body alterations (e.g., piercing) Indirect self-harm Failure to care for self Overt self-injury	Frequency Types of self-injury Reasons	Internal consistency: fair to good Test-retest reliability: excellent	Content Convergent Divergent

Measure						
Self-Harm Behavior Questionnaire (Guttierez, Osman, Barrios, & Kopper, 2001)	No	Yes	Suicide attempts NSSI Suicidal threats Suicidal ideation	Frequency Severity Medical tx required Context	Internal consistency: good to excellent Inter-rater reliability: 95 to 100% agreement	Content Construct Convergent Discriminant
Deliberate Self-Harm Inventory (Gratz, 2001)	No	Yes	NSSI	Frequency Severity Duration Type of self-harm	Internal consistency: good Test-retest reliability: good to excellent	Content Construct Convergent Discriminant
Ottawa Self-Injury Inventory (Nixon & Cloutier, 2002)	Yes	Yes	NSSI Suicidal ideation Suicide attempts	Method Frequency Reasons Context Addictive properties Effectiveness of behavior at regulating negative affect Motivation for change	Test-retest: fair to good	Content

TABLE 7.1 Overview of Measures of Self-Injury (continued)

Measure	Developed for adolescents	Has been used with adolescents	Self-injurious behavior measured	Characteristics of self-injury	Reliability[a]	Validity[b]
Self-Harm Survey and Motivations Underlying Self-Harm Questionnaire (Laye-Gindhu & Schonert-Reicht, 2005)	Yes	Yes	Self-injury ideation, Overt self-injury, Risk-taking behavior, Suicide history	Frequency, Context, Reasons	Internal consistency: excellent (for motivations underlying self-harm), Inter-rater reliability: 97% agreement for coding qualitative data	Content
STRUCTURED INTERVIEWS						
Suicide Attempt Self-Injury Interview (Linehan, Comtois, Brown, Heard, & Wagner, 2006)	No	No	Suicidal self-injury, NSSI	Frequency, Method, Severity, Context, Intent, Reasons, Functional outcomes	Internal consistency: unacceptable to excellent (subscales)	Content, Construct

Measure	Content[b]	Construct[b]		Method	Reliability[a]
Self-Injurious Thoughts and Behaviors Interview (Nock, Holmberg, Photos, & Michel (2007))	Yes	Yes	Suicidal ideation Suicidal plans Suicidal gestures Suicide attempts NSSI	Frequency Severity Reasons Context Self-reported future probabilities of each type of self-injurious thoughts and behaviors	Inter-rater reliability: excellent Test-retest reliability: fair to good

[a] Test reliability guidelines (Cicchetti, 1994): Internal consistency (usually coefficient alpha, <.70 = level of clinical significance is unacceptable; .70–.79 = fair; .80–.89 = good; .90 and above = excellent); Inter- and Intrarater reliability: kappa, weighted kappa, intraclass correlation coefficient (<.40 = level of clinical significance = poor; .40–.59 = fair; .60–.74 = good; .75 and over = excellent).

[b] See text for details of available validity data.

Self-Injury Inventory

The Self-Injury Inventory (SII; Zlotnick et al., 1996) is a self-report measure designed to assess the frequency, duration, and types of self-injurious behavior over a respondent's lifetime. Neither the number of items, nor the completion time has been reported in the literature. The SII was developed on a sample of female inpatients admitted to a women's psychiatric unit (Zlotnick et al., 1996). It has also been used with other populations, including adolescent and young adult inpatients in a psychiatric hospital (Zlotnick, Wolfsdorf, Johnson, & Spririto, 2003) and young adults and adults admitted to an inpatient substance abuse treatment program at a private hospital (Zlotnick et al., 1997). There are two subscales: the "self-injury" subscale, based on self-destructive acts, or acts of indirect bodily harm, commonly reported in the literature (e.g., impulsive behaviors such as bingeing, driving recklessly, having unprotected sex, shoplifting, and consuming large amounts of drugs or alcohol), and the "self-mutilation" subscale (which is more consistent with our definition of NSSI), which assesses behaviors that are deliberate, direct acts of harm to one's body, without intent to die (e.g., cutting, burning, and banging one's body to the point of bruising). The self-mutilation subscale has been shown to have good internal consistency (α = .80; Zlotnick et al., 2003). No data have been published with regard to the validity of the SII. Means and standard deviations have been published for samples of adolescent and young adult suicide attempters and ideators (Zlotnick et al., 2003).

The SII can be used as a screening measure in the course of mental health assessment to plan the intensity of treatment required for specific individuals. The inclusion of the two subscales allows for either a broad-based or a narrower focus of assessment of self-destructive and self-injurious behaviors. Given that the SII is designed to assess incidence and frequency of a broad spectrum of self-injury over the respondent's lifetime, it would have limited utility in measuring treatment outcome.

Functional Assessment of Self-Mutilation

The Functional Assessment of Self-Mutilation (FASM; Lloyd, Kelly, & Hope, 1997) is a self-report measure designed to provide information regarding the frequency and motivations of different types of self-injury in adolescents (Guertin, Lloyd-Richardson, Spirito, Donaldson, & Boergers, 2001; Lloyd et al., 1997; Nock & Prinstein, 2004, 2005). This brief measure takes between 5 to 10 minutes to complete. Measure items were selected based on past research and items generated through focus groups with psychiatric inpatient adolescents who had engaged in self-injury. The first section of the measure uses a yes/no response format and consists of 11 items representing different methods of self-injury along with one additional item labeled "other." This section is rated in terms of frequency and need for medical treatment. Principal components analysis of these items yielded two subscales with internal consistencies of .65 and .66 (Guertin et al., 2001). The subscales differed by severity of method of self-injury. The second section of the measure consists of six dichotomous and categorical questions regarding the contextual features of the self-injury, including intent, impulsiveness, relationship to drugs and alcohol, experience of pain, age of onset, and self-injury prior to the past year.

The final section asks how often the adolescent engages in self-injury for any of 22 specified reasons plus one "other" option. Each reason is rated on a four-point scale (0 = never, 1 = rarely, 2 = some, 3 = often). Based on this last section of the measure, Nock and Prinstein (2004, 2005) demonstrated the structural validity of a four-function model. Reliability analysis revealed internal consistencies for each function: automatic-negative reinforcement (α = .62), automatic-positive reinforcement (α = .69), social-negative reinforcement (α = .76), and social-positive reinforcement (α = .85). The low internal consistency for automatic-negative and automatic-positive reinforcement may be due to the small number of items that load on each of these factors. One item from the reasons for self-injury did not load on any factor and was removed. This four-factor model was recently replicated in a community sample of adolescents (Lloyd-Richardson, Perrine, Dierker, & Kelly, 2007).

This brief measure can be used to assess the severity of self-injury and the adolescent's reasons for engaging in self-injury. It can help determine if motivations are primarily intrapersonal, automatically reinforcing (e.g., tension reduction), or socially reinforcing and if the reinforcement is positive or negative. These distinctions could be used in tailoring an individualized treatment plan.

Self-Harm Inventory

The Self-Harm Inventory (SHI; Sansone, Wiederman, & Sansone, 1998) is a brief, 22-item self-report measure designed to assess respondents' lifetime histories of engaging in a variety of self-injurious behaviors. A yes/no response format is used, and the total score reflects the total number of self-injurious behaviors endorsed (i.e., the number of "yes" responses). Individual items were chosen based on behaviors described in the literature and in the clinical experience of the authors and their multidisciplinary treatment teams (Sansone et al., 1998). Examples of self-injurious behaviors listed in the measure include overdose, cutting, substance abuse, self-starvation, engaging in emotionally abusive relationships, and suicide attempts. The SHI was developed on three subsamples: obese women presenting for nonemergent care with a family physician, men and women with eating disorders and/or substance abuse disorders, and mothers of obese and normal-weight adolescent girls presenting to a family physician for nonemergent care (Sansone et al., 1998). The SHI has subsequently been used with adult psychiatric inpatients in community hospitals (Sansone, Gaither, Songer, & Allen, 2005; Sansone, Songer, & Sellborn, 2006).

The SHI has been shown to have good internal consistency (α = .80; Sansone et al., 2006), and validation studies have demonstrated high correlations with measures of borderline personality disorder (BPD; r = .76 with the Diagnostic Interview for Borderlines [DIB] and r = .73 with the BPD scale of the Personality Diagnostic Questionnaire Revised [PDQ-R]; Sansone et al., 1998). A cutoff score of 5 or greater has demonstrated 84% accuracy in diagnosing BPD in adults. Means and standard deviations have been published for samples of suicide attempters and nonsuicide attempters (Sansone et al., 2006).

The SHI may be useful as a screening measure for BPD. It could be used for planning the intensity of treatment needed for specific individuals. Its brevity makes it convenient for use as a screening tool in a variety of clinical settings. As with the SII, the lifetime history framework limits its utility as a measure of treatment outcome.

Self-Injury Motivation Scale-II

Originally designed for adult patient groups, the Self-Injury Motivation Scale-II (SIMS-II; Osuch, Noll, & Putnam, 1999) is a self-report measure designed to quantify the motivations for self-injurious behavior from the respondent's perspective. They rate the degree to which each of 36 reasons accounts for their self-injurious behavior. Ratings are on an 11-point scale from 0 (never a reason) to 10 (always a reason) and are tallied to yield a total score. This measure takes approximately 7 to 15 minutes to complete. Items for this measure are based on past research and the authors' clinical experience. The original version of the SIMS (version 1) consisted of 35 items. Preliminary factor analysis conducted on data from 99 adult psychiatric inpatients revealed six factors that accounted for 85% of the scale variability. The factors are affect modulation, desolation, punitive duality, influencing others, magical control, and self-stimulation. Internal consistency as measured by Cronbach's alpha for the total SIMS was .96 and ranged from .81 to .93 for the six factors. Test-retest reliability was demonstrated over a range of 2.5 to 11 weeks (r = .70). Concurrent validity was demonstrated by means of correlation with a number of measures of psychopathology. Demographic variables were not found to affect SIMS scores, with the exception of age (r = −.22) (Osuch et al., 1999).

Two extra items that were drawn from write-in answers obtained during testing were added to the SIMS-II, and one of the original items from the SIMS was omitted due to redundancy with another item. The SIMS-II version of the measure was assessed in 50 adolescent psychiatric inpatients (Kumar, Pepe, & Steer, 2004). Internal consistencies with the adolescent patient population were .91 for the total score and from .51 to .81 for the factor scores (Kumar et al., 2004). There is also some evidence of convergent validity with the punitive duality subscale correlating with a history of sexual abuse ($r = .40$). It has yet to be determined if the factor structure that was obtained in the adult sample is the same as that for an adolescent sample and whether the same factor structure would hold for both sexes.

The SIMS-II may be a useful instrument for evaluating the motivations for self-injury in adolescent patients. Its brief self-report format makes it useful for a rapid assessment of the motives behind SI, which can be used in determining an individualized treatment plan.

Self-Injury Questionnaire

The Self-Injury Questionnaire (SIQ; Alexander, 1999) is a 30-item self-report measure designed to assess the frequency, type, and functions of various self-injurious behaviors (Santa Mina et al., 2006). It was originally developed by Alexander (1999) on a community sample of undergraduate students and later tested by Santa Mina and colleagues (2006) on an adult clinical sample recruited from the crisis service and the inpatient mental health unit of an inner city teaching hospital. The SIQ was conceptualized from the trauma literature, specifically from Connors' (1996) classification of four types of self-injury: body alterations (e.g., piercing, tattoos), indirect self-harm (e.g., smoking marijuana, fasting), failure to care for self (e.g., avoiding the doctor when ill, having unprotected sex), and overt self-injury (e.g., cutting, burning). Participants indicate whether they have ever engaged in any of the 30 behaviors on purpose; if they have, they indicate the reasons for engaging in each behavior. The reasons included in the SIQ reflect eight themes: regulation of feelings, regulation of realness, safety, communication with self, communication with others, fun, social influence, and regulation of body sensations.

Behaviors from the SIQ can be examined individually, as a total score of all behaviors reported, or as a subtotal for each of the four self-injury subtypes. The reasons can be examined individually or scored according to the eight themes. Internal consistency for the total SIQ scale is reported as $\alpha = .83$, and alphas for the subscales range from .72 to .77 (Santa Mina et al., 2006). Test-retest reliability of the SIQ summary scores (SIQ total and the four Connors subscales) over a 2-week period ranged from $r = .76$ to $r = .96$ (Alexander, 1999). Santa Mina et al. (2006) created two SIQ subscales, the affective subscale and the dissociation subscale, to test construct validity. With regard to convergent validity, a weak positive correlation was obtained between the affective subscale and a measure of affect regulation, and a moderate positive correlation was obtained between the dissociation subscale and a measure of dissociation. In terms of divergent validity, a weak negative correlation was obtained between the item for "instead of suicide or to avoid suicide" and measures of suicide.

The SIQ is helpful in delineating the various types of self-injury used by the respondent and the reasons for each type endorsed by the respondent. The SIQ could therefore be used in designing individualized treatment plans. The flexible scoring system allows for broad-based assessment or more fine-grained analysis.

Self-Harm Behavior Questionnaire

The Self-Harm Behavior Questionnaire (SHBQ; Gutierrez, Osman, Barrios, & Kopper, 2001) is a brief self-report measure that evaluates self-injury, thoughts, or verbalizations as well as intent, lethality, and outcome. The measure is laid out in four sections, each beginning with a yes/no question (i.e., [a] Have you ever hurt yourself on purpose? [b] Have you ever attempted suicide? [c] Have you ever threatened to commit suicide? [d] Have you ever talked or thought about wanting to die? Have you ever talked or thought about committing suicide?) Respondents who answer affirmatively to any of the questions go on to provide more detail regarding the frequency, method, age of onset, last episode, whether or not they told anyone about their behavior, and whether or not they required medical attention with respect to the behavior in question. Sections regarding suicidal behaviors also evaluate related events, intent, and whether or not any preparations had been made (Fliege, et al., 2006). Factor analysis conducted on data from 342 university undergraduate students revealed four nonredundant factors (i.e., past suicide attempts, self-harm, suicide threat, suicide ideation), which accounted for 80% of variance in the data (Gutierrez et al., 2001). Internal consistencies of the factors range from .89 to .96. Convergent validity is evidenced by significant correlations with other validated measures of suicidality. Scores on the SHBQ also discriminated between level of current and past suicide-related behaviors. A German translation of this instrument has been developed and used with hospitalized adolescents (Fliege et al., 2006).

The authors provide a comprehensive coding system, which includes a single numerical value to represent the severity of each of the four types of self-harm behaviors. Inter-rater reliability for the scoring of the measure is reported as percentage agreement and ranges from 95% to 100% (Gutierrez et al., 2001).

This measure was developed to bring together the ease and cost effectiveness of a self-report questionnaire along with the rich detail of a clinical interview to assess history and current risk of suicide-related behaviors.

Deliberate Self-Harm Inventory

The Deliberate Self-Harm Inventory (DSHI; Gratz, 2001) is a 17-item behavior-based self-report measure evaluating the frequency, severity, duration, and type of deliberate self-injury without conscious suicidal intent. It takes approximately 5 minutes to complete. The types of self-injurious behaviors included in the questionnaire are based on the research literature, clinical observation, and patient testimonials. Two scale scores have been derived from the measure: (a) a dichotomous self-injury variable that classifies respondents as ever having engaged in any of the deliberate self-injury items (score = 1) and those never having engaged in any of the deliberate self-injury items (score = 0); and (b) a continuous variable measuring the total frequency of self-injurious behavior, derived by adding the frequency of all reported self-injurious behaviors. Preliminary psychometric data were established using data from 150 undergraduate psychology students.

The measure displays good internal consistency (α = .82), good test-retest reliability for the dichotomized variable (Φ = .68) over 2–4 weeks, and excellent test-retest reliability for the continuous frequency variable (r = .92). With regard to construct validity, a positive association between the dichotomized DSHI variable and other dichotomized measures of self-injury ranged from .35 to .49 (mean r = .42; Gratz, 2001). In terms of convergent validity, a significant positive correlation was obtained with a measure used to assess experiences, behaviors, and beliefs in individuals with BPD (Gratz, 2001). Finally, discriminant validity was established via low correlations with variables thought to be unrelated to self-injury (Gratz, 2001). The DSHI has also been used to evaluate symptom changes following treatment in clinical samples of adults with BPD (Gratz & Gunderson, 2006; Gratz, Lacroce, & Gunderson, 2006). A German translation of this instrument has been developed and has essentially replicated the psychometric properties of the original English version (Fliege et al., 2006).

The DSHI is based on a clear definition of self-injury whereby the respondent is specifically directed to report only behaviors that do not involve intent to die. The frequency of self-injurious behaviors—not simply the presence or absence of the behaviors—is reported. This measure may be helpful for monitoring treatment progress over time.

Ottawa Self-Injury Inventory

The Ottawa Self-Injury Inventory (OSI; Cloutier & Nixon, 2003) is a self-report questionnaire designed to identify clinical and psychosocial correlates of self-injury in adolescents. It is a modification of work done by Epstein and colleagues at the Queen's University Department of Child and Adolescent Psychiatry. Since that time, the measure has undergone numerous revisions including evaluating past and present aspects of self-injurious behavior to elucidate the evolution of the behavior. The OSI is composed of 27 items covering cognitive, affective, behavioral, and environmental aspects of self-injury and requires approximately 20 minutes to complete. One question that addresses the reasons for starting and continuing to self-injure is composed of 33 items that are answered on a 5-point scale (i.e., 0 = never a reason, 2 = sometimes a reason, 4 = always a reason). The motivations for self-injury in the OSI were chosen based on previous research literature (e.g., Nock & Prinstein, 2004; Osuch et al., 1999; Shearer, 1994), feedback from clinicians (psychologists, psychiatrists) who work with this population, and feedback from adolescent inpatients and outpatients as well as researchers who examine self-injury in community samples.

The OSI does not yield a total score or diagnostic categories. The items yield answers that are both quantitative (dichotomous, categorical, continuous) and qualitative (answers to open-ended questions). Cloutier and Nixon (2003) have examined the test-retest reliability of an earlier version of the OSI over a short testing period (7 to 14 days). Test-retest reliability was evident in reasons for engaging in self-injury, average number of addictive symptoms endorsed, and reported lack of motivation to stop self-injuring (correlations range from .52 to .74). The measure has been used in adolescent psychiatric inpatient research (Nixon et al., 2002). The psychometric properties of this measure are currently being evaluated in a multisite adolescent inpatient study in Canada and the United States. A computerized version of the measure is also under development.

The OSI departs from existing measures in several areas. These include items related to addictive properties of the behavior, scales assessing self-reported effectiveness of self-injury at regulating negative affect, and a scale to measure the motivation to stop engaging in self-injurious behavior. The OSI is the only measure to evaluate the evolution of self-injury by exploring whether the motivations for continuing to self-injure differ from the motivations for first trying the behavior. The OSI may therefore be useful in individualized treatment planning and monitoring for adolescents.

Self-Harm Survey and Motivations Underlying Self-Harm Questionnaire

Laye-Gindhu and Schonert-Reichl (2005) developed two measures of self-injury for a study examining the prevalence, nature, and reasons for self-injury in a community sample of adolescents. The Self-Harm Survey is a 44-item self-report questionnaire tapping 6 dimensions: (a) self-harm ideation; (b) self-harm action and emotions; (c) risk-taking behavior; (d) suicide history; (e) disclosure and professional help; and (f) peer self-harm. Response formats include 29 forced-choice and 15 open-ended questions. The authors obtained a 97.3% rate of agreement between two independent coders who coded the responses into conceptually meaningful categories. No further psychometric information is available about this measure.

The Motivations Underlying Self-Harm Questionnaire is a 29-item self-report questionnaire that presents a series of motivational statements derived from a review of the literature and discussion with adolescents and with clinicians with expertise in adolescent self-injury. The statements were developed according to the following categories: self-punishment, self-anger, interpersonal anger, tension and distress, curiosity, substance use, dissociation, escape, boredom, control, suicide urge, attention, and communication. Respondents indicate how true each statement is for them on a four-point Likert-type scale ("always true" to "not at all/never"). An additional open-ended item allows respondents to describe a motivation not reflected in the questionnaire. Internal consistency for this measure was shown to be excellent (α = .90; Laye-Gindhu & Schonert-Reichl, 2005). No data have been published with regard to the validity of this questionnaire.

These measures could be helpful in delineating the types of self-injury used by the respondent and the reasons for each type endorsed by the respondent. They could therefore be useful in designing individualized treatment plans. Given that the measures were developed for use with a community sample of adolescents, they may be particularly useful as screening measures that could be implemented in community settings (e.g., schools, youth drop-in centers).

STRUCTURED INTERVIEWS

Suicide Attempt Self-Injury Interview

The Suicide Attempt Self-Injury Interview (SASII; Linehan, Comtois, Brown, Heard, & Wagner, 2006) is a structured interview designed to assess the frequency, method, severity, context, intent, reasons, and outcomes of self-injurious behavior (e.g., fatal and nonfatal, suicidal and nonsuicidal). Items were developed on the basis of existing measures of suicidal behavior and on the characteristics of suicide attempts and self-injury described in the literature. The measure was developed with a few clinical samples of adults, including patients admitted to a psychiatric unit or to the emergency room of a teaching hospital due to a suicide attempt or intentional self-injury and women seeking treatment for BPD. The SASII includes a combination of open-ended, checklist, forced-choice, Likert-type, and yes/no questions. Self-report and interviewer-rated items are included. Several items have objective referents (i.e., item scores bear specific, standardized meanings in terms of severity, lethality, intent, etc.). There are six subscales: suicide intent (four items), interpersonal influence (eight items), emotion relief (six items), suicide communication (two items), lethality (three items), and rescue likelihood (two items); two additional isolated items do not form part of these subscales (suicide note and impulsiveness of episode).

Means and standard deviations have been published for samples of emergency room patients and women seeking treatment for BPD.

Internal consistency of the subscales ranges from unacceptable to excellent (from .63 for both emotion relief and suicide communication to .93 for suicide intent) (Linehan, Comtois, Brown, et al., 2006a). Inter-rater reliability for the 11 interviewer-rated items ranges from intra-class correlations of .84–.96 (Linehan, Comtois, Brown, et al., 2006). Evidence for the construct validity of the SASII is seen in the relatively high levels of agreement between SASII reports of self-injury episodes and therapists' psychotherapy case notes (83% for presence or absence of intentional self-injury; 76% for number of episodes) and high consistency (intraclass correlations = .91) between SASII reports and daily participant diary cards for the number of self-injurious acts. The SASII has been shown to be sensitive to change in treatment outcome studies with suicidal adults (Linehan, Armstrong, Suarez, Allmon, & Heard, 1991; Linehan, Comtois, Murray, et al., 2006).

The SASII offers a flexible scoring system, which allows one to study specific variables of interest (e.g., method, severity, or intent of self-injurious acts). Although it was developed primarily as a research measure, it also has clinical utility, allowing for detailed risk assessment and identification of specific targets for intervention. The SASII may be helpful in delineating the precipitants and consequences of self-injurious acts in particular individuals. It may also be helpful in the ongoing monitoring of treatment outcomes in dialectical behavior therapy for BPD.

Self-Injurious Thoughts and Behaviors Interview

The Self-Injurious Thoughts and Behaviors Interview (SITBI; Nock, Holmberg, Photos, & Michel, 2007) is a 169-item structured interview composed of five modules that evaluate the presence, frequency, and characteristics of (a) suicidal ideation; (b) suicidal plans; (c) suicidal gestures; (d) suicidal attempts; and (e) NSSI. It was developed and evaluated in a sample of adolescents recruited from community and psychiatric clinics. The interview is conducted for only those modules that receive a positive endorsement for the lifetime presence of that thought or behavior. The characteristics assessed by the measure include age of onset, methods, severity, functions, precipitants, experience of pain, use of alcohol and drugs during self-injurious thoughts and behaviors, impulsiveness, peer influences, and self-reported future probabilities of each type of self-injurious thoughts and behaviors (Nock, et al., 2007). The SITBI requires 3 to 15 minutes to complete. Average inter-rater reliability is excellent ($k = .99$, $r = 1.0$), and average test-retest reliability over a 6-month period is $k = .70$, intraclass correlations = .44 (Najmi, Wegner, & Nock, 2007; Nock et al., 2007). Interinformant agreement (parents-adolescents) on the presence or absence of each type of self-injurious thought and behavior ranged from $k = .21$ for suicidal gesture to $k = .91$ for NSSI, with an average κ of .60. Construct validity was demonstrated by examining the correspondence between SITBI and measures of suicidal ideation (mean $k = .54$), suicide attempt (mean $k = .65$), and NSSI (mean $k = .87$).

Recent modifications to this measure include the addition of items assessing thoughts of NSSI, which will help elucidate the relationship between thoughts and behaviors. A short form of the measure has also been created for use in situations where little time is available. The shortened version excludes items related to the functions of the behavior, experience of pain, and the influence of peers (Nock et al., 2007).

The SITBI examines differences between five self-injurious thoughts and behaviors using clear and consistent definitions and methods. This allows the clinician to compare the characteristics of the different forms of self-injurious thoughts and behaviors. The authors of the measure suggest that it be administered as an initial broad screening measure, which can be followed up with more focused, detailed measures as required.

MEASURE SELECTION FOR ADOLESCENT SELF-INJURY

Brief Screening Measures

Four measures can be used as a brief screen to assess the frequency, duration, and type of self-injury (SII, SHI, SHBQ, DSHI). Only the DSHI explicitly looks at NSSI, with the remaining measures covering both direct and indirect self-injury with or without intent to die. All measures are self-reports with developed scoring methods. All are quite straightforward to administer and score and are available by request from the authors (see Table 7.2). All measures have demonstrated good reliability, with the SHBQ, DSHI, and the SHI also having been evaluated for validity; however, more work remains to be done in this area. The SII, DSHI, and SHBQ were developed using adult samples but have also been used on adolescents. Only the SHI has not been used or evaluated for adolescents. Nonetheless, it may still have potential to be relevant to this population. An interesting development in the design of new measures to screen for adolescent self-injury can be seen in Nock and Prinstein's (2006) efforts to use real-time assessment of adolescent self-injury by way of electronic diaries. This is a promising avenue for future research in the measurement of self-injury in adolescent populations, for whom electronic media may be particularly appealing and approachable. At the present state of measure development and evaluation, we would recommend the SHBQ as the brief screening measure of choice, as it has established psychometric properties and a comprehensive scoring system with established inter-rater reliability and has the advantage of covering contextual features of the behavior while remaining quite brief.

TABLE 7.2 Contact Information for Measures

Self-reports	Contact name	Address	Telephone numbers	e-mail address
Functional Assessment of Self-Mutilation	Elizabeth Lloyd-Richardson, Ph.D.	Brown Medical School The Miriam Hospital Weight Control and Diabetes Research Center 196 Richmond Street Providence, RI 02903	Tel: (401) 793-8150 Fax: (401) 793-8944	erichardson@lifespan.org
Self-Harm Inventory	Randy Sansone, M.D.	Sycamore Primary Care Center 2115 Leiter Road Miamisburg, OH 45342	Tel: (937) 384-6850 Fax: (937) 384-6938	Randy.sansone@ kmcnetwork.org
Self-Harm Survey and Motivations Underlying Self-Harm Questionnaire	Aviva Laye-Gindhu, M.A.	University of British Columbia Faculty of Education Dept. of Educational and Counselling Psychology 2125 Main Mall Vancouver, BC V6T 1Z4		aviva23@telus.net or alaye@interchange.ubc. ca
Self-Harm Behavior Questionnaire	Peter M. Gutierrez, Ph.D.	VA Eastern Colorado Health Care System/ VISN 19 MIRECC 1055 Clermont Street, 8D130 Denver, CO 80220	Tel: (303) 399-8020 x2280 Fax: (303) 370-7519	peter.gutierrez@va.gov

Self-Injury inventory	Caron Zlotnick, Ph.D.	Department of Psychiatry and Human Behavior Brown Medical School Butler Hospital 345 Blackstone Blvd Providence, RI 02906	Tel: (401) 455-6529 Fax: (401) 455-6539	czlotnick@butler.org
Self-Injury Motivation Scale II	Elizabeth Osuch, M.D.	Department of Psychiatry London Health Science Centre 339 Windermere Road London, ON N6A 4G5 Canada		elizabeth.osuch@lhsc.on.ca
Self-Injury Questionnaire	Elaine E. Santa Mina, Ph.D. (not the original author of the SIQ but has adapted it for use in a clinical population)	POD 460 D School of Nursing Ryerson University 350 Victoria Street Toronto, ON M5B 2K3 Canada		esantami@ryerson.ca
Deliberate Self-Harm Inventory	Kim L. Gratz, Ph.D.	Center for Addictions, Personality, and Emotion Research (CAPER) Department of Psychology University of Maryland College Park, MD 20742	Tel: (301) 405-3551 Fax: (301) 405-3223	klgratz@aol.com Web: http://www.addiction.umd.edu

TABLE 7.2 Contact Information for Measures (continued)

Self-reports	Contact name	Address	Telephone numbers	e-mail address
Ottawa Self-Injury Inventory	Mary Kay Nixon, M.D. Paula Cloutier,MA	Centre for Youth & Society PO Box 3050 STN CSC Victoria, BC V8W 3P3 Canada	Tel: (250) 952 5073 Fax: (250) 952 4546	mary.nixon@viha or cacloutier@cheo.on.ca
Suicide Attempt Self-Injury Interview	Marsha M. Linehan, Ph.D., ABPP	Department of Psychology Box 351525 University of Washington Seattle, WA 98195-1525	Tel: (206) 543-9886 Fax: (206) 616-1513	linehan@u.washington. edu Web: http://faculty. washington. edu/linehan/ http://www.brtc.psych. washington.edu
Self-Injurious Thoughts and Behaviors Interview	Matthew Nock, Ph.D.	Department of Psychology Harvard University William James Hall, 128033 Kirkland Street Cambridge, MA 02138	Tel: (617) 496-4484 Fax: (617) 496-9462	nock@wjh.harvard.edu

Comprehensive Baseline Assessment

Four of the measures (SASII, SITBI, OSI, SIQ) might be considered well suited for use in a comprehensive clinical assessment, to help determine the nature, scope, intensity, and motivations of a client's self-injury and thus aid in diagnosis and treatment planning. The SASII and SITBI are both structured interviews, whereas the OSI and SIQ are self-report measures, which may therefore be less costly to administer. The SITBI and OSI were developed and used with adolescents and young adults, whereas the SASII and SIQ were developed for use with adults (or young adults) and do not appear to have been used in adolescent populations to this point. The latter two measures may nevertheless hold relevance to adolescents as well.

The SASII, SITBI, and SIQ offer flexible administration and scoring procedures to allow clinicians to focus on specific areas of interest. Methods of administration and scoring are relatively straightforward for all four of the measures. The SASII and corresponding instruction manual are available online, and the remaining measures are available by request from the authors (see Table 7.2). A computerized scoring system for the SASII is under development. The SASII uses objective referents for several of the items, allowing for clear interpretation of scores. The psychometric properties of the SITBI, SASII, and SIQ have been relatively well established, including reliability and validity data (although the SASII and SIQ have been validated on adult and young adult samples only). The OSI is in an earlier stage of development and validity data are being gathered in a current multisite study. The SITBI includes items pertaining to the influence of peers on the initiation and maintenance of self-injury, a subject of particular relevance to adolescents. This measure may help elucidate the contagious nature of self-injury, an area that has been identified as requiring further study (Hawton, Rodham, K., & Evans, 2006). At the present state of measure development and evaluation, we would recommend the SITBI as the comprehensive assessment measure of choice given its high relevance to adolescent populations, established psychometric properties, flexible administration and scoring procedures, and clear differentiation between different categories of self-injury.

Determining Reason for Self-Injury

Seven measures can be used to help identify the functions of self-injury (FASM, MUSHQ, OSI, SASII, SIMS, SITBI, SIQ). Of these, three focus either uniquely (SIMS, MUSHQ) or primarily (FASM) on the motivations for self-injury. The SIMS and the FASM were developed for clinical purposes to evaluate the motivations for self-injury with or without intent to die, and both have been successfully used with adolescent clinical samples. The FASM has also been used in nonclinical samples. The MUSHQ was developed to evaluate self-injury without suicidal intent in an adolescent community sample and therefore may be particularly useful for use in schools and community centers. All three self-report measures require little time to complete and are easy to score. In terms of psychometrics, all have established reliability, with the SIMS and the FASM also having demonstrated construct validity. These measures are available by request from the authors (Table 7.2). The remaining four measures (OSI, SASII, SITBI, SIQ) include an evaluation of reasons for self-injury along with data evaluating the nature, scope, and intensity of the behavior. These measures have been summarized in the previous section. They are more comprehensive and therefore may ground the reasons for self-injury within a broader context.

Among the measures that focus primarily or exclusively on the reasons or motivations for self-injury, we recommend the FASM for use in both clinical and nonclinical settings due to its high relevance to adolescents, established psychometric properties, and brief overview of the nature and scope of the behavior. This measure would be particularly useful when time does not permit a more comprehensive assessment. The SIMS is also relevant to the adolescent clinical population but may best be used in combination with one of the brief screening measures such as the SHBQ to gain a more thorough understanding of the behavior.

SUMMARY AND FUTURE DIRECTIONS

For mental health professionals, other clinicians, or school personnel wanting to use questionnaires or structured interviews to screen for or assess NSSI in adolescents, a number of useful measures are currently available to gather relevant information that might lead to appropriate intervention. This chapter has reviewed and summarized the main self-report measures and structured interviews for NSSI that have been published in the literature as well as several measures that have yet to be published. For the most part, these are all relatively brief and straightforward to administer and score. Some allow for a brief screening of the presence and extent of the full spectrum of self-injuring behavior, whereas others provide the opportunity to explore in a more comprehensive fashion the contextual factors and reasons underlying self-injury in youth. Not all of these measures were designed specifically for use with adolescents, although some have been used with adolescent populations and most would be deemed appropriate. Nevertheless, the publication of more normative data for adolescents will be an important area for research in the near future. Further evaluation of psychometric properties is also required for some of the measures.

A promising area for future research is the development of more electronic formats for responding to questionnaires about NSSI. Given the facility with which many adolescents make use of computers and other electronic media, this would likely offer an appealing assessment approach for many youth, thus potentially increasing response rates and perhaps reducing response biases through increased comfort and "anonymity." Another novel area of development is that of performance-based assessment. The Self-Injury Implicit Association Test is a behavioral test that uses response times to measure the implicit associations individuals hold about self-injury and may offer a complement to more traditional self-reports (Nock & Banaji, 2007). Continued research in the development and validation of NSSI measurement tools is critical given their utility for clinical assessment, treatment planning and monitoring, outcomes measurement, and research.

REFERENCES

Alexander, L. A. (1999). *The functions of self-injury and its link to traumatic events in college students.* UMI ProQuest Digital Dissertations, 24-p. preview, 9932285.

Ciarlo, J. A., Brown, T. R., Edwards, D. W., Kiresuk, T. J., & Newman, F. L. (1986). National Institute of Mental Health. Series FN No. 9, *Assessing mental health treatment outcome measurement techniques.* DHHS Publication No. ADM 86-1301. Washington, DC: U.S. Government Printing Office.

Cicchetti, D. V. (1994). Guidelines, criteria, and rules of thumb for evaluating normed and standardized assessment instruments in psychology. *Psychological Assessment, 6,* 284–290.

Claes, L., Vandereycken, W., & Vertommen, H. (2005). Clinical assessment of self-injurious behaviors: An overview of rating scales and self-reporting questionnaires. In A. Columbus (Ed.), *Advances in psychology research* (Vol. 36, pp. 183–209). Hauppauge, NY: Nova Science.

Cloutier, P. F., & Nixon, M. K. (2003). The Ottawa Self-Injury Inventory: A preliminary evaluation. Abstracts to the 12th International Congress European Society for Child and Adolescent Psychiatry. *European Child & Adolescent Psychiatry, 12* (Suppl 1): I/94.

Connors, R. (1996). Self-injury in trauma survivors: 1. Functions and meanings. *American Journal of Orthopsychiatry, 66,* 197–206.

Favazza, A. R., & Conterio, K. (1988). The plight of chronic self-mutilators. *Community Mental Health Journal, 24,* 22–30.

Fliege, H., Kocalevent, R., Walter, O. B., Beck, S., Kim S., Gratz, L., et al. (2006). Three assessment tools for deliberate self-harm and suicide behavior: Evaluation and psychopathological correlates. *Journal of Psychosomatic Research, 61,* 113–121.

Gratz, K. L. (2001). Measurement of deliberate self-harm: Preliminary data on the Deliberate Self-Harm Inventory. *Journal of Psychopathology and Behavioral Assessment, 23,* 253–263.

Gratz, K. L., & Gunderson, J. G. (2006). Preliminary data on an acceptance-based emotion regulation group intervention for deliberate self-harm among women with borderline personality disorder. *Behavior Therapy, 37,* 25–35.

Gratz, K. L., Lacroce, D. M., & Gunderson, J. G. (2006). Measuring changes in symptoms relevant to borderline personality disorder following short-term treatment across partial hospital and intensive outpatient levels of care. *Journal of Psychiatric Practice, 12,* 153–159.

Guertin, T., Lloyd-Richardson, E., Spirito, A., Donaldson, D., & Boergers, J. (2001). Self-mutilative behavior in adolescents who attempt suicide by overdose. *Journal of the American Academy of Child and Adolescent Psychiatry, 40,* 1062–1069.

Gutierrez, P. M., Osman, A., Barrios, F. X., & Kopper, B. A. (2001). Development and initial validation of the self-harm behavior questionnaire. *Journal of Personality Assessment, 77,* 475–490.

Hawton, K., Rodham, K., & Evans, E. (2006). *By their own young hand: Deliberate self-harm and suicidal ideas in adolescents.* London: Jessica Kingsley.

Hawton, K., Rodham, K., Evans, E., & Weatherall, R. (2002). Deliberate self-harm in adolescents: A self report survey in schools in England, *British Medical Journal, 325,* 1207–1211.

Kumar, G., Pepe, D., & Steer, R. (2004). Adolescent psychiatric inpatients' self-reported reasons for cutting themselves. *Journal of Nervous and Mental Disease, 192,* 830–836.

Lambert, M. J., & Hawkins, E. J. (2004). Measuring outcome: Implementing, monitoring and evaluating outcome in clinical practice. *Professional Psychology: Research and Practice, 35,* 492–498.

Laye-Gindhu, A., & Schonert-Reichl, K. (2005). Non-suicidal self-harm among community adolescents: Understanding the "whats" and "whys" of self-harm. *Journal of Youth and Adolescence, 34,* 447–456.

Linehan, M. M., Armstrong, H. E., Suarez, A., Allmon, D., & Heard, H. L. (1991). Cognitive-behavioral treatment of chronically parasuicidal borderline patients. *Archives of General Psychiatry, 48,* 1060–1064.

Linehan, M. M., Comtois, K. A., Brown, M. Z., Heard, H. L., & Wagner, A. (2006). Suicide Attempt Self-Injury Interview (SASII): Development, reliability, and validity of a scale to assess suicide attempts and intentional self-injury. *Psychological Assessment, 18,* 303–312.

Linehan, M. M., Comtois, K. A., Murray, A. M., Brown, M. Z., Gallop, R. J., Heard, H. L., et al. (2006). Two-year randomized trial + follow-up of dialectical behavior therapy vs. therapy by experts for suicidal behaviors and borderline personality disorder. *Archives of General Psychiatry, 63,* 757–766.

Lloyd, E. E., Kelley, M. L., & Hope, T. (1997). *Self-mutilation in a community sample of adolescents: Descriptive characteristics and provisional prevalence rates.* Poster presented at the Annual Meeting of the Society for Behavioral Medicine, New Orleans.

Lloyd-Richardson, E. E., Perrine, N., Dierker, L., & Kelley, M. L. (2007). Characteristics and functions of non-suicidal self-injury in a community sample of adolescents. *Psychological Medicine, 37,* 1183–1192.

Najmi, S., Wegner, D. M., & Nock, M. K. (2007). Thought suppression and self-injurious thoughts and behaviors. *Behavior Research and Therapy, 45,* 1957–1965.

Newman, F. L., Rugh, D., & Ciarlo, J. A. (2004). Guidelines for selecting psychological instruments for treatment planning and outcomes assessment. In M. E. Maruish (Ed.), *The use of psychological testing for treatment planning and outcomes assessment: Vol. 1. General considerations* (3rd ed., pp. 197–214). Mahwah, NJ: Lawrence Erlbaum Associates.

Nixon, M. K., Cloutier, P. F., & Aggarwal, S. (2002). Affect regulation and addictive aspects of repetitive self-injury in hospitalized adolescents. *Journal of the American Academy of Child and Adolescent Psychiatry, 41,* 1333–1341.

Nock, M. K., & Banaji, M. R. (2007). Assessment of self-injurious thoughts using a behavioral test. *American Journal of Psychiatry, 164,* 820–823.

Nock, M. K., Holmberg, E. B., Photos, V. I., & Michel, B. D. (2007). The Self-Injurious Thoughts and Behaviors Interview: Development, reliability, and validity in an adolescent sample. *Psychological Assessment, 19,* 309–317.

Nock, M. K., & Prinstein, M. J. (2004). A functional approach to the assessment of self-mutilative behavior. *Journal of Consulting and Clinical Psychology, 72,* 885–890.

Nock, M. K., & Prinstein, M. J. (2005). Contextual features in behavioral functions of self-mutilation among adolescents. *Journal of Abnormal Psychology, 114,* 140–146.

Nock, M. K., & Prinstein, M. J. (2006, November). Real-time measurement of self-injurious thoughts and behaviors using electronic diaries. In J. J. Muehlenkamp (Chair), *Understanding non-suicidal self-injury in adolescents from macro- to micro-level.* Paper presented at the annual convention of the Association for Behavioral and Cognitive Therapies, Chicago, IL.

Nunnally, J. C., & Bernstein, I. H. (1994). *Psychometric theory* (3rd ed.). New York: McGraw-Hill.

Osuch, E. A., Noll, G. G., & Putnam, F. W. (1999). The motivations for self-injury in psychiatric inpatients. *Psychiatry, 62,* 334–346.

Ross, S., & Heath, N. (2002). A study of the frequency of self-mutilation in a community sample of adolescents. *Journal of Youth and Adolescents, 31,* 67–77.

Sansone, R. A., Gaither, G. A., Songer, D. A., & Allen, J. L. (2005). Multiple psychiatric diagnoses and self-harm behavior. *International Journal of Psychiatry in Clinical Practice, 9,* 41–44.

Sansone, R. A., & Sansone, L. A. (2002). Assessment tools for self-harm behavior among those with eating disorders. *Eating Disorders, 10,* 193.

Sansone, R. A., Songer, D. A., & Sellbom, M. (2006). The relationship between suicide attempts and low-lethal self-harm behavior among psychiatric inpatients. *Journal of Psychiatric Practice, 12,* 148–152.

Sansone, R. A., Wiederman, M. W., & Sansone, L. A. (1998). The Self-Harm Inventory (SHI): Development of a scale for identifying self-destructive behaviors and borderline personality disorder. *Journal of Clinical Psychology, 54,* 973–983.

Santa Mina, E. E., Gallop, R., Links, P., Heslegrave, R., Pringle, D., Wekerle, C., et al. (2006). The Self-Injury Questionnaire: Evaluation of the psychometric properties in a clinical population. *Journal of Psychiatric and Mental Health Nursing, 13,* 221–227.

Shearer, S. L. (1994). Phenomenology of self-injury among inpatient women with borderline personality disorder. *Journal of Nervous and Mental Disease, 182,* 524–526.

Zlotnick, C., Shea, M. T., Pearlstein, T., Simpson, E., Costello, E., & Begin, A. (1996). The relationship between dissociative symptoms, alexithymia, impulsivity, sexual abuse and self-mutilation. *Comprehensive Psychiatry, 37,* 12–16.

Zlotnick, C., Shea, M. T., Recupero, P., Bidadi, K., Pearlstein, T., & Brown, P. (1997). Trauma, dissociation, impulsivity, and self-mutilation among substance abuse patients. *American Journal of Orthopsychiatry, 67,* 650–654.

Zlotnick, C., Wolfsdorf, B. A., Johnson, B., & Spirito, A. (2003). Impaired self-regulation and suicidal behavior among adolescent and young adult psychiatric inpatients. *Archives of Suicide Research, 7,* 149–157.

8

Assessment of Nonsuicidal Self-Injury in Youth

NANCY L. HEATH AND MARY K. NIXON

In this chapter, the practitioner will gain an understanding of:

- How to employ a hierarchal step approach to assessment to be more effective
- Essential elements of basic and complex assessments of NSSI
- When and how to make referrals
- How assessment guidelines are used in practice
- How to ensure that assessment informs intervention

This chapter presents an overview of an approach to the assessment of nonsuicidal self-injury (NSSI) that would be applicable across settings and professionals. Initially, previous work on the assessment of NSSI using the biopsychosocial model is summarized. The utility of employing a biopsychosocial model of NSSI as a framework for assessment is emphasized. This chapter, however, goes beyond previous work by offering a multilevel approach to the assessment of NSSI to meet the needs of all settings and professionals. Previous literature has exclusively described a full comprehensive assessment that is often neither feasible nor recommended in all settings or situations. The model presented here describes three levels of assessment: first, the *triage* to determine the risk level of the youth; second, the *basic assessment for intervention* for use in referral or creation of a skill-based intervention; and, third, the *comprehensive assessment* for purposes of an intensive intervention.

A hierarchical stepwise approach may function more efficiently and effectively than a unitary comprehensive assessment (see Figure 8.1).

Little has been written about assessment approaches and NSSI, and no research exists regarding the effectiveness or utility of one approach to assessment over another. Therefore, whereas this chapter considers, and cites, previously proposed models, the proposed stepwise model relies heavily on clinical experience as well as legal and ethical considerations and knowledge in related areas (e.g., suicide research). Throughout, case applications of each step will be provided.

Currently, the two books that offer assessment chapters most useful to mental health professionals are those by D'Onofrio (2007) and Walsh (2006). Both employ the understanding of self-injury as a biopsychosocial phenomenon and recommend a detailed assessment consistent with this model. The biopsychosocial model of self-injury posits that the occurrence and maintenance of NSSI is a result of contributing factors from one or more of five domains: affective, behavioral, biological, cognitive, and environmental. These domains do not function in isolation and are intertwined and interact upon each other. D'Onofrio and Walsh suggest a wealth of information one can gather concerning all aspects of the NSSI in these different domains through listing elements within each domain (Walsh, 2006) or more simply the questions one could ask to tap these elements (D'Onofrio, 2007). Table 8.1 summarizes the information that is subsumed within each domain.

In a number of settings, a range of professionals can benefit by keeping this framework in mind as they move through the different levels of assessment. If the practitioner conceptualizes the levels of assessment of NSSI and is aware of the following five interacting domains they will be guided through this process. In the Level 3, more complex, assessment a clinician may be conducting an assessment similar to that suggested by D'Onofrio (2007) and Walsh (2006), but the time and resources necessary to complete such a detailed and comprehensive assessment are not always available or required. This assessment focuses less on documenting all aspects of the client's self-injury than on directing services to maximize outcome. Not all clients require a profusion of services. Through a tiered assessment protocol, it is our hope that those in need of specific services have better access to them.

FIRST CONTACT AND INITIAL RESPONSE

In the initial phase of assessing youth who self-injure, one is also working on developing a positive alliance. This may present challenges. Frequently, youth who self-injure have difficulty expressing themselves and forming therapeutic relationships. They are often concerned about how their self-injury will be perceived. In a survey of high school counselors about NSSI in the schools, one of their primary concerns was how to react when confronted with the behavior (Heath, Toste, & White Kress,

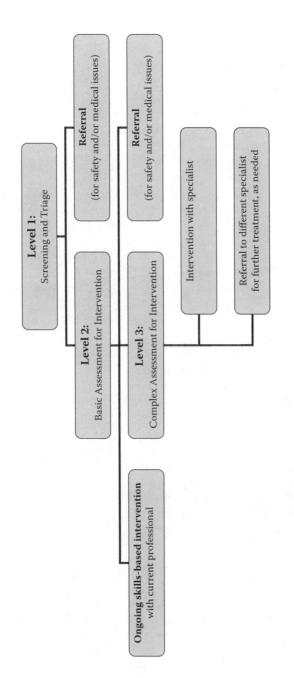

Figure 8.1 Hierarchical Step Approach to Assessment

TABLE 8.1   Biopsychosocial Model for Self-Injury

Domain	Elements
Affective	Emotion profile or style, experiencing of emotions in general Emotions prior, during, and after NSSI Dissociation
Behavioral	Behavior style (e.g., avoids close relationships, uncommunicative) Behaviors prior, during, and after NSSI (e.g., argument with parent, choosing isolation, rituals)
Biological	Neurochemical dysregulation (e.g., serotonin, dopamine, noradrenaline systems), manifesting as mood disorder, affective instability, anxiety disorder, impulse control disorder, etc. In some with repetitive NSSI, hypotheses about addictive behavior versus low pain sensitivity
Cognitive	Cognitive style, thoughts, beliefs about self and others, past and future Thoughts prior, during, and after NSSI
Environmental	Current family environment and history History of physical and sexual abuse Youth's social support Peer and romantic relations School and community Cultural and religious

2007). Several studies have demonstrated that even experienced medical and mental health professionals find self-injuring behavior one of the most difficult and upsetting behaviors they encounter (e.g., Connors, 2000; Dieter, Nicholls, & Pearlman, 2000). Several basic recommendations are made below to promote the optimal initial response to NSSI by professionals and to maximize the opportunity to develop a positive therapeutic alliance.

When a youth's self-injury is first revealed, either intentionally or unintentionally by the individual themselves or by a friend, it is important not to over- or underreact. An overreaction of shock, revulsion, or excessive concern can negatively affect the relationship with the youth. A matter-of-fact, calm response is needed, which focuses on listening to the youth's perspectives on his or her overall emotional well being. The discussion should then move quickly from a basic understanding of the self-injuring behavior to the underlying reasons for NSSI, stressors, and contributing factors. Figure 8.2 gives examples of helpful versus unhelpful first response questions and statements.

Helpful	Non-Helpful
"I would appreciate if you could help me to understand better about your self-injury."	"Why do you do (self-injure*)?"
	"What is wrong that you need to do this?"
"Would you be willing to share what ever you feel comfortable discussing with me?"	
	"Describe what you do ..."
"Tell me when it first started, describe briefly what you would do, tell me about what that time was like for you and what was going on in your life, has the behavior changed since you started? If so, how?"	"Is it something about the blood that makes you do this?"
	"Why are you telling me this?"
"I know this may sound unusual but, some individuals tell me that self-injuring somehow helps them, at least on a temporary basis, what might SI, if anything, do for you?"	"Do you think you do this to get attention?"
	"Is this a 'cry for help'?"
"You must feel that (self-injuring) helps you in some way, can you tell me more about that?	
"Help me understand what is going on with you."	
"In terms of how you are feeling these days, are there things that you would like to share with me."	
"Tell me about yourself."	
"I know it is so hard for you to tell about how you feel ... but can you walk me through your feelings about your (self-injury)."	

* Use the youth's own terminology

Figure 8.2   Sample "Helpful" versus "Non-Helpful" Initial Responses

The quality of the relationship, or alliance, between client and therapist is one of the best predictors of a variety of positive outcomes independent of therapeutic orientations (e.g., Barber, Connolly, Crits-Cristoph, Gladis, & Siqueland, 2000; Horvath, 2000; Martin, Garske, & Davis, 2000; Norcross, 2002). In 2002, Horvath and Bedi, in reviewing the study of alliance, suggested that it could best be understood as including aspects of affective bonds (trust, liking, respect, and caring), cognitive elements (agreement about goals and means to achieve them), and partnership (shared and understood responsibilities and tasks). Regarding self-injury, it has been argued that the attachment-relationship aspect of the therapeutic process may be the most important component of any intervention (Connors, 2000; Farber, 2000; Ivanoff, Linehan, & Brown, 2001). Based on this premise, the quality of contact that occurs prior to the assessment is critical in paving the way for a positive alliance.

LEVEL 1 ASSESSMENT: SCREENING AND TRIAGE

In Level 1, initial assessment, the NSSI has usually already been established. However, in many cases the clinician may have reason to suspect NSSI but have no confirmation. Additionally, in a number of settings and under certain circumstances, it can be helpful to screen for NSSI during an initial interview. One way of screening for NSSI without suggesting the behavior to the youth is to use the "How I Deal with Stress" (HIDS) survey (Figure 8.3; Ross & Heath, 2002; Heath & Ross, 2007), either to use as interview questions or as a self-report measure for youth. The HIDS embeds the question of whether the youth has ever "hurt themselves on purpose" in a series of questions about how they deal with stress. If the youth indicates he or she has done this, a series of follow-up questions probe the nature of the injury. This has been found to be effective in identifying youth who engage in self-injury without pathologizing the behavior.

In a Level 1 assessment, variations in the complexity of the assessment are based on possible time constraints and who is conducting the assessment. For example, when a school counselor is doing a Level 1 assessment of a student who was referred by a teacher for NSSI, he or she would complete a less comprehensive Level 1 assessment than a mental health clinician or psychiatrist in a hospital who is requested to evaluate a youth who was brought into the emergency room for NSSI. Despite this variability, certain core assessment issues need to be addressed at this level. The essentials of a Level 1 assessment are outlined below, and, where necessary, reference to the range of complexity will be made across settings and professions.

A Level 1 assessment across settings should minimally consist of a suicide risk assessment, an injury risk assessment, and consideration of common co-occurring mental health issues. See Table 8.2 for a summary of suicide risk assessment. Not all risk factors should be equally weighted in the assessment of risk. For example, suicide ideation is extremely common among adolescents, and although it should always be followed up, it does not by itself constitute a high risk indicator (Lieberman, 2007). Similarly, poor social support or change in recent stressors, do not, on their own, suggest a high risk for suicide. However, a youth engaging in self-injury (even low lethality) who indicates suicide intent, plan, or personal, family or friend history of suicide should be immediately considered high risk (Joiner, Walker, Rudd, & Jobes, 1999).

A second factor to be considered in the initial triage assessment is the evaluation of physical injury (Silverman, Berman, Sanddal, O'Carroll,

& Joiner, 2007). Self-injury by definition results in physical injury, but to determine the overall risk category, it is important to determine the level or severity of physical injury. Occasionally, a youth will not appear to be a suicide risk according to all the indices mentioned above, but when the risk for physical injury is evaluated, it becomes apparent that the youth is engaging in forms of self-injury that put him or her at risk for severe physical injury or death (see Table 8.3).

The last element of the initial triage is the evaluation for commonly co-occurring mental health issues. The triage for suicide risk and physical injury is standard, but the evaluation of mental health status is more complex. As discussed in Chapter 5, NSSI may co-occur with a number of psychiatric conditions, and clinicians need to conduct a comprehensive and detailed assessment for *Diagnostic and Statistical Manual–*, text revision (*DSM-IV-TR*) Axis I and Axis II disorders. This assessment can be extremely complex and requires both a significant amount of time and expertise. However, the practitioner who is aware of the common related issues as described in Chapter 5 can determine through some screening questions the possible presence of major mental health issues. If the youth has multiple difficulties in addition to the self-injury or depending on the severity of related issues, they may be considered higher severity or complexity, requiring more intensive services. Table 8.4 provides a checklist of related mental health issues. If there are positive responses to the following screening questions, further evaluation by a professional trained in diagnostic assessment is indicated.

In summary, along with following the appropriate initial response and understanding the importance of developing a positive therapeutic alliance from the beginning, the Level 1 assessment must include a suicide risk assessment, a physical injury risk assessment, and a mental health status evaluation. Although this information seeks to determine the risk category of the youth, it is important to acknowledge that no simple formula exists for differentiating when an individual is high risk or low risk. If there is higher risk of suicide or physical injury or the presence of significant mental health concerns, then the risk status level increases. Furthermore, it is essential that the practitioner revisit risk assessment on a regular basis, as risk levels may change over time, particularly when all contributing factors are not fully apparent. Ongoing aspects of assessment should be integrated within the intervention process. This serves as a means to gather further, as well as new or changing, information that can then inform the treatment approach.

Completion of a Level 1 assessment that indicates a high risk for the youth, from the safety or medical perspective, should result in immediate referral to the appropriate facility or professional, for example, medical interventions such as sutures and referral to inpatient or crisis intervention services. Those who are not at high risk regarding safety may continue to a Level 2 assessment, either with the same professional who completed the risk assessment or as part of the initial steps by the professional who receives the youth as a new referral.

Please begin by completing the following information:

Age: Sex: ❏ Male   ❏ Female

What **languages** do you speak at home?   ❏ English   ❏ French
                                                         ❏ Other (please specify): _____

Country of **permanent residence**   ❏ Canada   ❏ USA
                                                         ❏ Other (please specify): _____

Country of **birth**   ❏ Canada   ❏ USA
                                                         ❏ Other (please specify): _____

Young adults have to deal with a lot of stress. In a recent survey, young adults said they used the following list of strategies to help them deal with problems. We are interested in knowing if you have also used any of these strategies to help you deal with stress.

Please read each item and indicate whether you:
    never used this strategy (0)
    used this strategy **only once** (1)
    used this strategy a **few times** to cope with stress (2)
    frequently used this strategy to cope with stress (3)

➤ Please note that some items are printed in **bold**. If you answer that you have used a bolded strategy (once, a couple of times, or frequently), please fill out the follow-up questions at the end of the survey.

Coping strategies	*Never*	*Once*	*Few times*	*Frequently*
1. Try not to think about it	0	1	2	3
2. Spend time alone	0	1	2	3
3. Go out	0	1	2	3
4. **Talk to someone**	0	1	2	3
5. Try to solve the problem	0	1	2	3
6. Do something to keep myself busy	0	1	2	3
7. Say to myself it doesn't matter	0	1	2	3
8. Listen to music	0	1	2	3
9. Exercise	0	1	2	3
10. Play sports	0	1	2	3
11. Read	0	1	2	3
12. Go shopping	0	1	2	3
13. Eat	0	1	2	3
14. Stop eating	0	1	2	3
15. Drink alcohol	0	1	2	3
16. Hit someone	0	1	2	3
17. Get into an argument with someone	0	1	2	3
18. Do drugs	0	1	2	3
19. Smoke	0	1	2	3
20. **Do risky things**	0	1	2	3
21. **Physically hurt myself on purpose**	0	1	2	3
22. Cry	0	1	2	3
23. Sleep	0	1	2	3
24. Pray or engage in other religious	0	1	2	3
25. Other: _____	0	1	2	3

Figure 8.3   How I Deal With Stress (HIDS)

"Talk to someone"

Please fill out this section if you answered that you indicated that you have used this strategy.

Who do you talk to? (circle all that apply)

Parents	Other family members	Friends
Romantic partner	Teachers	Other (specify):_____

How helpful is this strategy? (circle one)
0 – Never helpful
1 – Sometimes helpful
2 – Usually helpful
3 – Always helpful

"Do risky things"

Please fill out this section if you answered that you indicated that you have used this strategy.

What kind of risky activities have you engaged in? (circle all that apply)

Reckless driving	Uncontrolled alcohol abuse	Drug abuse
Theft	Promiscuous/unprotected sex	Vandalism
Excessive gambling	Other (specify): _____	

How did the risky activities make you feel?

"Physically hurt myself on purpose"

Please fill out this section if you answered that you indicated that you have used this strategy.

Please circle any way that you have intentionally hurt yourself (*without suicidal intent*):

1. Cut your wrists, arms, or other areas of your body
2. Burned yourself
3. Scratched yourself, to the extent that scarring or bleeding occurred
4. Banged your head against something, to the extent that you caused a bruise to appear
5. Punched yourself, to the extent that you caused a bruise to appear

How old were you when you first hurt yourself on purpose?   _____

When was the last time you hurt yourself on purpose?   _____

How many years have you been hurting yourself on purpose? (If you are no longer doing this, how many years did you do this before you stopped?)   _____

Think of the longest period in which you engaged in self-injury (this could be in days, months, or years). How long was this period?   _____

Has this behavior ever resulted in hospitalization or injury severe enough to require medical treatment?   ❑ Yes   ❑ No

Have you ever hurt yourself with the intent to kill yourself?   ❑ Yes   ❑ No

How many times have you hurt yourself on purpose throughout your life? (circle one)

One time	2 to 4 times	5 to 10 times
11 to 50 times	51 to 100 times	More than 100 times

TABLE 8.2   Suicide Risk Assessment

Suicide Risk Factors	Present	Absent
Suicide ideation "Have you thought about killing yourself?"	"I have thought a lot about killing myself."	"I haven't really thought about killing myself."
Suicide intent "You did this because you wanted...?"	"I wanted to die."	"I wanted to feel better."
Plan "You say you want to die. Have you thought about how you would do that?"	"Yeah, I would jump in front of the subway." "Yeah, my Dad has a hunting rifle and I know where the keys are to the gun cabinet."	"No... I don't know."
Hopelessness "Can you see how this might get better in time?"	"No, it's just never going to change. I am never going to feel better."	"Yeah, if I could just get out of school." "Yeah, it is just a bad time now for me."
Suicide history, personal "Have you ever attempted suicide before?" (Medical treatment required?)	"Yeah, I took an overdose of Tylenol and had to have my stomach pumped."	"No, I have never actually done anything."
Suicide history, family or friend "Has anyone you know ever attempted or committed suicide?"	"Yeah, my dad shot himself when I was nine." "Yeah, a girl I knew took a whole bunch of Tylenol and her liver died or something and she died."	"No, not really... well there was a kid in my class in grade 9 who hung himself."
Poor social support "Is there someone who you can talk to when you feel bad or are in trouble?"	"Umm... maybe... but not really cause I don't want to upset my Mom. She can't handle it, and mostly I am not that close to anyone."	"Sure, I have a really good friend and we talk about everything. And my older sister... she's good."

TABLE 8.2   Suicide Risk Assessment (continued)

Suicide Risk Factors	Present	Absent
Recent change in stress "Are there things that are really bothering or stressing you out right now?"	"Well yeah, exams... you know? I know I have to do well and I just don't think... I just don't know..., but yeah exams." "My girlfriend. She's going to break up with me. I hate that. I wish I could stop it."	"Ummm... I guess the usual. My parents on my back, school. But nothing special—you mean one thing? Not really."

The following case illustrates the benefits of sometimes using a checklist to facilitate disclosure and the need to continually reassess suicide risk.

C.D. was a 15-year-old female, seen initially by her school counselor regarding concerns of self-injury. It was her friends who suggested that she go talk with the counselor, as they were becoming concerned regarding her behavior. They had not directly discussed their concern with C.D. because they did not feel comfortable. Each time that they had approached her, she continually denied any difficulty and became angry that her friends were intruding in her personal life. C.D. reluctantly agreed with her friends to meet with the school counselor, mostly to appease them. She was initially adamant that she was doing "fine" and that her friends were "ganging up on me." The school counselor took a low-key approach, and they both agreed to simply review how things were going with her at school and how she was coping.

Because C.D. was reluctant to talk much, the counselor suggested that she use a brief questionnaire "to review what stressors might be there and how you feel you are coping." C.D. appeared relieved that she would not have to discuss things in detail directly with the counselor and sat quietly while she filled out the questionnaire. When she revealed in the self-report measure that she was using self-injury to cope, the counselor asked if she would be willing to discuss this further. C.D. then revealed that she had been self-injuring on and off for the past three months, starting after the breakup with her boyfriend. She denied any suicidal ideation, and on inspection, the cuts to her forearm were superficial and did not require medical attention. C.D. stated that she wished to finish the interview, as she had found the encounter somewhat stressful but at the same time helpful to finally disclose to someone regarding her behavior. C.D. was willing to return to see the counselor again in three days.

At the follow up appointment the counselor probed for more information and in so doing came to understand that C.D. had been experiencing low mood for the past three months since the breakup with her ex-boyfriend. Her sleep was disrupted, and she was having difficulty focusing on her school work. Her parents were also pressuring her because her last report card was a distinct drop from her previous average. She had always been a high achiever

TABLE 8.3   Physical Injury Assessment

Severe Physical Injury Risk Factors	Present	Absent
Other high-risk methods of self-harm "What other types of self-harm have you done? Thought of? Have you ever taken an overdose of a drug (prescribed, over the counter, or illegal)?	"I know some kids who do that strangulation thing to get a rush... I haven't done it, but I have thought of it" "One time when I was really upset after the breakup with my boyfriend I impulsively took 30 Tylenol just to numb myself from the emotional pain."	"I have..." [lists other low lethality forms of NSSI)
Exposure to injury "Have you ever been sexually or physically abused?" If yes, check current status and risk	"Ever? Yeah, I was sexually abused by my Uncle for two years when I was 7." (Probe) "No, now he moved to XXX, we never see him"	"No."
Unintentional injury "Have you ever hurt yourself more severely than you meant to? How often?"	"Oh yeah, every now and then I cut way too deep without meaning to."	"Only ever once... I am pretty careful. I know what I am doing."
Medical history "Have you ever had to seek medical attention (e.g., for stitches)? How often?"	"Yeah, a few times for stitches."	"No, never."

Escalation of self-injury "Are you hurting yourself differently now than when you started? More severe? More injuries?"	"Uh huh.... I used to just cut lightly two or three times and that worked... then I had to cut more, maybe five or six times to get it to work. Now I am cutting pretty deep and sometimes I hit my head on the wall.... It doesn't work as well. I need more."	"Sometimes I cut and sometimes I just scratch.... Since I started I have tried some different things.... like sometimes I use my ID card over and over on my knuckles until they bleed.... (Probe) "But not more severe, just different." "No I have my routine, my ritual.... It hasn't changed."
Shared tool "Have you ever shared a _____?"	"Yes, we sometimes sit around and pass the blade."	"No."
Substance abuse and self-injury "Have you ever self-injured while drunk or high? How often?"	"Lots. Sometimes my friends have to stop me because I am so f***ed up I don't know what I'm doing."	"No." "Maybe once or twice but mostly, no."

at school and was frustrated that she could not meet her own expectations. C.D. was not experiencing any suicidal ideation. She agreed that the school counselor could call her parents to discuss concerns regarding her mood, but she was adamant that the counselor could not discuss her cutting. C.D. indicated that she would be willing to see a mental health professional, which her parents would be asked to facilitate, if the school counselor attended the first appointment with her. C.D. also agreed to meet with the school counselor on a regular basis for ongoing support. The school counselor also suggested, and C.D. agreed, that she have deferred deadlines for one project and one exam that were due in the next week. The school counselor agreed to discuss this with the teachers, without breaking confidentiality at this time.

Over the weekend and after the second session with the school counselor, during which further assessment of risk and coping strategies was done and no change was determined, C.D. decided to meet with her ex-boyfriend. This encounter did not go well, as she had hoped for reconciliation, which did not occur. Her mood dropped and she felt hopeless to the point of feeling suicidal. She had not disclosed to her parents or the school counselor upon questioning whether she had a means to harm herself that she had kept a bottle of acetaminophen in her room to treat pain from a sports injury. She overdosed on thirty pills when she returned home, with the intent being to take her life. She felt rejected by her ex-boyfriend and stressed by the fact that she could not keep up with her school work. She felt she had failed completely and that the pain of failure was intolerable.

Fortunately, her mother, who had been observing her more closely since the call from the school counselor, noted that something was not quite right, and C.D. eventually confessed regarding her overdose and was immediately taken to the hospital, where she was treated medically and assessed by the on-call psychiatrist. The assessment concluded that she had symptoms of major depression, that there was a previous history of depression one year ago, and that the stress of the breakup with her boyfriend, academic difficulties, and peer alienation related to recent behavior were also contributing factors. In addition, she was typically not one who sought out support or assistance but felt she should manage all her problems herself. C.D. indicated that although she had suicide thoughts, she admitted she had "scared" herself regarding the impulsive nature and severity of her overdose and the extent of professional intervention that it had required. She indicated that she was willing to be seen by the crisis intervention service the next day to consider treatment of her depression and developing a range of coping skills.

The following day, at her appointment, she was seen alone and with her family. C.D. felt in some ways relieved that she no longer had to cope "with all these problems" alone. The crisis intervention worker, in discussion with the school counselor, and with permission and consent, agreed to jointly support C.D. and her family. The school counselor would provide support regarding her academic program and minimizing stress in that regard and would provide a place for her to come and talk on a regular basis as well as on an as needed basis if she felt overwhelmed. The crisis intervention worker in conjunction with the team psychiatrist would further evaluate symptoms of major depression and presence of suicidal ideation and make recommendations regarding treatment. The school counselor was informed that they could notify the crisis intervention worker directly, as well as the parents, if there were any concerns regarding safety.

TABLE 8.4   Mental Health Issues Checklist

Does the youth suffer from...?

- Mood disorder
    - o Do you often have low mood? Have you lost interest in your usual activities?
    - o Do you often have severe and/or frequent mood swings?
- Anxiety disorder
    - o Do you fear being humiliated in public?
    - o Do you feel tense and nervous when you are around people?
    - o Do you frequently get panicky?
    - o Do you have thoughts that go over and over in your head that you can't get rid of?
    - o Do you have things you must do over and over again?
- Impulse control problems or conduct problems
    - o Do you often find that you do things without thinking?
    - o Do you take risks that most others would not?
    - o Have you had problems with the law, or broken the law but not been caught?
- Uncontrolled anger
    - o Do you find that it is difficult to control your anger/rages?
- Borderline traits such as affective instability, difficulty being alone, rejection sensitivity
    - o Do your emotions fluctuate frequently?
    - o Do you find it difficult to be alone?
    - o Do you feel you are sensitive to feelings of rejection?
- Alcohol and/or substance abuse
    - o Do you use alcohol or substance? If so, how much and what?
- Eating disorders
    - o Do you purposefully restrict your food intake?
    - o Do you purge or abuse laxatives as a means to control your weight?
    - o Do you believe that you are overweight when others tell you that you are not?

LEVEL 2: BASIC ASSESSMENT FOR
DETERMINING INTERVENTIONS

Level 2 assessment focuses on the assessment of the self-injuring behavior and its function. This assessment needs to be completed regardless of assessed risk, as it provides a fuller understanding of the behavior. Chapter 7 reviews measures of self-injury, and in assessing self-injury, these may be helpful either as a checklist or to provide a guideline to structure an interview. Assessment of self-injury varies depending on the setting and the expertise of the professional completing the assessment. Below, the basics of an assessment of self-injury are listed. Although one can certainly do a more comprehensive assessment of the self-injury itself, this must be done with caution. Collecting detailed information about all aspects of the self-injury should only be done when it is clear to the clinician how this will inform and contribute to treatment.

Often, the first step in a basic assessment is having the youth describe the most recent incident of self-injury in a nonthreatening manner that elicits the youth's perspective. Use of the Self-Assessment Sheet (SAS; Nixon, 2007; Figure 8.4) enables the youth to describe in a somewhat structured but narrative form, elements of the event including potential triggers, related cognitions and emotions, the extent of self-injury, and consequences. The assessor can then use these descriptions as starting points to assess what types of triggers, if any, and what typical cognitions and emotions may accompany the youth's acts of self-injury as well as an assessment of his or her ability to manage or cope differently, if at all. The SAS may be used in the assessment of the behavior and during the course of an intervention as a log of the behavior and associated factors. Table 8.5 provides some core features of self-injurious behavior that should be assessed.

In completing the Level 2 assessment of the self-injuring behavior, the goal is to gain a better understanding of the scope and severity of the behavior. Often, youth who self-injure will not reveal much about the self-injury except in response to direct questions. Clinicians frequently may not be aware of the variety of indices that should be tapped to attain necessary information. Although ultimately, the self-injury should not be the focus of the intervention, it is important for the clinician to have an accurate and current representation of the behavior.

Another facet of the Level 2 assessment is a functional assessment of the self-injury, done by completing an analysis of the behavioral, cognitive, and emotional factors that may contribute to the need to engage in NSSI. This type of functional analysis is integral to both the more complex assessment described below as well as in determining potential interventions Furthermore, as described in Chapter 3, the functions that NSSI serves may vary. The assessment of these functions is directly and indirectly tapped in the more complex assessment described below and frequently only becomes apparent in the course of treatment. In

SAS (Self Assessment Sheet)

Please help to describe, in your own words, aspects around a recent self-injuring episode.

Was there a "trigger" for your SI? (Was there something that upset you?) If so, what was the trigger?

Where were you at the time? ————————————————————————
Was there anyone else there, or were you alone? _____

What were you thinking at the time? (What was going through your head?)

How upset were you? Circle one.

1	2	3	4	5
Very Upset	Really	Moderately	Mildly, but still OK	Not at all

What did you do? How did you handle the situation?

Did you use any techniques to cope differently with your distress?

How well did you feel you handled yourself? Circle one.

1	2	3	4	5
Poorly	Not so well	Okay	Good	Great

What were the consequences? What happened as a result of how you handled yourself?

Would you do anything differently? If so, what would you do?

Figure 8.4   Self-Assessment Sheet

TABLE 8.5   Level 2 Assessment of NSSI

Social contributors to the NSSI
*   How did they start? Friend?
*   Do they have friends who NSSI?
*   Do they NSSI alone or in groups or both?
*   Who have they told?

History of NSSI
*   Family History of NSSI
*   Age of onset
*   Longest period free of self-injury
*   Lifetime frequency of self-injury
*   Current frequency of self-injury
*   Changes in self-injury over time (frequency, severity, type, location)

Current State
*   Desire to stop
*   History of attempts to stop and interventions?

the present, more limited assessment context the focus is to identify antecedent events, specific triggers, and reinforcing consequences of the behavior within the framework of these empirically derived functions. When the antecedent events and triggers are identified, one can assist the client in developing more adaptive coping skills to manage the events and associated triggers. Similarly, when the reinforcing consequences are uncovered, they are eliminated where possible, and other pathways to achieve the reinforcing consequences are explored. Table 8.6 lists some common examples of antecedent events, triggers, and reinforcing consequences by function category. It is important to remember that (a) the most common function that has been found in NSSI is affect regulation; (b) there is rarely only one function of the behavior; and (c) functions may vary over time.

The strength of using evidence-based functional analysis of NSSI (as described in Table 8.6) is not necessarily in the detail, but is in the broader conceptual understanding of the behavior that it provides to the practitioner. When the practitioner is aware that NSSI may serve one or more key functions, the assessment of the behavior will be more accurate, leading to a more targeted and efficient assessment, referral, and intervention process.

Following Level 2, which includes the assessment of the self-injury and a preliminary assessment of the possible function of the NSSI, the practitioner may choose from three possible paths. First, as suggested above, if issues of medical or safety concerns became apparent in Level 2, an immediate referral to appropriate care is needed. Second, if the Level 2 assessment reveals that severe or complex issues exist around specific areas of functioning (for example, it is apparent that family

TABLE 8.6   Functional Assessment of Self-injury

Functional category	Antecedent events (behavioral, cognitive, emotional)	Sample triggers	Reinforcing consequences
Affect regulation	Behavioral: exams Cognitive: "I am going to fail, I can't fail, it will ruin everything." Emotional: anxiety, tension	Being alone, seeing the pin on the bureau	Feeling relaxed
Self-punishment	Behavioral: taunted for being overweight by peers Cognitive: "I am a fat, ugly, loser." Emotional: self-hatred, tense, angry	Being alone, visiting a website on NSSI	Relaxed, feeling "purified"
Interpersonal or social influence	Behavioral: relationship break up Cognitive: "I feel bad. S/he can't do this to me." Emotional: angry, sad	Going through pictures of "us"	Friends concerned, upset, sympathize; ex is worried, concerned and re-involved
Sensation-seeking or risk-taking	Behavioral: bored and seeking excitement Cognitive: "I bet I can do this." Emotional: excited, "hyped"	Seeing or hearing of someone else's NSSI	Feeling high, like s/he accomplished something Reaction of others: shock or horror
Anti-dissociation	Behavioral: variable Cognitive: "I need to feel something, even if it is pain." Emotional: feeling numb	Seeing a tool or blood or seeing someone expressing emotion (e.g., crying)	Feeling pain and relief, ending dissociation
Anti-suicide	Behavioral: having suicidal thoughts and feelings Cognitive: "I will use (self-injuring behavior) instead of acting on these thoughts." Emotional: depressed, anxious, tense, desperate	No trigger may be apparent or there may be cumulative stressors and/or an acute stressor	Reinforced by effectiveness in averting acting on suicidal thoughts

Note: Based on Klonsky, 2007

interaction is problematic or there is possible psychiatric disorder), then a directed referral to the appropriate clinician would be indicated. The third path is for the youth who is assessed as not being at immediate risk for safety or medical issues and has no severe or complex presenting issues. In this case the clinician may choose to proceed from the focused functional assessment to a focused intervention building on identified skill deficits.

The following case illustrates how an individual received ongoing assessment while receiving a psychotherapeutic intervention for NSSI.

A.J. was a 17-year-old female who participated in the self-harm group at her regional mental health clinic for children and youth. She was initially referred to the group by her therapist due to her symptoms of affective instability and use of self-cutting to relieve these dysphoric feelings. In the course of the group meetings, with the use of self-assessment sheets that delineated triggers, distorted cognitions, behavioral responses, and self-rating scales, it became apparent that in addition to mood changes without triggers that prompted self-cutting, she also experienced increased tension and self-loathing when dealing with peers. She used self-cutting to reduce the intense feeling of tension and temporarily provide a sense of "relief" as well as to self-punish, as she felt inferior to her friends and had significant difficulties asserting herself or feeling understood and accepted in her peer group. She described self-cutting as a means to punish herself because she felt inferior, and NSSI was used as a reinforcing behavior regarding negative self-image and peer interactions. "I cut myself, so I am weird, which is just what my friends think of me." The clinician's assessment based on a formulation from the functions of NSSI indicated that A.J. required a more detailed assessment regarding the presence of an affective instability. Group therapists made note of the need to focus on addressing negative self-image and developing interpersonal skills.

LEVEL 3: COMPLEX ASSESSMENT FOR DETERMINING INTERVENTIONS

The final level of assessment should be undertaken by a professional with expertise in the area of adolescent mental health. More specifically, these professionals would have training in diagnostic assessment or family assessment and have the ability to formulate a comprehensive understanding of all predisposing, precipitating, perpetuating, and protective factors. Despite the complexity of this level of assessment, several guiding principles will simplify and assist the professional in how best to develop a formulation. In certain cases, this level of assessment may be completed by a team of professionals, for example, a psychologist or psychiatrist to complete the diagnostic assessment and a family therapist to explore detailed family issues and assist in completing the formulation. Aspects from the Level 2 assessment can act as a guide regarding which steps to initiate first in terms of the Level 3 assessment. In more complex cases, where several professionals are involved, it is recommended that one individual act also in a case management role to ensure that all levels of assessment are integrated and that important information is shared, with consent, among those doing specific aspects of the Level 3 assessment.

To start, use of the SAS (see Figure 8.4) can be helpful. If the youth is willing, previous SAS sheets can be shared with the professional so information does not have to be repeated, and successive SAS sheets over the assessment period can build on the information gained. The ongoing use of the SAS provides both a predicable method for the youth to describe his or her behavior, an opportunity for the youth to gain awareness of potential contributing factors, as well as an indication of what he or she might be trying, if anything, to do differently.

An additional tool that may be helpful at this level is a self-report functions of NSSI measure that asks more specific questions regarding the extent of motivations or roles of NSSI in the domains previously outlined in Level 2. Figure 8.5 contains the Ottawa Self-Injury Inventory (OSI) Functions self-report measure that can be used to identify these aspects both from the perspective of when the youth started self-injuring and what functions it continues to serve on a repeated basis. A "summary key" is also provided in Table 8.7 so that the assessor can calculate the number of items that are endorsed under each function category as well as obtain a cumulative score. This self-report can then act as a way to be comprehensive in this respect as well as to obtain further information that guides which aspects of assessment might be most important to address first. For example, whereas hearing a voice that tells them to self-injure may not be a common presentation, this comprehensive review will ensure that those types of questions are included. In rare cases where this is the primary reason for self-injury, the next step regarding psychiatric assessment for psychotic symptoms is clearly identified.

If, for example, family issues such as parent-child conflict are considered the major precipitating and/or perpetuating factors as identified at the Level 2 assessment or based on more self-report (see interpersonal boundary and interpersonal influence questions on the OSI-F that may be related to parent-child conflict), a referral to a family therapist would be recommended. Chapter 12 outlines specifics of what a professional, familiar with family assessment, should consider in evaluating families in which youth present with NSSI. If psychiatric symptoms are deemed a prominent feature, a referral for diagnostic assessment is recommended. Chapter 5, on co-occurrence of psychiatric disorders, outlines recommended standard assessment tools in this domain. If such tools are not available to the assessor, the use of *DSM-IV-TR* criteria (American Psychiatric Association, 2000) can act as a guide to a systematic diagnostic interview. It is not uncommon that several sessions and further collection of data, using charting and collaborative information beyond the youth and parents (e.g., school information, information from previous mental health assessments), may be essential to gather prior to confirming a particular diagnosis.

Figure 8.5 Ottawa Self-Injury Inventory – Functions(OSI-F)

| Name: _____ | Sex ____ Male ____ Female |

| Today's Date:____ DD ____ MM____YY | Date of Birth ____ DD ____ MM____YY |

Why do you think you started and if you continue, why do you still self-injure (without meaning to kill yourself)? Please circle the number that best represents how much your self-injury is due to that reason.

Circle "0" if it has never been a reason that you self-injure and "4" if it has always been a reason that you self-injure.

WHY DID YOU START?

IF YOU CONTINUE, WHY DO YOU CONTINUE?

	never a reason / sometimes a reason / always a reason		never a reason / sometimes a reason / always a reason
1. to release unbearable tension	0 1 2 3 4	1. to release unbearable tension	0 1 2 3 4
2. to experience a "high" that feels like a drug high	0 1 2 3 4	2. to experience a "high" that feels like a drug high	0 1 2 3 4
3. to stop my parents from being angry with me	0 1 2 3 4	3. to stop my parents from being angry with me	0 1 2 3 4
4. to stop feeling alone and empty	0 1 2 3 4	4. to stop feeling alone and empty	0 1 2 3 4
5. to get care or attention from other people	0 1 2 3 4	5. to get care or attention from other people	0 1 2 3 4
6. to punish myself	0 1 2 3 4	6. to punish myself	0 1 2 3 4
7. to provide a sense of excitement that feels exhilarating	0 1 2 3 4	7. to provide a sense of excitement that feels exhilarating	0 1 2 3 4
8. to relieve nervousness/fearfulness	0 1 2 3 4	8. to relieve nervousness/fearfulness	0 1 2 3 4
9. to avoid getting into trouble for something I did	0 1 2 3 4	9. to avoid getting into trouble for something I did	0 1 2 3 4

Figure 8.5   Ottawa Self-Injury Inventory – Functions(OSI-F)

10. to distract me from unpleasant memories	0 1 2 3 4	10. to distract me from unpleasant memories	0 1 2 3 4
11. to change my body image and/or appearance	0 1 2 3 4	11. to change my body image and/or appearance	0 1 2 3 4
12. to belong to a group	0 1 2 3 4	12. to belong to a group	0 1 2 3 4
13. to release anger	0 1 2 3 4	13. to release anger	0 1 2 3 4
14. to stop my friends/ boy-girlfriend from being angry with me	0 1 2 3 4	14. to stop my friends/ boy-girlfriend from being angry with me	0 1 2 3 4
15. to show others how hurt or damaged I am	0 1 2 3 4	15. to show others how hurt or damaged I am	0 1 2 3 4
16. to show others how strong or tough I am	0 1 2 3 4	16. to show others how strong or tough I am	0 1 2 3 4
17. to help me escape from uncomfortable feelings or moods	0 1 2 3 4	17. to help me escape from uncomfortable feelings or moods	0 1 2 3 4
18. to satisfy voices inside or outside of me telling me to do it	0 1 2 3 4	18. to satisfy voices inside or outside of me telling me to do it	0 1 2 3 4
19. to experience physical pain in one area, when the other pain I feel is unbearable	0 1 2 3 4	19. to experience physical pain in one area, when the other pain I feel is unbearable	0 1 2 3 4
20. to stop people from expecting so much from me	0 1 2 3 4	20. to stop people from expecting so much from me	0 1 2 3 4
21. to relieve feelings of sadness or feeling "down"	0 1 2 3 4	21. to relieve feelings of sadness or feeling "down"	0 1 2 3 4
22. to have control in a situation where no one can influence me	0 1 2 3 4	22. to have control in a situation where no one can influence me	0 1 2 3 4
23. to stop me from thinking about ideas of killing myself	0 1 2 3 4	23. to stop me from thinking about ideas of killing myself	0 1 2 3 4

Figure 8.5   Ottawa Self-Injury Inventory – Functions(OSI-F)

24. to stop me from acting out ideas of killing myself	0 1 2 3 4	24. to stop me from acting out ideas of killing myself	0 1 2 3 4
25. to produce a sense of being real when I feel numb or "unreal"	0 1 2 3 4	25. to produce a sense of being real when I feel numb or "unreal"	0 1 2 3 4
26. to release frustration	0 1 2 3 4	26. to release frustration	0 1 2 3 4
27. to get out of doing something that I don't want to do	0 1 2 3 4	27. to get out of doing something that I don't want to do	0 1 2 3 4
28. for no reason that I know about - it just happens sometimes	0 1 2 3 4	28. for no reason that I know about - it just happens sometimes	0 1 2 3 4
29. to prove to myself how much I can take	0 1 2 3 4	29. to prove to myself how much I can take	0 1 2 3 4
30. for sexual excitement	0 1 2 3 4	30. for sexual excitement	0 1 2 3 4
31. to diminish feeling of sexual arousal	0 1 2 3 4	31. to diminish feeling of sexual arousal	0 1 2 3 4
32. other (please specify) _____	0 1 2 3 4	32. I am "addicted" to doing it	0 1 2 3 4
		33. other (please specify) _____	0 1 2 3 4

CONCLUSION

This guide to the assessment of youth with NSSI is the first to delineate a stepwise approach that considers the range of settings and professionals who might encounter and need to evaluate, at some level, these youth. In certain circumstances, the assessment will, by necessity, be limited in time and focussed on issues such as risk or triage regarding specific needs and services. Assessment of NSSI may require, and often benefits from, the opportunity to revisit and discuss difficulties, both as the youth feels more comfortable disclosing as a therapeutic alliance develops and as additional information becomes available. It is also important to note, as illustrated in the case example, that risk level can change over time such that each encounter, including preliminary intervention or treatment sessions, should include a brief assessment in these areas.

TABLE 8.7   Summary Key for the Ottawa Self-Injury Inventory Functions (OSI-F)*

Affect Regulation: to alleviate acute negative affect/aversive affective arousal

1	to release unbearable tension
4	to stop feeling alone and empty
8	to relieve nervousness/fearfulness
10	to distract me from unpleasant memories
13	to release anger
21	to relieve feelings of sadness or feeling "down"
26	to release frustration

Number of items endorsed (out of 7) as 2 or higher: ___

Anti-dissociation: to end the experience of depersonalization or dissociation

17	to help me escape from uncomfortable feelings or moods
19	to experience physical pain in one area, when the other pain I feel is unbearable
25	to produce a sense of being real when I feel numb and "unreal"

Number of items endorsed (out of 3) as 2 or higher: ___

Anti-Suicide: to replace, compromise with or avoid impulse to commit suicide

23	to stop me from thinking about ideas of killing myself
24	to stop me from acting out ideas of killing myself

Number of items endorsed (out of 2) as 2 or higher: ___

Interpersonal boundaries: to assert one's autonomy/distinction between self and others

11	to change my body image and/or appearance
22	to have control in a situation where no one can influence me

Number of items endorsed (out of 2) as 2 or higher: ___

Interpersonal Influence: to seek help/influence

3	to stop my parents from being angry with me
5	to get care or attention from other people
9	to avoid getting into trouble for something I did
12	to belong to a group
14	to stop my friends/boyfriend/girlfriend from being angry with me
15	to show others how hurt or damaged I am
16	to show others how strong or tough I am

TABLE 8.7   Summary Key for the Ottawa Self-Injury Inventory Functions (OSI-F)*

20	to stop people from expecting so much from me
27	to get out of doing something that I don't want to do

Number of items endorsed (out of 9) as 2 or higher: ___

Self Punishment: to derogate/express anger towards oneself

6	to punish myself

Number of items endorsed (out of 1) as 2 or higher: ___

Sensation seeking: to generate exhilaration or excitement

7	to provide a sense of excitement that feels exhilarating
29	to prove to myself how much I can take
30	for sexual excitement
31	to diminish feeling of sexual arousal

Number of items endorsed (out of 6) as 2 or higher: ___

Addictive Features:

2	to experience a "high" that feels like a drug high
32	I am "addicted" to doing it

Number of items endorsed (out of 2) as 2 or higher: ___

Other:

18	to satisfy voices inside or outside of me telling me to do it
28	for no reason that I know about - it just happens sometimes

* These categories are based on the literature regarding functions of NSSI and are currently under evaluation.

We are also aware that with co-occurring psychiatric disorders, symptoms can change over time, as the youth do not necessarily present at the initial assessment with the threshold of symptoms needed to make a specific diagnosis. In another domain, specific family dynamics or family problems such as alcohol and substance abuse in parents or abuse may be information that is withheld until a solid therapeutic alliance is established. All aspects of the assessment process therefore benefit from a repeated review based on these features.

These guidelines and tools presented for assessment of youth with NSSI provide a practical approach for practitioners. Specific assessment tools are available dependent on need, level of expertise, and level of assessment. It is our hope that providing these tools and guidelines will diminish the often confusing and complicated appearance of this behavior as well as the heightened anxiety that can occur in those who are required to evaluate these youth. Finally, assessment guidelines can be given, but as clinicians are aware, there is no "recipe" or strict approach to the process, as each individual case differs. Ultimately, an effective and insightful assessment is the result of an intuitive, informed, and skilled professional. The guidelines and tools are therefore not a rigid format but suggestions and options for the clinician; one cannot substitute the use of tools or guidelines for the skills and craftsmanship of an experienced professional.

REFERENCES

American Psychiatric Association. (2000). *Diagnostic and statistical manual of mental disorders* (text revision). Washington, DC: Author.

Barber, J. P., Connolly, M. B., Crits-Christoph, P., Gladis, L., & Siqueland, L. (2000). Alliance predicts patients' outcome beyond in-treatment change in symptoms. *Journal of Clinical and Consulting Psychology, 68*(6), 1027–1032.

Connors, R. E. (2000). *Self-injury: Psychotherapy with people who engage in self-inflicted violence.* Northvale, NJ: Jason Aronson.

Dieter, P. J., Nicholls, S. S., & Pearlman, L. A. (2000). Self-injury and self-capacities: Assisting an individual in crisis. *Journal of Clinical Psychology, 56*, 1173–1191.

D'Onofrio, A. A. (2007). *Adolescent self-injury: A comprehensive guide for counselors and health care professionals.* New York: Springer.

Farber, S. K. (2000). *When the body is the target: Self-harm, pain, and traumatic attachments.* Northvale, NJ: Jason Aronson.

Heath, N. L., & Ross, S. (2007). *How I deal with stress.* Unpublished measure.

Heath, N. L., Toste, J. R., & White Kress, V. (2007). [School counselors' experiences with non-suicidal self-injury]. Unpublished raw data.

Horvath, A. O. (2000). The therapeutic relationship from transference to alliance. *Journal of Clinical Psychology/In Session: Psychotherapy in Practice, 56*, 163–173.

Horvath, A. O., & Bedi, R. P. (2002). The alliance. In J. C. Norcross (Ed.), *Psychotherapy relationships that work: Therapist contributions and responsiveness to patients.* New York: Oxford University Press.

Ivanoff, A., Linehan, M. M., & Brown, M. (2001). Dialectical behavior therapy for impulsive self-injurious behaviors. In D. Simeon and E. Hollander (Eds.), *Self-injurious behaviors: Assessment and treatment* (pp. 149–173). Washington, DC: American Psychiatric Publishing.

Joiner, T. E., Walker, R. L., Rudd, M. D., & Jobes, D. A. (1999). Scientizing and routinizing the assessment of suicidality in outpatient practice. *Professional Psychology: Research and Practice, 30*(5), 447–453.

Klonsky, E. D. (2007). The functions of deliberate NSSI: A review of the evidence. *Clinical Psychology Review, 27*, 226–239.

Martin, D. J., Garske, J. P., & Davis, M. K. (2000). Relation of therapeutic alliance with outcome and other variables: A meta-analytic review. *Journal of Consulting and Clinical Psychology, 68*, 438–450.

Lieberman, R. (2007). *Understanding and responding to self-injurious students.* Presentation to the Wyoming Chapter of the Council for Exceptional Children.

Nixon, M. K., Cloutier, P., & Aulakh, H. (2007). Self-Assessement Sheet (SAS). Unpublished measure.

Norcross, J. C. (2002). *Psychotherapy relationships that work*. New York: Oxford Press.

Ross, S., & Heath, N. L. (2002). A study of the frequency of self-mutilation in a community sample of adolescents. *Journal of Youth and Adolescence, 1,* 67–77.

Silverman, M. M., Berman, A. L., Sanddal, N. D., O'Carroll, P. W., & Joiner, T. E. (2007). Rebuilding the Tower of Babel: A revised nomenclature for the study of suicide and suicide behaviors: Part 2. Suicide-related ideations, communications, and behaviors. *Suicide and Life-Threatening Behavior, 37,* 264–277.

Walsh, B. (2006). *Treating self-injury: A practical guide*. New York: Guilford.

Intervention and Prevention Issues

Intervention and Prevention in the Community

JANIS WHITLOCK AND KERRY L. KNOX

In this chapter, the practitioner will gain an understanding of:

- The role development, social, and physical environments may play in the initiation and maintenance of NSSI in community populations
- The nomenclature and a taxonomy that is useful for thinking about community-level intervention and prevention in mental health
- Specific examples of NSSI intervention and prevention efforts
- Issues in prevention related to development, culture, and NSSI

The notion of community, though easy to wield in the abstract, is exceptionally difficult to operationalize in practice. Communities consist of individuals, clusters of individuals, such as families, and institutions with implicit and explicit contracts that guide the complex transactions between and among them. In contemporary use, community is fluid, dynamic, and multifaceted and may be bounded by common location; vocation or experience; history; or social, religious, economic, and political interests. Traditional notions of community and research methods used to study them are increasingly complicated by the diminished role geographic boundaries play in the formation of groups, by proliferation of instantaneous communication modalities, such as the Internet and cell phone technology, and by substantial individual and familial migration in and out of communities. Internet communities are, perhaps, the best example of this because they render obsolete the role of geopolitical boundaries in social exchange, establishment of norms, and perceptions of group membership and belonging.

Despite its elusive nature, community is a common unit of study and intervention. For this to be effective, however, there must be clarity about what constitutes the boundaries of the community of interest and, most importantly, *whose* behavior is of interest in assessment, intervention, and prevention. In psychiatric epidemiology, "community" populations of youth are those identified through community settings such as schools or through nationally representative studies, such as those conducted of self-injury in Great Britain (Hawton & Rodham, 2006). For the purposes of this chapter, *community* will be used to refer to nonclinical settings in which youth are found in high concentration. This may include, but is not limited to, neighborhoods, youth-serving programs, and secondary school and college settings. Although youth communities are increasingly virtual, Internet-based intervention and prevention efforts for virtually defined communities may be quite different than those for geographically defined areas. Although we do offer some suggestions about the need to acknowledge and address the role that virtual communities play in nonsuicidal self-injury (NSSI), we will not discuss strategies for intervening in or preventing NSSI in on-line communities.

This chapter is dedicated to a broad review of literature germane to intervention and prevention of adolescent NSSI in community populations. Because the developmental period in which intervention and prevention efforts take place is an important consideration in crafting effective prevention efforts, we begin with a summary of NSSI in a developmental context. From there we move into a discussion of the NSSI in community contexts intended to build on prior chapters by highlighting the theoretical role that community-level mechanisms play in fostering the initiation and maintenance of NSSI among significant numbers of cognitively intact youth not found in clinical settings. The final segment of this chapter will set forth promising practices for community-level NSSI prevention efforts.

SELF-INJURY IN A DEVELOPMENTAL CONTEXT

There is broad agreement that community-level prevention efforts with youth, regardless of the focus, are most successful when grounded in an understanding of the developmental tasks and processes at play in the populations of interest (Bronfenbrenner, 1979; Eccles & Gootman, 2002; Lerner, 1991). This is particularly true for NSSI because the behavior occurs most often during adolescence (Conterio & Lader, 1998; Favazza, 1996; Walsh, 2006), which suggests that developmental stage plays a role in receptivity and reliance on NSSI as a coping mechanism. Adolescence, regardless of how it is defined, is a distinct stage of life from both childhood and adulthood. Physical and sexual maturity coupled with the need to acquire skills necessary for carrying out adult roles mandate increasing independence and a realignment of social interconnections (Erikson, 1968; Feldman & Elliott, 1990). It is the life period in which childhood gives way to intense concentration on development of the skills, attitudes, and capacities required for adulthood (Erickson, 1968; Havighurst, 1972).

Only early childhood, in which rapid physical, cognitive, social, and emotional changes are obvious, rivals adolescence in the speed and breadth with which changes occur. Over a period of just a few years, childhood bodies become adult bodies with concomitant desires and capacities, needs for physical and emotional intimacy with peers intensify, questions about one's sexual capacities and identity emerge and demand address, the desire for autonomy from parents and other adults clashes with the enduring need for connection and validation from these same individuals, needs for belonging and affirmation of likely success outside family realms emerge, and vocational possibilities and skills must be catalogued and developed. All of these tasks, in turn, must be resolved in a way that permits integrated development of a set of values and behaviors capable of guiding adult actions and decisions and, most importantly, of providing a sense that life is fundamentally meaningful and worthwhile. The brain-behavior-social context interactions that occur during this period have profound implications for emotion and motivation—the depth of which has only just begun to be explored (Dahl, Spear, Kelley, Shaikh, & Clayton, 2004).

The number and complexity of tasks a human being needs to accomplish during adolescence is complicated by variations in the timing with which various cognitive, emotional, and physical capacities are accomplished. For example, studies consistently show few age differences in cognitive processes relevant to risk taking and decision making between adolescents and adults (Steinberg & Cauffman, 1996). Instead, differences in risk behaviors in adolescence and adulthood are attributable to age differences in psychosocial factors that influence self-regulation, namely disjunction between novelty and sensation-seeking (both of which increase dramatically at puberty) and the development of self-regulatory competence (which does not fully mature until early adulthood) (Steinberg, 2004). When timing issues such as these are coupled with psychosocial factors that frustrate or delay healthy developmental processes such as early childhood trauma, biological imbalances or difficult temperamental dispositions, overly demanding or challenging environments, and persistent inconsistency in the nature of the demands of various social environments (e.g., family, peers, school, community), detrimental consequences are likely to result (Lerner & Steinberg, 2004).

Such factors render it unsurprising that less than healthy methods of coping, such as NSSI, emerge with regularity, particularly because NSSI is thought to involve dysregulation of the endogenous opioid system and other limbic system functions that regulate emotion responses (Konicki & Shulz, 1989; Symons, 2002).

Whereas attraction to the violence of the practice may be puzzling, the need met by the function is not. NSSI is an act that is universally acknowledged to be undertaken in cognitively intact youth to regulate emotional imbalance and to communicate distress to the self or others (Chapman, Gratz, & Brown, 2006; Klonsky, 2006; Nock & Prinstein, 2004), and as Conterio and Lader (1998) so aptly point out, NSSI may literally and figuratively serve as an outlet for the "growing pains" of adolescence. Their extensive clinical experience with self-injurious adolescents suggests that NSSI gives form and expression to discomfort with physical changes and sexual impulses, confusion about the twin need for autonomy and connection, the need to perform perfectly in all social situations, and the need for psychological reconciliation of past family or childhood hurt and dysfunction.

Not surprisingly, empirical evidence validates the importance of these four areas (see Yates, 2004 and Walsh, 2006 for review), and it is likely that further investigation into the relationship between NSSI and development will place the behavior as one of multiple contemporary adolescent expressions of angst. However, although a number of biological and intrapersonal processes are clearly at work, the self-mutilative nature of NSSI and the concerning level of prevalence with which it is currently found in youth populations belies the influence of environmental forces as well. Indeed, a large and growing body of research demonstrates that a common set of environmental precursors are largely responsible for the stress and vulnerability that serve as pathways for multiple forms of psychopathology. As Levine and Smolak (2006) so aptly point out in a recent review of literature on eating disorders, "Mental disorders, behavioral problems, and ill health in general flourish when people have too much stress, too little respect for themselves and others, too few personal relationships and too little perceived support, and too few personal, social, and physical resources for meeting their needs" (p. 135). Comments such as the following self-injury message board post exemplify these pathways well:

> I cut myself for two reasons. To feel something and to commit violence that doesn't hurt anyone else. Like many young people who don't "fit" in the average American high school, I swung back and forth between a numbness that I still find scary, and an all-consuming rage at the life I had. At the same time, unlike the Columbine boys, who I had more in common with than I care to think about, I never wanted to hurt anyone else...since I hated myself for not being "normal", I made an excellent target.... One of the things I liked about it was how it continued to burn and ache, like a reminder that I was still there, a klaxon telling me I hadn't actually ceased to exist.

Large and growing numbers of cognitively intact young people are unable to meet core developmental needs to belong, exercise voice, and experience mastery in key developmental areas without engaging in self-injurious behavior of all sorts. This challenging problem cannot be addressed by "fixing" the person without fixing the environments in which they learn and grow. Indeed, from an ecological (Bronfenbrenner, 1979; Lerner, 1995) and public health perspective, NSSI may be best viewed as one of several emerging symptoms that suggest that even relatively average adolescents are finding contemporary western societies increasingly difficult to successfully navigate. Not only have a growing number of books been dedicated to this general thesis (Garbarino, 1995; Hersch, 1998; Levine, 2006; Twenge, 2006), but empirical study of changes in anxiety and psychiatric disorders over the past several generations suggest linear upward trends in rates of mental disorders in youth over the past half century for reasons not solely attributable to biological changes or differences in detection and classification of psychiatric disorders (Benton, Robertson, Tseng, Newton, & Benton, 2003; Birmaher et al., 1996; Erdur-Baker, Aberson, Barrow, & Draper, 2006; Twenge, 2000, 2006).

Whether or not rates of youth struggling to meet developmental needs or deal with childhood adversity have increased, methods of providing short-term relief from distress find fertile soil in populations of adolescents. The combination of high need for self-expression, high drama, and willingness to try out new behaviors and identities can make "alternative" behaviors appealing to individuals or subgroups of youth. Because of the emphasis on being simultaneously accepted by peers and proving oneself unique is a pillar of adolescent development, novel and extreme behaviors may be adopted and passed along, covertly or overtly, quite readily. Successful intervention and prevention are thus likely to be most effective when both developmental stage and processes are taken into consideration. It is also important, however, to consider and address the mechanisms through which behaviors spread in communities of youth.

NSSI IN THE COMMUNITY CONTEXT

When Barent Walsh wrote his dissertation on NSSI in 1987, the behavior was virtually unheard of in community populations. Regarded as a disorder primarily associated with significant cognitive or emotional impairment such as psychosis or borderline personality disorder, it was largely confined to clinical settings (B. Walsh, personal communication, November, 11, 2006). To some extent, this fact reflects the dearth of epidemiological study of NSSI in any population; the only two recognized epidemiological studies prior to the late 1980s (Clendenin & Murphy, 1971; Weissman, 1975) were based on emergency room populations. It also reflects a lack of awareness about the behavior among youth-serving professionals, although whether this is due to ignorance of the behavior or very low prevalence in community populations is not clear.

Unfortunately, lack of baseline data will forever prevent an accurate accounting of historical trends. What is clear at this point is that the behavior is both prevalent and acknowledged among those who work with youth in nonclinical settings (Heath, Toste, Nedecheva, & Charlebois, 2008; Kress, Gibson, & Reynolds, 2004; Ross & Heath, 2002; Whitlock, Eckenrode, & Silverman, 2006; Whitlock, Purington, Eells, & Cummings, 2008). Although growing awareness has prompted research on the phenomenon in community samples, robust assessment of the differences between NSSI in clinical and community populations is currently lacking. What we do know suggests that whereas there are important similarities in form and function across individuals in clinical and community samples, there may be important differences in comorbidity, help-seeking, life trajectories, and contextual contributors to initiation, duration, and meaning. Because community samples often contain some individuals who might also be found in clinical samples, assuming discrete differences between the two samples imposes artificial boundaries that are unlikely to exist. However, studies on community samples suggest the presence of self-injurious individuals who do not fit the clinical profile (Adler & Adler, 2007; Hawton & Rodham, 2006).

Although clearly speculative at this juncture, it is likely that some of the differences in NSSI expression and patterns between clinical and nonclinical samples arise as a result of the fact that NSSI often goes undetected for long periods or indefinitely in community populations of youth (see Hawton & Rodham, 2006, for review). For example, in a recent study of NSSI in a representative sample of college students from two northeastern U.S. universities, 36% reported that no one knew that they self-injured, and only 21.4% indicated that they had discussed their NSSI with a mental health professional (Whitlock, Eckenrode, et al., 2006). The clear capacity of some individuals to function well enough on a day-to-day basis to avoid detection suggests that, if present, conditions that commonly accompany NSSI in clinical populations, such as emotion and cognition regulation disorders, may be less detectible or not present at all in community populations of youth. This leads to questions about whether initiation of NSSI in community samples stems from similar motivations and is maintained by similar mechanisms as in clinical samples.

ROLE OF THE COMMUNITY IN THE INITIATION AND MAINTENANCE OF NSSI

If the widespread assumption that NSSI has increased in prevalence in community populations of youth is correct, we must then ask how awareness of the behavior has spread and through what mechanisms it has been made appealing to large numbers of youth. Although lacking NSSI-specific data germane to this question, studies of the social contexts of behavior consistently show that positive and negative behaviors are socially patterned and often clustered (Berkman & Kawachi, 2000; Evans, 2004; Sameroff & Siefer, 1995). Such nonrandom distribution suggests that social and physical environments play an important role in the way behaviors move from one individual and context to another. With this in mind, social epidemiologists have identified four primary mechanisms through which social environments influence behavior: (a) shaping of norms; (b) providing social (re)enforcement of behaviors; (c) providing (or limiting) opportunities to engage in the behavior; and (d) facilitating or inhibiting the antecedents for the behavior (Berkman & Kawachi, 2000). Considered together, these mechanisms provide a useful framework for understanding how NSSI might spread in community populations of youth.

Rarely can a social setting be held responsible for initiation or perpetuation of a particular behavior. Individuals bring into environments biological predispositions as well as norms, experiences, and expectations derived from other settings they inhabit (families, for example). However, recognition of the role social environments play in behavior adoption and maintenance contains important implications for intervention and prevention. Studies have documented, for example, that within confined institutional spaces populated by individuals susceptible to NSSI, such as inpatient treatment centers or floors, initiation of NSSI by a patient can spur a mini-epidemic among residents (Matthews, 1968; Ross & McKay, 1979; Taiminen, Kallio-Soukainen, Nokso-Koivisto, Kaljonen, & Helenius, 1998). In this case, the setting is populated by individuals who possess many of the biological, experiential, and psychological antecedents often linked to NSSI, contains individuals for whom the practice of other self-damaging behaviors is normative, and often inadvertently rewards those who practice NSSI with much desired staff attention. Although opportunities to employ tools common in NSSI, such as knives and razor blades, may be limited, access to fingernails, sharp corners, and the points of eating utensils are difficult for staff to banish or regulate.

There are, of course, important limitations to generalizing from institutional settings to settings in which a diverse cross section of youth are found, such as schools, neighborhoods, and youth groups. It would be rare in these settings to encounter social environments that concentrate the risk of NSSI in the same way institutional settings might. Nonetheless, the notable prevalence of NSSI in community samples of youth suggests that the social mechanisms through which NSSI spreads are present in community settings as well. Moreover, because adolescents tend to group themselves by common interest and behavioral practices, it is possible that NSSI behavior in community settings among youth is both diffuse (found in individuals who conform to the stereotypical secretive and isolated image) and concentrated in subgroups where it may performed as a part of group membership. A recent study of NSSI in "Goth" groups in the UK (Young, Sweeting, & West, 2006) supports this assumption. Similar findings have been documented in unpublished data collected by Young and Sweeting, which is undergoing analysis. In a survey of secondary school nurses and counselors in secondary school settings across New York state, a quarter of the 300 respondents indicated seeing students who injured themselves alone or together as a part of group membership. In light of these trends and the ubiquitous assumption that NSSI is increasingly prevalent in community settings, prevention efforts will be aided by consideration of the ways in which pro-self-injury norms, opportunities, reinforcement, and antecedents are established and maintained in community settings.

SELF-INJURY NORMS, OPPORTUNITIES, REINFORCEMENT, AND ANTECEDENTS IN COMMUNITY SETTINGS

Although identifying the point at which NSSI began to surface in community populations in more than isolated pockets is impossible, it is possible to trace the point at which it began to enter mainstream culture and media. Unpublished data collected by Whitlock shows that from 1993 to 2004, over 14 pop icons revealed self-injurious habits in various media outlets; similar disclosures by popular stars prior to that time were rare. Although not all possessed widespread popular appeal, some did. Princess Diana, Johnny Depp, Angelina Jolie, and Christina Ricci all publicly admitted to NSSI and shared detailed information about the medicative and calming sensation the behavior produced for them.

The same period saw a large increase in the number of mainstream movies, music, and news articles with NSSI scenes or themes (Whitlock, Purington, & Gershkovich, in press). NSSI scenes and themes have also appeared in television dramas such as *Grey's Anatomy* and *Seventh Heaven* and even comedies such as *Will and Grace*. While some of the media attention dedicated to the behavior is aimed to educate or to portray fictitious events and characters, the net result may highlight NSSI as a cognitively available emotional outlet for individuals predisposed to the behavior, similar to the pattern Brumberg (1992) observed in the spread of anorexia nervosa in the 1980s. The concomitant popularity of tattooing and piercing that emerged in the late 1980s as well as the emphasis on "extreme" behaviors obvious in television programming and advertisements may also contribute to normalizing NSSI.

Increased awareness and popularity of any behavior assumes an entirely new dimension when coupled with the ascension of the digital age. Youth born in 1985 and after, otherwise known as "Digital Natives," tend to use the Internet as the first stop in information gathering and socializing (Lenhart, Madden, & Hitlin, 2005). The power of the Internet to bring individuals together based on shared interests in a variety of forums—from message boards to sites where homemade videos can be uploaded and shared such as YouTube—provides historically unparalleled opportunity.

The Internet may be particularly appealing to adolescents and young adults because healthy social and emotional development relies on their ability to find acceptance and belonging in social groups, establish meaningful relationships, and to establish interpersonal intimacy (Reis & Shaver, 1988; Sullivan, 1953). Among those who self-injure, on-line anonymity may assist in managing the shame, isolation, and distress that so often accompany the behavior (McKenna & Bargh, 2000; Whitlock, Powers, & Eckenrode, 2006). Because on-line exchange can fill-in where off-line exchange fails, virtual interaction may provide the sense, illusory or real, that core developmental needs for community, intimacy, and honesty are met—at least for a while (Whitlock, Lader, & Conterio, 2007). Unfortunately, it is also possible that the ease with which one can identify NSSI communities, share stories, and solicit information enhances opportunities for NSSI to become normative both on- and off-line (Whitlock, Lader, et al., 2007).

Moreover, growing evidence that participation in virtual communities is a factor in off-line behavior (Brodie et al., 2000; Rideout, 2002; Wilson, Peebles, Hardy, & Litt, 2006) suggests a mechanism through which virtual life and experiences affect nonvirtual life. On-line discussion of techniques, triggers, and attitudes toward off-line help-seeking may shape behavioral choices outside of the virtual realm that are later brought back, shared, and used to assure support and membership. As has been documented with disordered eating and violence in the media (Bushman & Huesman, 2000; Donnerstein & Smith, 2000; Malamuth & Impett, 2000), proliferation of NSSI on the Internet may fundamentally reinforce NSSI as a behavioral option. In addition to cultural reinforcement, the biological, intrapsychic, and social functions cited by self-injurious youth for initiating the behavior also serve to maintain it (see Chapter 4). Also, as is true for other risk behaviors, once present in any concentration within highly youth-populated settings such as schools, the opportunity for the spread of NSSI may be enhanced. This is particularly true where the practice is distributed among a variety of social groups or used as part of group membership, as there is growing evidence to suggest (Walsh, 2006; Young et al., 2006).

Environments in which antecedents to NSSI are found in high concentration are the final mechanism through which the social epidemiology framework used here suggests NSSI might spread (Berkman & Kawachi, 2000). As reviewed in Chapter 13 (on inpatient treatment), among clinical populations, the most commonly identified antecedents of NSSI are a history of trauma (most often sexual abuse), emotion and personality disorders, disordered eating, social isolation, suicidality, and being female or a member of a minority sexual orientation group. Community settings with high proportions of individuals possessing these traits may be at higher risk for initiating and maintaining NSSI.

INTERVENTION AND PREVENTION OF
NSSI IN COMMUNITY SETTINGS

NSSI behavior is frightening and worrisome for many youth and adults. This is particularly true for adults who did not grow up with NSSI as part of their social landscape and who tend to view it as a suicidal gesture. The clear and pervasive presence of the behavior in community settings, however, raises the need for detection, intervention, and prevention approaches likely to be efficacious in a variety of community settings.

COMMUNITY-LEVEL PREVENTION
AND INTERVENTION

Because *community* is such an all-encompassing term, defining the target population for a particular intervention or prevention is a crucial first step. The target population consists of the individuals or entities to which services are focused and in which it is hoped change will be effected. When the community is defined as a setting with clearly defined physical or institutional boundaries, such as a school, detention facility, or other youth-serving program, the tasks associated with NSSI intervention and prevention necessarily occur within the scope and reach of the physical and associational boundaries of the community. A school, for example, typically identifies as its target population the student body (or particular individuals at heightened risk within its student body) and focuses detection, intervention, and prevention efforts only on this group. Larger community-level interventions, however, often occur across geopolitically defined areas, such as neighborhoods or school districts and thus are concerned with a much larger and more diverse population of youth.

Although approaches vary, there are important commonalities. The Institute of Medicine nomenclature for understanding intervention and prevention (Mrazek & Haggerty, 1994) offers a useful taxonomy for thinking about community-level intervention and prevention in mental health. As illustrated in Table 9.1, the Institute of Medicine breaks prevention into three levels that differ by approach, target, and objective. It is important to note that prevention subsumes intervention and detection because depending on the level of prevention specified and the setting in which it takes place, it includes intervention and detection activities.

Universal prevention approaches target an entire population without regard to the particular level of risk among individuals or groups within the population. Universal prevention is typically (a) targeted to groups rather than individuals; (b) focused on groups of individuals assumed to be healthy, although possibly at risk of the behavior by virtue of their circumstance (such as their age, in this case); (c) intended to change group norms, policies, or practices; and (d) founded on credible evidence or theory (Cowen, 1973, 1983). Examples specific to NSSI include teaching or promoting media literacy or incorporating coping skills training into educational curricula likely to reach large numbers of students.

Selective prevention approaches focus on nonsymptomatic individuals considered at high risk due to biological, psychological, and sociocultural factors. These approaches are designed to target risk factors believed to predispose individuals to the disorder in question. Examples specific to NSSI include focused emotion regulation training or reduction of help-seeking stigmas to individuals or groups of youth identified as at risk of NSSI.

Indicated, also called targeted, prevention focuses on individuals with very clear precursors to the behavior of interest, such as episodes of dissociation or presence of borderline personality disorder symptoms. Indicated prevention efforts are time and cost intensive in community settings where detailed mental health assessments are not typical or feasible. For this reason, we will only discuss frameworks and practices likely to be effective in universal and selective prevention efforts. It is also important to stress that, to our knowledge, there have been *no* evaluated prevention initiatives specific to NSSI. We can, however, make recommendations based on the review earlier in this chapter as well as lessons learned from suicide and disordered eating prevention programs because both of these have been strongly linked to NSSI (Favazza & Conterio, 1989; Favazza, DeRosear, & Conterio, 1989; Pattison & Kahan, 1983; Whitlock, Eckenrode, et al., 2006).

UNIVERSAL PREVENTION APPROACHES FOR NSSI

Population approaches, which include community-level interventions to prevent NSSI, are by no means the norm. Prevention research in the mental health arena often has struggled to ensure that interventions are theoretically and empirically tied to known risks, even as it appears that theory-driven interventions are more likely to be rigorously evaluated and to result in the desired outcomes (Mrazek & Haggerty, 1994). Although there now is a growing body of research regarding risk factors for NSSI, this has yet to be tied in a systematic fashion to prevention efforts that would be likely to affect a large proportion of young adults.

Models such as that posited by Levine and Smolak (2006)—the nonspecific vulnerability-stressor model (NSVS)—bring together empirical and theoretical knowledge about both adolescent development and underlying social-environmental causes of maladaptive behaviors. Derived from a broad and sound body of empirical study and theoretical principles, NSVS tenets apply well to what is known about NSSI specifically and meld developmental considerations with an emphasis on setting-level intervention (e.g., families, schools, peer groups, youth groups, etc.). The NSVS model stresses the teaching of life skills for coping with stress, provision of opportunities to attain

TABLE 9.1 Application of the Institute of Medicine Nomenclature to NSSI

Terminology	Target population	Prevention goal	Examples of NSSI-specific objectives
Universal prevention	Entire population	Changes in group norms or practices, present in the larger population, known or theoretically believed to reduce risk and increase protective factors.	• Involve multiple social ecologies (school, neighborhood, peer groups, youth groups, families, etc.) • Capacity to cope • Medial and digital literacy • Social connectedness • Social isolation • Promote help-seeking when signs of distress are present • Train individuals working with youth to recognize and respond to signs of SI and its precursors • Equip youth to recognize signs of distress • Equip parents to recognize and respond to signs of NSSI • Develop protocols for dealing with NSSI behavior in specific settings (such as schools and youth programs)
Selective (or targeted) prevention	Individuals or subgroups at significantly higher than average risk of developing mental disorders or adverse outcomes.	Changes in attitude, knowledge, and behavior of target population	• Train individuals who work with youth to identify those at risk • Enhance capacity to cope and help-seeking coping capacity in target group • Provide counseling services for target youth aimed at reducing risk and enhancing coping • Youth voice? • Engage parents and/or other key adults in lives of target population in achieving objectives
Indicated preventive	High risk individuals with detectable precursors to the condition of interest	Reduction of precursor and prodromal signs and symptoms	• Increase screening for target population • Vigorously treat youth with early NSSI behavior (e.g., single NSSI incident) • Provide counseling services for target youth aimed at reducing risk and enhancing coping • Actively identify and engage self-injurious youth in therapy

goals and feelings of competence and mastery, and a focus on increasing social connectedness at the individual and setting level. Prototypical elements of the approach emphasize:

- Broad incorporation of personal and interpersonal exercises for understanding and improving self-esteem, internal locus of control, and individual identity
- Peer and individual group-level instruction in ways to increase life skills
- Student involvement and engagement in development of environments that produce positive change
- Focus on altering attitudes and behaviors of adults, institutions, and peer groups to create supportive environments, with healthier norms and a manageable number of stressors (Levine & Smolak, 2006, p. 146).

Many of the elements featured in the NSVS model resonate with approaches commonly used in clinical settings to treat self-injurious youth. For example, dialectical behavior therapy, of which enhancing capacity to cope and mindfulness is a major element, is used often with significant success (Comtois, 2002; Hawton et al., 1998; Linehan, Armstrong, Suarez, Allmon, & Heard, 1991; Walsh, 2006). Similarly, Conterio and Lader (1998) use a dynamic and relation-based approach with which they report significant success.

Although not focused on youth, the U.S. Air Force's (USAF) Suicide Prevention Program illustrates a universal prevention initiative designed to change setting-level norms, provide (re)enforcement for positive help-seeking, and intervene in behavioral antecedents (Knox, Litts, Talcott, Feig, & Caine, 2003). One of the primary components includes identification and training of community gatekeepers to reach and refer those individuals at immediate risk of suicide and other self-damaging behaviors. Community gatekeepers are those with consistent access to enlistees, such as USAF commanders. Gatekeeper training is coupled with changes in policies that affect help-seeking, such as reduction in confidentiality policies for those seeking help from mental health services. By limiting confidentiality for disclosures to gatekeepers, the number of self-referrals to ambulatory mental health services increases which, in turn, enhances the likelihood that enlistees in danger of suicide are detected and assisted early. Another major target of the training includes institutionalizing a buddy system in which all USAF members are trained to recognize early signs and symptoms of someone in danger of harming him- or herself. This enhances capacity to recognize distress in oneself and others and reinforces the value and likelihood of help-seeking.

Case Study: Suicide Prevention in the U.S. Air Force

The USAF suicide prevention program is one of the only community-level, persistent, multidimensional approaches to suicide prevention. A multidimensional approach captures all of the aspects likely to be predictors of successful implementation. These include characteristics of communities (in the USAF, these include the geographical location and size of the various USAF bases, or communities); the theoretical framework of each of multiple interventions (in the USAF, the Eleven Initiatives), and the integrated strategic approach (universal, selective, or indicated) chosen to deliver multiple interventions. Taken together, this multidimensional universe will likely require institutionalization at the community level to support both implementation and ongoing fidelity.

The USAF's Eleven Initiatives were designed to alter social norms, increase knowledge and awareness, promote early help-seeking, and alter policies that might impede help-seeking and treatment for suicidality. They include leader awareness education and training, incorporation of suicide prevention practices into professional curricula, development of detection and referral policies, increased prevention focus among mental health personnel, establishment of a seamless system of services, tools for assessing behavioral heath, and central surveillance. Evaluation of the program has shown tremendous success in reducing the rate of suicide in the USAF (Knox et al., 2003) and is now being adapted to college settings.

Nine years worth of outcome data show consistent reduction in the rate of suicide and related outcomes. For example, there have been measurable reductions in risk for accidental death, homicide, and moderate and severe family violence (Knox et. al., 2003). The effectiveness of the initiative has led to an adaptation of the main components in a college setting under the lead of the second author, Knox. Although NSSI is well understood to not represent a suicidal attempt or gesture, a growing body of evidence suggests that it is a risk factor for suicide (Muehlenkamp & Guiterrez, 2004; Nock, Joiner, Gordon, Lloyd-Richardson, & Prinstein, 2006; Whitlock & Knox, 2007). Such evidence suggests that similar community-level risk reduction strategies may be effective for NSSI.

Negotiating and balancing connectedness and autonomy is a core and often difficult task for adolescents in western countries. Providing environments simultaneously capable of fostering a sense of individual accomplishment and connection with others may emerge as a critical component of both universal and targeted prevention efforts. In the case of NSSI, helping peers and parents recognize early signs of distress, of which NSSI is one, is imperative because these are the groups most likely to be those first "gifted" with knowledge of the behavior. Because the first response to such disclosures plays a large role in what is subsequently shared (Conterio & Lader, 1998; Walsh, 2006), peers and parents are quite literally the "front line" in NSSI prevention and intervention. In light of the role that media and the Internet may play in spreading knowledge of NSSI, inclusion of media and virtual literacy campaigns is also warranted. Whereas these need not be focused specifically on NSSI, teaching youth to discern between healthy and unhealthy examples of coping may help prevent a variety of behaviors linked to poor coping mechanisms including, but not limited to, NSSI.

A note of caution in designing universal prevention strategies is warranted. Because resources for universal prevention efforts are often limited, efforts to raise awareness through one-shot assemblies or awareness campaigns are common. In their review of eating disorder prevention strategies and research, Levine and Smolak (2006) summarize research that suggests that single-shot awareness raising strategies (e.g., educational assemblies or workshops) are, at best, either not effective or only effective in raising short-term knowledge. At worst, they are linked to increases in the behavior they intend to stop—particularly in high school and college populations. Similarly, repeated and rigorous evaluation of the popular DARE program aimed at reducing drug use among youth has also been shown to be ineffective and, at worst, harmful (Brown, D'Emidio-Caston, & Pollard, 1997; Lynam et al., 1999). Although the reasons for the ambivalent findings in studies aimed at evaluating time-delimited awareness raising are not clear, they may mirror some of the same mechanisms at work in studies that find suicide risk to be heightened by press coverage of a recent completed suicide (see Gould, Jamieson, & Romer, 2003, for review). Known as the "Werther effect," scholars have documented evidence for the hypothesis that promoting awareness of suicide may appeal to those susceptible to the behavior (Gould et al., 2003; Phillips, 1974). It is thus important that universal prevention efforts be grounded in sound theory, be mindful of possible unintended consequences, and be focused as much on addressing underlying behavioral mechanisms as in raising awareness about the phenomenon itself (particularly within the broad youth population; adult stakeholders will need specific information).

Case Study: Reduction of Mental Illness in a College Population

The success of the USAF suicide prevention project has led to replication in other settings. One of these involves an adaptation of the approach in college settings where it has been broadened to include NSSI as well as other forms of mental illness and distress. Although designed with the same overarching goals as the USAF suicide prevention project, activities associated with the college project are tailored to meet different contextual capacities and demands than those confronted in the USAF project. The college adaptation includes three primary components: baseline and ongoing population surveillance (via Internet-based survey of mental health and well-being outcomes of interest), enhancement of clinical competency in effective treatment of mental health issues, and gatekeeper training for rapid detection and intervention. The primary objective is to change institutional norms and procedures, to raise awareness and capacity to detect and respond to mental distress, and to encourage student help-seeking. In the college project gatekeepers consist of residence hall advisors, faculty, and administrative and custodial staff with consistent student contact. Each of these groups is trained to recognize and respond to signs of student distress through presentations and role plays. College mental health providers are trained in clinical methods empirically demonstrated to reduce distress and the subsequent likelihood of self-harm. These components are complimented by university-wide campaigns intended to reduce stigma related to help-seeking and foster adoption of positive coping strategies.

SELECTIVE (OR TARGETED) PREVENTION APPROACHES FOR NSSI

Selective prevention approaches differ from universal approaches largely in the population they strive to reach. Whereas specific activities may vary somewhat from those associated with universal approaches aimed at addressing underlying mechanisms, many of the goals do not. In selective prevention, those deemed at risk of developing self-injurious behaviors are those to whom resources and intervention are directed. In keeping with this, selective prevention activities are often more narrow in scope and center on development and maintenance of a system for detecting and intervening with specific youth at higher than average risk. In the case of NSSI, youth at higher than average risk may be those who evidence a number of characteristics known to be associated with NSSI (see review above and Chapter 5). These characteristics may include poor coping mechanisms, a history of trauma and familial difficulties, a history of emotional or personality disorders, the presence of disordered eating or other self-harming behaviors such as drug or alcohol use and smoking, bisexual or questioning sexual orientation, self-depreciating cognitive appraisal style, or strong negative emotionality. Physiological problems associated with NSSI include sleep disorders and the tendency to somaticize stress. Association with friends who self-injure is another risk factor.

Because so many of these risk factors are associated with a myriad of other unhealthy behaviors, all targeted prevention approaches with this population may be more widely effective when aimed at enhancing interpersonal, intrapersonal, and environmental mechanisms known to serve as protective factors in NSSI and other risk behaviors. They are also likely to be most effective when mindful of the ways in which each setting might inadvertently support NSSI norms, social reinforcement, opportunities, and antecedents and when addressing salient development-related struggles and needs.

At the individual level, this broader approach might include training at-risk youth related to positive coping mechanisms, balanced cognitive appraisal styles, and emotion regulation. It may also include facilitating access to individuals and opportunities to experience mastery, enhance interpersonal skills, and develop other developmentally appropriate skills. At the institution level, selective prevention efforts should focus on the development of protocols for detecting and responding to NSSI behaviors, identifying and intervening in individuals and groups for which NSSI is or may become normative, structuring responses to avoid inadvertently rewarding and thus reinforcing the behavior, and limiting opportunities for self-injurious practices (if possible). In line with this and as described in the previous chapter, protocols typically include staff training on the signs and symptoms of NSSI (and, ideally, other forms of mental distress) and designation of one or more point people to whom self-injurious youth are referred. Easily accessible therapeutic resources for youth deemed at higher than average risk are also important. As with universal prevention approaches, targeting settings of particular influence on the young person's life outside the institution or group in question, such as families and peer groups, enhances likelihood of success since because parents and peers wield influence. This influence, depending on its nature, may strengthen or undermine targeted prevention efforts.

ISSUES IN PREVENTION: DEVELOPMENT, CULTURE, AND UNINTENDED CONSEQUENCES

All prevention efforts are strengthened when universal, selective, and indicated approaches are pursued simultaneously. Selective and indicated prevention strategies, for example, will be stronger when coupled with efforts to change norms, policies, and practices across the multiple ecologies in which youth develop. Likewise, universal prevention approaches are most powerful when concentrated services for youth at particular risk can be offered in tandem. Similarly, they will be most effective when developmental trajectories of individuals and health conditions are taken into consideration as well. For example, delivering interventions at key periods of transition, such as entry into elementary, middle school, or college helps establish norms and expectations at junctures when youth are particularly receptive to acquiring them. Another approach focuses more on immediate risk factor reduction among those at risk during a critical window relative to the behavior. For example, adolescent drug prevention programs teach social skills and resistance training just before the major period of exposure to drugs (Botvin, Baker, Dusenbury, Botvin, & Diaz, 1995). Similar approaches are used in the prevention of HIV/AIDS (Kim, Stanton, Li, Dickersin,

& Galbraith, 1997). Finally, no prevention effort will be successful if it is not undertaken in a manner that is both mindful and respectful of the cultural values in which they are to be a part. As Armando Favazza (1996) so aptly points out in his anthropological study of NSSI that the meaning of NSSI differs radically across time, culture, and context. Although empirical study extending Favazza's observations is sorely lacking, anyone designing prevention efforts in populations other than their own is well advised to understand thoroughly the meanings as well as intended and possibly unintended consequences of their actions.

REFERENCES

Adler, P. A., & Adler, P. (2007). The demedicalization of self-injury from psychopathology to sociological deviance. *Journal of Contemporary Ethnography, 36*, 537–570.

Benton, S. A., Robertson, J. M., Tseng, W. C., Newton, F. B., & Benton, S. L. (2003). Changes in counseling center client problems across 13 years. *Professional Psychology: Research and Practice, 34*(1), 66–72.

Berkman, L. F., & Kawachi, I. (2000). A historical framework for social epidemiology. In L. F. Berkman & I. Kawachi (Eds.), *Social epidemiology.* Oxford, UK: Oxford University Press.

Birmaher, B., Ryan, N. D., Williamson, D. E., Brent, D. A., Kaufman, J., Dahl, R. E., et al. (1996). Childhood and adolescent depression: A review of the past 10 years. *Journal of the American Academy of Child and Adolescent Psychiatry, 35*(11), 1427–1439.

Botvin, G. J., Baker, E., Dusenbury, L. D., Botvin, E. M., & Diaz, T. (1995). Long-term follow-up results of a randomized drug abuse prevention trial in a white middle-class population. *Journal of the American Medical Association, 273*, 1106–1112.

Brodie, M., Flournoy, R. E., Altman, D. E., Blendon, R. J., Benson, J. M., & Rosenbaum, M. D. (2000). Health information, the Internet, and the digital divide. *Health Affairs, 19*(6), 255–265.

Bronfenbrenner, U. (1979). *The ecology of human development: Experiments by nature and design.* Cambridge, UK: Harvard University Press.

Brown, J. H., D'Emidio-Caston, M., & Pollard, J. A. (1997). Students and substances: Social power in drug education. *Educational Evaluation and Policy Analysis, 19*, 65–82.

Brumberg, J. J. (1992). From psychiatric syndrome to "communicable" disease: The case of anorexia nervosa. In C. Rosenberg & J. Golden (Eds.), *Framing disease* (pp. 134–154). Piscataway, NJ: Rutgers University Press.

Bushman, B. J., & Huesmann, L. R. (2000). Effects of televised violence on aggression. In D. G. Singer & J. L. Singer (Eds.), *Handbook of children and the media.* Thousand Oaks: CA: Sage.

Chapman, A. L., Gratz, K. L., & Brown, M. Z. (2006). Solving the puzzle of deliberate self-harm: The experiential avoidance model. *Behavior Research and Therapy, 44*(3), 371–394.

Clendenin, W. W., & Murphy, G. E. (1971). Wrist cutting. *Archives of General Psychiatry, 25*, 465–469.

Comtois, K. A. (2002). A review of interventions to reduce the prevalence of parasuicide. *Psychiatric Services, 53*(9), 1138–1144.

Conterio, K., & Lader, W. (1998). *Bodily harm: The breakthrough healing program for self injurers.* New York: Hyperion Press.

Cowen, E. L. (1973). Social and community intervention. *Annual Review of Psychology, 24,* 423–472.

Cowen, E. L. (1983). Primary prevention in mental health: Past, present, and future. In L. A. Jason, J. N. Moritsugu, & S. S. Farber (Eds.), *Preventive psychology: Theory, research, and practice* (pp. 11–25). New York: Pergamon.

Dahl, R., Spear, L. P., Kelley, A., Shaikh, R., & Clayton, R. (2004). Preface. *Annals of the New York Academy of Sciences, 1021,* xi–xii.

Donnerstein, E., & Smith, S. (2000). Sex in the media: Theory, influences, and solutions. In D. G. Singer & J. L. Singer (Eds.), *Handbook of children and the media.* Thousand Oaks, CA: Sage.

Eccles, J. S., & Gootman, J. A. (2002). *Community programs to promote youth development.* Washington, DC: National Academy Press.

Erdur-Baker, O., Aberson, C. L., Barrow, J. C., & Draper, M. R. (2006). Nature and severity of college students' psychological concerns: A comparison of clinical and nonclinical national samples. *Professional Psychology: Research and Practice, 37*(3), 317–323.

Erikson, E. H. (1968). *Identity: Youth and crises.* New York: W. W. Norton.

Evans, G. W. (2004). The environment of childhood poverty. *American Psychologist, 59*(2), 77–92.

Favazza, A. R. (1996). *Bodies under siege: Self mutilation and body modification in culture and psychiatry* (2nd ed.). Baltimore, MD: Johns Hopkins University Press.

Favazza, A. R., & Conterio, K. (1989). Female habitual self-mutilators. *Acta Psychiatry Scandinavia, 79,* 283–289.

Favazza, A. R., DeRosear, L., & Conterio, K. (1989). Self-mutilation and eating disorders. *Suicide & Life-Threatening Behavior, 19*(4), 352–361.

Feldman, S. S., & Elliott, G. R. (Eds.). (1990). *At the threshold: The developing adolescent.* Cambridge: Harvard University Press.

Garbarino, J. (1995). *Raising our children in a socially toxic environment.* San Fransico: Josey-Bass.

Gould, M., Jamieson, P., & Romer, D. (2003). Media contagion and suicide among the young. *American Behavioral Scientist, 46*(9), 1269–1284.

Havighurst, R. J. (1972). *Developmental tasks and education.* New York: David McKay.

Hawton, K., Arensman, E., Townsend, E., Bremner, S., Feldman, E., Goldney, R., et al. (1998). Deliberate self-harm: Systematic review of efficacy of psychosocial and pharmacological treatments in preventing repetition. *British Medical Journal, 317*(7156), 441–447.

Hawton, K., & Rodham, K. (2006). *By their own young hand: Deliberate self-harm and suicidal ideas in adolescents.* London: Jessica Kingsley.

Heath, N. L., Toste, J. R., Nedecheva, T., & Charlebois, A. (2008). An examination of non-suicidal self-injury among college students. *Journal of Mental Health Counseling, 30*(2), 1–20.

Hersch, P. (1998). *A tribe apart: A journey into the heart of American adolescence.* New York: Ballantine.

Kim, N., Stanton, B., Li, X., Dickersin, K., & Galbraith, J. (1997). Effectiveness of the 40 adolescent AIDS-risk reduction interventions: A quantitative review. *Journal of Adolescent Health, 20*(3), 204–215.

Klonsky, E. D. (2006). The functions of deliberate self-injury: A review of the evidence. *Clinical Psychology Review, 27,* 226–239.

Knox, K., Litts, D. A., Talcott, G. W., Feig, J. C., & Caine, E. D. (2003). Risk of suicide and related adverse outcomes after exposure to a suicide prevention programme in the US Air Force: Cohort study. *British Medical Journal, 327:* 1376–1380.

Konicki, P. E., & Shulz, S. C. (1989). Rationale for clinical trials of opiate antagonists in treating patients with personality disorders and self-injurious behavior. *Psychopharmacology Bulletin, 25,* 556–563.

Kress, V. E. W., Gibson, D. M., & Reynolds, C. A. (2004). Adolescents who self-injure: Implications and strategies for school counselors. *Professional School Counseling, 7*(3), 195–200.

Lenhart, A., Madden, M., & Hitlin, P. (2005). Youth are leading the transition to a fully wired and mobile nation. *Pew Internet and American Life Project, Teens and Technology,* 1–48.

Lerner, R. M. (1991). Changing organism-context relations as the basic process of development: A developmental contextual perspective. *Developmental Psychology, 27*(1), 27–32.

Lerner, R. M. (1995). *America's youth in crisis: Challenges and options for programs and policies.* Thousand Oaks: Sage.

Lerner, R. M., & Steinberg, L. (Eds.). (2004). *Handbook of adolescent psychology* (2nd ed.). Hoboken, NJ: John Wiley & Sons.

Levine, M. (2006). *The price of privilege: How parental pressure and material advantage are creating a generation of disconnected and unhappy kids.* New York: Harper Collins.

Levine, M. P., & Smolak, L. (2006). *The prevention of eating problems and eating disorders.* Mahwah, NY: Lawrence Erlbaum Associates.

Linehan, M. M., Armstrong, H. E., Suarez, A., Allmon, D., & Heard, H. L. (1991). Cognitive-behavioral treatment of chronically parasuicidal borderline patients. *Archives of General Psychiatry, 48*(12), 1060–1064.

Lynam, D. R., Milich, R., Zimmerman, R., Novak, S. P., Logan, T. K., Martin, C., et al. (1999). Project DARE: No effects at 10-year follow-up. *Journal of Consulting and Clinical Psychology, 67*(4), 590–593.

Malamuth, N. M., & Impett, E. A. (2000). Research on sex in the media: What do we know about effects on children and adolescents? In D. G. Singer & J. L. Singer (Eds.), *Handbook of children and the media.* Thousand Oaks, CA: Sage.

Matthews, P. C. (1968). Epidemic NSSI in an adolescent unit. *International Journal of Social Psychiatry, 14,* 125–133.

McKenna, K. Y. A., & Bargh, J. A. (2000). Plan 9 from cyberspace: The implications of the Internet for personality and social psychology. *Personality and Social Psychology Review, 4*(1), 57–75.

Mrazek, P. J., & Haggerty, R. J. (Eds.). (1994). *Reducing the risks for mental disorders: Frontiers for prevention intervention research (report of the Institute of Medicine's Committee on Prevention of Mental Disorders).* Washington, DC: National Academy Press.

Muehlenkamp, J. J., & Gutierrez, P. M. (2004). An investigation of differences between self-injurious behavior and suicide attempts in a sample of adolescents. *Suicide and Life Threatening Behavior, 34,* 12–23.

Nock, M. K., Joiner, T. E., Gordon, K. H., Lloyd-Richardson, E., & Prinstein, M. J. (2006). Non-suicidal self-injury among adolescents: Diagnostic correlates and relation to suicide attempts. *Psychiatry Research, 144*(1), 65–72.

Nock, M. K., & Prinstein, M. J. (2004). A functional approach to the assessment of self-mutilative behavior. *Journal of Consulting and Clinical Psychology, 72*(5), 885–890.

Pattison, E. M., & Kahan, J. (1983). The deliberate self-harm syndrome. *American Journal of Psychiatry, 140*(7), 867–872.

Phillips, D. P. (1974). The influence of suggestion on suicide: Substantive and theoretical implications of the Werther effect. *American Sociological Review, 39,* 340–354.

Reis, H. T., & Shaver, P. (1988). Intimacy as an interpersonal process. In S. Duck (Ed.), *Handbook of personal relationships* (pp. 367–389).

Rideout, V. (2002). Generation Rx.com: What are young people really doing online? *Marketing Health Services, Spring,* 27–30.

Ross, S., & Heath, N. (2002). A study of the frequency of self-mutilation in a community sample of adolescents. *Journal of Youth and Adolescence, 31*(1), 66–77.

Ross, R. R., & McKay, H. B. (1979). *Self mutilation.* Lexington, MA: Lexington Books.

Sameroff, A. J., & Siefer, R. (1995). Accumulation of environmental risk and child mental health. In H. E. Fitzgerald, B. M. Lester & B. S. Zuckerman (Eds.), *Children of poverty: Research, health, and policy issues* (pp. 233–254). New York: Garland.

Steinberg, H., & Cauffman, E. (1996). Maturity of judgment in adolescence: Psychosocial factors in adolescent decision-making. *Law and human behavior, 20,* 249–272.

Steinberg, L. (2004). Risk taking in adolescents: What changes, and why? *Annals of the New York Academy of Sciences, 1021,* 51–58.

Sullivan, H. S. (1953). *The interpersonal theory of psychiatry.* New York: W. W. Norton.

Symons, F. S. (2002). Self-injury and pain: Models and mechanisms. In S. R. Schroeder, M. L. Oster-Granite, & T. Thompson (Eds.), *Self-injurious behavior: Gene–brain–behavior relationships* (pp. 223–234). Washington, DC: American Psychological Association.

Taiminen, T. J., Kallio-Soukainen, K., Nokso-Koivisto, H., Kaljonen, A., & Helenius, H. (1998). Contagion of deliberate self-harm among adolescent inpatients. *Journal of the American Academy of Child & Adolescent Psychiatry, 37*(2), 211–217.

Twenge, J. M. (2000). The age of anxiety? Birth cohort change in anxiety and neuroticism, 1952–1993. *Journal of Personality and Social Psychology, 79*(6), 1007–1021.

Twenge, J. M. (2006). *Generation me: Why today's young Americans are more confident, assertive, entitled—and more miserable than ever before.* New York: Free Press.

Walsh, B. W. (2006). *Treating NSSI: A practical guide.* New York: Guilford Press.

Weissman, M. (1975). Wrist cutting: Relationship between clinical observations and epidemiological findings. *Archives of General Psychiatry, 32*(9), 1166–1171.

Whitlock, J., Eckenrode, J., & Silverman, D. (2006). Self-injurious behaviors in a college population. *Pediatrics, 117,* 1939–1948.

Whitlock, J. L., & Knox, K. (2007). The relationship between suicide and self-injury in a young adult population. *Archives of Pediatrics and Adolescent Medicine. 161*(7), 634–640.

Whitlock, J. L., Lader, W., & Conterio, K. (2007). "The role of virtual communities in self-injury treatment: Clinical considerations." *Journal of Clinical Psychology/In Session, 63,* 1135–1143.

Whitlock, J. L., Powers, J. L., & Eckenrode, J. (2006). The cutting edge: The Internet and adolescent NSSI. *Developmental Psychology, 42*(3), DOI: 10.1037/0012-1649.1042.1033.1000.

Whitlock, J. L., Purington, A., Eells, G., & Cummings, N. (2008). *Self-injurious behavior in college populations: Perceptions and experiences of college mental health providers.* Manuscript submitted for publication.

Whitlock, J. L., Purington, A., & Gershkovich, M. (in press). Influence of the media on self injurious behavior. In M. Nock (Ed.), *Understanding nonsuicidal self-injury: Current science and practice.* Washington, DC: American Psychological Association Press.

Wilson, J. L., Peebles, R., Hardy, K. K., & Litt, I. F. (2006). Surfing for thinness: A pilot study of pro-eating disorder web site usage in adolescents with eating disorders. *Pediatrics, 118*(6), 1635–1643.

Yates, T. M. (2004). The developmental psychopathology of self-injurious behavior: Compensatory regulation in posttraumatic adaptation. *Clinical Psychological Review, 24,* 35–74.

Young, R., Sweeting, H., & West, P. (2006). Prevalence of deliberate self harm and attempted suicide within contemporary Goth youth subculture: Longitudinal cohort study. *British Medical Journal, 332,* 1058–1061.

10

Nonsuicidal Self-Injury in the Schools

Prevention and Intervention

RICHARD A. LIEBERMAN, JESSICA R. TOSTE,
AND NANCY L. HEATH

In this chapter, the practitioner will gain an understanding of:

- Best approaches to universal and program-based prevention strategies
- The role of various personnel and professionals within the school
- School policy and protocol surrounding the issue of NSSI
- School-based approaches to intervention with students engaging in NSSI

M.J. was a 13-year-old girl experiencing difficulties in school. She would have periods of time where she would miss days of school and then suddenly return to class. She tried to keep up with her homework but was unable to manage her course load. One day, when reviewing her assignment that she had received an extension on, I noticed a series of fresh cuts on the inner aspect of her wrist, which she was attempting to hide with several bracelets wrapped around her wrist. She looked away when it became apparent that I had noticed several fresh cuts and then indicated that she felt she needed to leave and would return at a later time to discuss the assignment. After her departure, I pondered what to do with the information I had. I felt both concerned and confused. Did her parents know about this behavior? How long had this been going on for? If I did not bring this to someone's attention, would something more serious happen? What were my responsibilities as her teacher?

I chose to set up a meeting time with the school counselor to discuss my observations at the end of that day. It certainly felt better to review the situation with a colleague. It was agreed that I would continue to support her in her desire to get her credits for the course that I was responsible for, that I would continue to feed forward to the school counselor any further observations or concerns that I might have, and that the school counselor, who had seen her in the past, would invite M.J. to meet with her to have a discussion about how she was doing. As a high school teacher, I decided that I needed to understand this behavior better, so I did an internet search and had difficulty knowing which sites were reliable. There was a wealth of opinion offered on many websites but I found only several sites that were helpful from my perspective. The following day, at our staff meeting, there were very mixed opinions and a heated discussion among the staff regarding the self-injurious behaviors of students. Some felt students use this behavior to get the attention of others or to avoid attending school. Some felt a student that cuts themselves intentionally must be experiencing some form of personal difficulty and that the self-injury was undoubtedly a "symptom."

Nonsuicidal self-injury (NSSI) is a growing concern among professionals working with youth (Shaw, 2002; Zila & Kiselica, 2001). As detailed in Chapter 2 "Self-Injury Today: Review of Population and Clinical Studies in Adolescents," the most recent studies exploring the occurrence of NSSI in high schools indicate that between 15 and 20% of students admit to having engaged in NSSI at least once (e.g., Laye-Gindhu & Schonert-Reichl, 2005; Muehlenkamp & Gutierrez, 2007; Nixon, Cloutier, & Aggarwal, 2002; Ross & Heath, 2002). When provided with a checklist of behaviors considered self-injurious, more than 30% indicate that they have cut, carved, or burned their skin or hit themselves on purpose (Lloyd-Richardson, Perrine, Dierker, & Kelley, 2007). The alarming numbers of adolescent students engaging in NSSI pose a challenge to all school personnel, particularly school-based professionals who are often called on to consult with school staff and parents when students engage in NSSI.

Although media attention has raised awareness about this behavior and its occurrence among adolescents, misconceptions persist in the general public regarding the correlates and function of NSSI. As concern grows within educational circles about the appropriate response to NSSI in the schools, these misconceptions may be detrimental to the quality of support and treatment provided to adolescents who engage in this behavior. A particular concern for school-based professionals is that NSSI can be contagious, often increasing among peer groups, grade levels, or campus clubs (Lieberman & Poland, 2006).

This chapter will address concerns related to the occurrence and management of NSSI within school settings. First, school-wide prevention strategies and preparedness will be discussed. The following section will present guidelines for developing a school protocol to respond to NSSI and detail each step of this school response including initial response, referral, assessment, and school-based interventions. Finally, the chapter will conclude with a summary of ethical and legal considerations, as these are issues critical to the management of NSSI in school settings.

PREVENTION IN THE SCHOOLS

Universal Prevention Strategies

Schools have an obligation to offer a safe and secure environment, as well as programs and experiences, that foster resilience in youth. Resiliency factors that can be developed within schools include access to mental health services, family-school connectedness, lack of access to lethal weapons, strong adult help-seeking behavior, good relations with peers, and the development of problem-solving and coping skills (Brock, Sandoval, & Hart, 2006). Our schools can become a place of connectedness for students through the provision of an environment where youth are able to express themselves, discuss issues and concerns, engage with peers and adults in a safe space, and seek out resources if they experience difficulties. This connectedness empowers students and serves as a universal strategy for preventing NSSI and other risky behaviors among youth.

These universal prevention strategies can also reduce the occurrence of NSSI in the schools. For example, NSSI in adolescence is most commonly characterized by difficulty in expression of emotions, self-derogation, anxiety, and poor distress tolerance (Klonsky, 2007; Muehlenkamp, 2006; Walsh, 2006). Schools can be an excellent environment in which to work with adolescents preventatively to provide information on more adaptive methods for coping with these types of difficulties and stress in general. Specifically, school-based professionals might offer activities within the curriculum or offer small group workshops on stress management and emotional awareness. These types of alternatives provide school-based professionals with the opportunity to help adolescents develop multiple ways to manage or express emotions, perhaps even before some youth attempt NSSI.

School-Based Prevention Programs

A number of evidence-based prevention programs have been used successfully in schools to address adolescent health risks, such as depression, alcohol and substance abuse, bullying, and suicide. The U.S. Substance Abuse Mental Heath Services Administration (SAMHSA) provides guidance to schools through the National Registry of Evidence-Based Programs and Practices (http://nrepp.samhsa.gov). Promoting trusting relationships with youth, as well as environments where students feel welcomed and respected, are related benefits of any primary prevention program (Webster & Browning, 2002), and such programs can be effective in preventing NSSI as well.

Prevention programs exist that are directed toward the entire student body and may aid in the detection of at-risk individuals. For example, the SOS (Signs of Suicide) program has documented evidence of reducing adolescent suicide attempts (Aseltine & DeMartino, 2004). SOS is a school-based program designed for middle and high school students and combines gatekeeper training for students with depression screening. The components of the program include an educational video and depression screening instrument. The video delineates suicide warning signs and emphasizes the critical significance of seeking adult assistance and using crisis hotlines. A brief depression questionnaire is also expected to be completed and scored by the students. If the child's score falls into the range that is considered a clinically significant indicator of depression, the interpretation sheet encourages the student to seek help immediately. The program aims to raise awareness in teens of depressive and suicidal symptoms while teaching them how to appropriately seek help for themselves or friends.

The Columbia University TeenScreen Program is another screening program designed to screen youth for depression and other mental disorders associated with suicidal thoughts or behaviors. Teens are given a variety of mental heath screening paper and pencil or computerized assessments after having consent from a parent. If the screening measures indicate a potential mental health problem, a follow-up interview with a mental health affiliate is conducted, and, if necessary, appropriate community resources are then provided. Researchers have found that the TeenScreen program is able to detect at-risk youth who have not previously been identified (Columbia University TeenScreen Program, 2005).

Presumably, improved help-seeking skills should also reduce students' risk for NSSI; however, the screening instruments used in SOS and TeenScreen do not specifically address NSSI. The SOS Middle School Program does, however, have a self-injury packet that provides suggestions for school-based mental health professionals, teachers, and parents. School psychologists must continue to promote prevention strategies while remaining up to date in their knowledge regarding identifying and intervening with youth who engage in NSSI (Lieberman, Poland, & Cassel, 2008).

Crisis Team Preparedness

When intervention is required for a student or group of students who are engaging in NSSI, it is essential that the school has a well-developed school response protocol (discussed in more detail later in the chapter) that allows for appropriate and rapid response. For the best response to self-injurious behavior, schools should have a crisis team established in advance. This team should include all professionals involved in school assessment or treatment, and they should be trained in first response and intervention for a wide variety of problems, including NSSI. It is also critical for school teams to collaborate with child and family services and other community organizations. School crisis teams provide an opportunity for collaboration between the school's administration and school mental health and medical staff (e.g., psychologists, counselors, nurses, social workers), as well as a critical link to the mental health resources in their communities (Poland & McCormick, 1999).

School-based professionals can play an important role in the referral of students to qualified professionals in their communities, and they are urged to update their lists of mental health resources on a regular basis. They need to be knowledgeable about the practitioners and treatment centers that have specific training in the management of NSSI, as well as resources that provide culturally responsive services. If possible, school-based professionals might use an in-service day to visit local treatment facilities and determine the steps a student would go through in seeking help and receiving treatment. When school-based professionals are more aware of what the referral and treatment process will be, they can better help students and their families make decisions and develop intervention plans (White Kress, Gibson, & Reynolds, 2004).

Teacher Training

Schools are very busy communities, with many adults who each take on very different roles. Whereas school-based professionals (e.g., school psychologists, counselors, social workers, nurses) should be conducting interventions with youth who engage in NSSI, it is important to note that other school personnel (e.g., teachers, librarians, coaches, and service staff) may be among the first adults to recognize the behavior. It is essential that teachers are aware of and knowledgeable about NSSI as students often disclose their behavior to a teacher whom they trust and respect. Often students go to a teacher and either tell the teacher about the behavior or reveal scars on their bodies. Recent studies have noted that teachers feel unprepared and uncertain about NSSI and would like to receive training in the area (Best, 2006; Heath, Toste, & Beettam, 2006). Although teachers may not be directly involved in the assessment of NSSI or intervention with youth who engage in this behavior, it is critical that they are provided with basic information such as warning signs and suggestions for reaching out to help youth who self-injure (see Tables 10.1 and 10.2).

It is important for teachers to know how to handle a situation in which a student discloses that he or she is engaging in self-injurious behaviors. The following points outline the role of the teacher in responding to NSSI:

TABLE 10.1   Warning Signs for NSSI

Frequent or unexplained bruises, scars, cuts, or burns

Black and blue marks on the neck

Consistent, inappropriate use of clothing designed to conceal wounds that often appear on the arms, thighs, or abdomen

Secretive behaviors, such as spending unusual amounts of time in the student restroom or isolated areas of campus

Risk-taking behaviors such as playing with guns, sexual acting out, running into traffic, or jumping from high places

Evidence of eating disorder or substance abuse

General signs of depression, social isolation, and disconnectedness

Possession of sharp implements (razor, shards of glass, thumb tacks)

Evidence of self-injury in work samples, journals, or art projects

Adapted from: Lieberman, R., & Poland, S. (2006). Self-mutilation. In G. G. Bear & K. M. Minke (Eds.), *Children's needs III: Development, prevention, and intervention.* Washington, DC: National Association of School Psychologists. [http://www.nasponline.org]

- Know that it is all right to talk to youth about this behavior. Be open to listening to them in an open and nonjudgmental way.
- Be informed about the risk factors and warning signs of NSSI.
- Upon observing any warning signs, a teacher should immediately refer the youth to a school-based professional and maintain the chain of supervision (e.g., escort the student to the appropriate team member, follow-up to make sure student met with the school-based professional). Teachers need to know that they cannot stop the NSSI and that their primary role is to identify and refer any adolescent who they suspect is engaging in this behavior to the designated school-based professional.
- Every teacher should be a collaborative member of the crisis team if they refer a student, as they are often able to provide critical information about the student to which only teachers have access (e.g., writing in class, interactions with peers).

Through advocacy and education, school-based professionals can work with teachers to dispel myths and misconceptions about NSSI. It is important to inform all school personnel, parents, and students that NSSI is not necessarily a sign of underlying psychopathology (Heath, Toste, & Zinck, 2008) but can be understood as a means of attempting to help one's self. A teacher who is aware that a student is self-injuring may not report the behavior, as he or she may perceive it as trivial or as a

TABLE 10.2   Suggestions for Teachers: Helping Youth Who Self-Injure

Many teachers have not been trained in and do not know how they should handle a student who shows signs of engaging in NSSI. It is important for teachers to know the do's and don'ts of how to handle such situations.

Do:

- Try to approach the student in a calm and caring way.
- Accept him or her even though you may not accept the behavior.
- Let the student know how much you care about him or her and believe in his or her potential.
- Understand that this is his or her way of coping with the pain he or she feels inside.
- Refer that student to your school-based professional (e.g., psychologist or counselor).
- Offer to go with that student to see the professional helper.
- Listen! Allow the student to talk to you. Be available.
- Discover what the student's personal strengths are and encourage him or her to use those strengths.
- Help him or her get involved in some area of interest (club, sport, or peer program).

Don't:

- Say anything to cause the student to feel guilt or shame (e.g., "What did you do to yourself?").
- Act shocked or appalled by his or her behavior.
- Talk about the student's NSSI in front of the class or around his or her peers.
- Try to teach the student what you think he or she should do.
- Judge the student, even if you do not agree with him or her.
- Tell the student that you won't tell anyone if he or she shares information about self-injuring behaviors with you.
- Use punishment or negative consequences if a student does self-injure.
- Make deals in an effort to get the student to stop.
- Make promises to the student that you can't keep.

Adapted from: Bowman, S., & Randall, K. (2004). *See my pain: Creative strategies and activities for helping young people who self-injure.* Chapin, SC: YouthLight. [http://www.youthlightbooks.com]

way for the student to receive attention but, with education, the teacher may be more likely to seek help and refer the student. Providing teachers with training about NSSI will help them feel more comfortable in addressing the issue within classrooms and schools.

The primary role of all school personnel is to be aware of the warning signs of NSSI and how to identify the behavior. In a recent survey of school counselors' experiences with NSSI, the major concern expressed when asked what they most needed to know about managing this behavior in the schools was knowing the signs of NSSI and how to identify a youth who is self-injuring (Heath, Toste, & White Kress, 2007). Clearly, identification of NSSI is a skill that school-based professionals must have in their repertoires. One of the most common indications of NSSI is peer flagging (Lieberman, 2004; Walsh, 2006), when a student who is engaging in NSSI tells a peer who then discloses the information to an adult in the school. In a recent study of young adults, 66% of participants reported that they had told a friend, whereas fewer than 30% had told a doctor, psychologist, counselor, or teacher (Heath, Holly, & Toste, 2007). In schools, another common indicator of NSSI is through creative work (e.g., composition, poetry, songs, art) that depicts the behavior (Lieberman & Poland, 2006). Other warning signs include the observation of cuts or scars on the arm or leg, continually wearing long sleeves, wrist bands, or long pants despite hot weather, and refusing to be involved in physical activities that would involve revealing skin, such as swimming (Carlson, DeGeer, Deur, & Fenton, 2005).

The most effective factor in improving identification of NSSI in schools is improving awareness of the prevalence of the behavior and ensuring that all school personnel are aware that the behavior requires immediate assessment and intervention. It is not "just a fad," or a way to seek attention or manipulate others. These may be serious warning signs and a marker of difficulties in a number of spheres.

SCHOOL RESPONSE PROTOCOL

One of the most important roles a school has in the management of NSSI in adolescents is the identification of and immediate response to youth who are engaging in NSSI. For this process to proceed smoothly and without alienation of the youth, it is recommended that every school have a self-injury protocol. A school protocol is an agreement among all school personnel about how incidents or reports of NSSI will be handled. Table 10.3 presents a sample protocol adapted from Walsh (2006) for responding to NSSI within the schools. Each section of this school protocol will be detailed in the next section, "Intervention in the Schools."

Although this sample provides a specific structure for a school protocol, it is important to note that the most critical factor in ensuring success of such a protocol is agreement on the guidelines by all staff and administration, as well as wide dissemination to all school personnel.

TABLE 10.3   Sample School Protocol for Nonsuicidal Self-Injury

Response to NSSI

• Schools should have assigned school-based professionals (e.g., school psychologist or counselor) for NSSI referral issues. There must be a key referral person if the school-based professional is not regularly available. This person would be responsible for contacting and collaborating with the school psychologist or counselor should any students be referred.

• All staff should have training and information about NSSI so that reactions are consistent, appropriate, and conform to protocol.

Referral

• Any school personnel who learns of a student's NSSI will immediately refer to a school-based mental health professional, maintain the chain of supervision, and remain involved with the school team that is conducting the intervention with this student.

Assessment

• The school-based professional conducts an initial (Level I) assessment. If it is found that the student is at any risk of suicide (current thoughts, previous attempts, self-harm, or current plan with access to means), then procedures will be followed for suicide risk (parents contacted, referral to community or hospital-based mental health professional for fuller evaluation, or, if urgent, emergency room crisis evaluation).

• If it is found that the student is engaging in NSSI as a maladaptive coping strategy and is not currently suicidal ensure that the student receives a more complete assessment and appropriate school interventions that include parent involvement are implemented.

• The school-based professional should conduct a fuller assessment and determine if more individualized, intensive therapy is required.

Parent Contact

• If it is deemed that outside therapy is required, the school-based professional will make the decision to contact the parent. Although it is best practice to involve parents at all times, not all adolescents who have engaged in NSSI *must* have parents contacted. Be aware of state or provincial laws regarding the school's obligation to contact parents.

A school response protocol cannot be imposed but must be created with all stakeholders involved. Nevertheless, regardless of the specific school protocol that is developed, all school policies related to NSSI should address the following issues:

• When should school personnel report a student suspected of self-injuring behaviors?

- To whom should school personnel report these behaviors?
- To what extent is the school administration involved with students who self-injure?
- To what extent are the school mental health professionals or school nurse involved?
- What is the school policy on parental notification and involvement?

It is essential that all school personnel (administrators, mental health personnel, and staff) are aware and knowledgeable about the school protocol. A cautionary suggestion is that the school policy should have built-in flexibility, as there is a great deal of variability in the underlying dynamics, issues, and needs of students who self-injure. An overly strict or rigid policy may not serve the best interests of some students.

INTERVENTION IN THE SCHOOLS

The following section provides information regarding intervention strategies for NSSI in the schools. In particular, guidelines are offered for school-based professionals involved in the various facets of working with youth who engage in NSSI: disclosure, referral, and intervention. The intervention component includes primary assessment, parent contact, and school-based interventions. This section also discusses the issue of contagion within the schools and strategies for preventing or limiting contagion.

In general, it may be difficult to work with youth who engage in NSSI, and it is not uncommon for school personnel to have strong emotional reactions to this behavior. These feelings can include intense horror and repulsion, and reactions to the adolescent can range from helplessness, anger, guilt, and sadness to utter frustration (Heath et al., 2006; White Kress et al., 2004). School-based professionals must continually monitor and manage their personal reactions and recognize their limitations. The first step is for the practitioner to assess his or her own comfort in working with a student who is engaging in NSSI. If a school-based professional does not feel that he or she will be comfortable completing a thorough assessment or intervention, he or she must be prepared with the appropriate resources for an immediate referral of the student. Further consideration must be made of the logistical limitations, such as the ratio of staff to students and other work demands. Each practitioner should work with only a few students engaging in NSSI at one time to ensure that they are receiving effective intervention. However, even when intervention may not be feasible, school-based professionals should continue to address the identification and referral of students who engage in NSSI to experts in the community.

Response to Student Disclosure

Students often disclose their NSSI to an adult in the school whom they trust. The initial response they receive to this disclosure will play a critical role in their future help-seeking behavior, as well as their willingness to discuss the issue and participate in an intervention program. School counselors recognize the importance of an appropriate first response but are often unsure of the most appropriate way to respond to a disclosure of NSSI (Heath, et al., 2008). Although there can never be an exact script, and the professional's responses may differ depending on the individual student, some general guidelines do exist. First, the response to student disclosure should show a respectful willingness to listen in a nonjudgmental fashion. The practitioner should use similar language to the youth in describing the behavior (e.g., if they describe "cutting," identify the behavior as such in your discussions) and should avoid the use of suicide terminology (Walsh, 2006).

In the initial response and discussions that follow, one should not express shock, revulsion, or discomfort; nor should the practitioner overreact and show too much concern for the adolescent. These types of reactions could alienate the youth and damage the trust within the working relationship. In attempting to assess the behavior or begin intervention, the practitioner should not show excessive interest in the behavior (e.g., permitting the client to relive in detail the experiences of NSSI itself), as this can be a trigger for further self-injurious behaviors.

Referral

Following the initial assessment, the school-based professional working with a student must determine whether this adolescent is at any risk for suicide or other mental health issues. Risk for suicide is low if the student is reporting current thoughts that were revealed in something they said (direct or indirect threats) or wrote (journals). Risk is considered moderate when in addition to current thoughts, the student (or parent or teacher) reports previous suicide attempts or there is evidence of self-injurious behaviors such as fresh or recent wounds. Risk is considered high when the student has a plan to kill him- or herself and has access to means. If the youth is at high risk, the school-based mental health professional should immediately refer and seek involvement of the appropriate emergency mental health services through community or hospital resources for the adolescent. If risk is deemed low to moderate, supervising and handing off the student directly to parents or guardians is recommended. In any case, the school-based professional should continue to monitor the student's attendance and return to school.

It is important to note that school-based professionals may lack the time or diagnostic expertise to respond to the therapeutic needs of students referred for exhibiting NSSI. Although school-based professionals may be able to implement many of the prevention and intervention strategies discussed in this chapter, their primary role (once the student has been identified) is to assess the adolescent for immediate risk, communicate with parents (if necessary), and direct the youth to the appropriate district and community mental health resources. Decisions about referral should be made based on the information gathered in the primary assessment of the behavior and potential suicide risk. In addition, after a student has found treatment, the school-based professional can focus on facilitating communication between the adolescent, school, home, and community mental health agencies, essentially creating a "circle of care" around the student. All referrals should be conducted in a sensitive manner, with the full knowledge and support of the student so that the adolescent feels empowered and supported by the adult in whom he or she originally confided.

Assessment in Schools

In Chapter 8 "Assessment of Nonsuicidal Self-Injury in Youth," guidelines for the assessment and triage of NSSI are discussed in detail, across settings. This section will focus on assessment issues that are specific to the school setting. Once a student has disclosed the behavior or been identified as engaging in NSSI, it is essential that a trained mental health professional complete an initial assessment and evaluate potential suicide risk (Level I assessment or triage, as described in Chapter 8). School-based professionals who serve as the primary contact person for NSSI issues in their schools must familiarize themselves with the levels of assessment. Frequently, in schools where the school psychologist or school counselor may not be regularly available, other school personnel such as a school nurse or administrator may serve as the key referral person (e.g., youth who are identified as engaging in NSSI are brought to them to be supervised until a school-based mental health professional can be consulted). Although it is not recommended that these individuals conduct a complete initial assessment, they do need to be aware of the necessity to evaluate a student's level of risk and be prepared to consult with the school team. Within the school system it is important to assess for possible suicidal behaviors or intent due to the legal responsibility to notify the parent, discussed below. Legal and ethical considerations in dealing with NSSI in the schools are discussed later in this chapter.

Parent Contact

Contacting parents about their child's self-injurious behavior must be done with patience, tolerance, and cultural responsiveness. Upon completing an initial assessment, the school-based professional must break confidentiality and contact parents if the adolescent is an immediate risk to him- or herself or others. However, if a suicide risk assessment is done, and a mental health status suggests no serious concerns, then

NSSI, like other high-risk behaviors (e.g., drug use), may not require parental contact, although this remains a controversial issue among school-based professionals. If parents are already aware of the behavior or if the adolescent is willing to discuss it with them, it can be beneficial for some youth to have the additional support in their home environment. For suggestions on how to communicate with parents and strategies for working with families of youth who engage in NSSI, consult Chapter 12, "Working with Families and Adolescents with NSSI."

School-Based Interventions

Interventions for NSSI within the schools should be evidence-based and consistent with recommendations for good practice, as outlined in Chapter 11, "Psychosical Interventions for Adolescents." As noted above, logistical or professional constraints may make intervention by school-based professionals difficult. As previously mentioned, youth who are deemed at high risk should be referred to appropriate services outside of the school setting to receive the most effective treatment. Although the interventions described below may be effective for some students, for more complex cases it is often a combination of biological, psychosocial, and environmental factors that lead to the NSSI. To deal with the combination of factors in addition to the self-injuring behavior, some youth require intervention and treatment in an individual and intensive setting that is not often available within the school.

Prior to beginning any intervention, it is important to understand that for youth who engage in NSSI, this behavior often serves as a coping mechanism. Thus, a well-intentioned adult such as a teacher should not try to stop the behavior through demands (e.g., "If I see signs that you have cut, then you will not be able to attend class."). Demanding that an adolescent stop self-injuring without having first suggested alternative coping strategies may be potentially harmful at worst and ineffective in terminating the behavior at least (Lieberman, 2004; Muehlenkamp, 2006; Walsh, 2006).

One caution in providing services to students who engage in NSSI in the school setting is the possible dangers of offering peer support groups specific to this behavior. This is strongly discouraged unless the group facilitator has extensive training in managing issues of contagion. However, groups that focus on empowerment, exercise and tension release, or grief resolution are worthwhile alternatives. Such groups should be governed by strict rules that prohibit discussion of the details of NSSI, and they should include teaching new skills (e.g., emotion regulation, mindfulness, self-soothing, distress tolerance) and discussing behaviors (e.g., physical activity) that the youth can do when they are feeling overwhelmed and filled with tension.

In addition to the primary response steps already discussed, several common elements across intervention approaches may have utility for school-based personnel and have been effective in decreasing

NSSI. These elements include alliance-building, communication skill–building, behavioral interventions, and cognitive restructuring (Dallam, 1997; Lieberman & Poland, 2006; Muehlenkamp, 2006; Walsh, 2006).

Alliance Building

Forming a supportive and collaborative therapeutic alliance is paramount to successfully treating self-injurious behaviors (Muehlenkamp, 2006; Walsh, 2006). Frequently, these youth do not have a full and open relationship with anyone and work to hide much of what they are feeling. Therefore, the formation of an honest and open relationship with the therapist is in itself therapeutic. Thus, the youth and mental health professional work as a team throughout the intervention. Specific to working with youth who engage in NSSI, it is important to develop the alliance by acknowledging the pain that the client is likely to be in, as well as the functional component that the self-injurious behavior is serving. This is essential because it shows the adolescents that there is a willingness to understand them without judgment.

Another way to demonstrate an empathetic stance is for the professional to understand that NSSI serves a specific function for the student, even before starting to work with an adolescent who self-injures. Although the behavior may be a maladaptive coping strategy, it still is important in helping to manage the adolescents daily life. Having the clients communicate how they feel the behavior is helping them cope can make them more receptive to discussions of why the NSSI may not be the best way to deal with their emotions. More details concerning how to do this is offered in Chapter 8, "Assessment of Nonsuicidal Self-Injury in Youth" and Chapter 11, "Psychosocial Interventions for Adolescents" (motivational interviewing). Once a strong therapeutic alliance is formed, the focus can shift to developing alternative, more adaptive coping mechanisms. The focus should never be directly on the elimination of the NSSI; rather, the occurrence of the self-injurious behaviors should be understood as an indicator of how well, or poorly, the new more adaptive coping mechanisms are functioning.

Communication Skill–Building

NSSI may serve as a means for an adolescent to communicate overwhelming feelings of anger, sadness, pain, or despair to others (Klonsky, 2007; Levenkron, 1998). Communication skill–building is essential in helping an adolescent develop more adaptive coping strategies to deal with life stressors. Youth who self-injure often have great difficulty communicating negative emotions to those they care about. Role-playing and practicing how to communicate more effectively are helpful. In addition, adolescents should be encouraged to identify and talk with trusted adults at home or at school about their feelings.

However, when adults are unavailable, the school-based professional can help the youth vent his or her emotions using written journals or art projects. One example of journaling is a "trigger log" in which the students record each time they engage in NSSI and identify the precipitating events (Bowman & Randall, 2004). They can also compare their experiences to days they did not self-injure.

Behavioral Interventions

The school-based professional can guide adolescents in finding alternative ways to understand, manage, and express their emotions. For example, stress management and tension release exercises and substitute behaviors empower adolescents with alternatives to NSSI. Techniques such as diaphragmatic and controlled breathing, meditation, and visualization can be effective exercises to reduce tension when these skills are learned and practiced regularly. A good suggestion for the management of depressive symptoms, poor self-esteem, and negative body image that often accompany NSSI, is good "self-care" (Lieberman & Poland, 2006). Adolescents who can manage to exercise every day or every other day for 3 weeks will not only feel better (physically and about themselves), but they will also sleep and eat better. Recently, there has been some early investigation into the possibility that when an individual has an impulse to self-injure, the substitution of aerobic exercise may be effective (Klonsky, 2007). Finally, although the technique is somewhat controversial, clinicians have anecdotally reported some success with individuals who have been encouraged to substitute putting ice against their skin for cutting or to snap a rubber band around the wrist when the impulse to self-injure overwhelms them (Lieberman & Poland, 2006; Walsh, 2006). School mental health personnel are urged to fully discuss alternatives with the adolescent and his or her parents.

Cognitive Restructuring

Youth who self-injure often have a number of negative automatic thoughts about themselves or others, their bodies, their ability to cope with distress, and their futures. Walsh and Rosen (1985) identify four key beliefs common to individuals who engage in NSSI; the recurrence of these beliefs is likely to start and continue the behavior. Youth who self-injure often believe that (a) the behavior is acceptable or necessary; (b) they are disgusting and deserving of punishment; (c) this action is needed to reduce unpleasant feelings or to solve immediate crises; and (d) this overt action is required to communicate their feelings to others and to have others understand the deep emotional pain they are experiencing. Common internal talk for individuals centers on the inability to regulate emotion. Statements such as "I can't stand this feeling" or "It is unbearable, something terrible will happen if I don't do something" are typical (see Chapter 4, "Psychosocial Risk and Protective

Factors" for further discussion on this topic). It is important to explore the individual's personal internal dialogue and help the youth challenge the maladaptive beliefs that are serving to maintain the NSSI.

No-Harm Agreements

No-harm agreements, also referred to as no-harm contracts or individual safety plans, although not uniformly supported (Lewis, 2007), have been used with youth who may pose a suicide risk (Lieberman & Poland, 2006). Current thinking on the treatment of NSSI suggests that an agreement with the youth about the necessity for trying an agreed upon alternative course of action in response to the self-injurious impulse is not a "contract," and it develops as the youth develops skills in employing the alternative behaviors (Muehlenkamp, 2006; Walsh, 2006). For a brief discussion regarding the limitations of no-harm contracts, refer to Chapter 11, "Psychosocial Interventions for Adolescents."

Contagion in the Schools

A sequence of events in which an individual engages in self-injurious behavior and is imitated by others in the environment is referred to as contagion of NSSI. We know that social contagion, or the spread of NSSI, is a problem for youth within the schools (Lieberman, 2004; Walsh, 2006). In these situations, multiple students who know each other self-injure within short periods of time. These youth often appear to be communicating frequently about NSSI and, in effect, triggering the behavior in each other. In some situations the contagion is immediate and direct. Youth may self-injure in each other's presence and may even share the same tools or implements or take turns injuring the body of others (Walsh, 2006). This "shared self-injury" may be more prevalent in males (Lloyd-Richardson et al., 2007). School administrators have observed self-injurious behaviors spread through peer groups, grade levels, and campus clubs. NSSI may serve as an occasional "rite of togetherness" used to cement certain friendships and romances (Froeschle & Moyer, 2004). As illustrated in the case of D.R., sometimes an adolescent will pick up the behavior from older siblings or peer group leaders and seek acceptance and inclusion through NSSI. Although every student referred for NSSI should be assessed for suicide risk, mental health professionals should expect that many students will inevitably assess as low risk. Studies have demonstrated repeatedly that with appropriate interventions, the majority of students develop better coping skills, and NSSI behaviors diminish.

Youth may trigger NSSI in each other because the behavior produces feelings of cohesiveness (e.g., "There is a special bond among people who cut themselves."); the behavior has powerful communication aspects (e.g., "My friend must really be upset to cut herself so many times."); the behavior may be viewed as outrageous and provocative (e.g., "It really freaks out my parents when we do this."); the behavior may also be inadvertently reinforced by adults (e.g., "Finally, my parents believe I'm in a lot of pain.").

> *D.R., a 14-year-old boy, was identified as "gifted" and attended a special gifted program in middle school. He was quiet and well behaved and had a group of friends. D.R. felt he was not really that close to his friends and just hung out with them. He reported that he felt different from most of his peer group; he was interested in world issues and wanted to make a difference. He felt a lot of his peer group just wanted to succeed financially and academically. He identified himself as a "loner," although neither his parents nor teachers felt this was accurate. D.R.'s mother noticed burns on his arms when he pulled up his sleeve to clean something. When she asked him about it, he admitted that he had burned himself with a cigarette at a party the previous week with a couple of other guys. According to him, all three guys took turns burning while in the presence of a number of other kids. The mother called the school, and a parent-school meeting was called to discuss the issue.*

> *Finally, it came out that at the party a number of kids, including the three boys who were burning, were smoking marijuana. The school sent out information to all the parents about NSSI and what to look for as well as about drug use. The school counselor met individually with the three boys who had burned. All three refused to talk about it, saying, "It wasn't a big deal." The counselor recommended that all three see a psychiatrist. D.R. went once and refused to return. Two years later D.R. reported he burned a couple more times within the following couple of months "just to piss the school off," once with others and once alone, and then stopped. When asked what made him stop he replied, "There was no point."*

Preventing Contagion

Because contagion may play a role in NSSI, it is prudent to disseminate materials carefully when responding to an outbreak of self-injurious behaviors in the school population. Educators must refrain from school-wide communications in the form of general assemblies or intercom announcements. When students within a particular peer group are referred together, it is appropriate to divide the group up among different support staff and respond to each adolescent individually.

School professionals should consider three main interventions to minimize the risk of contagion (Walsh, 2006). First, reduce communications about NSSI among members of the peer group. Explaining to individual adolescents that talking or emailing or instant messaging about self-injurious behaviors has a negative effect on peers. Further, it is necessary to reduce the public exhibition of scars and wounds in the school. School professionals should first meet with a student displaying scars alone and directly request that he or she cover the scars with clothing or jewelry when at school. Finally, the behavior should be treated using individual counseling methods and not group therapy, with a few exceptions.

When educating youth about NSSI, it is recommended that you keep information about specific behaviors very general and within the context of seeking help from a trusted adult. School professionals should explain to youth that NSSI is a problem in coping that can be managed; they should describe the signs of emotional stress and alternative coping strategies, as well as identify adults within the school who are trained to help students. Demonstrating that adults are aware that this is a fairly common maladaptive coping behavior can decrease the appealing "shock" value of the behavior while making help-seeking less intimidating. See Table 10.4 for suggestions for limiting behavioral contagion in school settings.

ETHICAL AND LEGAL CONSIDERATIONS

School-based professionals must often weigh legal and ethical responsibilities when responding to a student engaging in NSSI. A critical consideration within the schools is documentation. School boards and districts must establish guidelines for NSSI prevention and intervention

TABLE 10.4   Suggestions for Reducing Contagion of NSSI

- NSSI should not be discussed *in detail* in school newspapers or other student venues. This can serve as a "trigger" for individuals who engage in NSSI.

- Those who engage in NSSI should be discouraged from revealing their scars because of issues of contagion. This should be discussed, explained, and enforced.

- In general, a designated person should be clear with the student that although the fact of NSSI can be shared, the details of what is done and how should not be shared, as it can be detrimental to the well-being of the student's friends.

- Educators must refrain from school-wide communications in the form of general assemblies or intercom announcements that address self-injury.

- Health educators should reconsider the classroom presentation of certain books, popular movies, and music videos that glamorize such behaviors and instead seek appropriate messages in the work of popular artists.

- Divide students who are referred for a group rite of passage and have each assessed and responded to individually. When numerous students within a peer group are referred, assessment of every student will often identify an "alpha" student whose behaviors have set the others off. This student should be assessed for more serious emotional disturbance. Although most students participating in a group event will assess at low risk, identifying moderate and high risk students and targeting them for follow up is critical.

- School mental health professionals should refrain from running specific groups that focus on cutting, rather focusing on themes of empowerment, exercise and tension relief, and grief resolution.

in collaboration and consultation with the crisis team (which includes all school personnel). These policies must be in alignment with individual state or provincial laws, as well as any other policies already established by the school to manage risky behaviors. Further, they must be clearly written and shared with any school personnel who may identify (through referral or through student disclosure) an adolescent's NSSI. Froeschle and Moyer (2004) provide succinct recommendations to assist in responding to these issues:

- Clarify the limits of confidentiality with both students and parents. When students are at risk for suicide, school professionals have a duty to warn parents and ensure that the youth receives mental health services.
- Practitioners should recognize the limits of their abilities; maintain accurate and objective records; familiarize themselves with state or provincial law, school district policies, and procedures; collaborate and confer with colleagues regularly to make decisions in the best interest of their students; and maintain liability insurance coverage.
- Discuss with administration in your school awareness and support for the above and how it relates to your duties and NSSI.

CONCLUSION

Although there is some debate concerning whether the increase of NSSI in our schools is an increase of occurrence or of disclosure, there is no doubt that our school-based professionals and personnel have to cope with youth who engage in NSSI in ever growing numbers. This chapter focused on all aspects of the management of NSSI within the schools. The school-wide prevention strategies highlighted the importance of working to prevent NSSI through increasing support and decreasing stressors. The chapter described specific guidelines for responding to NSSI on a personal and systems level, and outlined school-based interventions that are appropriate for use. Finally, the chapter discussed ethical and legal issues concerning the management of NSSI in the schools.

School-based professionals and personnel are required to deal with NSSI in their schools. Although many feel overwhelmed and poorly prepared to handle this worrisome behavior, it is our hope that, providing them with clear guidelines for how to proceed will make them feel better able to work with youth who engage in NSSI.

REFERENCES

Aseltine, R. H., & DeMartino, R. (2004). An outcome evaluation of the SOS suicide prevention. *American Journal of Public Health, 94,* 446–451.

Best, R. (2006). Deliberate self-harm in adolescence: A challenge for schools. *British Journal of Guidance and Counselling, 34*(2), 161–175.

Bowman, S., & Randall, K. (2004). *See my pain: Creative strategies and activities for helping young people who self-injure.* Chapin, SC: YouthLight.

Brock, S. E., Sandoval, J., & Hart, S. (2006). Suicidal ideation and behaviors. In G. G. Bear, K. M. Minke, and A. Thomas (Eds.), *Children's needs III: Development, prevention and intervention* (pp. 225–238). Bethesda, MD: National Association of School Psychologists.

Carlson, L., DeGeer, S. M., Deur, C., & Fenton, K. (2005). Teachers' awareness of self-cutting behavior among the adolescent population. *Praxis, 5,* 22–29.

Columbia University TeenScreen Program. (2005). *How the program works.* Retrieved April 28, 2006, from http://www.teenscreen.org.

Dallam, S. J. (1997). The identification and management of self-mutilating patients in primary care. *Nurse Practitioner, 22*(5), 151–165.

Froeschle, J., & Moyer, M. (2004). Just cut it out: Legal and ethical challenges in counseling students who self-mutilate. *Professional School Counseling, 7,* 231–236.

Heath, N. L., Holly, S., & Toste, J. R. (2007). *Social influence and functions of non-suicidal self-injury in a sample of university students.* Unpublished master's thesis. McGill University, Montreal.

Heath, N. L., Toste, J. R., & Beettam, E. (2006). "I am not well-equipped": High school teachers' perceptions of self-injury. *Canadian Journal of School Psychology, 21*(1), 73–92.

Heath, N. L., Toste, J. R., & White Kress, V. (2007). [School counselors' experiences with non-suicidal self-injury]. Unpublished raw data.

Heath, N. L., Toste, J. R., & Zinck, L. (2008). Understanding adolescent self-injury from a resilience perspective: A model for international interpretation. In L. Liebenberg & M. Ungar (Eds.), *Resilience in action: Working with youth across cultures and contexts.* Toronto: University of Toronto Press.

Klonsky, E. D. (2007). The functions of deliberate self-injury: A review of the evidence. *Clinical Psychology Review, 27,* 226–239.

Laye-Gindhu, A., & Schonert-Reichl, K. A. (2005). Non-suicidal self-harm among community adolescents: Understanding the "whats" and "whys" of self-harm. *Journal of Youth and Adolescence, 34*(5), 445–457.

Levenkron, S. (1998). *Cutting: Understanding and overcoming self-mutilation.* New York: W. W. Norton.

Lewis, L. M. (2007). No-harm contracts: A review of what we know. *Suicide and Life Threatening Behavior, 37,* 50–57.

Lieberman, R. (2004). Understanding and responding to students who self-mutilate. *Principal Leadership (High School Ed.), 4,* 10–13.

Lieberman, R., & Poland, S. (2006). Self-mutilation. In G. G. Bear & K. M. Minke (Eds.), *Children's needs III: Development, prevention, and intervention* (pp. 795–804). Washington, DC: National Association of School Psychologists.

Lieberman, R., Poland, S., & Cassel, R. (2008). Suicide intervention. In A. Thomas & J. Grimes (Eds.), *Best practices in school psychology V.* Bethesda, MD: National Association of School Psychologists.

Lloyd-Richardson, E. E., Perrine, N., Dierker, L., & Kelley, M. L. (2007). Characteristics and functions of non-suicidal self-injury in a community sample of adolescents. *Psychological Medicine, 37,* 1183–1192.

Muehlenkamp, J. J. (2006). Empirically supported treatments and general therapy guidelines for non-suicidal self-injury. *Journal of Mental Health Counseling, 28,* 166–185.

Muehlenkamp, J. J., & Gutierrez, P. M. (2007). Risk for suicide attempts among adolescents who engage in non-suicidal self-injury. *Archives of Suicide Research, 11,* 69–82.

Nixon, M. K., Cloutier, P. F., & Aggarwal, S. (2002). Affect regulation and addictive aspects of repetitive self-injury in hospitalized adolescents. *Journal of the American Academy of Child & Adolescent Psychiatry, 41*(11), 1333–1341.

Poland, S., & McCormick, J. (1999). *Coping with crisis: Lessons learned.* Longmont, CO: Sopris West.

Ross, S., & Heath, N. L. (2002). A study of the frequency of self-mutilation in a community sample of adolescents. *Journal of Youth and Adolescence, 31*(1), 67–77.

Shaw, S. N. (2002). Shifting conversations on girls' and women's self-injury: An analysis of the clinical literature in historical context. *Feminism & Psychology, 12*(2), 191–219.

Walsh, B. W. (2006). *Treating self-injury: A practical guide.* New York: Guilford Press.

Walsh, B. W., & Rosen, P. (1985). Self-mutilation and contagion: An empirical test. *American Journal of Psychiatry, 142*(1), 119–120.

Webster, L., & Browning, J. (2002). Child maltreatment. In S. E. Brock, P. J. Lazarus, & S. R. Jimerson (Eds.), *Best practices in school crisis prevention and intervention* (pp. 503–530). Bethesda, MD: National Association of School Psychologists.

White Kress, V. E., Gibson, D. M., & Reynolds, C. A. (2004). Adolescents who self-injure: Implications and strategies for school counselors. *Professional School Counseling, 7*(3), 195–201.

Zila, L. M., & Kiselica, M. S. (2001). Understanding and counseling self-mutilation in female adolescents and young adults. *Journal of Counseling & Development, 79,* 46–52.

11

Psychosocial Interventions for Adolescents

MARY K. NIXON, HARJIT AULAKH,
LAUREL TOWNSEND, AND MEGHAN ATHERTON

In this chapter, the practitioner will gain an understanding of:

- Factors to consider when treating youth who self-injure, such as motivation for treatment, help-seeking behavior in youth, and the importance of interdisciplinary collaboration and communication
- The current evidence for treatment of NSSI in youth
- A range of psychosocial treatments available for treating youth who engage in NSSI, including their theoretical basis and application.

Despite the prevalence of nonsuicidal self-injury (NSSI) in youth and their frequent presentation in clinical settings, evidence of effective psychosocial treatments for NSSI in youth remains extremely limited. This chapter will review both adult and adolescent psychosocial interventions that have been evaluated and outline a range of potential treatment options for NSSI in this age group. Aspects related specifically to the engagement of adolescents in treatment and the need for developmentally sensitive and flexible approaches will also be discussed.

Many youth who self-injure do not seek help and may be reluctant to discuss their behavior or consider engaging in counseling. Whitlock, Eckenrode, and Silverman (2006), in their Internet-based survey of self-injuring college students, indicated that only a very small percentage (3.2%) of self-injurers had disclosed to a medical professional, whereas somewhat more (21.4%) had discussed their behavior with a mental health professional. In a population-based study of Western Canadian youth (Nixon, Cloutier, & Jansson, 2008), 56% (51/91) of those who self-harmed indicated that they had sought help or support for their self-harm. Of that same group, 56% sought help from a friend, 54% from a psychologist or psychiatrist, and 48% from a family member. Those who self harmed repeatedly (more than three times) sought help more frequently than those who did not. Barriers to seeking help may include the impression that the behavior is not problematic, fear of disclosing the behavior due to their sense of shame or guilt, and lack of resources or lack of knowledge regarding available resources. In a recent study of mental health service use in Canadian youth with major depression and suicidality, Cheung and Dewa (2007) noted that almost half of these youth had not received service. Matching youth in need with available resources remains challenging, and discussion regarding this is beyond the scope of this chapter.

In this Internet age, certain youth may prefer not to access direct service and substitute using the Internet for "self-help" and to gather information regarding self-injury and its treatment. Shame and secrecy often associated with NSSI can lead to feeling marginalized, and the Internet provides these youth with an anonymous venue where they can share their experiences and seek support (Whitlock et al., 2006). It is unclear how many self-injuring youth access these websites (not all of which are reputable) and what outcomes arise from their use. For further discussion and a review of this topic and a list of recommended websites regarding NSSI in youth, refer to Chapter 15 "Resource Guide for Working with Youth."

POINTS FOR CONSIDERATION PRIOR TO INITIATING TREATMENT

The preceding chapters on psychosocial risk and protective factors, co-occurring conditions with NSSI, and assessment of NSSI provide an overview of aspects related to NSSI and the importance of adequate and collaborative assessment, both to engage youth and families in treatment and to lay out a framework for considering which interventions may be most appropriate. The timing of provision of specific interventions is also important to consider. For example, if the youth is severely depressed and concentration or motivation are affected, skill-based therapies may not be of much benefit until these symptoms have improved. This might involve managing the environment by reducing stress, providing therapeutic support, and monitoring a medication trial until symptoms improve. Timing is also important in terms of recognizing that youth may be at different stages of readiness for change regarding their behavior. The use of techniques such as motivational interviewing (reviewed in more detail in the interventions section of this chapter) permit the counselor or therapist to work with the individual and set a preliminary framework from which to consider other possible interventions.

In general, training of therapists involved in providing specific psychosocial treatments for NSSI is limited. Nonetheless, therapists trained in key psychotherapies that have evidence of efficacy in the treatment of child and youth mental health disorders (e.g., cognitive behavioral therapy (CBT) for major depression, social anxiety disorder, and obsessive compulsive disorder) can be valuable, as some key principles and approaches can be of benefit in the treatment of NSSI. Training is now available for dialectical behavioral therapy (DBT) specific for suicidal adolescents, many of whom engage in NSSI.

Therapists working with youth who self-injure and their families may benefit from support and advice from other therapists with experience in this area. Youth with recurrent NSSI who are in treatment may have more than one professional involved in their care (e.g., family therapist and psychologist, psychologist and psychiatrist, group therapist and school counselor, etc.). The importance of open communication (with consent), defining the roles of each professional, and joint treatment planning cannot be underestimated in their contribution to successful outcomes. Members of a treatment team can also be key informants regarding the status of symptoms and behavior or new events, with which informed team members can make more accurate and informed decisions and recommendations regarding treatment interventions.

Although setting parameters and boundaries regarding the therapeutic process are important, the efficacy of signed "contracts" between the treatment team or clinician and the individual with NSSI has not been formally evaluated. A recent review (Lewis, 2007) of "no harm contracts" for suicidal individuals concluded that, despite it being widely practiced, existing research did not support it as a method for the prevention of suicide, nor was it protection for the clinician regarding malpractice in the event of suicide. Barent Walsh (2006), in his book *Treating Self-Injury*, suggests that safety contracts, without established efficacy, may be harmful, driving the behavior underground and expecting change without giving the individual an opportunity to develop alternate skills. Guarding against creating a sense of failure by avoiding setting unrealistic expectations is an important therapeutic goal. Whereas Walsh discounts safety contracts per se, he refers to the use of a "contingency management" approach (2006, pp. 116–124), where frequency of NSSI is captured over several weeks, and a "self protection contract" is written that identifies goals such as stated amount of reduction of self-injury over a specific time period, use of replacement skills, and rewards.

Whereas adolescents may benefit from structure within their treatment setting, it remains unclear whether such written contracts have any success in reducing self-injury or engaging further commitment from youth. Adolescents' perception of the utility of such interventions may play a pivotal role in their meaning and therefore outcome.

An intervention perceived as imposed, without choice, or as an unrealistic expectation of treatment (i.e., you must stop self-injuring starting today), without understanding or meaning to the youth, is likely to have limited or no success. At the same time, some youth return to a follow-up appointment or comment in group that they have "promised" a friend, boyfriend, girlfriend, grandparent, or other person that they will stop self-injuring. Some may even go so far as to indicate that this is the "one thing" that has been most helpful in making them stop. It may be that this kind of promise and associated change is more a reflection of the acknowledgment and commitment to a caring, meaningful relationship than the actual verbal promise itself.

CURRENT EVIDENCE FOR PSYCHOTHERAPIES IN CHILDREN AND ADOLESCENTS WITH AXIS I DISORDERS

Although it is not the objective of this chapter to review in detail therapies that have proven efficacy in the treatment of major mental health disorders in children and youth, a very brief summary is provided in order to be comprehensive in our understanding of treating youth with NSSI and its co-occurring disorders. Level 1 evidence (positive outcome in a double-blind randomized controlled trial) exists for a number of psychotherapies used in the treatment of mental health disorders among children and youth, such as for major depression and individual- or group-based CBT (Lewinsohn, Clark, Hops, & Andrews, 1990; Weisz, Valerie, McCarty, & Moore, 1999). Kahn, Kehle, Jenson, and Clark (1990) found that all three treatment interventions (CBT, relaxation, and individual self-modeling) for depression were equally effective against a control group, indicating that efficacy may not be specific to a single treatment type in this case. Interpersonal therapy (Mufson et al., 1994) focuses on improving the overall social networks by focusing, with adolescents and their parents, on problem areas such as grief, interpersonal role disputes, role transitions, interpersonal deficits, and single-parent families. Interpersonal therapy has demonstrated level 1 evidence for the treatment of major depression in this age group (Mufson, et al., 2004). Other researchers have employed a double-blind randomized design for CBT for anxiety disorders in youth such as generalized anxiety, separation anxiety, and social anxiety (Compton et al., 2004) and for obsessive-compulsive disorder, incorporating exposure and response prevention (March, Franklin, Nehon, & Foa, 2001). A description of the key aspects of CBT will be reviewed further on in this chapter.

Monitoring responses to intervention and changes in symptoms, as in the example of major depression, while at the same time monitoring frequency and functions of NSSI assists clinicians in their formulation of the role of NSSI and assists in further refining treatment interventions and goals. For example, a youth whose depression improved with therapy may no longer feel the need to self-injure, may present as more confident in his or her ability to problem solve, and may view his or her circumstances from a more positive perspective. The clinicians' therapeutic goals would then move toward the development and practice of adaptive coping skills and rational cognitions in the event of a relapse of depression or onset of stressors or triggers for NSSI.

For the treatment of disruptive behavior disorders, a number of therapies have been shown to be effective, including behavioral classroom interventions and behavioral parent training in the treatment of attention deficit disorder with hyperactivity and behavioral parent training and videotape modeling for parent training in the treatment of oppositional defiant disorder and conduct disorder (Roberts, Lazicki-Puddy, Puddy, & Johnson, 2003). Multisystemic therapy (intensive home- and family-based combined, i.e., CBT and systemic treatment) has also been studied for the treatment of conduct disorder, youth with multiple problems, and inpatients with suicidal behaviors (Borduin, 1999; Huey et al., 2004; Schoenwald, Ward, Henggeler, & Rowland, 2000) and appears promising.

PSYCHOSOCIAL TREATMENTS IN YOUTH WHO SELF-INJURE

Two key review papers have been published on the efficacy of psychosocial treatments for self-injurious and self-harming behavior in adolescents and adults. Muehlenkamp, in her 2006 review, collapsed studies including both NSSI and suicidal behaviors (many did not differentiate behaviors but did report on NSSI as an outcome measure). Hawton et al. (1999) published their Cochrane review, which provides a summary and analysis of treatments for deliberate self-harm (DSH).

The Cochrane review points out that nearly all trials reviewed (both psychosocial and medication treatments) include too few participants for statistical power to detect a meaningful change in repetition of DSH. Table 11.1 outlines interventions that have been formally evaluated and may be applicable to the treatment of NSSI in youth.

The following subsections review promising interventions, including a brief theoretical background for each therapy. Key aspects of the treatment and considerations when applying these to youth with NSSI are discussed. Specific aspects related to which type of NSSI might be best suited to a particular therapy are also explored.

Psychoeducation

Psychoeducation regarding NSSI in youth is considered an important aspect of treatment during the initiation phase as a means to clarify and establish a mutual understanding of this behavior among treatment participants. In the chapter on family interventions (Chapter 12), more specific information is reviewed in regard to how information about NSSI is shared, including demystifying the behavior (Selekman, 2002). We also refer the reader to the chapter on inpatient treatment (Chapter 13), which discusses a more detailed review of the role of psychoeducation.

Crisis Intervention and Problem Solving Therapy

The goal of crisis intervention is to provide quick access to service, which can then provide a targeted assessment, brief duration interventions, and coordination of access to further service as necessary. A main component of the assessment is to evaluate the level of suicide risk and gain information about the circumstances of the episode of NSSI and its functions. Identification of acute and chronic stressors, potential contributing factors, and preliminary problem solving may take one to three sessions. Although no research has been done regarding the efficacy of crisis intervention in the initial phase of treatment of NSSI, best practice suggests that it has an important role in deescalating certain situations and can be considered the point of departure for further recommendations and interventions.

Theory regarding the use of problem-solving therapy (PST) assumes that maladaptive or disordered coping mechanisms are related to disordered problem solving. Table 11.1 reviews components and results of meta-analysis research on the efficacy of PST in adults who self-harm. Although PST may not be effective in reducing self-harm behavior itself, problem-solving techniques incorporated into a CBT approach may enable the participant to understand and address any triggers associated with NSSI.

Motivational Interviewing

A more recently developed therapeutic approach, motivational interviewing (MI), was born out of the merger of humanistic therapy principles (e.g., empathy, reflection; Rogers, 1951) and cognitive behavioral techniques targeting the client's particular stage of change at that time (Prochaska, DiClemente, & Norcross, 1992). It has demonstrated particular benefit with clients in the contemplation stage by exploring their ambivalence and increasing intrinsic motivation to change (Miller & Rollnick, 2002). In the precontemplation stage, MI may be used to raise awareness, whereas the action phase may involve enhancement of the client's desire to change. A number of studies during the past decade have established the efficacy MI in drug and alcohol interventions (Miller, Benefield, & Tonigan, 1993; Project MATCH Research Group, 1997; Stephens, Roffman, & Curtin, 2000), whereas other studies have begun to examine its use in various clinical populations (Hettema, Steele, & Miller, 2004).

TABLE 11.1 Therapies for Self-Injury or Self-Harm: Main Goals and Components of Interventions

Type of therapy	Goals of therapy	Therapy components	Evidence: adult and/or adolescents	Comments
Emergency card provision	Card permits direct admission to hospital, considered a novel method to reduce the incidence of further DSH due to offering a temporary escape from the adolescent's environment and getting help.	Those given the token, a green card, on discharge from hospital, were permitted to use it as a "passport" for re-admission to the pediatric ward of their local hospital. They were instructed that if they ever felt suicidal and the urge to self-harm, they would be given admission if a bed was available. The control group received standard outpatient follow up.	DSH (Cotgrove, Zirinsky, Black, & Weston, 1995) Randomized control trial, adolescents 16 and under N = 105 ER card for admission and routine care vs. routine care	Lower repetition of DSH in ER card group but not statistically significant
INDIVIDUAL THERAPY:				
Problem-solving therapy (PST)	Identify and resolve problems Teach coping and problem-solving skills by breaking down components	Problem identification Goal setting (e.g., via a behavioral analysis) Brainstorming Review potential solutions Implement a potential solution Evaluate outcome	Meta-analysis of PST in adults (Townsend et al., 2001)	PST reduced depression, hopelessness, level of problems; not conclusive concerning significantly reducing self-harm

TABLE 11.1 Therapies for Self-Injury or Self-Harm: Main Goals and Components of Interventions (continued)

Type of therapy	Goals of therapy	Therapy components	Evidence: adult and/or adolescents	Comments
		INDIVIDUAL THERAPY:		
Manual assisted CBT	Short-term, combined therapies to reduce repetitive SI via: Managing emotions Changing negative thinking	PST plus: Cognitive Behavioral Interpersonal Six sessions	Adults (Tyrer et al., 2003) Randomized trial (N = 480) MACT vs. TAU	6- and 12-month follow up: some individuals may require a longer period than this brief model provides
Dialectical behavior therapy (DBT)	Reduction in life-threatening behaviors, therapy-interfering behaviors, and quality-of-life-interfering behaviors via generalization of behavioral coping skills with enhancement of self-acceptance and self-respect	Combines PST, dialectical, and validation strategies Individual and family skills training (24-session program conducted in 12 weeks) mindfulness, distress tolerance, emotional regulation, interpersonal and communication skills	Parasuicidal adolescents in DBT (N = 29) vs. TAU (N = 82) (Rathus & Miller, 2002)	Reduced psychiatric hospital admissions; improved retention rates to outpatient treatment. Overall reduction in number of suicide attempts, but no significant group differences

GROUP THERAPY:

Developmental group psychotherapy (DGP)	Focus on adolescents going through difficulty by using positive corrective therapeutic relationships. Goals: reduce self-harm, reduce depression	Combined: Problem solving, CBT, DBT Psychodynamic psychotherapy Open groups: Acute phase: six themes including relationships, school problems, personal relationships, family problems, anger management, depression and self-harm, hopelessness and feelings about the future Long term group: emphasis on group process	Evaluation(N=62) single-blind randomized controlled trial; DGP and routine care vs. routine care alone (Wood et al., 2001)	DGP group less likely to self-harm; had better school attendance and lower behavioral problems on follow up (7 months) than those in routine care; no significant change in levels of depression, suicidal thinking, or global outcome

Note: TAU = treatment as usual

Miller and Rollnick (1991) described five core principles in MI. The first of these, expressing empathy, specifically involves use of reflective listening (as described by Rogers, 1951) to not only establish rapport, but accept and mirror the client's experiences as a means of increasing their awareness of the need for change. This principle allows the client greater insight through the idea that "I learn what I believe as I hear myself speak."

The second core principle, developing discrepancy, focuses on using specific types of questions, along with selective reflections, to focus the client on the discrepancy between their present behavior and broader personal values. The aim of this principle is to point out not the positive and negative aspects of the behavior, but the discrepancy between what the client is currently doing and would like to do to increase the motivation to change. Whereas aspects of MI are somewhat directive, the therapist is to avoid advocating for change, as it must be the client who presents the reasons for change.

To more fully illustrate this principle, therapists may use techniques such as first asking the client about the good things (e.g., "What are some of the good things about...?" "What would you miss if you weren't...?"), followed by the not so good things related to their behavior (e.g., "What are some of the not so good things about...?" "How do you see yourself in a year from now if you don't change?"). To further develop the discrepancy between their current behavior and values, the therapist may also employ specific questions (e.g., "What sort of things are important to you"? "What would it be like for you if you were no longer...one year from now?" "How does your cutting fit in with your goals?").

The third and fourth principles of MI are avoiding argumentation and rolling with resistance. Miller and Rollnick (1991) suggest therapists should respond to client resistance with acceptance and reflective listening (rather than opposition) if they are to maintain momentum toward change. MI can target youth who are at the precontemplative or contemplative phase regarding their NSSI and assist in moving them toward more active engagement.

Cognitive Behavioral Therapy

CBT, first described in the 1950s and 1960s, took its early beginnings from social learning theory and cognitive psychology and is best described as a general category of therapy rather than a distinct technique. Several approaches to treatment fall within this category, the best known being Ellis' rational emotive therapy (Ellis, 1984), Beck's cognitive therapy (Beck, Rush, Shaw, & Emery, 1979; Beck, Emery, & Greenberg, 1985), and Meichenbaum's cognitive behavior modification (Meichenbaum, 1977). CBT is one of the most well-researched types of therapy and has demonstrated efficacy with a number of Axis I disorders, including major depression, social anxiety, posttraumatic stress disorder, separation anxiety, obsessive-compulsive disorder, schizophrenia, and bulimia (Lewinsohn et al., 1990; March, Amaya-Jackson, Murray, & Schult, 1998; Wilson, 2005), across developmental stages (e.g., childhood, adolescence, adulthood, and old age; Compton et al., 2004; Wright & Beck, 1995).

Most cognitive-behavioral therapies involve a number of common principles:

- Cognition, not external factors, both mediate and cause one's feelings and overt behaviors, allowing clients to change their maladaptive beliefs in order to feel and behave more adaptively, even if little in the environment around them changes.
- Client beliefs are primarily the result of learning experiences and thus can be changed; the goal of treatment is often to unlearn related maladaptive feelings and behaviors by identifying those that are irrational and generating more rational alternate beliefs.
- More emphasis should be put on the here and now and situationally specific beliefs and behaviors rather than general or stable personality traits.
- The essence of effective therapy is to assist clients in developing more awareness of the role their irrational beliefs play in distress and helping them change those beliefs. CBT recognizes that these irrational beliefs are more common among persons with anxiety, depression, and so on and are based upon errors in reasoning or logic.

CBT is a highly structured, systematic, and time-limited intervention (typically 12–20 sessions) where the therapist plays an active role in helping clients identify and work toward specific treatment goals. Although it requires a strong therapeutic alliance, this relationship is not a focus of treatment. CBT makes use of the Socratic method of questioning to assist clients in understanding and challenging their own beliefs and establishes rational thinking on the basis of fact. Homework is also a central principle, encouraging clients to practice the techniques learned in session between sessions to reinforce learning and encourage behavioral change. CBT involves behavioral interventions (e.g., activity scheduling, graded exposure, etc.) designed to reduce maladaptive behaviors (e.g., avoidance, withdrawal, etc.) and improve cognitive functioning. Treatment can often be described as occurring in three phases, with the first of these focused on establishing a strong therapeutic alliance and reviewing CBT principles, using, if possible, examples from the client's own situation to demonstrate the relationships between thoughts, feelings, and behaviors. The second phase of therapy typically involves modifying patterns of irrational beliefs and maladaptive behavior through use of thought recording, identifying cognitive errors, examining evidence for and against beliefs, developing rational alternatives, activity scheduling, or desensitization or graded exposure procedures. The third phase of therapy involves reinforcing previously

TABLE 11.2   Relationships Between Thoughts, Feelings, and Behavior in CBT

	Thoughts	Feelings	Behavior
Irrational	I am all alone, no one cares about me	Tense, anxious, depressed	Isolates, scratches skin with paper clip
Rational	I have good friends who care about me	Calm, confident, content	Accepts invite for coffee

learned skills, preparing clients to manage their problems independently, and reducing the risk of relapse.

The relationships between thoughts, feelings, and behaviors examined in CBT may be best illustrated by the example given in Table 11.2. In this situation the client has perceived rejection by peers and is encouraged to examine his or her irrational beliefs and generate alternate ones based upon fact. The premise is that by doing so, the client will positively impact his or her subsequent feelings and behaviors.

Self-injuring adolescents whose triggers may be associated with significant symptoms of anxiety or depression, as well as those with marked irrational thoughts and a range of maladaptive behaviors, may be best suited to CBT as an initial intervention.

Dialectical Behavior Therapy

Dialectical behavioral therapy (DBT) therapy, originally developed by Linehan (1987a, b) to treat parasuicidal adults with borderline personality disorder, was later adapted by Miller and colleagues to treat NSSI and suicidal adolescents (Miller, Rathus, Linehan, Wetzler, & Leigh, 1997; Miller, Rathus, & Linehan, 2007). DBT synthesizes change-based behavioral, problem-solving, and skill-training techniques with Zen Buddhist ideas of acceptance and tolerance. DBT's underpinning in dialectic philosophy emphasizes youth finding balance between the opposing need to make change with developing self-acceptance and tolerance of distress. The therapist embodies and models this dialectical balance by accepting the adolescents for who they are in the moment and validating their feelings while challenging maladaptive behavior and pushing for change. DBT case conceptualization is informed by the perspective that psychological disorders are systemic dysfunctions resulting in emotional dysregulation. Linehan's (1993a) biosocial theory guides case conceptualization and posits a transactional individual-environment relationship, whereby individuals with biological vulnerabilities interact within invalidating environments resulting in susceptibility to emotional dysregulation and self-destructive behaviors.

DBT can be delivered using four modes: individual (outpatient and inpatient; see Chapter 13), phone consultation, therapist consultation meetings, and in-group skills training. Family therapy sessions are often integrated into treatment as a means of addressing any obstacles to therapy and furthering the generalization of skills. DBT begins with a pretreatment phase when adolescents and their families are oriented to the process and an agreement is made upon the goals of therapy. Subsequently, a hierarchical four-stage treatment model guides treatment targets (Miller et al., 2007). The core therapeutic strategies used in balance throughout the four stages of treatment include validation, dialectic, and problem-solving strategies. Stage one, which is the primary focus of DBT with adolescents addresses: (a) decreasing life-threatening behaviors; (b) decreasing behaviors that interfere with therapy; (c) decreasing quality-of-life-interfering behaviors; and (d) increasing behavioral skills. Coping skills that are taught include interpersonal skills, mindfulness, emotional regulation, distress tolerance, and walking the middle path skills. In their recent book, Miller and colleagues (2007) discuss in detail the core DBT adolescent skills and the corresponding dysregulation issues that these skills are applied toward (see Table 11.3 for a summary).

Once self-destructive behaviors are under control, stage two focuses on the reduction of any posttraumatic stress as well as helping adolescents cope with invalidating environments. Stage three of DBT involves increasing self-respect and helping adolescents identify and achieve individual short-term and long-term goals. Finally, treatment is concluded in stage four by assisting youth to enhance their capacity to experience joy. DBT targets youth with both NSSI and suicidal behavior where emotional dysregulation, inability to tolerate distress, and an invalidating environment are contributing factors to these behaviors.

Combined Group Therapies

Wood, Trainor, Rothwell, Moore, and Harrington (2001) evaluated the efficacy of group therapy using a randomized trial comparing developmental group therapy and routine care versus routine care alone for repeat deliberate self-harming adolescents. The goals, structure, and outcome of the evaluation of "developmental group psychotherapy" is outlined in Table 11.1. Although this study is only preliminary due to the small number of participants, results, from the behavioral perspective, appear promising. Symptoms such as depression and suicidal ideation, however, did not improve, suggesting that certain symptoms may be less responsive to this type of intervention.

The use of group therapy in the treatment of NSSI requires much consideration in terms of the level of skill of therapists, controls and limits on group discussion and behavior, screening of group participants, and regular ongoing communication between the group and individual therapists. Nixon, McLagan, Landell, Carter, and Deshaw

TABLE 11.3   Summary of DBT Skill Modules

DBT skill module	Core skills	Skill is useful for
Mindfulness skills	Learn to differentiate between emotional, reasonable, and wise mind. Learn how to achieve wise mind (e.g., don't judge, observe, describe, be in the moment, participate, do what works)	Self-dysregulation (e.g., dissociation, identity confusion)
Emotional regulation skills	Learn to mindfully observe and describe emotions, increase experience of positive emotions and reduce vulnerability to intense negative emotions (e.g., improve physical health, sleep, diet, get exercise, avoid drugs, build mastery)	Emotion dysregulation (e.g., emotional lability, depression, anxiety, guilt, anger)
Interpersonal effectiveness skills	Learn effective communication skills (e.g., be gentle, act interested, be fair, be truthful, stick to values, describe the issue, express, assert, reinforce, appear confident, negotiate, stay mindful, etc.)	Interpersonal dysregulation (e.g., interpersonal conflicts, chronic family disturbance as well as abuse and neglect)
Distress tolerance skills	Crisis survival skills: Distraction techniques, self-soothing techniques using the five senses, improving the moment skills (e.g., imagery), assessing the pros and cons of tolerating distress Acceptance skills: Radical acceptance, turning the mind to acceptance, willingness (to do what's needed)	Behavioral dysregulation (e.g., parasuicidal behaviors, impulsive behaviors such as drug use or aggression)
Walking the middle path	Learning to think and act dialectically, learning how to validate self and others, learning to use behavioral principals on self and others.	Cognitive dysregulation (e.g., poor problem solving and judgment, rigid black and white thinking)

Note: From Miller, Rathus, & Linehan, 2007

(2004) developed and piloted a combined group therapy program for repetitive self-injuring adolescents and their parents as an adjunct treatment. Youth are screened regarding level of motivation, reasons for self-injury, acuity of suicidal ideation, and level of substance and alcohol abuse prior to group entry. Those with moderate to high motivation and nonattention seeking and nonsensation seeking forms of NSSI (most participants are using NSSI for affect regulation and stress management) and who are not actively suicidal are offered the group, along with their parents or guardians. Youth whose abuse of substances or alcohol is considered primary or significant are requested to engage in a treatment program that focuses on addressing abuse issues. Dependent on the outcome of this intervention, youth may be offered the next group series if NSSI remains.

Table 11.4 outlines components of this group-based modality that incorporates a modified DBT-based skills component and therapeutic support group for teens and a separate group for parents. Group therapy of this kind is suited to the moderately motivated youth, who benefits from the opportunity to identify with those who also self-injure, accepts group rules regarding behavior, and benefits from group learning and reinforcement regarding skill development and practice. While a formal evaluation of this group has not yet been undertaken, a number of group series have been completed, with the majority of adolescents and parents finding aspects of the group helpful and recommending this group to others in similar circumstances.

Family Therapy

The role of family therapy in the range of psychosocial treatment interventions for NSSI in adolescents is discussed in detail in Chapter 12.

CONCLUSION

Psychosocial treatment interventions may be multiple and sequential. Addressing any co-occurring disorders with specific treatments that have evidence for success may diminish or eliminate NSSI based on the primary functions of NSSI. Engaging and treating youth and their families with NSSI can be both challenging and rewarding. Reasonable expectations regarding the recommended length of treatment, possibilities for relapse, and role of maintenance or "booster" sessions may also be considered. Reviewing outcomes from preliminary interventions, ongoing evaluation of any residual difficulties, and the fact that many youth with NSSI may have emerging mental health disorders are aspects of treatment that are best addressed by both a flexible approach and an ongoing assessment component. Although not all adolescents are fully engaged or ready to participate in the treatment process on the first round, those initial encounters and the ability for youth and families to

TABLE 11.4 Modified and Combined DBT and Therapeutic Support Groups

Community-based group for self-harming adolescents and their parents (Nixon et al., 2004)	Therapeutic objectives	Therapy components
Adolescent group: 12–14 sessions, weekly	Adolescent DBT portion (Miller, Miller, Wagner, & Rathus, 2004): validation introduction of new skills and concepts practice, reinforcing of new skills Therapeutic support for adolescents (Fine, Forth, Gilbert, & Haley, 1991): process oriented; based on experiential, interpersonal, and insight-oriented approach; provides milieu where adolescents use their peers to facilitate separation from parents; supportive environment within which change can be facilitated	DBT skills: mindfulness, distress tolerance, emotional regulation, interpersonal effectiveness Modifications to DBT: use of one-page self-assessment sheet in lieu of self-injury diary and behavioral sheet, simplified handouts and homework assignments, no multifamily skills group
Parent group: 6–7 sessions, biweekly	Facilitate separation and individuation of parents and adolescents; therapeutic support for parents and parental skill building	Parent sessions: psycho-education, therapeutic support, parental skill building (e.g., mindfulness, family interactions and communication, affect identification)

re-engage when youth are more willing can promote a positive rapport and demystify what it means to participate in a therapeutic process.

PSYCHOSOCIAL TREATMENTS AND INTERNET SITES

Dorset Mental Health Services (sponsored by the UK National Health Service): Provides useful handouts on all core DBT skills as well as coping strategies for a variety of mental health issues. (http://www.dorset-pct.nhs.uk/mental_health_services/ services_ for_users_and_carers/dbt/dbt_main/index.asp)

Kaiser Permanente Center for Health Research: Provides access to free copyrighted downloadable CBT therapist manuals as well as teen and parent workbooks for depression and for youth at risk for depression. These materials are for the use of mental health professionals to deliver group cognitive-behavioral treatment or prevention to teenagers. These are not self-help materials for the direct use of depressed teenagers and their families. (http://www.kpchr.org/public/acwd/acwd.html)

Dealing With Depression: Sponsored by the BC Ministry of Children and Families. This link provides access to a free downloadable workbook for youth to help them learn CBT skills to deal with depression. (http://www.mcf.gov.bc.ca/mental_health/pdf/ dwd_printable.pdf)

Anxiety BC: Created by BC Partners for Mental Health and Addiction Information to provide resources of self-help information and programs, as well as resources about anxiety issues for parents and caregivers. Many CBT tools and strategies are highlighted. (http://www.anxietybc.com)

Motivational interviewing: Resources on motivational interviewing, including general information, links, discussion board, training resources, and information on reprints. (http://www.motivation-alinterview.org)

Note: Refer to Chapter 15 for general resources regarding NSSI. The above list is not a complete list of all internet resources available and is not intended to be an endorsement of the information contained on these websites.

REFERENCES

Beck, A. T., Emery, G., & Greenberg, R. L. (1985). *Anxiety disorders and phobias: A cognitive perspective.* New York: Basic Books

Beck, A. T., Rush, A. J., Shaw, B. F., & Emery, G. (1979). *Cognitive therapy of depression.* New York: Guilford

Borduin, C. (1999), Multisystemic treatment of criminality and violence in adolescents. *Journal of the American Academy of Child and Adolescent Psychiatry, 40,* 495–499.

Cheung, A., & Dewa, C. (2007). Mental heath service use among adolescents and young adults with major depressive disorder and suicidality. *Canadian Journal of Psychiatry, 52,* 228–232.

Compton, S., March, J., Brent, D., Albano, A. M., Weersing, R., & Curry, J. (2004). Cognitive-behavioral psychotherapy for anxiety and depressive disorders in children and adolescents: An evidence based medicine. *Journal of the American Academy of Child and Adolescent Psychiatry, 43*(8), 930–959.

Cotgrove, A., Zirinsky, L., Black, D., & Weston, D. (1995). Secondary prevention of attempted suicide in adolescence. *Journal of Adolescence, 18*(5), 569–577.

Ellis, A. (1984). Rational emotive therapy. In R. Corsini (Ed.), *Current psychotherapies* (3rd ed.). Itasca, IL: Peacock

Fine, S., Forth, A., Gilbert, M., & Haley, G. (1991). Group therapy for adolescent depressive disorder: A comparison of social skills and therapeutic support. *Journal of the American Academy of Child and Adolescent Psychiatry, 30*(1), 79–85.

Hawton, K., Townsend, E., Arensman, E., et al. (2001) Psychosocial and pharmacological treatments for deliberate self-harm. (Cochrane) *The Cochrane Library,* Issue 4. Oxford.

Hettema, J., Steele, J., & Miller, W. (2005). Motivational interviewing. *Annual Review of Clinical Psychology, 1,* 91–111

Huey, S., Henggeler, S., Rowland, M., Halliday-Boykins, C., Cunningham, P., Pickrel, S., et al. (2004). Multisystemic therapy effects on attempted suicide by youth presenting psychiatric emergencies. *Journal of the American Academy of Child and Adolescent Psychiatry, 43*(2), 183–190

Kahn, J. S., Kehle, T. J., Jenson, W. R., & Clark, E. (1990). Comparison of cognitive-behavioral, relaxation and self-modeling interventions for depression among middle-school students. *School Psychology Review, 19*(2), 196–211.

Lewinsohn, P. M., Clark, G. N., Hops, H., & Andrews, J. (1990). Cognitive-behavioral treatment for depressed adolescents. *Behavior Therapy, 21,* 385–405.

Lewis, L. M. (2007). No-harm contracts: A review of what we know. *Suicide and Life-Threatening Behavior, 37,* 50–57.

Linehan, M. M. (1987a). Dialectical behavior therapy: A cognitive behavioral approach to parasuicides. *Journal of Personality Disorders, 1,* 328–333.

Linehan, M. M. (1987b). Dialectical behavior therapy for borderline personality disorder: Theory and method. *Bulletin of Meninger Clinic, 51,* 261–276.

Linehan, M. M. (1993a). *Cognitive behavioral treatment of borderline personality disorder.* New York: Guilford Press.

March, J., Amaya-Jackson, L., Murray, M. C., & Schult, A. (1998). Cognitive-behavioral psychotherapy for children and adolescents with posttraumatic stress disorder after a single incident stressor. *Journal of the Academy of Child and Adolescent Psychiatry, 57*(6), 585–593

March, J., Franklin, M., Nehon, A., & Foa, E. (2001). Cognitive-behavioral psychotherapy for pediatric obsessive-compulsive disorder. *Child Psychology, 30* (1), 8–18

Meichenbaum, D. (1977). *Cognitive behavior modification: An integrative approach.* New York: Plenum Press.

Miller, A. L., Rathus, J. H., & Linehan, M. M. (2007). *Dialectical behavior therapy with suicidal adolescents.* New York: Guilford Press.

Miller, A. L., Rathus, J. H., Linehan, M. M., Wetzler, S., & Leigh, E. (1997). Dialectical behavioral therapy adapted for adolescents. *Journal of Practical Psychiatry and Behavioral Health, 3,* 78–86.

Miller, A. L., Wagner, E. E., & Rathus, J. H. (2004) Dialectical behavior therapy for suicidal adolescents: An overview. In H. Steiner (Ed.), *Handbook of mental health interventions in children and adolescents: An integrated developmental approach* (pp. 659–684). San Francisco: Jossey-Bass.

Miller, W. R., Benefield, R. G., & Tonigan, J. S. (1993). Enhancing motivation for change in problem drinking: A controlled comparison of two therapist styles. *Journal of Consulting and Clinical Psychology, 61,* 455–461.

Miller, W. R., & Rollnick, S. (2002). *Motivational interviewing: PReparing people for change.* New York: Guilford Press.

Miller, W., & Rollnick, S. (1991). *Motivational interviewing: Preparing people to change addictive behavior.* New York: Guilford Press.

Muehlenkamp, J. (2006). Empirically supported treatments and general therapy guidelines for non-suicidal self-injury. *Journal of Mental Health Counselling, 28*(2), 166–185.

Mufson, L., Dorta, K. P., Wickramaratne, P., Nomura, Y., Olfson, M., & Weissman, M. M. (2004). A randomized effectiveness trial of interpersonal psychotherapy for depressed adolescents. *Archives of General Psychiatry, 61,* 577–584.

Mufson, L., Moreau, D., Weissman, M. M., Wickramaratne, P., Martin, J., & Samoilov, A. (1994). Modification of interpersonal psychotherapy with depressed adolescents (IPT-A): Phase I and II studies. *Journal of the American Academy of Child and Adolescent Psychiatry, 33*(5), 695–705.

Nixon, M. K., Cloutier, P., & Jansson, M. (2008). Non-suicidal self-harm in youth: A population based survey. *Canadian Medical Association Journal, 178*(5), 306–312.

Nixon, M. K., McLagan, L., Landell, S., Carter, A., & Deshaw, M. (2004). Developing and piloting community-based self-injury treatment groups for adolescents and their parents. *The Canadian Child and Adolescent Psychiatry Review, 13*(3), 62–67.

Prochaska, J. O., DiClemente, C. C., & Norcross, J. C. (1992). In search of how people change: Applications to addictive behaviors. *American Psychologist, 47,* 1102–1114.

Project MATCH Research Group. (1997). Matching alcoholism treatments to client heterogeneity: Project MATCH posttreatment drinking outcomes. *Journal of Studies on Alcohol, 58,* 7–29.

Rathus, J. H., & Miller, A. L. (2002). Dialectical behavior therapy adapted for suicidal adolescents. *Suicide and Life-Threatening Behavior, 32*(2), 146–157.

Roberts, M., Lazicki-Puddy, T., Puddy, R., & Johnson, R. (2003). The outcomes of psychotherapy with adolescents: A practitioner-friendly research review. *Journal of Clinical Psychology: In Session, 59*(11), 1177–1191.

Rogers, C. R. (1951). *Client-centered therapy.* Boston: Houghton-Mifflin.

Schoenwald, S., Ward, D. M., Henggeler, S. W., & Rowland, M. D. (2000). Multisystemic therapy versus hospitalization for crisis stabilization of youth: Placement outcomes 4 months post referral. *Mental Health Services Research, 2,* 3–12.

Selekman, M. (2002). *Living on the razor's edge: Solution-oriented brief family therapy with self-harming adolescents.* New York: Norton.

Stephens, R. S., Roffman, R. A., & Curtin, L. (2000). Comparison of extended versus brief treatments for marijuana use. *Journal of Consulting and Clinical Psychology, 68,* 898–908.

Townsend, E., Hawton, K., Altman, D. G., Arensman, E., Gunnell, D., Hazell, P., et al. (2001). The efficacy of problem-solving treatments after deliberate self-harm: Meta-analysis of randomized controlled trials with respect to depression, hopelessness and improvement in problems. *Psychological Medicine, 31,* 979–988.

Tyrer, P., Thompson, S., Schmidt, U., Jones, V., Knapp, M., Davidson, K., et al. (2003). Randomized controlled trial of brief cognitive behavior therapy versus treatment as usual in recurrent deliberate self-harm: The POPMACT study. *Psychological Medicine, 33,* 969–976.

Walsh, B. W. (2006). *Treating self-injury: A practical guide.* New York: Guilford Press.

Weisz, J. R., Valeri, S. M., McCarty, C. A., & Moore, P. S. (1999) Interventions for child and adolescent depression: Features, effects and future directions. In C. A. Essau & F. Petermann (Eds.), *Depressive disorders in children and adolescents* (pp. 383–435). Northvale, NJ: Harwood.

Whitlock, J., Eckenrode, J., & Silverman, D. (2006). Self-injurious behaviors in a college population. *Pediatrics, 117,* 1939–1948.

Wilson, T. (2005) Psychological treatment of eating disorders. *Annual Review of Clinical Psychology, 1*(1), 439–465.

Wright, J. H., & Beck, A. T. (1995). Cognitive therapy. In R.E. Hales, S. E. Yudofsky, & J. A. Talbott (Eds.), *American psychiatric press textbook of psychiatry* (2nd ed., pp. 1083–1114). Washington, DC: American Psychiatric Press.

Wood, A., Trainor, G., Rothwell, J., Moore, A., & Harrington, R. (2001). Randomized trial of group therapy for repeated deliberate self-harm in adolescents. *Journal of the American Academy of Child and Adolescent Psychiatry, 40*(11), 1246–1253.

12

Working with Families and Adolescents with NSSI

HEATHER VALE, MARY K. NIXON,
AND ANNA KUCHARSKI

In this chapter, the practitioner will gain an understanding of:

- The evidence regarding working with families with NSSI
- The theoretical basis for working with families with self-injuring youth
- The role and aspects important to family assessment
- Components of family interventions, whether with individual families or in group sessions with parents

Treating nonsuicidal self-injury (NSSI) within adolescent populations often encompasses the family environment of the client. This chapter will start with a review of the current literature on family risk, protective factors of adolescent self-injury, and clinical interventions involving family members in the treatment of NSSI. The role of psychoeducation and family assessment in NSSI will also be explored in this chapter. An outline of two basic models of working with families will provide clinicians with the requisite knowledge to deliver their own family intervention. Modifying the family interactions of self-injuring adolescents through family participation in therapy may provide optimal surroundings to develop more healthy coping skills.

FAMILY RISK AND PROTECTIVE FACTORS

Although no specific family factors have been clearly identified in research as risk factors associated with adolescent self-injury, certain patterns of interaction and communication appear to be more common in self-injuring adolescents. Researchers have documented relationships between self-injury and adverse childhood experiences such as sexual abuse (Tyler, Whitbeck, Hoyt, & Johnson, 2003; Whitlock, Eckenrode, & Silverman, 2006; van der Kolk, Perry, & Herman, 1991; Ystgaard, Hestetun, Loeb, & Mehlum, 2004), physical abuse (Evren & Evren, 2005; Green, 1978), and emotional neglect (Lipschitz et al., 1999). As discussed in Chapter 4, "Psychosocial Risk and Protective Factors," the importance of specific types of abuse has yet to be determined by clinical researchers. Some studies have reported sexual assault as being more predictive of NSSI, whereas others have found physical abuse to be more predictive of NSSI in adolescents. In a review of the developmental psychopathology of self-injury, Yates (2004) explored the existing literature with respect to parent-child incest. She reported that intrafamilial sexual abuse has been associated with NSSI across multiple studies. She advises that clinicians working with clients or families where incest is suspected or verified must be vigilant for signs of NSSI in adolescents.

Other family environment variables have been implicated in the presence of NSSI among adolescents. Tulloch, Blizzard, and Pinkus (1997) studied 52 self-injuring adolescents aged 14–19 years and a matched control group (N = 52). The researchers hypothesized that impaired communication between parent and adolescent has a significant role in the development of self-injuring behavior. Family communication was measured by the Parent-Adolescent Communication Scale, family cohesion and adaptability was measured by the Family Adaptability and Cohesion Evaluation Scale, and an estimate of family stress was obtained through use of the Family Inventory of Life Events. Adolescents, especially those with an internal locus of control and lacking a family confidant, were more likely to engage in self-injurious behavior. Communication deficiencies between parent and adolescent had a strong dose response effect, that is, the poorer the communication, the greater the risk of self-injury.

Correspondingly, Evans, Hawton, and Rodham, (2005) found that adolescents who thought of, or engaged in, an episode of deliberate self-harm were less able to "talk about things which really bothered them" than were nonself-injuring controls. Females with repeat episodes were "less able to talk to family members about things which bothered them" than were single-episode females. These results suggest the importance of healthy communication between family members when working with self-injuring adolescents.

Rubenstein, Halton, Kasten, Rubin, and Stechler (1998) surveyed 272 grade 10 and 11 students. They found that those who had tried to injure themselves in the past year scored approximately 62% higher on a measure of total stress, which included family-related stressors, than adolescents who had not tried to hurt themselves. Sources of family stress that were significantly related to adolescent self-injuring behavior included family suicidality, family illness, family conflict, and personal loss. Family cohesiveness and intactness appeared to be protective factors against self-injury and suicidality. Family cohesiveness was defined by the level of interpersonal closeness within the family, demonstrated by positive emotional involvement of family members, time together, consultative decision-making, and common interests and activities. The level of family intactness was also related to suicidality; students from intact families were less likely to be suicidal, students from separated or divorced families were at intermediate risk, and students living in remarried families had the highest risk. The authors of this study suggest that the "particular vulnerability in remarried families may be understood in the context of lower levels of cohesive family interaction and higher levels of stress."

In a similar study, Sourander et al. (2006) attempted to predict self-harming behavior and suicidal ideation in a cohort of 15 year olds using measures of childhood problems at 3 and 12 years of age. At the second data collection point, age 12, researchers incorporated measures of parental health and family intactness and functioning. Interestingly, at age 15, early childhood psychopathology did not predict adolescent self-harming behavior and suicidal thoughts. However, at age 12 important family factors that predicted later self-harming behavior included maternal reports of poor health and living in a nonintact family. Other relevant factors at age 12 that had significant predictive power three years later included mental health issues such as internalizing problems and aggression levels.

Marchetto (2006) studied the role of parental bonding, personality, and gender in 517 consecutive repetitive self-injuring adults who attended a general hospital setting. He found that retrospective accounts of parental care and overprotection did not discriminate between borderline personality disorder patients who engaged in self-injury from borderline personality disorder patients who did not engage in self-injury. However, when borderline personality disorder patients were excluded from the analysis, the "repetitive skin-cutting" group recalled significantly higher levels of overprotection from both mothers and fathers but lower care from mothers. The author of this study cautioned that these results must be replicated in a larger sample before they could be applied to the general population.

EVIDENCE FOR FAMILY INTERVENTIONS
WITH SELF-INJURING YOUTH

The effectiveness of adjunct family therapy specifically for nonsuicidal self-injuring adolescents has not been studied (Comtois & Linehan, 2006); however, certain factors can be taken into consideration when working with these families. For example, Harrington et al., (1998) conducted a clinical trial of brief family therapy for adolescents with suicidal ideation who deliberately poisoned themselves. The results indicated that there was a difference in response dependent on the presence of major depressive disorder (MDD).

The objective of the randomized trial of home-based family therapy was to decrease suicidality in adolescents who deliberately poisoned themselves as well as improve the functioning level of the family unit. The intervention consisted of five home-based therapy sessions, an assessment session, and four follow-up visits. In general, parents within the intervention group reported greater satisfaction with home-based treatment, but the researchers found no significant differences in suicidal thoughts between the intervention and control groups. Further analysis revealed that a subgroup of adolescents, without MDD, significantly benefited from the home-based family intervention.

Continuing this work, Harrington et al. (2000) reanalyzed the 1998 data to identify potential mechanisms for the treatment differences between self-poisoning adolescents with and without MDD. When the researchers compared the pretreatment assessments of the groups to determine possible mediators of treatment efficacy, they found that the groups were adequately matched on demographic and family variables. The only difference between the treatment group and control at follow-up was that the intervention group had fewer symptoms of depression. Regression analysis revealed that positive effects of the family-based intervention for nondepressed adolescents were partially independent of the treatment effects on the depressed adolescents. No significant differences in family functioning were found between depressed adolescents and nondepressed adolescents, ruling out the possibility that depressed youth had families with increased problems. Significant elevations did occur in the magnitude of suicidal thinking and hopelessness of depressed adolescents. The researchers concluded that improvement in suicidal ideation of the nondepressed adolescents was not due to increased family functioning but was due to the fact that they were not depressed. The authors cautioned that these results must be replicated in larger clinical interventions and that extending the duration or intensity of the family-based treatment regime may lead to greater improvements in decreasing suicidal ideation.

The use of family therapy in the treatment of adolescent depression has been more extensively studied and could be helpful for clinicians treating NSSI, where depression is often co-occurring in these youth.

Recently, Trowell et al., (2007) conducted a randomized controlled trial in which the depressed adolescents were treated with individual or family therapy. Individual therapy was hypothesized to be more effective in alleviating moderate to severe depression, but findings indicated that significant changes occurred in both treatment groups. These findings and others (see the review of family therapy and adolescent depression by Diamond & Josephson, 2005) demonstrate that family therapy has a potential role in the treatment of MDD.

Theoretical underpinnings for family therapy for self-injuring adolescents have been discussed by a number of authors including Miller, Glinski, Woodberry, Mitchell, and Indik (2002), Miller, Wagner, and Rathus (2004), Selekman (2002), and Walsh (2006). Linehan (1993), in her work on dialectical behavior therapy (DBT), proposes that one of the core dialectics (i.e., opposing factors or forces) is between the emotional vulnerability of the individual and exposure to invalidating environments. An example of this dialectic is when adolescents' responses are chronically categorized as incorrect, wrong, or defective (Miller et al., 2002; Woodberry, Miller, Glinski, Indik, & Mitchell, 2002). Invalidation might include punishment of emotional displays, intermittent reinforcement of emotional escalation, or the oversimplification of solving life's problems (Linehan, 1993). Woodberry et al. (2002) suggested that the treatment of families with depressed, suicidal, or self-injuring adolescents should include the following objectives:

- Decreasing family risk factors (e.g., abuse or psychopathology)
- Reducing skill deficits in parents (e.g., affect identification and management)
- Increasing affect identification and management
- Enhancing potential protective factors (e.g., warmth and adaptability)
- Improving interpersonal interactions (e.g., parents decrease reactivity).

They suggested that the most important aspect of improving family relationships is teaching family members how to validate each other's emotional experiences. Pragmatic strategies for therapists include helping families identify common dilemmas such as vacillating between excessive leniency and authoritarianism. Once rigid, extreme behavioral patterns are identified within the family, therapists may prompt to help families find a constructive middle ground between the two ends of the continuum (Miller et al., 2002). Interventions for adolescent self-injury can be multifaceted and dependent on the determinants of the behavior. Based on the outcome of a thorough family assessment, therapists can model and propagate these processes in families through a variety of therapeutic techniques including family and/or individual therapy.

WORKING WITH FAMILIES:
THE ROLE OF PSYCHOEDUCATION

Family involvement can be initiated through participation and engagement in psychoeducation programs about youth with mental health problems. Researchers have found that psychoeducation is an effective adjunct therapy for treatment of adolescent bipolar disorder (Miklowitz et al., 2004). In a study of adjunctive family psychoeducation in the treatment of adolescent MDD, Sanford et al. (2006) found that adolescents with MDD who participated in a treatment program that included a family psychoeducation component "showed greater improvement in social functioning and adolescent-parent relationships" than those who received treatment "as usual." The adjunct program that was presented to all family members in the family home focused on increasing knowledge about adolescent depression and its effect on the family, strengthening family communication, reducing isolation, fostering supportive interactions, and enhancing coping skills, problem solving skills, and crisis and relapse management skills. Importantly, parents who participated in the psychoeducational group found the treatment more satisfying than the control group.

The role of psychoeducation in the treatment of adolescent NSSI is addressed in the inpatient treatment chapter (Chapter 13). Table 12.1 provides a brief summary for families and caregivers regarding NSSI in youth. Psychoeducation is best conducted on an ongoing and as-needed basis as the clinician evaluates over time how parents and other family members are able to process this information.

CRISIS INTERVENTION WITH FAMILIES

School counselors and psychologists, mental heath clinicians, and physicians may encounter families with youth with NSSI at a "crisis stage." To determine appropriate interventions and management of NSSI, a thorough assessment is required. A more detailed assessment is outlined in Chapter 8, "Assessment of Nonsuicidal Self-Injury in Youth." Table 12.2 outlines tips families can use to manage immediate crisis situations and may be used as a handout.

FAMILY ASSESSMENT IN YOUTH WITH NSSI

Selekman, in his 2002 book *Living on the Razor's Edge*, outlines a multisystem approach to working with families of self-harming adolescents. This approach includes a multisystem family assessment, provides a framework for formulating and evaluating types of interventions, and highlights the importance of selecting meaningful questions. He follows

TABLE 12.1   Psychoeducation for Parents and Caregivers Regarding NSSI

Estimate of prevalence of NSSI

• Prevalence of moderate to severe NSSI has been estimated to range from 4 to 28% in adolescents.

• The age of onset of NSSI is frequently during the period of adolescence.

• Some studies have reported that females are more likely to self-injure than their male counterparts. However, no conclusive results are as yet available.

Signs of NSSI

• Unexplained injuries such as cuts or bruises.

• Dressing inappropriately for the season (i.e., wearing a turtleneck in the summer).

• Having friends who self-injure.

Continuum of NSSI

• The range of NSSI is still undetermined, with some adolescents reporting hurting themselves on only one occasion, whereas other adolescents engage in NSSI more frequently and self-injure repeatedly throughout the teenage years in a continuous or episodic fashion.

Common types of self-injury

• Cutting of body tissue

• Scratching

• Self-hitting

• Overdose of medication

• Ingesting illicit drugs or alcohol (sometimes considered indirect forms of NSSI)

Factors that contribute to NSSI

• Environmental factors such as family, school or relationship problems.

• Biological factors such as co-occurring mental health problems including depression.

• Cognitive factors such as low body satisfaction and the habitual internalization of problems.

Types of treatment for NSSI

• Individual, group, or family therapy.

• Medication to treat significant co-occurring mental health problems such as depression.

Things parents and guardians can do to help adolescents who self-injure

• Help the youth find professional help.

• Gather information about self-injury for the youth.

• Educate yourself about NSSI and associated factors.

• Support doctor and therapist appointments.

TABLE 12.2   Approach for Parents and Families when Managing a Crisis

Do:
- Stay clam (e.g., keep emotions and reactions in check).
- Encourage the adolescent to talk with you or someone he or she feels comfortable with. Demonstrate support. Intervene as necessary.
- Determine further steps jointly with the adolescent.
- Encourage the adolescent to find alternative ways to express him- or herself (e.g., writing, drawing).
- Consult your family physician, mental health clinician, school counselor, psychiatrist, or other health professional. Focus on the facts.
- Collaborate with others who may have an understanding of extenuating circumstances, stressors, other important observations, and so on. Be reasonable in whom you might ask, and if at all possible seek permission from the youth to speak with others.
- Engage the adolescent in the process of problem-solving.
- Take a temporary self-imposed break or time-out from discussions when they become sidetracked or out of control.

Don't:
- Overreact, particularly if behavior is deemed nonlife threatening.
- Digress from getting information you need to determine what to do next.
- Interpret behavior.
- Engage in power struggles, arguments, or secondary issues during the crisis.

a somewhat eclectic approach that includes cognitive skills training and mood management techniques, solution-oriented approaches with families including the possibility of "one person family therapy when family therapy is not possible due to lack of engagement or is contraindicated or counterproductive. Goal maintenance and solution enhancing strategies are discussed in the contexts of family "helpers," specifically, regarding monitoring of potential triggers and enhancing "positive triggers" (i.e., specific solution-maintaining patterns).

Walsh (1998) identified three key processes related to family resilience and protective factors: *Belief systems* include making meaning of adversity, having a positive outlook, and experiencing transcendence and spirituality. *Organizational patterns* include flexibility, connectedness, and social and economic resources. *Communication processes* include clarity, open emotional expression, and collaborative problem solving. In 2006, Walsh outlined a basic approach to working with families that focused on the varying levels of family functioning and levels of intervention required with self-injuring adolescents. This approach highlights the use of cognitive behavioral therapy and psychoeducation with families. The role of family members as "skill practice allies" includes three key roles:

- Noticing triggers and reminding the adolescent when cues have occurred
- Encouraging the adolescent to practice these skills and help identify when they have been effective
- Practicing skills with the adolescent

Walsh's model shares features of the multifamily skill development group developed by Miller and colleagues (2002). Miller suggested that family members attend group sessions to learn DBT components such as mindfulness, affect identification, and management. Family members are then encouraged to help the adolescent practice DBT skills within the family context.

Another important component of Miller and colleagues' (2002) therapy is "walking the middle path," a skill for dealing with common conflicts or dilemmas in the parent-teen relationship. By learning skills such as validation and reinforcement, parents are able to disengage from power struggles, which could potentially decrease NSSI.

From the first contact with a family member, information is available regarding, at minimum, how the family is responding and reacting both to their adolescent's behavior and to the clinician's interaction with them and the clinician's inquiries. A standard approach to a basic family assessment can be extremely helpful in identifying contributing and protective factors related to NSSI. Understanding that assessment of family functioning may occur over a number of encounters, the following list highlights key aspects that should be covered:

- Parents' understanding of the problem and level of validation or invalidation related to NSSI
- Potetial family-related triggers to incidents of NSSI, (e.g., parent-child conflict; communication difficulties; family dynamics; family stressors such as loss, separation, divorce, financial difficulties)
- Past history or current history of physical or sexual abuse
- Presence of factors that may enhance or protect youth in families, (e.g., level of warmth, adaptability, cohesion, respect for adolescent developmental processes such as separation and individuation)
- Assessment of parental skills, (e.g., level of reactivity, affective expression, ability to negotiate, listening skills)
- Presence of parental psychopathology (e.g., major depression, substance and alcohol abuse, anxiety, borderline personality disorder, history of abuse, history of self-harming behaviors)

Certain standardized measures such as the Family Assessment Device (Epstein, 1983) can be used to objectively collect a range of perspectives regarding family functioning from each family member. This model identifies six dimensions of family functioning: problem solving, communication, roles, affective responsiveness, affective involvement, and behavior control. This can then be used as another tool in identify-ing family issues that may benefit from family intervention.

Working with Families: Reviewing Basic Needs

The main goals of working with families of adolescents are to maintain a predictable family environment, continue or promote positive family interactions, preserve and build family connections, and understand and assist aspects of adolescent development such as separation and indi-viduation. Starting with a discussion regarding family functioning with a focus on "basic needs" within the family can provide a nonthreatening approach to the discussion of levels of family function. In the early stages, a discussion of Rosenberg's (1999) basic needs may be helpful to caregiv-ers of adolescents who self-injure. He identifies seven basic needs:

- Physical nurturance
- Autonomy
- Interdependence
- Integrity
- Celebration
- Play
- Spiritual communion

Rosenberg (1999) suggests that when people, in this case parents, understand what needs are not being met, they will focus on meeting those needs rather than engaging in conflict, thereby enhancing the pos-sibility of achieving resolution.

Promoting a Predictable Family Environment

Parenting of adolescents requires flexibility balanced with setting limits and appropriate expectations. Parents of self-injuring adolescents often describe "tip-toeing-like" behaviors to avoid discussions and/or disagree-ments, fearing conflict may lead to further self-injurious behavior. This trepidation can virtually paralyze the parental role if one is not care-ful. To be effective, parental limits should be consistent, predictable, and, unless safety is at issue, negotiable. These limits are more effective when developed and agreed to by the entire family.

Improving Family Interactions and Communication

Reinforcing and building upon effective family interactions as well as assisting in diminishing habitual and maladaptive responses improves family interactions and communications. Parents and adolescents can be helped to identify effective and ineffective interactions and communica-tion patterns as well as habitual responses that may perpetuate problematic interactions and communication within the family. Parenting self-injuring adolescents requires the ability to judge a situation and determine when to be flexible and when to enforce limits in a nonrigid manner.

Increasing Emotional Connectedness

Derouin and Bravender (2004) suggest that one of the primary treatment goals for adolescents who self-injure is to decrease environmental stress by increasing emotional connectedness to parents and other supportive members of the community. Selekman (2002) includes connection building in his solution-oriented model because "all children need to feel a sense of place or belonging in their families."

Gottman and DeClaire (2001) offer parents practical suggestions regarding the recognition of "bids for connection" and opportunities to "turn toward" their adolescent. Once recognized, these bids and opportunities can be the first steps in connecting emotionally with the adolescent. These authors also highlight the importance of family time and describe "rituals" as opportunities for emotional connection and bonding. Rituals of connections are described as being "repeated, predictable, and [having] symbolic meaning" and may involve individuals, family, or extend to the community. They may include "morning rituals, leavetaking, reuniting, mealtimes, homework time, bedtime, family chores, support for sports, arts, academic achievements, holiday celebrations, rites of passage, discipline, apologies, and forgiveness."

Enabling Adolescent Developmental Tasks

Parents may also need assistance in understanding normative development of adolescence to ensure that parenting, direct or indirect, is facilitating and not hampering maturity. Developmental tasks of adolescents include identity formation, sexual maturation, cognitive and social development, separation, and individuation (Santrock, 2003). A helpful resource for parents is the facts sheets on the American Academy of Child and Adolescent Psychiatry website (http://www.aacap.org), which provides a comprehensive outline of normative adolescent development.

When parents initially learn that their adolescent is engaging in self-injurious behavior, they often react with fear and mistrust of the adolescent. They may react by becoming hypervigilant and overprotective. However, this desire to protect should be balanced with support for the adolescent's progress toward separation and individuation, particularly when parents are able to determine that their youth is safe.

Parental Functioning and Parental Factors

During the treatment process, parents may also experience mental health-related problems. These problems often affect their ability to function effectively as a parent. Problems may include disclosure of historical abuse, unresolved mental health difficulties such as mood disorders (major mood disorder, bipolar disorder, and substance abuse), or marital conflict or breakdown. Initially, parents seek treatment for their adolescent, unprepared or unaware of the need to address their own difficulties. Understanding the effect of parental difficulties on adolescent well-being has the potential to be either transformative or guilt inducing for parents and must be approached sensitively.

As professionals working with these families, we must carefully choose the timing and approach used to address and explore these sensitive issues with parents. We must establish rapport, or parents may withdraw themselves and their adolescent from treatment. Parents may be encouraged to address these issues as a way to model for their adolescent accepting help and support; however, some parents may choose to keep these issues confidential.

Exploring the early-life experiences of parents can be helpful to the therapeutic process and treatment outcome. Research indicates that if parents have had difficult childhoods but have made sense of their experiences, they are not bound to recreate the same negative interactions with their children (Siegel & Hartzell, 2003). In families where a parent has a substance abuse or mental health problem, an adolescent may take on a more parental role within the family. In these instances, parent-adolescent roles and boundaries must be redefined and rebalanced.

Single parents may experience stressors that include financial difficulties and limited personal and parental time. In these instances, parents may benefit from a problem-solving approach that emphasizes the importance of meeting basic needs and developing and utilizing a more comprehensive support network. Setting priorities for personal care and family involvement are often paramount in these discussions.

Significant marital conflict may also be a contributing factor to adolescent behavior. With support, parents may be willing to take the necessary steps to examine the more personal aspects of their lives in family or couples therapy. For some families, working through separation and divorce may also be an aspect of therapy. Family separation may create further crisis and family instability. The outcome often depends upon the maturity of the couple and their ability to put their adolescent's mental health needs above their own emotional needs. The role of the family therapist can be critical in assisting with this balance of needs.

In addition, parents may benefit from acquiring and refining skills related to developing relaxation and coping techniques, modeling healthy communication and effective negotiation, and regulating appropriate affect. In addition to obtaining and supporting professional assistance for their adolescent, two key approaches a parent can implement to positively affect the outcome of adolescent self-injury are practicing patience and providing stability and consideration. Parents can be reminded that patience does not necessarily mean complacency, and that commitment means steadfastly remaining focused on the goals outlined in therapy.

The following case illustrates family factors associated with adolescent NSSI and how these were addressed through treatment.

K.M., a 13-year-old female, presented with her mother to an urgent care service for assessment of suicide risk. She had no previous history of contact with mental health services. K.M. lived alone with her mother, who had been divorced for many years. She had no recent contact with her father. K.M. had been self-injuring on and off for the past several months. Her chief complaint regarding stress was the ongoing conflict with her mother, noting that she typically cut after she and her mother had an argument or disagreement.

During the initial interview, K.M.'s mother expressed her anger about her daughter's behavior, as she was not complying with house rules, was not regularly attending school, and, she felt, was not contributing positively to the mother-daughter relationship. She also expected that by referring K.M for individual assessment and treatment, her daughter would cease cutting. K.M's mother was observed to be highly emotionally reactive to her daughter.

Over a period of three weeks, K.M was also assessed by a psychiatrist. Concerned that she was depressed, her family physician had prescribed a Selective Serotonin reuptake inhibitor (SSRI). The psychiatric assessment concluded that a trial of medication made sense, as she did not meet the criteria for MDD. The mother was encouraged to disengage during conflict and to work with the clinician on crisis management and parenting techniques. She had difficulty with this approach and continued to negatively reinforce her daughter's behavior when expectations were not met.

A referral was made to a group for adolescents who self-injure and their families. After attending the group for 5 weeks, K.M. voluntarily moved from her family's home to a friend's. This move was planned with her mother's consent. While participating in the parent group, K.M.'s mother realized and accepted the need for individual counseling and support for herself. Parenting issues that required further work included minimizing reactivity and disengaging from power struggles related mostly to adolescent separation and individuation issues.

K.M. benefited most from the distress tolerance aspect of the skill-building component of the adolescent group. During the therapeutic support part of the group, she was able to share and problem-solve regarding conflicts she experienced with her mother. After being out of the home for several months K.M. commented that "you only have one mother" and began to have more realistic expectations regarding her relationship with her mother. K.M. completed the group and reported no further self-injury, although she continued to have disagreements with her mother.

PARENTS AS EFFECTIVE ADVOCATES

Effective parental advocacy requires preparation, persistence, inquiry, and involvement. Adequate preparation requires parents to be ready to answer questions about:

- Family history
- Changes in adolescent mood and behavior
- Level of adolescent functioning in home, community, and school settings
- Events and circumstances that may have led to current difficulties or precipitated changes to adolescent mood and behavior
- Strategies that have been tried and their level of success or failure

Effective persistence requires parents to adequately convey their level of concern about all adolescent symptoms. They must not give up when faced with systemic barriers or resistance from the adolescent. Community advocacy and support groups can provide parents with an opportunity to meet with other parents who understand and may be able to offer advice and support.

Knowledge about self-injury and how it presents during adolescence can assist parents in accessing appropriate treatment and services in a timely manner. Libraries and the Internet provide a wealth of information regarding self-injury. Treatment of self-injury often involves a number of professionals and agencies. Parents may find it useful to have someone act as a case manger to assist with coordinating the care and treatment for their adolescent. Parents need to remain involved and committed throughout the prescribed course of treatment. Consistent attendance at medical appointments and treatment sessions is essential to adolescent recovery and requires a strong commitment from parents.

TWO MODELS OF WORKING WITH FAMILIES

Family work can occur within two basic models. The first is with the adolescent and the family; the second is a group model. The first model is a family therapy model that includes the self-injuring adolescent and key family members. Key members may include parents, siblings, extended family, and significant others. Each session may include all family members or may be with the adolescent or parents on their own. Much depends on a thorough assessment of family dynamics. Family therapy is contraindicated in the presence of ongoing abuse or protection issues in the family home. Creation of a safe therapeutic environment is paramount to a successful therapeutic outcome. The four phases in this model include: (a) family assessment; (b) psychoeducation; (c) improving family interactions and communication; and (d) closure.

Individually Based Family Therapy

Phase One: Family Assessment

The first phase of treatment is designed to build rapport with the adolescent and family and assess the levels of functioning in the adolescent and family. This phase, usually lasting two or three sessions, includes a thorough assessment of the severity and duration of the self-injuring behavior. As with all treatment approaches to self-injury, the therapist must begin by ensuring that the adolescent is safe and stable. A separate session with the parents may be necessary to develop a safety plan.

During this phase of treatment, a thorough family history is gathered and a family tree created. The family and the therapist identify areas of family resiliency and note patterns of destructive behavior. Identifying patterns of destructive behavior in a family may highlight intergenerational vulnerabilities. Family interactions during these sessions may also highlight patterns of family interaction that may be unwittingly contributing to adolescent and family distress.

Phase Two: Psychoeducation

Psychoeducation for the family includes providing information about the prevalence and features of self-injury, crisis information and management, and skills training regarding mindfulness and distress tolerance. This phase of therapy lasts two or three sessions and often overlaps with the assessment phase. Tables 12.1 and 12.2 provide detailed information about psychoeducation.

Phase Three: Improving Family Interactions and Communication

The third phase is the lengthiest phase of therapy, and the number of sessions is determined by the level of family function and engagement. During this phase, family members explore current patterns of interaction and experiment with alternate ways of relating, increase emotional connectedness, identify and consider the developmental tasks of adolescence, and refine emotional regulation and effective interpersonal skills. Separate sessions with the parents may be needed to address individual parent issues or couple issues that may be affecting the adolescent's recovery and well-being.

Phase Four: Ending Therapy

Once the family's therapeutic goals have been met, family therapy comes to an end.Goals are reviewed, changes are highlighted, and possible next steps are discussed. Sometimes parents or the individual adolescent need further therapeutic intervention.

A family therapy approach with parents may still be helpful if an adolescent does not want to attend family sessions. An adolescent may be more willing to attend individual or group therapy initially; however, as the adolescent gains skills and confidence from individual or group therapy and possibly sees parenting changes, s/he may be willing to engage in family therapy.

Parent Group for Parents of Self-Injuring Youth

The second model incorporates a parent group that may be used either as the principal component of family-based work or as an adjunct to individualized family sessions based on the needs of parents and their level of functioning and motivation. This program (Nixon et al., 2004) is based on six sessions conducted over 12 weeks in combination with a separate 12-week adolescent DBT-supportive psychotherapy group. The parent group sessions last for 2 hours, are conducted in the late afternoon to accommodate work hours, and run with two cotherapists. The following is a brief outline of the six sessions:

Session One: Introduction

1. Introduction of members and therapists, including brief synopsis of personal goals for this group from parents
2. Overview of parent group sessions
3. Discussion and agreement of group goals and guidelines
4. Psychoeducation about self-injuring behavior in adolescence
5. Crisis intervention, management, and planning
8. Wrap up
9. Feedback and evaluation

Session Two: Basic Needs and Self-Care

1. Check in with each parent present
2. Review of group guidelines
3. Review and discussion of basic needs
4. Review and discussion of parental self-care
5. Introduction to mindfulness and mindfulness exercise
6. Wrap up
7. Feedback and evaluation of session

Session Three: Family Interactions

1. Check in
2. Review of family interactions
3. Review of family communication

4. Discussion: creating a safe environment
5. Mindfulness exercise
6. Wrap up
7. Feedback and evaluation of session

Session Four: Effect of Family History

1. Check in
2. Review of self-understanding of parental influences
3. Discussion of family values and beliefs
4. Mindfulness exercise
5. Wrap up
6. Feedback and evaluation of session

Session Five: Parental Modeling

1. Check in
2. Parental modeling: affect regulation, interpersonal skills, distress tolerance
3. Family rules
4. Mindfulness exercise
5. Wrap up
6. Feedback and evaluation of session

Session Six: Review: Where To Go from Here

1. Check in
2. Review and further discussion of previous material
3. Next steps
4. Mindfulness exercise
5. Wrap up
6. Feedback and final evaluation

At the end of each session, participants are asked to fill out a one-page feedback form that therapists can use to tailor group topics and meet the specific needs of participants, with the possibility of increasing the number of sessions, if necessary.

SUMMARY

Incorporating knowledge of risk and protective factors into assessment protocols of NSSI can help clinicians devise effective treatment plans. Differentiating adolescents presenting with major mental health problems such as MDD from those without can provide clinicians with a framework for developing a therapeutic intervention that addresses how best to include family members in the treatment of adolescent NSSI. Utilizing components of DBT and traditional family therapy may potentiate existing interpersonal skills and create new ways of coping with conflicting situations within the family. Future research needs to address the potential role of the family environment in development and maintenance of adolescent NSSI to tailor effective interventions. Evaluation of treatment programs for adolescent NSSI that include families is also required.

REFERENCES

Comtois, K. A., & Linehan, M. M. (2006). Psychosocial treatments of sui-cidal behaviors: A practice friendly review. *Journal of Clinical Psychology*, *62*(2), 161–170.

Derouin, A., & Bravender, T. (2004). Living on the edge: The current phe-nomenon of self-mutilation in adolescents. *American Journal of Maternal/ Child Nursing*, *29*(1), 12–18.

Diamond, G., & Josephson, A. (2005). Family based treatment research: A 10 year update. *Journal of the American Academy of Child and Adolescent Psychiatry*, *44*(9), 872–887.

Epstein, N. B. (1983). The McMaster Family Assessment Device. *Journal of Marital and Family Therapy*, *9*(2), 171–180.

Evans, E., Hawton, K., & Rodham, K. (2005). In what ways are adolescents who engage in self-harm or experience thoughts of self-harm different in terms of help-seeking, communication and coping strategies. *Journal of Adolescence*, *28*, 573–587.

Evren, C., & Evren, B. (2005). Self-mutilation in substance-dependent patients and relationship with childhood abuse and neglect, alexithymia, and temperament and character dimensions of personality. *Drug and Alcohol Dependence*, *80*, 15–22.

Gottman, J., & DeClaire, J. (2001). *The relationship cure: A 5 step guide to strengthening your marriage, family, and friendships*. New York: Three Rivers.

Green, A. H. (1978). Self-destructive behavior in battered children. *American Journal of Psychiatry*, *135*, 579–582.

Harrington, R., Kerfoot, M., Dyer, E., McNiven, F., Gill, J., Harrington, V., et al. (1998). Randomized trial of a home-based family intervention for chil-dren who have deliberately poisoned themselves. *Journal of the American Academy of Child and Adolescent Psychiatry*,*37*(5), 512–518.

Harrington, R., Kerfoot, M., Dyer, E., McNiven, F., Gill, J., Harrington, V., et al. (2000). Deliberate self-poisoning in adolescence: Why does a brief family intervention work in some cases and not others? *Journal of Adoles-cence*, *23*, 13–20.

Linehan, M. M. (1993). *Cognitive behavioral therapy of borderline personality disorder*. New York: Guilford Press.

Lipschitz, D. S., Winegar, R. K., Nicolaou, A. L., Hartnick, E., Wolfson, M., & Southwick, S. M. (1999). Perceived abuse and neglect as risk factors for suicidal behavior in adolescent inpatients. *Journal of Nervous and Mental Disease*, *187*(1), 32–39.

Marchetto, M. J. (2006). Repetitive skin-cutting: Parental bonding, personality, and gender. *Psychology and Psychotherapy: Theory, Research, and Practice, 79,* 445–459.

Miklowitz, D. J., George, E. L., Axelson, D. A., Kim, E. Y., Birmaher, B., Schneck, L., et al., (2004). Family-focused treatment for adolescents with bipolar disorder. *Journal of Affective Disorder, 82*(1), 113–128.

Miller, A. L., Glinski, J., Woodberry, K. A., Mitchell, A. G., & Indik, J. (2002). Family therapy and dialectical behavior therapy with adolescents: Part I: Proposing a clinical synthesis. *American Journal of Psychotherapy, 56*(4), 568–584.

Miller, A. L., Wagner, E. E., & Rathus, J. H. (2004). Dialectical behavior therapy for suicidal adolescents: An overview. In H. Steiner (Ed.), *Handbook of mental health interventions in children and adolescents: An integrated developmental approach* (pp. 659–684). San Francisco: Jossey-Bass.

Nixon, M. K., McLagan, L., Landell, S., Carte, A., & Deshaw, M. (2004). Developing and piloting community-based self-injury treatment groups for adolescents and their parents *Canadian Academy of Child and Adolescent Psychiatry Review, 13*(3), 62–67.

Rosenberg, M. B. (1999). *Nonviolent communication: A language of compassion.* Del Mar, CA: Puddle Dancer

Rubenstein, J. L., Halton, A., Kasten, L., Rubin, C., & Stechler, G. (1998). Suicidal behavior in adolescents: Stress and protection in different family contexts. *American Journal of Orthopsychiatry, 68*(2), 274–284.

Sanford, M., Boyle, M., McCleary, L., Miller, J., Steele, M., Duku, E., & Offord, D. (2006). A pilot study of adjunctive family psychoeducation in adolescent major depression: Feasibility and treatment effect. *Journal of the American Academy of Child and Adolescent Psychiatry, 45*(4), 386–395.

Santrock, J. W. (2003). *Adolescence* (9th ed.). New York: McGraw-Hill

Selekman, M. (2002). *Living on the razor's edge: Solution-oriented brief family therapy with self-harming adolescents.* New York: Norton.

Siegel, D., & Hartzell, M. (2003). *Parenting from the inside out: How a deeper self-understanding can help you raise children who thrive.* New York: Jeremy P. Tarcher.

Sourander, A., Aromaa, M., Philakoski, L., Haavisto, A., Rautava, P., Helenius, H., et al. (2006). Early predictors of deliberate self-harm among adolescents: A prospective follow-up study from age 3 to age 15. *Journal of Affective Disorder, 93,* 87–96.

Trowell, J., Joffe, I., Campbell, J., Clemente, C., Almqvist, F., Soininen, M., et al. (2007). *European Child & Adolescent Psychiatry, 16*(3), 157–167.

Tulloch, A. L., Blizzard, L., & Pinkus, Z. (1997). Adolescent-parent communication in self-harm. *Journal of Adolescent Health, 21,* 267–275.

Tyler, K. A., Whitbeck, L. B., Hoyt, D. R., & Johnson, J. D. (2003). Self-mutilation and homeless youth: The role of family abuse, street experiences and mental disorders. *Journal of Adolescent Research, 13*(4), 457–474.

van der Kolk, B. A., Perry, J. C., & Herman, J. L. (1991). Childhood origins of self-destructive behavior. *American Journal of Psychiatry, 148,* 1665–1671.

Walsh, F. (1998). *Strengthening family resilience.* New York: Guilford Press.

Walsh, B. W. (2006). *Treating self-injury: A practical guide.* New York: Guilford Press.

Whitlock, J., Eckenrode, J., & Silverman, D. (2006). Self-injurious behaviors in a college population. *Pediatrics, 117,* 1939–1948.

Woodberry, K. A., Miller, A. L., Glinski, J., Indik, J., & Mitchell, A. E. (2002). Family therapy and dialectical behavior therapy with adolescents: Part II. A theoretical review. *American Journal of Psychotherapy, 56*(4), 585–602.

Yates, T. M. (2004). The developmental psychopathology of self-injurious behavior: Compensatory regulation in posttraumatic adaptation. *Clinical Psychology Review, 24,* 35–74.

Ystgaard, M., Hestetun, I., Loeb, M., & Mehlum, L. (2004). Is there a specific relationship between childhood sexual and physical abuse and repeated suicidal behavior? *Child Abuse and Neglect, 28,* 863–875.

13

Adolescent Nonsuicidal Self-Injury in an Inpatient Setting

NICHOLAS LOFTHOUSE AND LAURENCE KATZ

In this chapter, the practitioner will gain an understanding of:

- The current evidence specific to the presentation of hospitalized youth who engage in NSSI
- The current evidence specific to the treatment of hospitalized youth who engage in NSSI
- Special considerations that relate to this population (e.g., potential for contagion and trigger effects for NSSI in the hospital setting and the importance of discharge planning)

Due to the use of multiple terms, definitions, and mixed adolescent and young adult samples further complicating the study of this already challenging phenomenon, to impart greater clarity on this subject, we focus our discussion in this chapter on the presentation, assessment, and treatment of nonsuidical self-injury (NSSI) among adolescents (12–18 years). More specifically, in the first part of our chapter we report on the prevalence of NSSI in this population, discuss why the study of NSSI in this context is important, and then review the current literature on NSSI among adolescent inpatients. We devote the second half of this chapter to clinical issues and recommendations associated

with adolescent NSSI at this level of care including assessment, empirically supported treatments, and clinical treatment guidelines.

RECENT TRENDS IN INPATIENT SERVICES
FOR CHILDREN AND ADOLESCENTS

In 2003, the president of the United States' New Freedom Commission on Mental Health recognized acute inpatient services as part of
the "essential components of a balanced system of mental health." This
is certainly the case for children and adolescents in the United States,
for whom psychiatric disorders are the leading reason for hospitalization, accounting for approximately 33% of all hospital days and approximately 50% of annual mental health costs (Geller & Biebel, 2006). Of
the 1.3 million U.S. youth accessing mental health services in 1997,
21.8% received inpatient care, which is a 142.7% increase in utilization
since 1986 (Pottick et al., 2002). More recent data demonstrate a continued increase, with a 58.5% rise in discharges between 1996 and 2004
(Blader & Carlson, 2007). However, irrespective of the greater need for
this "essential component of mental heath," over the past two decades
managed health care organizations in the United States have dramatically reduced coverage for such services (Pottick et al., 2002), resulting in the median length of stay plummeting 63%, from 12.2 days in
1990 to 4.5 days in 2000 (Case, Olfson, Marcus, & Sigel, 2007). Finally,
despite these statistics, "youth with severe psychopathology [self-
injurious behavior included] who are treated in the inpatient setting,
particularly have been overlooked in much of the published research"
(Kaplan & Busner, 1997, p. 77).

PREVALENCE OF NSSI AMONG
ADOLESCENT INPATIENTS

We are aware of only three publications reporting the prevalence of
NSSI among adolescent inpatients. The first, published, by Lipschitz et
al. in 1999, examined, via clinical interviews, 71 adolescent admissions
in a U.S. hospital over a one-year period and identified 28 (39%) cases
of NSSI (mostly cutting) within the previous year. Three years later,
Nixon, Cloutier and Aggarwal (2002) assessed all 12- to 18-year-olds
admitted to either an inpatient or acute youth partial hospital program
in Canada over a four-month period. They found 27 of 91 (29.7%) inpatients and 15 of 39 (38.5%) partial hospitalization patients who met
criteria for repetitive NSSI during the past six months, with over 80%
engaging in such acts at least once per week. In 2004, Makikyro et al.
examined 157 12- to 17-year-olds admitted to an inpatient unit in Finland over a 15-month period and identified 84 (67.7%) adolescents with
occasional or frequent NSSI.

Although the study by DiClemente, Ponton, and Hartley (1991) is often cited with regard to the prevalence of NSSI among adolescent inpatients, their reported 61.2% may not be a valid estimate for this age range because their sample was actually composed of 12- to 21-year-olds. Similarly, although the 40% incidence rate reported by Darche (1990) is frequently cited, this was actually based on a citation of Pattison and Kahan (1983), who in turn were referring to a study by Green (1967). This original study may not be truly representative of inpatient adolescent NSSI, either, because it examined 52 5- to 12-year-olds with schizophrenia in a residential setting, 17 (40%) of whom engaged in self-harm (intent to die or not was not reported).

REASONS TO STUDY NSSI IN ADOLESCENT INPATIENTS

Apart from its large and increasing prevalence, another reason to examine NSSI in adolescent inpatients is that very few empirical studies of this behavior have been conducted in this population. This is surprising considering NSSI is probably at its most severe in terms of frequency, duration, and impairment when adolescents are admitted to a psychiatric hospital. A second reason for studying NSSI among adolescent inpatients is that it is a high-risk behavior, associated with irreversible damage to body tissue (Nock & Prinstein, 2005), severe psychopathology, and suicidal behaviors (Nock, Joiner, Gordon, Lloyd-Richardson, & Prinstein, 2006). In fact, Nock et al. found 50–75% of adolescents with a history of NSSI also had a past suicide attempt. Third, despite its prevalence and the recent increase in research and public attention devoted to NSSI, it is a symptom of only one diagnosis (borderline personality disorder) in the *Diagnostic and Statistical Manual of Mental Disorders,* Fourth Edition (*DSM-IV;* American Psychiatric Association [APA], 1994). However, only half of those adolescents who engage in NSSI meet criteria for borderline personality disorder (Nock et al., 2006). This problem of classification is further complicated by the extensive co-occurrence displayed by adolescents with NSSI (see Chapter 5).

Related to the difficulty of classifying NSSI, a fourth incentive to its further examination is the lack of evidence-based screens and assessments for NSSI in adolescence. Most inpatient assessments for this age range focus primarily on *DSM-IV* disorders and suicide, often neglecting to measure NSSI and its functions. Fifth, an exploration of the risk and protective factors and other correlates associated with NSSI among adolescents receiving inpatient services may open a window on the biological and psychosocial etiological mechanisms of this phenomenon in general. Sixth, because no longitudinal studies have been conducted on NSSI in community or clinical populations, we are unaware of the onset, course, impairment, and outcome, particularly after hospitalization, of these problems. Seventh, as we have very few empirically supported pharmacological or nonpharmacological treatments or preventions for NSSI in general, evidence-based interventions for adolescent inpatient settings are sorely needed. Finally, as NSSI is being increasingly seen in inpatient hospitals that have experienced dramatically reduced insurance coverage (Pottick et al., 2002) and plunging lengths of stay (Case et al., 2007), we need to identify cost- and time-efficient ways to identify, evaluate, and treat adolescents with NSSI on our units.

RESEARCH ON NSSI IN ADOLESCENT INPATIENTS

We conducted a review of the literature on NSSI in adolescent inpatients via two methods: (a) A PsychInfo (1872 to October 2007) and Medline (1950 to October 2007) abstract search;* and (b) examination of citations in articles on adolescent NSSI. This approach yielded 42 peer-reviewed publications. Unfortunately, most of these do not differentiate NSSI from suicidal self-harm either theoretically in terms of the study's definition or methodologically by asking and reporting the intent of participants' behavior. Therefore, we can only report on eight studies that specifically examined NSSI in samples of adolescent inpatients (excluding samples with mental retardation, developmental delays, or schizophrenia). To our knowledge, this is the first detailed review of studies specifically examining NSSI in adolescent-only inpatient samples.

One of the earliest studies we identified was conducted by Darche in 1990. Via a chart review spanning three years of admissions to a US inpatient facility, she identified 48 13- to 17-year-old females (ethnicity not reported) who endorsed two or more acts of NSSI in their past or during hospitalization. Darche also identified a clinical control group of 48 female patients who did not report any past or present NSSI. Compared to this group, the NSSI group had significantly more sleep, eating, anxiety, and affective disorders; higher scores on measures of depression, anxiety, somatization, hostility, body comfort, and global psychopathology; more sexual abuse; and more treatment with psychotropic medications. However, the NSSI group had significantly fewer diagnoses of conduct or adjustment disorder and lower scores on an index of confidence. Furthermore, a discriminant function analysis, based on sleep disorders, depression, and anxiety scores correctly classified 71.9% of the NSSI group.

Regarding the previously described study by Lipschitz et al. (1999), 28 adolescents with NSSI (specific data on gender and ethnicity not reported) were identified and compared to "a control group without this behavior" (p. 36). Results indicated the NSSI group was significantly

---

* Using the terms "self-injury" or "self-injurious" or "self-mutilation" or "self-mutilate" or "self-harm" or "cutting" and "child" or "children" or "adolescent" or "adolescence" or "youth" or "juvenile" and "inpatient" or "hospital" or "hospitalized."

more likely to be female and report sexual, physical, and emotional abuse and neglect. In addition, for the entire sample of 71 adolescents (i.e., those who did and did not engage in NSSI), those who had made suicide attempts were also significantly more likely to report past "self-mutilation" (p. 35).

In Nixon et al.'s (2002) previously described study of 27 inpatient and 15 partial hospitalization adolescents with NSSI (85.7% female, ethnicity not noted), the majority reported daily urges to cut or scratch themselves and engaging in acts more than once a week. Most identified the source of the idea to engage in NSSI as internal urges occurring after a stressful event, and the most common body location as their lower arm or wrist. Similarly, the majority of adolescents described the act as a solitary activity and reported making up stories to account for the inflicted injuries. Furthermore, many adolescents described using other behaviors, the most common being talking with others, to distract themselves from NSSI when they could not engage in it. Few adolescents reported disclosing their NSSI to anyone and that few hurt themselves after consuming substances. Regarding why they engaged in NSSI, adolescents reported an average of 8.2 reasons, with most endorsing eight or more reasons. Nearly all endorsed affect-related reasons, the two primary ones being "to cope with feelings of depression" and "to release unbearable tension." After the act, the majority reported relief but also negative feelings such as shame, guilt, and disappointment. Nearly all endorsed three or more addictive symptoms from a list of seven (e.g., behavior occurs more often and/or severity has increased). In addition, Nixon et al. reported that adolescents who engaged in NSSI had poor psychosocial functioning; problems with eating disorders, substances, depression, and internalized and externalized anger; and had been sexually, physically, or emotionally abused. In particular, those with clinically elevated levels of internalized anger appeared at greater risk for more addictive features of NSSI. Finally, most of the adolescents who engaged in NSSI also reported daily suicidal ideation and a history of suicide attempts in the past six months.

Two years later, in Makikyro et al.'s (2004) previously described study (66.6% female, ethnicity not noted), NSSI was found to be significantly more frequent among girls, girls who smoked, and those with affective disorders. Also in 2004, Kumar, Pepe and Steer identified 50 13- to 17-year-olds (62% females, 64% Caucasian) from a U.S. facility who described a history of one form of NSSI, cutting, with a mean age of onset of 13.5 years. Diagnostically, the majority had unipolar depression and other comorbid disorders; less than a third had a disruptive, anxiety, substance, or bipolar disorder or reported a history of physical or sexual abuse. Kumar and colleagues found more than half recalled using razors and/or knives to cut and nearly all identified their forearms as the most common area. Most noted that cutting was never serious enough to require medical attention, but nearly all said their cutting behavior had sometimes been misinterpreted as a suicide attempt. Half of the sample claimed they never cut to experience physical pain, whereas the majority described cutting as being impulsive but also denied discovering any unremembered cuts or alcohol or substances affecting their decision to cut. Most described affect modulation as the common reason for cutting, a sense of relief after the act, and the experience of seeing or feeling blood as being important to them.

In the same year, Nock and Prinstein (2004) applied a functional approach to the assessment of NSSI among 108 (70.1% girls; 72.2% Caucasian) 12- to 17-year-olds in a U.S. inpatient hospital. Nearly the entire sample reported at least one incident of NSSI, about half reported 19 or more incidents over the previous year and a mean age of onset of 12.8 years. Multiple methods of NSSI were reported, the most common ones being erasing skin to draw blood, pulling out hair, burning skin, self-tattooing, inserting objects under skin or nails, picking at body to the point of drawing blood, biting, scraping skin to draw blood, and hitting oneself. Interestingly, cutting and carving skin was only reported by 26% of the sample. Regarding the function of NSSI, Nock and Prinstein found NSSI appeared to serve the four functions of automatic negative reinforcement, automatic positive reinforcement, social negative reinforcement, and social positive reinforcement (see Chapter 3 for details regarding these functions).

Using a subsample from their 2004 study, Nock and Prinstein (2005) examined the contextual features and behavioral functions of NSSI among 89 (74.2% girls, 76.4% Caucasian) of the 12- to 17-year-old inpatients. They found NSSI was typically performed impulsively, within a few minutes of contemplating it and in the absence of alcohol or drugs or physical pain. Additional analyses further supported Nock and Prinstein's (2004) theory of NSSI serving the two functions of social and automatic reinforcement. The majority of adolescents reported NSSI among their friends, suggesting the role of social modeling. Furthermore, the number of incidents by friends was associated with adolescents' endorsement of a social positive reinforcement function, indicating that some may believe their friend's NSSI was effective in obtaining rewarding social behavior, such as attention or assistance, from others. Interestingly, endorsement of the function of positive reinforcement for NSSI was associated with the absence of substance use, suggesting that, for some adolescents, NSSI is a more effective strategy than alcohol or substance use to obtain a favorable state. In addition, Nock and Prinstein found the experience of more physical pain with NSSI was associated with a longer time contemplating the act and the number of NSSI acts performed by friends.

Automatic negative reinforcement, reported in Nock and Prinstein's earlier study (2004) as the most common function of NSSI, was specifically associated with hopelessness (i.e., a negative feeling) and a history of suicide attempts (i.e., another common method used to "stop bad feelings," p. 141). They also found automatic positive reinforcement to be correlated with major depressive disorder and posttraumatic stress disorder, suggesting that NSSI may counter the associated lack of affect associated with these disorders by creating some sensation or feeling in order to "feel something, even if it is pain" (p. 141). Nock and Prinstein also reported a correlation between the function of social positive and negative reinforcement and social perfectionism, indicating NSSI may serve to obtain help from others or to escape others, respectively. Finally, both the positive and negative social reinforcement functions of NSSI were associated with younger age, ethnic minority status, and depression, suggesting that obtaining social rewards or escaping socially aversive experiences was important to younger adolescents, minorities, and the existence of depression. The latter association suggests that depression may lead to engaging in NSSI for social functions or the social outcome of NSSI may contribute to the development of depression.

More recently, Nock et al. (2006) were the first to use structured clinical interviews to examine the diagnostic correlates of adolescents with NSSI. Using the sample from their 2005 study, they examined the relationship between NSSI and suicide attempts. Nock and colleagues found evidence demonstrating extensive diagnostic heterogeneity for adolescents engaging in NSSI. The majority of adolescents met criteria for at least one *DSM-IV* Axis I diagnosis, with a mean of three and range of 0–8 diagnoses, mostly externalizing (conduct disorder and oppositional defiant disorder), internalizing (major depressive disorder), and substance disorders (nicotine abuse and cannabis dependence). In addition, the majority of adolescents also met criteria for an Axis II personality disorder, with the highest frequency for borderline, avoidant, and paranoid, respectively. There was considerable overlap between NSSI and suicide attempts, with most adolescents reporting a lifetime history of multiple suicide attempts. The main NSSI characteristics associated with suicide attempts were a longer history of NSSI, use of more methods, and the absence of physical pain during NSSI.

Summary

To date, we were only able to identify eight studies on the phenomenology of NSSI among adolescent inpatients. Most of these studies were on Caucasian females in American facilities, and just over a third of them were published by Nock and colleagues, who used the Functional Assessment of Self-Mutilation questionnaire (Lloyd, Kelley, & Hope, 1997) with the same sample recruited from a facility in New England. Synthesizing the results of all eight studies, the main findings suggest that NSSI among adolescent inpatients is a relatively high-frequency behavior that starts in early adolescence, is more common among females, is usually inflicted on the forearm, and is performed in the absence of alcohol and substances. It is not typically used to experience physical pain but as a function of negative or positive automatic or social reinforcement to decrease or increase emotional, physiological, or social experiences. NSSI usually leads to a sense of relief after the act and is associated with addictive properties, increasing its future frequency and intensity. Finally, NSSI has a high degree of co-occurrence, commonly associated with affective problems, particularly with depression; impulsivity, eating, anxiety, and alcohol and substance problems; a history of sexual, physical, and emotional abuse; and past suicide ideation and attempts.

Research Limitations and Future Directions

We did not include several of the studies found in our literature search because they failed to distinguish and directly report the intent of self-injury, used a mixed-age sample, or did not clearly document whether the clinical setting was actually an inpatient one. Even though NSSI, suicidality, and *DSM-IV* (APA, 1994) diagnoses are highly associated, not all the aforementioned studies contained comprehensive measures of suicidality and comorbid psychopathology. In addition, only half of the studies discussed used an evidence-based assessment to investigate NSSI in this treatment setting. Furthermore, as few studies used clinic control groups, some of the reported findings may not be specific to NSSI but associated with psychopathology in general. Related to this is the lack of studies investigating proximal-distal, causal-maintaining, and risk-protective factors specific to NSSI before and after discharge from the inpatient setting. Finally, as all of the studies were phenomenological in content, we know virtually nothing about which pharmacological or psychosocial interventions are helpful or unhelpful in treating NSSI among adolescent inpatients.

In light of these limitations, we encourage researchers to conduct future studies on NSSI among adolescent inpatients and to clearly distinguish, assess, and directly report both NSSI and suicidal behavior; focus on adolescent-only samples in clearly described clinic settings; use clinic control groups to identify and examine NSSI-specific proximal-distal, causal-maintaining, and risk-protective factors retrospectively and prospectively; and test the efficacy and effectiveness of pharmacological and nonpharmacological treatments.

INPATIENT ASSESSMENT OF NSSI

Because little research exists on the assessment of NSSI for adolescent inpatients, in this section we have incorporated information based on the previous literature review and clinical expertise. A thorough review of the tools available for the assessment of NSSI, suicidal behaviors as a whole, and measures evaluating dimensions of psychopathology related to NSSI is beyond the scope of our discussion and is available elsewhere (American Academy of Child and Adolescent Psychiatry, 2001; Nock, Wedig, Janis, & Deliberto, in press). As with all assessments, the fundamental purpose is to collect enough information to perform an individualized case-conceptualization that will guide treatment and assessment of treatment outcomes.

Due to the strong relationship between NSSI and suicidal behavior (see Chapter 5) and the potential implications for immediate treatment decisions, the primary goal is to uncover the perceived intent behind the adolescent's behavior. Any reported current or past suicidal intent, plan, or attempt should be fully evaluated for indication of current and future risk and treated accordingly. At the time of writing, there are no validated measures for the comprehensive assessment of NSSI, so this process remains a clinical one guided by measures used in previous research. Thus, we encourage the application of the Functional Assessment of Self-Mutilation questionnaire (Lloyd, et al., 1997), used in the studies by Nock and colleagues (2004, 2005, 2006), or the Queens/ Ottawa Self-Injury Questionnaire (now called the Ottawa Self-Injury Questionnaire, OSI), employed by Nixon et al. (2002), to evaluate the function of NSSI among adolescent inpatients.

Although the FASM or OSI can assist in understanding the function of NSSI but may not elucidate all the cognitive, emotional, interpersonal, perceptual, and behavioral determinants of this clinical phenomena. In the dialectical behavior therapy model (DBT; see below), behavioral chain analysis (Linehan, 1993; Miller, Rathus, & Linehan, 2007) is the primary structured clinical tool utilized to understand the functions and determinants of the behavior and ultimately inform both pharmacotherapeutic and psychotherapeutic interventions (Katz, Gunasekara, & Miller, 2002; Katz & Fotti, 2005). Behavioral chain analysis is a method of assessment in which the clinician uses detailed questioning to delineate the cognitive, behavioral, emotional, perceptual, and interpersonal determinants of a problem behavior (Linehan, 1993). The assessment includes a description of the periods prior to, during, and after the problem behavior occurred. Thus, in meeting with the patient, the clinician obtains a description of the moment-to-moment events (cognitions, emotions, behaviors, interpersonal experiences) occurring over the course of the day in which the problem behavior occurred (it is occasionally necessary to begin on the previous day if that is when the problem began). It may begin with a question such as "How were you feeling when you woke up that morning?" and it could then go on to ask "So what did you do after you got out of bed?" The events can be categorized into those that created a vulnerability to emotional dysregulation, precipitating events of the problem behavior, the problem behavior itself, and its consequences. To obtain and maintain cooperation of the patient in this process, validation of the patient's experience is essential. At the end of the analysis, the goal is to have created a chain starting at the beginning of the day, with the links on the chain consisting of the events over the course of the day that are relevant to the problem behavior. The chain allows for accurate formulation of the determinants of the problem behavior and thus development of an appropriately targeted pharmacotherapeutic or psychosocial intervention.

On an inpatient unit, the treatment team's dialectical dilemma in assessing these behaviors involves the need to evaluate the behavior and its function for the safety and treatment of the patient versus the risk of reinforcing the behavior through excessive attention (McClellan & Hamilton, 2006). In the adolescent inpatient DBT model (Katz, Cox, Gunasekara, & Miller, 2004; Katz et al., 2002; Katz & Cox, 2002), this dialectic is synthesized in a manner meant to ensure safety and reinforce functional behavior while not reinforcing dysfunctional behavior. The patient is oriented to this approach at the beginning of the inpatient admission. If a patient engages in NSSI, his or her immediate medical needs are attended to (e.g., suturing if required), but this occurs in a matter of fact manner and without discussion of the events that took place. Once medically stable, the patient is given a behavioral chain analysis form to complete, and all other activities are on hold for the remainder of the day, allowing for completion of this "work." The following day, the chain analysis is reviewed in detail with the patient. This allows the team to gain an understanding of the function and determinants of the behavior and to develop a solution analysis (Linehan, 1993) involving various behaviorally anchored psychotherapeutic strategies meant to influence future coping and prevent repetition of this behavior. This form of assessment (behavioral chain analysis as part of multimethod analysis) is integrated into a larger treatment approach to the management of NSSI on adolescent inpatient units.

In addition to the functional assessment and behavioral chain analysis of NSSI, its age of onset, initial causes, course, related stressors, protective factors, methods, severity (extent of damage), and addictive properties should also be measured. Furthermore, due to the high degree of co-occurrence, a comprehensive assessment of associated *DSM-IV* diagnostic correlates (both Axis I and II) and the adolescent's psychological, family, school, and social functioning is also required (see Chapter 5). To assess Axis I and II psychopathology among adolescent inpatients, once again we turn to what has been used in research on NSSI in this population and recommend the Diagnostic Interview Schedule for Children Version 2.3 (Shaffer et al., 1996) and the Diagnostic Interview for *DSM-IV* Personality Disorders (Zanarini, Frankenburg, Sickel, & Yong 1996) as used in Nock et al.'s (2006) study.

Due to the paucity of research in this area, there are numerous limitations to the assessment of NSSI on inpatient units and thus substantial areas for future study. For example, few studies have examined agreement across measurement methods (e.g., interview vs. self-report) or informants (i.e., adolescent vs. parent report) and the subsequent combining of this data. Also, the reliance on retrospective assessments introduces recall bias into the evaluation, so the development of real-time measures of these behaviors would be of benefit. Finally, currently available instruments have yet to be validated for tracking treatment progress. Research groups have begun working on these areas, and we hope we will have some guidance in the future.

EMPIRICALLY SUPPORTED INPATIENT
TREATMENT OF NSSI

As of 2007, we found no published studies on the treatment of NSSI among adolescent inpatients. However, a study conducted by one of the authors (Katz et al., 2004) appears to be the most relevant. This study examined the effect of DBT versus treatment-as-usual (TAU) on self- and other-harm behavior among 62 14- to 17-year-old inpatients (83.9% female, 72.6% Caucasian) admitted to one of two Canadian psychiatric inpatient units. With 32 adolescents, one unit used a two-week-long DBT protocol, modified from the 12-week adolescent outpatient program by Miller and colleagues (Miller, Rathus, Linehan, Wetzler, & Leigh, 1997; Rathus & Miller, 2002), while the other unit used TAU- with the remaining 30 adolescents. Behavioral incidents on the unit (i.e., nurse-reported violence toward self [NSSI and suicidal behavior] or others), depressive symptoms, suicidal ideation, hopelessness, hospitalizations, emergency room visits, and adherence to follow-up recommendations before and after treatment and at one-year follow-up was examined for both groups. During hospitalization, it was found that DBT was significantly more effective than TAU for reducing behavioral incidents, such as NSSI, suicidal behavior, and other-directed aggression, on the unit. At one-year follow-up, both treatment groups demonstrated highly significant reductions in parasuicidal behavior, depressive symptoms, and suicidal ideation. The DBT group had larger effect sizes in the improvement of suicidal ideation and depression, but these did not reach statistical significance with this sample size.

Although this is the only study of its kind to date, certain limitations need to be acknowledged, such as not separating NSSI from suicidal self-harm and aggression toward others, thus preventing one from knowing whether DBT would be specifically effective for the treatment of NSSI among adolescent inpatients. In addition, the nonrandomization of inpatients to the DBT or TAU groups makes it impossible to rule out other explanations for the results. Finally, this study was conducted in the Canadian health system, so the DBT program and its associated results may not generalize to U.S. adolescent inpatient units that have, on average lengths of stay of only 4.5 days (Case et al., 2007).

Despite these limitations, the results suggest that DBT might be helpful in managing adolescent patients' NSSI while they are on the unit and may have other long-term advantages that require further study with a larger sample size. In that respect, clinicians should consider these DBT components in addition to psychoeducation of the patient and family regarding NSSI and DBT, which also involves orientation to Linehan's biosocial theory of the etiology and maintenance of pervasive emotion dysregulation. Briefly, this theory states that emotion dysregulation is the end result of the transaction of an individual biologically predisposed to increased emotionality with an invalidating environment. For the adolescent inpatient, twice-weekly individual DBT sessions and daily DBT skills-training groups, involving behavioral strategies for managing emotional, behavioral, interpersonal, and self-dysregulation, should also be considered. In DBT sessions, the therapist utilizes a behavioral chain analysis assessment to gain an understanding of the function of the behavior. Then, by encouraging the adolescent to apply the skills learned in-group and the therapist's use of validation and other DBT change strategies, the therapist helps the adolescent develop more functional behaviors. In addition to psychoeducation, family members are also provided ongoing support and informal skills training. An essential element of delivering DBT and for treating NSSI in particular is regular treatment team consultation meetings. These allow the team to support each other and adhere to the treatment model in treating this multi-problem population.

CLINICAL TREATMENT GUIDELINES FOR NSSI AMONG ADOLESCENT INPATIENTS

Because the previously described study is the only published treatment study pertaining to NSSI among adolescent inpatients, we provide seven important clinical recommendations for the treatment of this condition. Our primary recommendation is that clinicians take a biopsychosocial approach to treatment. Biological intervention using pharmacotherapy is an essential part of inpatient treatment, but we can not cover this topic any further in this chapter because of the extensive review and clinical guidelines in Chapter 14 of this book. We believe that a fundamental part of the biopsychosocial approach is the conceptualization of NSSI as a solution, albeit a dangerous one, that the adolescent has acquired to temporarily cope with certain internal states or external situations. An empathic understanding of this, coupled with an emphasis on encouraging adolescents to abstain from hurting themselves while we assist them in acquiring less harmful coping strategies (taking prescribed medication included) in a collaborative and supportive relationship, should be directly communicated to the adolescents and their families. Although no research exists on family problems and NSSI among adolescent inpatients, on the basis of clinical experience with this population, we advocate for the inclusion of families in treatment, wherever possible, to be involved as part of the solution to their adolescent's destructive behavior (see Chapter 12 for a review of working with families).

In this age of U.S. managed health care cuts and a median length of stay of 4.5 days (Case et al., 2007), our second recommendation, psychoeducation, has become even more essential and at times, along with medication changes and psychosocial support, the sole thing we can provide for our patients in the short span that they are hospitalized. Psychoeducation differs from psychotherapy in that the former involves the patient and family's acquisition of biopsychosocial information about their psychiatric condition and the skills to recover from the condition. In contrast, psychotherapy is the subsequent individualized application of the information and skills to specific real-life problems inside and outside of therapy (Friedberg & McClure, 2002). Psychoeducation's theoretical mechanism of change is based on Sir Francis Bacon's centuries' old assumption that "knowledge is power" (Henry, 2002) and the Chinese proverb, "Give a man a fish, you feed him for a day; teach a man to fish and you feed him for a lifetime." In that respect, psychoeducation has the potential to give patients and their families cognitive and emotional power (empowerment) over their condition; accurate information, which may also correct previous misinformation and prevent future errors; and the ability to distinguish, access, and utilize efficacious and cost-effective mental health and educational services.

Unfortunately, no evidence-based psychoeducation programs currently exist for NSSI, so individual inpatient units have to develop their own materials. These should include age-appropriate handouts containing information on biopsychosocial components of NSSI and the skills to recover from this condition. Ideally, these psychoeducation handouts will be used to structure discussions with individuals, groups, and families on the inpatient unit. To help readers develop these materials, we suggest utilizing information from this and other chapters in this book. We also recommend materials from three websites, (Self-Injury and Related Issues [http://www.siari.co.uk], Self-injury: You are NOT the only one [formerly Secret Shame; http://www.palace.net/~llama/psych/injury.html], and National Self-harm Network [http://www.nshn.co.uk] two books (*A Bright Red Scream: Self-Mutilation and the Language of Pain* [Strong, 1999] and *The Scarred Soul: Understanding and Ending Self-Inflicted Violence* [Alderman, 1997]), and Bateman's (2004) article, *Self-Help Books on Deliberate Self-Harm*.

Furthermore, we recommend that psychoeducation include a definition of NSSI and information regarding adolescent inpatient and community prevalence, gender ratio and presentation, average age of onset, developmental course including its potentially addictive nature, causal and maintaining factors, four behavioral functions, common co-occurring conditions (particularly suicide), and pharmacological and non-pharmacological (therapy-, school-, and community-based) treatment approaches. Individuals can be educated to consider NSSI as a coping mechanism or solution, albeit a very dangerous, destructive, and ultimately ineffective one, that a person acquires to temporarily deal with certain highly distressing internal states or external situations. In addition, NSSI can be thought of as (a) a condition that someone has rather than something he or she is (e.g., cutter, self-injurer, self-mutilator, borderline); (b) a "no-fault disorder" (Koplewicz, 1997) caused by a combination of inherited biological vulnerabilities triggered by stressful life events, none of which the individual or family consciously chose; and (c) a "challenge," as in "It's not your fault, but it's your challenge" (Fristad

& Goldberg-Arnold, 2003) from which they ultimately need to recover with the help of their family, friends, and treatment team.

Psychoeducation regarding recovery skills can include basic cognitive-behavioral and DBT tools such as identifying and changing "unhelpful" thoughts, feelings, and behaviors into "helpful" thoughts, feelings, and behaviors: pleasant events scheduling; effective individual and collaborative problem-solving strategies; the adoption of healthy sleeping, eating, and exercise habits; mindful acceptance and validation; emotion regulation; distress tolerance; and interpersonal effectiveness skills.

Our third recommendation involves the application of a set of clinical guidelines developed by Kevin Epps, a British clinical and forensic psychologist, for the care of adolescents who engage in NSSI (Epps, 1997). Epps astutely and sensitively discusses several issues including, among others, (a) reducing access to objects used for NSSI; (b) how staff should respond to such acts; (c) use of physical restraint in "extreme instances" (p. 543); (d) the pros and cons and importance of strictly adhering to institutional and legal procedures when using pat, strip, or, in extreme circumstances, internal body searches; (e) what to do when adolescents refuse medical treatment despite infection and the risk of blood poisoning and gangrene; (f) increasing supervision and checks during the night, when some adolescents are at greater risk for NSSI; (g) the distressing or contagious effect of NSSI among peers; (h) the traumatic effect on staff and resulting staff-team splitting; and (i) understanding the limitations of conducting therapy in short-term secure environments.

Because research indicates that NSSI among adolescent inpatients usually serves one or more of four functions (Nixon et al., 2002; Nock & Prinstein, 2004, 2005), our fourth recommendation involves the assessment of these functions to help the adolescent and family become more aware of their association with NSSI and to develop less destructive strategies to meet the same function. Fifth, as described in the assessment section, adolescent inpatients with NSSI have a wide variety of additional psychiatric conditions. As the research on this co-occurrence and recommendations for treatment are discussed in detail in Chapter 5 of this book, we encourage readers to review that chapter to supplement these guidelines.

Sixth, although clinicians are frequently concerned about the possibility of the contagion of NSSI among inpatient adolescents, no studies have been conducted specifically on this phenomenon. Furthermore, Katz et al. (2004) did not find any evidence of contagion when they implemented their DBT program. However, research by Taiminen, Kallio-Soukainen, Nokso-Koivisto, Kaljonen and Helenius (1998), among others, found evidence of the contagion of general self-harm (i.e., intent not examined) among 12 Finnish adolescent inpatients. They reported that 10 of the 12 inpatients were involved in contagion episodes, usually cutting, and this was mostly performed by depressed females with borderline personality disorder as initiation rites to strengthen group cohesion. Based on these findings, Taiminen and colleagues recommended units avoid placing several females with borderline personality disorder on the same ward at the same time, or, if this is not practical, limiting hospitalization to two weeks, making access to the method of self-harm as difficult as possible, introducing healthy rites of togetherness, and openly discussing contagion with adolescents. As the reoccurrence of NSSI may be increased in the period immediately following discharge, our final recommendation is that patients receive timely referrals to outpatient mental health professionals who are experienced in working with this population.

CONCLUSION

NSSI appears to be a highly prevalent, growing, and severe problem in adolescent inpatients. Despite this, only eight studies on this phenomenon currently exist, the majority of which describe the frequency, age of onset, methods, body location, gender difference, function, addictiveness, and associated co-occurrence of NSSI. More research is required on the development and testing of screens, assessments, and biopsychosocial treatments for youth with NSSI on inpatient units. Until that time, the process of assessment and treatment remains a clinical one guided by existing research. Therefore, for the assessment of NSSI among adolescent inpatients, we encourage the application of functional assessment questionnaires, behavioral-chain analyses, and structured clinical interviews of Axis I and II psychopathology. For treatment, we recommend a biopsychosocial approach using pharmacotherapy, psychoeducation, DBT for the development of less destructive functional strategies, Epps' (1997) clinical guidelines, the reduction of co-occurring conditions, and timely transitions to outpatient therapists with experience treating adolescent NSSI.

REFERENCES

Alderman, T. (1997). *The scarred soul: Understanding and ending self-inflicted violence*. Oakland, CA: New Harbinger Publications.

American Academy of Child and Adolescent Psychiatry. (2001). Practice parameter for the assessment and treatment of children and adolescents with suicidal behavior. *Journal of the American Academy of Child and Adolescent Psychiatry, 40*, 24S–51S.

American Psychiatric Association. (1994). *Diagnostic and statistical manual of mental disorders* (4th ed.). Washington, DC: Author.

Bateman, A. W. (2004). Self-help books on deliberate self-harm. *British Journal of Psychiatry, 185*, 441–442

Blader, J. C., & Carlson, G. A. (2007). Increased rates of bipolar disorder diagnoses among U.S. child, adolescent and adult inpatients. *Biological Psychiatry, 62*, 107–114.

Case, B. G., Olfson, M., Marcus, S. C., & Siegel, C. (2007). Trends in the inpatient mental health treatment of children and adolescents in US community hospitals between 1990 and 2000. *Archives of General Psychiatry, 64,* 89–96.

Darche, M. A. (1990). Psychological factors differentiating self-mutilating and non-self-mutilating adolescent inpatient females. *Psychiatric Hospital, 21,* 31–35.

DiClemente, R. J., Ponton, L. E., & Hartley, D. (1991). Prevalence and correlates of cutting behavior: Risk for HIV transmission. *Journal of the American Academy of Child and Adolescent Psychiatry, 30,* 735–739.

Epps, K. (1997). The use of secure accommodation for adolescent girls who engage in severe and repetitive self-injurious behaviour. *Clinical Child Psychology and Psychiatry, 2,* 539–552.

Friedberg, R. D., & McClure, J. M. (2002). *Clinical practice of cognitive therapy with children and adolescents: The nuts and bolts.* New York: Guilford Press.

Fristad, M. A., & Goldberg-Arnold, J. S. (2003). *Raising a moody child: How to cope with depression and bipolar disorder.* New York: Guilford Press.

Geller, J. L., & Biebel, K. (2006). The premature demise of public child and adolescent inpatient psychiatric beds: Part I. Overview and current conditions. *Psychiatric Quarterly, 77,* 251–271.

Green, A. H. (1967). Self-mutilation in schizophrenic children. *Archives of General Psychiatry, 17,* 234–244.

Henry, J. (2002). *Knowledge is power. How magic, the government and an apocalyptic vision inspired Francis Bacon to create modern science.* Cambridge, UK: Icon Books.

Kaplan S. L., & Busner, J. (1997). Prescribing practice of inpatient child psychiatrists under three auspices of care. *Journal of Child and Adolescent Psychopharmacology, 7,* 275–286.

Katz, L. Y., & Cox, B. J. (2002). Dialectical behavior therapy for suicidal adolescent inpatients: A case study. *Clinical Case Studies, 1,* 81–92.

Katz, L. Y., Cox, B. J., Gunasekara, S., & Miller A. L. (2004). Feasibility of dialectical behavior therapy for suicidal adolescent inpatients. *Journal of the American Academy of Child and Adolescent Psychiatry, 43,* 276–282.

Katz, L. Y., & Fotti, S. (2005). The role of behavioral analysis in the pharmacotherapy of emotionally dysregulated problem behaviors. *Child and Adolescent Psychopharmacology News, 10,* 1–5.

Katz, L. Y., Gunasekara S., & Miller, A. L. (2002). Dialectical behavior therapy for inpatient and outpatient parasuicidal adolescents. In L.T. Flaherty (Ed.), *Adolescent psychiatry: The annals of the American Society for Adolescent Psychiatry* (pp. 161–178). New Jersey: Analytic Press.

Koplewicz, H. (1997). *It's nobody's fault: New hope and help for difficult children and their parents.* New York: Three Rivers Press.

Kumar, G., Pepe, D., & Steer, R. A. (2004). Adolescent psychiatric inpatients' self-reported reasons for cutting themselves. *Journal of Nervous and Mental Disease, 192,* 830–836.

Linehan, M. M. (1993). *Cognitive-behavioral treatment of borderline personality disorder.* New York: Guilford Press.

Lipschitz, D. S., Winegar, R. K., Nicolaou, A. L., Hartnick, E., Wolfson, M., & Southwick, S. M. (1999). Perceived abuse and neglect as risk factors for suicidal behavior in adolescent inpatients. *Journal of Nervous and Mental Disease, 187,* 32–39.

Lloyd, E., Kelley, M. L., & Hope, T. (1997). *Self-mutilation in a community sample of adolescents: Descriptive characteristics and provisional prevalence rates.* Presented at the annual meeting of the Society for Behavioral Medicine, New Orleans, LA.

Makikyro, T. H., Hakko, H. H., Timonen, M. J., Lappalainen, J. A. S., Ilomaki, R. S., Marttunen, M. J., et al. (2004). Smoking and suicidality among adolescent psychiatric patients. *Journal of Adolescent Health, 34,* 250–253.

McClellan, J. M., & Hamilton, J. D. (2006). An evidence based approach to an adolescent with emotional and behavioral dysregulation. *Journal of the American Academy of Child and Adolescent Psychiatry, 45,* 489–493.

Miller, A. L., Rathus, J. H., & Linehan, M. M. (2007). *Dialectical behavior therapy for suicidal adolescents.* New York: Guilford Press.

Miller, A. L., Rathus, J. H., Linehan, M. M., Wetzler, S., & Leigh, E. (1997). Dialectical behavior therapy adapted for suicidal adolescents. *Journal of Practical Psychiatry & Behavioral Health, 3,* 78–86.

New Freedom Commission on Mental Health (2003) *Achieving the promise: Transforming mental health care in America.* Rockville, MD: Department of Health and Human Services.

Nixon, M. K., Cloutier, P. F., & Aggarwal, S. (2002). Affect regulation and addictive aspects of repetitive self-injury in hospitalized adolescents. *Journal of the American Academy of Child and Adolescent Psychiatry, 41,* 1333–1341.

Nock, M. K., Joiner, T. E., Gordon, K. H., Lloyd-Richardson, E., & Prinstein, M. J. (2006). Non-suicidal self-injury among adolescents: Diagnostic correlates and relation to suicide attempts. *Psychiatry Research, 144,* 65–72.

Nock, M. K., & Prinstein, M. J. (2004). A functional approach to the assessment of self-mutilative behavior. *Journal of Consulting and Clinical Psychology, 72,* 885–890.

Nock, M. K., & Prinstein, M. J. (2005). Clinical features and behavioral functions of adolescent self-mutilation. *Journal of Abnormal Psychology, 114,* 140–146.

Nock, M. K., Wedig, M. W., Janis, I. B., & Deliberto, T. L. (in press). Evidence-based assessment of self-injurious thoughts and behaviors. In J. Hunsley & E. J. Mash (Eds.), *A guide to assessments that work.* New York: Oxford University Press.

Pattison, E. M., & Kahan, J. (1983). The deliberate self-harm syndrome. *American Journal of Psychiatry, 140,* 867–872.

Pottick, K. J., Warner, L. A., Issacs, M., Henderson, M. J., Milazzo-Sayre, L., & Manderscheid, R. W. (2002). Children and adolescents treated in specialty mental health care programs in the United States: 1968 and 1997. In R. W. Manderscheid & M. J. Henderson (Eds.), *Mental health, United States, 2002.* Washington, DC: U.S. Government Printing Office.

Rathus, J. H., & Miller, A. L. (2002). Dialectical behavior therapy adapted for suicidal adolescents. *Suicide and Life-threatening Behavior, 32,* 146–157.

Shaffer, D., Fisher, P., Dulcan, M. K., Davies, M., Piacentini, J., Schwab-Stone, et al. (1996). The NIMH Diagnostic Interview Schedule for Children Version 2.3 (DISC-2.3): Description, acceptability, prevalence rates, and performance in the MECA Study. *Journal of the American Academy of Child and Adolescent Psychiatry, 35,* 865–877.

Strong, M. (1999). *A bright red scream: Self-mutilation and the language of pain.* London: Virago.

Taiminen, T. J., Kallio-Soukainen, K., Nokso-Koivisto, H., Kaljonen, A., Kelenius, A., & Helenius, H. (1998). Contagion of deliberate self-harm among adolescent inpatients. *Journal of the American Academy of Child and Adolescent Psychiatry, 37,* 211–217.

Zanarini, M. C., Frankenburg, F. R., Sickel, A. E., & Yong, L. (1996). *The Diagnostic Interview for DSM-IV Personality Disorders (DIPD-IV).* Boston, MA: McLean Hospital.

14

Use of Medication in the Treatment of Nonsuicidal Self-Injury in Youth

PAUL L. PLENER, GERHARD LIBAL,
AND MARY K. NIXON

In this chapter, the practitioner will gain an understanding of:

- Models for the integration of pharmacotherapy in the treatment of NSSI
- A rationale for when to consider medication as part of the treatment as well as the types of medication that may be used for the treatment of NSSI and co-occurring psychiatric disorders or symptoms.
- A treatment algorithm to assist practitioners in their approach to psychopharmacologic treatment for NSSI in youth

As discussed in the chapters on psychosocial risk and protective factors and neurobiology of NSSI, it is essential to understand the underlying risk factors of a disorder, both from a psychosocial, as well as from a neurobiological perspective. Negative family environment, emotional dysregulation, as well as self-derogation predict a higher risk for NSSI, whereas from the biological perspective, dysregulation within the serotonergic, dopaminergic, and opioid systems has been identified in different populations as factors associated with NSSI.

Biopsychosocial factors interrelate, and neurobiological states can affect behavior, which then can be further impacted by biologically

$_{\jmath}$ feedback loops. It is at this level that therapeutic approaches
fy dysfunctional behavior. As discussed in the chapter on
biology of NSSI (Chapter 6), neurobiological "states" can be
d by both psychotherapeutic interventions and psychopharmacology, enabling the individual to change behavior that in turn affects
feedback circuits, altering neurobiology by new learning experiences.
The role of psychopharmacologic interventions for NSSI ought to be
considered in the context of these conditions and interactions.

KEY POINTS IN CONSIDERING THE ROLE
OF MEDICATION IN YOUTH WITH NSSI

In the following section, the practitioner will be informed about:

- When to consider intervening with medication
- How to inform parents and adolescents about what to expect from pharmacological treatment
- When a "shared-care" management approach with the family physician or pediatrician might be appropriate

The decision to initiate psychopharmacological treatment for NSSI is made on an individual basis. Determining the choice of the appropriate treatments ranging from psychosocial to psychopharmacological must be based on information gathered by a thorough diagnostic and psychosocial assessment (see Chapter 8, on assessment). Successful psychopharmacological interventions work as an adjunct to ongoing psychosocial treatments. Medication can be helpful in augmenting the effects of psychosocial interventions, for example, by improving mood and motivation in depression and thus, helping to relieve the burden of symptoms. Nevertheless, in the long run the patients benefit from learning effective skills and strategies to manage their biopsychosocial risk factors.

Psychopharmacological interventions should be considered in youth with NSSI when a co-occurring psychiatric disorder (with sufficient evidence for the role of medication) is not responsive to psychosocial interventions alone. NSSI, as a behavioral symptom itself, may need to be addressed with the use of medication. It is important to emphasize that a simplified approach to pharmacological treatment of NSSI does not exist. Thus far, no medication has been licensed for the treatment of NSSI specifically. Many medications described in this chapter would be considered "off-label" (meaning without approval of the drug regulation agencies such as the Federal Drug Administration [FDA], the European Medicines Agency [EMEA], or Health Canada). It is important to acknowledge and inform patients and families about this when obtaining informed consent and assent.

A "shared care" approach to medication management, for example, with the patient's family physician or pediatrician can be helpful, particularly when patients have long distances to travel to see a child and adolescent psychiatrist or when appointments with the specialist are limited. Open communication and sharing of information between the family physician and the child and adolescent psychiatrist enables better care; for example, symptoms and side effects can be monitored to effectively evaluate dosing, potential side effects, medication changes, and compliance.

In summary, psychopharmacological treatment is recommended:

- If other approaches to treating NSSI have failed or are insufficient, especially concerning managing significant symptoms
- If NSSI has significantly affected the individual from partaking in an age-appropriate social, school, and family life
- As part of a treatment regime that also includes psychosocial interventions such as psychotherapy

The following case of a youth with repetitive NSSI and co-occurring disorders illustrates how assessment for medication and its implementation were integrated and facilitated progress with psychosocial interventions.

A.B. was a young woman of 15 years living with her parents and referred to the self-harm group. She had a 1-year history of self-injury, bulimia, and distorted body image as well as symptoms of major depression. In addition, there were a number of psychosocial stressors related to her family. Her relationship with her mother was enmeshed, and she was not able to achieve the developmentally appropriate need to initiate separation and individuation.

Her early participation in group therapy was limited in that she was moderately anxious and found it difficult to talk and interact. A.B. also appeared to have difficulty focusing on the discussion or material, claiming that her "mind was elsewhere." After 6 weeks of group sessions, the group leaders recommended that A.B. have a further psychiatric consultation for medication review, as they felt that her lack of concentration and level of depression were affecting her ability to participate in therapy. During the psychiatric consultation A.B. revealed that she had previously been started on fluoxetine, up to 20 mg per day for less than 4 weeks. Due to her and her mother's concern about taking antidepressants, they reduced the dose to 10 mg a day on their own, and after another 4 weeks, feeling that it had not helped, discontinued completely. It was around this time that A.B. started the group in addition to her individual therapy. A.B. commented that her depressive symptoms became worse thereafter and that "the antidepressant did not help me when I took it." She also disclosed for the first time that she was hearing voices, mostly when she was extremely depressed, that would tell her that she was "no good" or that she should harm herself. She met criteria for major depressive disorder with psychotic features and bulimia with co-occurring NSSI.

In a joint session with A.B. and her mother, the psychiatrist spent some time discussing the importance of an adequate trial of an antidepressant (both in the length of the trial and the target dose) prior to concluding that a medication is not helpful. The role of treating the psychotic symptoms with an atypical antipsychotic was also discussed. A.B. and her mother agreed to a retrial of the fluoxetine and to consider the addition of a low dose of quetiapine (25–50 mg) to target auditory hallucinations if they remained. They reviewed side effects and restarted fluoxetine at 10 mg every morning for the first week then increased to 20 mg. They were seen weekly for follow up over the first month, and quetiapine 25 mg every evening was added at week 3. By week 4, psychotic symptoms had dissipated, and A.B.'s mood was starting to lift. Both her mother and therapist noted brighter affect, better eye contact, and more engagement socially. No side effects were noted with the fluoxetine, and sedation with the quetiapine resolved hallucinations.

Urges to self-injure remained, although A.B. acted on them less often, and they were associated with psychosocial stressors as opposed to low mood. She was more readily engaged in the later states of group therapy and continued thereafter with one-to-one therapy focusing on separation and individuation tasks as well as general coping, stress management, and her eating disorder symptoms. Her mother had several sessions with the therapist alone as well to support the goals of separation and individuation. In discussion with the psychiatrist, both A.B. and her mother found the medications helpful for her mood and voices and agreed to a 6-month period of maintenance on medication as A.B. returned fully to school and continued to work in therapy.

A REVIEW OF THE EVIDENCE FOR THE TREATMENT OF NSSI

This section will review:

- The use of levels of evidence in evaluating relevant findings in medication studies
- Current evidence for psychopharmacological treatment of NSSI
- Key neurobiological systems that are targeted by medications

In the rapidly developing field of psychopharmacology, it is important to assess the current level of scientific knowledge by rating studies according to their level of evidence (e.g., type of study) and comparability (e.g., setting, study population). Centers in Canada, the United States, and Great Britain have developed criteria to categorize the relevance of research findings. For example, Harbour and Miller's (2001) approach labels the level of research support for (psycho)pharmacological intervention as shown in Table 14.1. In this model, level 1 studies are those with the best research evidence, and level 4 studies are those with the least evidence.

Though the levels of evidence provide a system to explain and compare the quality standards of studies, a second step is needed when considering actual treatment recommendations. As Harbour and Miller (2001)

TABLE 14.1 Levels of Evidence for Medication Studies

Level	Type of study and evidence
1++	High-quality meta-analyses, systematic reviews of RCTs, or RCTs with a very low risk of bias
1+	Well-conducted meta-analyses, systematic reviews of RCTs, or RCTs with a low risk of bias
1-	Meta-analysis, systematic reviews of RCTs, or RCTs with a high risk of bias
2++	High-quality systematic reviews of case control or cohort studies or high-quality case control or cohort studies with a very low risk of confounding, bias, or chance and a high probability that the relationship is causal
2+	Well-conducted case control or cohort studies with a low risk of confounding, bias, or chance and a moderate probability that the relationship is causal
2-	Case control or cohort studies with a high risk of confounding, bias, or chance and a significant risk that the relationship is not causal
3	Nonanalytic studies, for example, case reports, case series
4	Experts' opinions

From: Harbour & Miller (2001)

Note. RCT = randomized control trial

TABLE 14.2 Summary of Grades of Recommendations

Level	Grades of recommendations
A	At least one meta-analysis, systematic review, or RCT rated as 1++ and directly applicable to the target population or a systematic review of RCTs or a body of evidence consisting principally of studies rated as 1+ directly applicable to the target population and demonstrating overall consistency of results.
B	A body of evidence including studies rated as 2++ directly applicable to the target population and demonstrating overall consistency of results or extrapolated evidence from studies rated as 1++ or 1+
C	A body of evidence including studies rated as 2+ directly applicable to the target population and demonstrating overall consistency of results or extrapolated evidence from studies rated as 2++
D	Evidence level 3 or 4 or extrapolated evidence from studies rated as 2+

From: Harbour & Miller 2001

Note. RCT = randomized controlled trial

pointed out, four grades of recommendations (ranging from A to D), which summarize the available evidence, are considered (Table 14.2).

To provide the reader with an overview of the current state of the literature, we performed a PubMed research search including literature published within the past 10 years. Different terms describing NSSI (e.g., self injury, deliberate self-harm, etc.) were searched for in conjunction with psychopharmacological treatment. On the whole, 140 published papers could be found, of which very few were eligible to be included in this review. Studies were excluded if they described psychopharmacological treatment in developmentally delayed or geriatric populations. In addition, books on NSSI and review papers were hand-searched for additional (cross) references. We followed the approach of Cardish (2007), who, with respect to suicidal behavior, included studies in his review that used outcome variables known to be predictors for suicidal behavior (such as impulsivity).

A review of medication studies in the treatment of self-injury is complicated by the fact that NSSI is not a diagnostic entity but rather a symptom within classificatory systems of *Diagnostic and Statistical Manual of Mental Disorders*, Fourth Edition (American Psychiatric Association, 1994), or International Classification of Diseases (World Health Organization, 2005). Therefore, NSSI itself was seldom used as a primary outcome factor. This makes it difficult to assess the efficacy of certain pharmacological interventions as specific treatments for this behavior. Therefore, studies on mental disorders with NSSI as part of their diagnostic criteria, such as borderline personality disorder (BPD), are of utmost importance, as it has been shown that up to 75% of patients with BPD exhibit self-harming behavior (Cardish, 2007). Although a range of studies report on treating self-injurious behavior in developmentally delayed individuals, these studies have been omitted from this review, as this is a distinctly different population. The following review is categorized based on targeted neurotransmitter systems (see Chapter 6, "Neurobiological Perspectives on Sef-Injury").

Serotonergic System

Psychopharmacological drugs influencing the serotonergic system are numerous, ranging from older tri- and tetracyclic antidepressants to the newer selective serotonin (SSRI) and serotonin-norepinephrine (SNRI) reuptake inhibitors. SSRIs are the most often recommended first- or second-line psychopharmacological treatment options for self-injury (Pies & Popli, 1995; Roberts, 2003). Antidepressants are a well-established pharmacological therapy for obsessive-compulsive disorder (OCD) in children and adolescents, and reports describe an improvement of co-occurring NSSI after antidepressant treatment of OCD (Primeau & Fontaine 1987). However, Hawton et al. (2006) pointed out that the pooled odds ratio for studies of antidepressants versus placebo eligible to be included in their 1998 Cochrane review (Hawton et al., 1998) does not indicate a benefit for patients with deliberate self-harm regarding the repetition of their behaviors. Although second generation antipsychotics are known to have serotonergic properties, they will be more fully discussed in the following section.

Dopaminergic System

Evidence about the possible influence of the dopaminergic system on self-injurious behavior stems primarily from animal research (Breese, Criswell, & Duncan, 1989; Criswell, Mueller, & Breese, 1989; Goldstein, Kuga, & Kusano, 1986; Wagner et al., 2003) and from the treatment trials of severely developmentally delayed patients with Cornelia de Lange or Lesch-Nyhan syndrome (Lloyd, Hornykiewicz, & Davidson, 1981; Mueller & Khan, 1982; Mueller, Saboda, Palmour, & Nyhan, 1982). Although these studies do not yet fully inform the development of a neurobiological hypothesis for NSSI in humans, a number of reports on successful treatments of NSSI using antipsychotics (medication that among other functions blocks dopamine receptors) exist. Medications targeting the dopaminergic system include the older first generation antipsychotics (e.g., haloperidol), the newer second generation antipsychotics (SGAs; e.g., risperidone, olanzapine, quetiapine, ziprasidone, clozapine), and newer developments such as aripiprazole. SGAs' advantage in the treatment of NSSI may be their influence on serotonergic as well as dopaminergic pathways.

Summarizing the evidence in the literature, the effectiveness of haloperidol, which again was never studied using NSSI as primary outcome but was tested as a treatment for patients with BPD and NSSI (see Table 14.2), remains difficult to assess and somewhat contradictory. Therefore, taking into account the potential for significant side effects ranging from acute dystonia to tardive dyskinesia, it is questionable whether haloperidol should be considered as a first-line choice to treat this population. SGAs, compared with first generation antipsychotics such as haloperidol, appear to have fewer side effects in some respects, but the long-term risks of weight gain and effects on glucose metabolism are of increasing concern (Cornell, 2007; Kumra et al., 2007), and the long-term risk of tardive dyskinesia is unknown. In clinical practice, excessive weight gain often is a major factor, limiting the patients' adherence and compliance, especially in the case of adolescent females.

Opioid System

As stated in the neurobiology chapter, the implications of the opioid system have been discussed with regard to both the sometimes addictive features of NSSI (Nixon, Cloutier, & Aggarwal, 2002) and pain perception. Therefore, the use of an opioid antagonist seems to be the appropriate approach for targeting possible reward system reactions after NSSI and thus decreasing the frequency of the acts (Karwautz, Resch,

Wöber-Bingöl, & Schuch, 1996; Konicki & Schulz, 1989). Although several reports indicate positive effects of this treatment approach on self-injurious behavior in children with developmental delay (Sandyk, 1985; White & Schultz, 2000), the literature on successful treatment with an opioid antagonist in individuals without developmental delay is limited to case reports in adults (Griengl, Sendera, & Dantendorfer, 2001; Sandman, Barron, Crinella, & Donnely, 1988; Sandman et al., 2000) and an open-label trial of naltrexone (Roth, Ostroff, & Hoffman, 1996). It may be justified to consider an opioid antagonist to control NSSI with significant addictive features after a series of failed pharmacological and psychosocial interventions.

Other Medications

Benzodiazepines

Contradictory results are reported for the treatment of NSSI with benzodiazepines (Bond, Mandos, & Kurtz, 1989; Cowdry & Gardner 1988). An important cautionary note is that benzodiazepines have significant addictive potential as well as so-called paradoxical reactions with a behavioral activation rather than sedation, especially in youth. Treatment should not exceed 4–6 weeks in length, nor should this group of medications be administered to those with a history of addiction. Benzodiazepines with shorter half-lives should also be avoided. In clinical practice, those with medium-duration half-lives (e.g., lorazepam) seem to be the most effective for the treatment of acute anxiety states and acute agitation that have not responded to other interventions or medication.

Clonidine

The alpha$_2$-adrenergic receptor agonist clonidine has been shown to reduce urges to self-injure, suicidal ideation, and inner tension in a pilot study of 14 women with BPD (Philipsen et al., 2004). No further randomized controlled trials (RCTs) are available so far.

Anticonvulsants (Mood Stabilizers)

Lithium is the most commonly used mood stabilizer in the treatment of bipolar disorder (Burgess 2001; Cipriani, Pretty, Hawton, & Geddes, 2005). Lithium has been promoted for its antisuicidal effects, although this claim remains disputed (Burgess et al., 2001). It is important to note that lithium is a drug that can be dangerous in overdosage, so that its use in suicidal adolescents, with often high impulsivity, needs to be strictly monitored (Soloff et al., 1993).

Aside from lithium, the anticonvulsants carbamazepine, oxacarbazepine, divalproex, topiramate, and lamotrigine were used as mood stabilizers in treatment studies of BPD (Cardish, 2007). Cardish (2007) pointed out that the studies using carbamazepine in BPD lack direct outcome measures (such as self-injury rate) and remain contradictory. For oxacarbazepine, Bellino, Paradiso, & Bogetto (2005) showed an improvement in several core traits of BPD but not for "parasuicidal behavior." Cardish (2007) stated that divalproex can be seen as the best-studied anticonvulsant in personality disorders, and studies overall suggest that there is an effect in reducing impulsive aggression. In addition to side effects such as sedation and weight gain, the potential for developing polycystic ovarian syndrome with subsequent hormonal imbalance is important to consider in young women. Baseline menstrual and gynecological history and ongoing monitoring, including possible ultrasound and referral to a specialist, is important to consider. Studies on the use of topiramate in BPD suggest that this agent is useful in reducing anger and impulsive aggression, but NSSI-specific outcome measures were not utilized in these studies (Loew et al., 2006; Nickel et al., 2004, 2005). Evidence for the use of lamotrigine in patients with BPD stems from one RCT and open-label trials, where lamotrigine proved useful in reducing suicidal behavior and anger (Pinto & Akiskal 1998; Tritt et al., 2005).

Omega-3 Fatty Acids

The role of Omega-3 fatty acids has been investigated in several studies. In a RCT, Zanarini and Frankenburg (2003) found the fatty acid ethyl-eicosapentaenoic (E-EPA) effective in diminishing aggression and depression in 30 women with BPD. Hallahan, Heibbeln, Davis, and Garland, (2007) conducted an RCT in 49 adult patients with self-harm using a combination of eicosapentaenoic acid and decosahexaenoic acid versus placebo. They observed an improvement in scores of suicidality and depression in the fatty acids group, but scores for impulsivity, aggression, and hostility did not differ significantly after 12 weeks. No significant difference could be observed in rates of self-harm between these two groups.

Overview of Psychopharmacological Trials with NSSI

As previously mentioned, no medications are licensed specifically for the treatment of NSSI. This review suggests that some promising psychopharmacological interventions can be considered and used as adjuncts to psychosocial treatments. In general, the level of evidence for psychopharmacological interventions in patients exhibiting NSSI is low, as published literature is mainly based on case descriptions and only a few controlled trials in adults. The literature concerning psychopharmacological treatment of self-injuring adolescents is extremely limited, having levels of evidence below 3. Grades of recommen-

TABLE 14.3 Review of Evidence for Medication in the Treatment of Self-Injury and Associated Disorders

Generic name	Reference	Type of study	Study population	Target symptoms or disorders	Outcome (primary and secondary)	Level of evidence
SEROTONERGIC SYSTEM						
Fluoxetine	Markovitz et al., 1991	OL	Adults (n = 22)	BPD	SI ↓	3
	Salzman et al., 1995	RCT	Adults (n = 22)	BPD or BPD traits	Improvement in both groups Anger ↓ in fluoxetine group	2-
	Coccaro & Kavoussi, 1997	RCT	Adults (n = 40)	Personality disorders (BPD and others)	Aggression ↓ Irritability ↓	2-
Fluoxetine + DBT	Simpson et al., 2004	RCT	Adults (n = 20)	BPD	No difference between fluoxetine and placebo	2-
Paroxetine	Verkes et al., 1998	RCT	Adults (n = 91)	Suicide attempters	Fewer suicidal attempts in paroxetine group but not statistically significant	2-
Fluvoxamine	Rinne et al., 2002	RCT	Adults (n = 38)	BPD	Anger ↓ Impulsivity ↓ in both groups; no difference to placebo	2-

Clomipramine/ Desipramine	Swedo et al., 1989	DBCT	Adults (n = 13)	Trichotillomania	Clomipramine relieves symptoms better than desipramine	2+
Mianserin	Montgomery et al., 1983	DBPC	Adults (n = 58)	Multiple episodes of suicidal behavior	Mianserin = placebo	2+
DOPAMINERGIC SYSTEM						
Haloperidol/ Phenelzine	Soloff et al., 1993	DBPC (haloperidol/ phenelzine/ placebo)	Adolescents and adults (age: 16–36) (n = 108)	BPD	Haloperidol only superior in ↓ of impulsive aggression	2+
	Cornelius et al., 1993	DBPC (haloperidol/ phenelzine/ placebo)	Adults (n = 54)	BPD	No benefit of continuation with Haloperidol except for irritability	2+
Flupenthixol	Montgomery & Montgomery, 1982	RCT	Adults (n = 30)	Suicide attempters (mostly BPD)	Suicidal attempts ↓ under flupenthixol	2-
	Kutcher et al., 1995	OL	Adolescents and young adults (n = 13)	BPD (impulsivity as indirect measure)	Impulsivity ↓	3

TABLE 14.3 Review of Evidence for Medication in the Treatment of Self-Injury and Associated Disorders (continued)

Generic name	Reference	Type of study	Study population	Target symptoms or disorders	Outcome (primary and secondary)	Level of evidence
Fluphenazine (comparison of "low" and "ultra-low" placebo-like dose)	Battaglia et al., 1999	RCT	Adults (n = 58)	Suicide attempters	Self-harm ↓ in both groups	2-
Clozapine	Chengappa et al., 1999	RCR	Adults (n = 7)	SI (in BPD with psychosis)	SI ↓	3
Olanzapine	Zanarini & Frankenburg, 2001	DBPC	Adults (n = 28)	BPD	Impulsivity ↓ Anxiety ↓	2+
	Hough, 2001	CR	Young adults (n = 2)	BPD	SI ↓	3
	Bogenschutz & Gorge, 2004	RCT	Adults (n = 40)	BPD	BPD symptoms ↓	2-
Olanzapine alone/ fluoxetine alone/ olanzapine + fluoxetine	Zanarini et al., 2004	RCT	Adults (n = 45)	BPD	Depression , and aggression ↓ in both combination and olanzapine group	2-
Olanzapine + DBT	Soler et al., 2005	RCT	Adults (n = 60)	BPD	Aggression ↓ Impulsiveness ↓	2-
Risperidone	Rocca et al., 2002	OL	Adults (n = 15)	BPD	Impulsive-aggressive behaviors ↓	3

	Study	Design	Population	Diagnosis	Outcome	
Quetiapine	Villeneuve et al., 2005	OL	Adults (n = 23)	BPD	Impulsivity ↓	3
	Bellino et al., 2006	OL	Adults (n = 14)	BPD	Impulsivity ↓ but no significant effect on parasuicidal behavior	3
	Perrella et al., 2007	OL	Adults (n = 29)	BPD	Hostility ↓ Aggression ↓ No changes in "suicidality"	3
(as augmentation of antidepressant medication)	Good, 2006	CR	Adolescents (n = 2)	Major depressive disorder	SI ↓	3
Ziprasidone/other AAs	Libal et al., 2005	RCR	Adolescents (n = 16)	SI (various D/O)	SI ↓	3
Aripiprazole	Nickel et al., 2006	DBPC	Adolescents and young adults (n = 52)	BPD	SI ↓	2+
	Nickel et al., 2007	18 months follow-up	Adults (n = 39)	BPD	SI ↓	2+

TABLE 14.3 Review of Evidence for Medication in the Treatment of Self-Injury and Associated Disorders (continued)

Generic name	Reference	Type of study	Study population	Target symptoms or disorders	Outcome (primary and secondary)	Level of evidence
OPIOIDS SYSTEM						
Naltrexone	Roth et al., 1996	OL	Adults (n = 7)	SI	SI ↓	3
	Griengl et al., 2001	CR	Adults (n = 1)	SI (in BPD)	SI ↓	3
ANTICONVULSANTS (MOOD STABILIZERS)						
Carbamazepine/ alprazolam/ trifluorperazine/ tranylcypromine/ placebo	Cowdry & Gardner, 1988	DBCT	Adults (n = 16)	BPD	Carbamazepine: "behavioural dyscontrol"	2+
Carbamazepine	De la Fuente & Lotstra, 1994	RCT	Adults (n = 20)	BPD	No differences	2-
Oxcarbazepine	Bellino et al., 2005	OL	Adults (n = 17)	BPD	Impulsivity ↓ Affective instability ↓ No change in parasuicidal behavior	3
	Cordás et al., 2006	CR	Adults (n = 2)	Bulimia	SI ↓	3

Medication	Study	Design	Sample	Diagnosis	Outcome	Rating
Divalproex	Frankenburg & Zanarini, 2002	RCT	Adults (n = 30)	BPD and bipolar II disorder	Anger ↓ Hostility ↓ Impulsive aggression →	2-
	Hollander et al., 2005	RCT	Adults (n = 52)	BPD	Impulsive aggression →	2-
Topiramate	Cassano et al., 2001	CR	Adult (n = 1)	BPD	SI ↓	3
	Nickel et al., 2004	DBPC	Adults (n = 29)	BPD	Anger ↓	2+
	Nickel et al., 2005	RCT	Adults (n = 44)	BPD	Anger ↓	2-
	Loew et al., 2006	RCT	Adults (n = 56)	BPD	Anger ↓ Hostility ↓ Interpersonal sensitivity ↓	2-
Lamotrigine	Tritt et al., 2005	RCT	Adults (n = 27)	BPD	Anger ↓	2-
OMEGA-3 FATTY ACIDS						
Ethyl-eicosapentaenoic acid	Zanarini & Frankenburg, 2003	DBPC	Adults (n = 30)	BPD	Aggression ↓	2+

TABLE 14.3 Review of Evidence for Medication in the Treatment of Self-Injury and Associated Disorders (continued)

Generic name	Reference	Type of study	Study population	Target symptoms or disorders	Outcome (primary and secondary)	Level of evidence
Eicosapentaenoic acid+ decosahexaenoic acid	Hallahan et al., 2007	RCT	Adults and adolescents (n = 49)	Self-harm	Suicidal behaviors ↓	2-
ALPHA-ADRENERGIC SYSTEM						
Clonidine	Philipsen et al., 2004	OL	Adults (n = 14)	BPD (most of them with SI)	Urge to SI ↓ Suicidal ideation ↓	3

Note: DBPC = double-blind placebo-controlled, DBCT = double-blind cross-over trial, OL = open label trial, CR = case report, RCR = retrospective chart review, BPD = borderline personality disorder, DBT = dialectical behavior therapy, SI = self-injury (suicidal intent not distinguished) dations can only be considered to be on the C or D level, as often results are not directly applicable to the target population, and studies are on very low levels of evidence. Table 14.3 presents an overview of psychopharmacological trials with NSSI and associated symptoms.

MODEL FOR INTEGRATING PSYCHOPHARMACOLOGIC TREATMENT

Developing an individually based psychopharmacological approach for the psychopharmacological treatment of personality disorders in adults, Kapfhammer (2003) proposed a three-level model that could be adapted to the treatment of NSSI: First, treat any underlying psychiatric disorder if it exists. If it does not, target associated symptoms and symptom clusters of NSSI that may be responsive to medication or, as a third step, consider treating NSSI as a symptom responsive to medication.

Katz and Fotti (2005) proposed another approach that considers pharmacotherapy of emotionally dysregulated problem behaviors, which include behaviors that involve aggression toward the self in the context of an emotionally dysregulated state. This approach, based on the concept of emotional dysregulation (Linehan, 1993), may be applicable to those seeking treatment for NSSI, as emotional dysregulation is one of the core states in NSSI (Klonsky, 2007). The authors recommend a thorough analysis of the problem behaviors and base the choice of the appropriate pharmacotherapeutic treatment on this analysis. If an Axis I disorder is clearly present, they recommend targeting this disorder first. In cases of NSSI and suicidal behavior they advise identifying the determinants of these behaviors and treating them accordingly.

These two models are similar in their first two steps, as they both propose to first treat underlying mental disorders that can then attenuate symptoms that secondarily reduce NSSI. As a second step, symptoms and symptom clusters in NSSI are targeted such as tension, anxiety, anger, irritability, and feelings of emptiness or perceived need of self-punishment (Jacobson & Gould, 2007). The models differ, though, with regard to whether NSSI can be treated directly, meaning that NSSI itself is a target symptom that responds to a specific medication. To date, there has been very limited experience in doing this, except, perhaps, with the use of Omega-3 fatty acids.

The following case demonstrates how symptoms of a major Axis I disorder may not be fully apparent when NSSI first presents. The importance of a thorough diagnostic evaluation when major psychiatric symptoms present as well as the medical management of a major Axis 1 disorder is outlined to illustrate its role in the treatment of NSSI.

C.D., age 16, sought assistance from her psychiatrist for help with severe mood swings and reoccurrence of her NSSI, which she had previously received therapy for at age 14. Her difficult home situation had remained unchanged

*despite family interventions and attempts to have her mother be assessed for
a mood disorder. C.D. explained to her physician how terrified she was by
the extreme mood swings and the extent of her impulsive behavior, feeling
that both contributed to "out of control" episodes of self-injury. No psychotic
symptoms were noted. She met criteria for bipolar II disorder after a thorough
diagnostic assessment and period of mood charting. Psychoeducation and
lifestyle choices and effects on mood were discussed. C.D. and her parents
agreed to a trial of lithium after the role of medication was reviewed and her
screening work up was completed. Within 3 weeks on lithium 300 mg BID,
C.D.'s mood symptoms were becoming more stable. She complained of some
polyuria, polydypsia, and nausea but felt that these side effects were tolerable
based on the improvement in mood symptoms that she had achieved. NSSI
episodes halted with improved mood stability during the trial period. Ongoing treatment was now focused on medication management and monitoring
and one-on-one therapy regarding stress and coping as well as issues regarding interpersonal relationships. She attended her sessions regularly, and two
brief episodes of NSSI reoccurred within the first 6 months. One was associated with a trial period off lithium that she initiated herself, and the second
was during a stressful break-up. She has had no further NSSI episodes in
the past year and continues in regular therapy sessions and is maintained on
Lithium 600 mg twice a day.*

A PROPOSED ALGORITHM FOR THE
PHARMACOLOGICAL TREATMENT
OF ADOLESCENT NSSI

This section will review:

- Previous algorithms proposed for the treatment of self-injury
- A new algorithm that incorporates previous models and identifies
  the need for individualizing the treatment regiment
- Important aspects to consider when using such an algorithm

Despite the fact that evidence from the literature on the treatment of
NSSI in youth is limited, several psychopharmacological treatment algorithms have been proposed. These algorithms may assist the practitioner
in discerning the steps required when considering medication treatment.
Pies and Popli (1995) and Villalba and Harrington (2000) developed psychopharmacological treatment recommendations for adults
with NSSI. Harper (2006) pointed out that, in considering psychopharmacological treatment of NSSI, the clinician must focus on current
behavior, associated clinical syndromes, and current life context. This
is especially important when it comes to understanding youth and their
ongoing development. It also seems crucial to include specific aspects of
the patient's history such as traumatic experiences (abuse, neglect, loss
of relevant others, etc.). Roberts (2003) has proposed a treatment algorithm for adolescent NSSI. As in the algorithms for adults mentioned

above, he recommended SSRIs as a first treatment choice. For several reasons, this recommended primary choice should not always be adopted. In recent years, more information has become available regarding safety issues with SSRIs in this age group. This includes emergence of suicidal behavior and self-harm behavior with the use of SSRIs (Donovan et al., 2000; King et al., 1991; Teicher, Glod, & Cole, 1993). In addition, SSRIs alone are contraindicated as the first-line treatment in individuals presenting with bipolar disorder due to the possibility of aggravating mood swings. More recently, second generation antipsychotics have seen increased use in general and specifically for the treatment of NSSI (Harper, 2006). A recent meta-analysis reported that antipsychotics as a class have a positive effect on core traits of BPD such as impulsivity, aggression, interpersonal relationships, and global functioning, whereas antidepressants and mood stabilizers are effective against affective instability and anger but not against the aforementioned traits (Nose, Cipriani, Biancosino, Grassi, & Barbui, 2006).

Based on the work of Roberts (2003), Harper (2006), Katz and Fotti (2005), Kapfhammer (2003), and Libal and Plener (2007), we propose an algorithm (see Figure 14.1) that takes into consideration the possible risks of SSRI use in certain populations and follows a symptom-oriented approach in 11 steps.

1. An algorithm should work on the premise that psychopharmacological interventions are used as an adjunct to psychosocial treatments. Before considering psychopharmacological treatment, make sure that sufficient psychosocial and psychotherapeutic support is available for the patient.
2. Detailed and age-adjusted discussion about the medication, including its desired benefits and potential side effects as well as duration of treatment ("as short as possible, but as long as necessary"), is important. Secure parental informed consent and adolescent assent, based on legal and ethical requirements, prior to treatment. If relevant, discuss the issue of prescribing certain medications off-label with reference to the available evidence in the literature.
3. Before administering medication, ensure that the adolescent has been assessed medically and that any contributing medical conditions, for example, thyroid disease, are ruled out. Prior to starting certain medications, baseline laboratory and other tests may be required. Standard evaluation of weight, pulse, and blood pressure can provide a baseline for further reference as necessary.
4. It is important to differentiate between the treatment of an underlying psychiatric disorder, the treatment of associated symptoms, and the direct treatment of NSSI. Rule in or rule out a major Axis I psychiatric disorder (e.g., major depression, bipolar disorder, psychotic disorder). If one is present, follow treatment guidelines

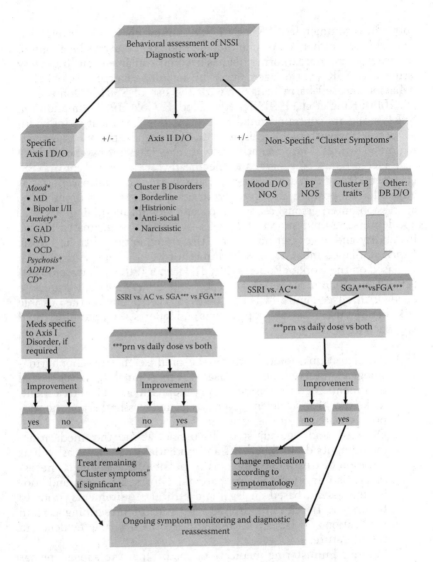

Figure 14.1 Proposed Treatment Algorithm for Adolesents with NSSI
*=follow medication guidelines for specific disorder (e.g. http://www.aacap.org
or http://www.nice.org.uk); **= choice of medication is dependent on key presenting features (e.g., low mood vs. affective instability vs. impulsivity and/or
aggression; ***= Use of antipsychotic medication may be given in lower doses,
see notes to algorithm; Ω 3 Fatty acids may be used as a supplement to diet in an
experimental approach for mood related symptoms; SGA: Second generation
antipsychotic; FGA: First generation antipsychotic; SSRI: Selective Serotonin
Reuptake inhibitor; AC: Anticonvulsant; MD: Major Depression; BP: Bipolar
Disorder; GAD: Generalized Anxiety Disorder; SAD: Social Anxiety Disorder; OCD: Obsessive Complusive Disode; ADHD: Attention Deficit Disorder;
CD: Conduct Disorder; DBD: Disruptive Behavior Disorders

according to the disorder (e.g., Practice Parameters of the AACAP [http://www.aacap.org or the UK National Institute for Health and Clinical Excellence guidelines [http://www.nice.org.uk/]).

5. If the diagnosis remains unclear, but a range of "cluster symptoms" (e.g., affective instability, impulsivity, difficulty concentrating or focusing, etc.) are present, medication should target symptoms that are the most debilitating or hinder a positive outcome from psychotherapeutic interventions.

6. If NSSI occurs together with affective lability, tension, impulsivity, anxiety, or depressive states (with sleeping problems or suicidal thoughts), psychopharmacological treatment could start with an SGA. It is highly relevant to discuss possible weight gain in adolescent patients. In general, it is wise to "start low, go slow and taper slowly," but some individuals may need a more rapid approach. In twice-a-day dosing, give the higher dose in the evening, with the intention of both minimizing possible side effects such as sedation, sleepiness, drowsiness, and concentration problems during daytime but also making use of these sedation effects for some patients.

7. If primary symptoms are depressive states, flashbacks, depression, compulsions, or bulimic symptoms, a SSRI could be used. If these symptoms co-occur with the symptoms mentioned above (affective lability, tension, impulsivity, etc.), the augmentation of a SGA with a SSRI might be justified. In youth, as well as in young adults, close monitoring for suicidal ideation and suicide risk is important, particularly in the initial period of treatment (Herpertz-Dahlmann & Fegert 2004; Simon, 2006). If augmentation therapy is successful and NSSI is reduced but associated symptoms still persist, consider reducing the SGA step by step and continue with SSRI monotherapy.

8. In case of significant affective lability or aggression (without significant psychosocial triggers), a trial of a mood stabilizer should be considered. When lithium is administered, closely monitor the patient for side effects as well as suicide risk, as this medication is toxic in overdosage.

9. If multiple addictive features of NSSI are present or if previous treatment steps failed to show sufficient effects, a treatment trial with an opiate-antagonist such as naltrexone either as monotherapy or in combination with a SGA or SSRI may be warranted.

10. In acute states of tension with urges to self-injure or for sleeping disorders, low-potency first generation antipsychotics can be helpful. Confine this treatment to the short term use only ("pro re nata" or PRN medication) due to its side effects profile (sedation, hypotension). Due to their potential for dependency, use benzodiazepines such as diazepam and lorazepam as an alternative only in selected cases.

11. Maintain an ongoing evaluation of symptoms and (re)consideration of diagnosis over time, in case sufficient symptoms arise to categorize an Axis I disorder.

Apart from the side effects discussed in detail in the Table 14.4, two classes of psychotropic medication need special consideration.

Selective Serotonin Reuptake Inhibitors

Treatment of adolescents with SSRIs was reviewed extensively after the first reports in 2004 led to warnings from the FDA and EMEA of the possibly increased risk of suicide and suicidal behavior in this age group (Brent, 2004; Bridge et al., 2007; Newman, 2004; Isacsson, Holmgren, & Ahlner, 2005; Whittington et al., 2004). Because adolescents exhibiting NSSI are seen as a high-risk group for increased suicidality (Zahl & Hawton, 2004), SSRIs need to be critically reviewed as a first-line treatment of NSSI in adolescents. A strong correlation was found between SSRI use and suicide attempts in a retrospective chart review of 16 self-injuring female adolescents (Plener, Fegert, & Libal, 2005). In a recently published meta-analysis, fluoxetine was considered the SSRI with the best benefit-risk ratios in adolescents (Hammad, Laughren, & Racoosin, 2006). In a recent UK study of 208 adolescents (aged 11–17) with moderate to major depression, participants received either an SSRI and routine care or an SSRI and cognitive behavioral therapy. The SSRI used most was fluoxetine. In this adolescent sample NSSI decreased over the 28 weeks of treatment in both groups (Goodyer et al., 2007).

The benefit of SSRI treatment seems to outweigh the risk of non-treatment of pediatric major depressive disorder, OCD, and non-OCD anxiety disorders. The effects of SSRIs are strongest in non-OCD anxiety disorders, intermediate in OCD and more modest in major depressive disorder (Bridge et al., 2007). Thus, whenever targeting one of these underlying Axis I psychiatric disorders, SSRIs remain the drug of choice. In the assessment, any symptoms or history of cyclothymia, hypomania, or mania as well as family history of bipolar disorder must be considered, as SSRIs have the potential to promote or aggravate these symptoms in those who experience them or may be predisposed.

Second Generation Antipsychotics

A key issue with second generation antipsychotics is weight gain (Allison & Casey, 2001). Therefore, it is best to start with a rather weight-neutral SGA (e.g., aripiprazol, ziprasidone) except in cases of anorexia, where weight gain is clinically desired and the patient has consented to doing so (Mitchell, deZwann, & Roerin, 2003). For all medication, it is important to follow the recommended guidelines regarding baseline investigations and ongoing monitoring requirements (Bezchlibnyk-

TABLE 14.4 Medications: Dosing for Children and Adolescents and Side Effect Profiles

Medication	Starting dose (mg/d)	Suggested therapeutic range (mg/d)	Side effects (most prominent)
SSRI			
Fluoxetine	Child: 5 Adolescent: 10	5–60 In youth with NSSI:* (5–)10–40(–60)	Drowsiness, insomnia, excitement, headache, fatigue, dry mouth, tremor, dizziness, GI distress, sexual disturbances, suicidal ideation, emerging hypomania or mania
Second generation antipsychotics			
Aripiprazole	2.5–5	Child: 5–10 Adolescent: 5–15 In youth with NSSI: *Child: (2.5 -) 5 - 10 Adolescent: 5 – 10	Drowsiness, sedation, insomnia, agitation
Clozapine	6.25–12.5 (day 1)	Child: 100–350 Adolescent: 225–450 In youth with NSSI: **Adolescent: 25–150 (-300)	Drowsiness, sedation, weight gain, agranulocytosis, akathisia, orthostatic hypotension, tachycardia, ECG abnormalities, anticholinergic effects
Olanzapine	2.5–5	Child: 5–10 Adolescent:10–15 In youth with NSSI: *Child: 2.5–10 Adolescent: 5–10	Drowsiness, sedation, weight gain, akathisia, anticholinergic effects

TABLE 14.4   Medications: Dosing for Children and Adolescents and Side Effect Profiles (continued)

Medication	Starting dose (mg/d)	Suggested therapeutic range (mg/d)	Side effects (most prominent)
Quetiapine	12.5	Child: 150–400 Adolescent: 250–550 In youth with NSSI: **Child: 12.5–75 Adolescent: 25–150 (-300)	Drowsiness, sedation, insomnia, agitation, orthostatic hypotension, weight gain
Risperidone	0.25	Psychosis and mania: Child: 1 2) Adolescent: 2.5–4 Impulse control deficit and NSSI: *Child: 0.5–1 (-2) Adolescent: 1–2.5	Drowsiness, sedation, insomnia, agitation, orthostatic hypotension, weight gain, akathisia, tachycardia
Ziprasidone	5	Child: 40–100A dolescent: 80–140 In youth with NSSI: *Child: 40–80 Adolescent: 40–80 (-120)	Drowsiness, sedation
First generation antipsychotics			
Flupenthixol		Child: 0.4–2 Adolescent: <3	Parkinsonism, akathisia, dystonic reactions, weight gain, anticholinergic effects

Anticonvulsants

Lithium	<25 kg: 600 25–39 kg: 900 40–50 kg:1200 >50 kg 1500	Weakness, fatigue, cognitive blunting, memory impairment, tremor, ECG changes, nausea, diarrhea, weight gain, hair loss or thinning, menstrual disturbances, hypothyroidism, polyuria, polydipsia, rash, leukocytosis
Carbamazepine	100–200 in divided doses	Child: 200–600 Adolescent: 300–1200	Drowsiness, sedation, weakness, fatigue, tremor, incoordination, dizziness, ataxia, diplopia, nausea, menstrual disturbances, polycystic ovary syndrome, rash, transient leukopenia
Lamotrigine	25–50 in divided doses	Max. 700	Drowsiness, sedation, headache, dizziness, ataxia, diplopia, blurred vision, nausea, rash
Valproate	125	Child: 1,000–1,200 Adolescent: 1,000–2,500	Drowsiness, sedation, headache, weakness, fatigue, dizziness, tremor, diplopia, nausea, diarrhea, weight gain, hair loss or thinning, menstrual disturbances, polycystic ovary syndrome, thrombocytopenia, transient enzyme elevation
Topiramate	Children: 1–3 Adolescents: 25–50	Children: 5–9 Adolescents: 400	Sedation; lethargy; fatigue; confusion; psychomotor slowing; deficits in word-finding, concentration and memory; anxiety; irritability; insomnia; nervousness; increased panic attacks; worsening of depression or psychosis; headache; tremors; ataxia; paresthesias; nausea and vomiting; blurred vision; sweating; rash; nystagmus; diplopia; cases of severe liver damage; dizziness; epistaxis; nephrolithiasis; metabolic acidosis

TABLE 14.4 Medications: Dosing for Children and Adolescents and Side Effect Profiles (continued)

Medication	Starting dose (mg/d)	Suggested therapeutic range (mg/d)	Side effects (most prominent)
Alpha2- adrenergic drugs			
Clonidine		0.05–0.5 (according to disorder and body weight)	Sedation, irritability, decreased memory, headache, hypotension, dry mouth
Opioid antagonists			
Naltrexone		0.5—2 mg/kg/d	Tremor, dizziness, hypertension, tachycardia

Based on Bezchlibnyk-Butler & Virani (2007)

Note: Drug treatment must be provided by an expert in child and adolescent psychiatry. Doses above need to be evaluated and potentially revised in every case, according to trained clinical judgement. No warranty is taken for appropriate dosing.

* These dosage recommendations in youth with NSSI are based on the authors' clinical experience. Low-dose SGAs have been used in certain cases of Bipolar Disorder not otherwise specified, Bipolar Disorder II, Borderline Personality Disorder, and mood disorders NOS. .

** Clozapine is not a first-line treatment approach to adolescent NSSI.

Butler & Virani, 2007). To avoid significant side effects, it is important to closely monitor effectiveness at the lowest dose. At the same time, target doses may be important to achieve, as medications are often not effective at dosages well below those identified as therapeutic.

Table 14.4 illustrates potential starting and target doses as well as key side effects to monitor during initiation of treatment. Some clinicians, for example, in outpatient settings, use even lower starting and therapeutic doses (e.g., of quetiapine, starting at 50 mg and increasing to 100–150 mg), with significant improvement in symptom clusters of mood instability, impulsivity, tension, anxiety, and NSSI that without treatment were significantly affecting functioning levels.

ETHICAL FRAMEWORK

Many ethical questions are involved in the decisions whether, if, and how to treat with medication. It is worthwhile to ask whether we should treat adolescents with newer drugs that may have a potential for not-yet-completely-known effects on a developing body and brain. On the other hand, if a drug has the potential for a positive effect in an individual, are we permitted to reject that improvement by focusing only on negative side effects? Children and adolescents are in danger of being "therapeutic orphans" because only very limited research is available in many areas of mental health. Nevertheless, as clinicians we have the obligation to develop an individually based "best practice" model whenever any intervention and, particularly, psychopharmacological support appears considerable.

CONCLUSION

This chapter informs the clinician about a flexible approach to using medication in youth with repetitive NSSI. The ideal therapeutic dose should have proven effects on the target symptoms (efficacy), a timely onset of response, few side effects, low toxicity, no potential for abuse, and a sustained effect in longer-term treatment (effectiveness). Treatment goals include the significant reduction or amelioration of symptoms and improvement of outcome in accompanying psychosocial treatments. The proposed algorithm may guide clinicians and assist them with delineating target symptoms. Duration of treatment is guided by the principle "as short as possible, but as long as necessary"; treatment should be continued as long as the individual's symptoms prevent her or him from participating in day-to-day life and meeting the developmental challenges of adolescence.

REFERENCES

Allison, D. B., & Casey, D. E. (2001). Antipsychotic-induced weight gain: A review of the literature. *Journal of Clinical Psychiatry, 62*(Suppl 7), 22–31.

American Psychiatric Association. (1994). *Diagnostic and Statistical Manual of Mental Disorders* (4th ed.). Washington, DC: Author.

Battaglia, J., Wolff, T. K., Wagner-Johnson, D. S., Carmody, T. J., & Basco, M. R. (1999). Structured diagnostic assessment and depot fluphenazine treatment of multiple suicide attempters in the emergency department. *International Clinical Psychopharmacology, 14,* 361-372.

Bellino, S., Paradiso, E., & Bogetto, F. (2005). Oxcarbazepine in the treatment of borderline personality disorder: A pilot study. *Journal of Clinical Psychiatry, 66,* 1111–1115.

Bezchlibnyk-Butler, K. Z., & Virani, A. S. (2007). *Clinical handbook of psychotropic drugs for children and adolescents.* Toronto, Ontario: Hogrefe & Huber.

Bogenschutz, M. P., & George Nurnberg, H. (2004). Olanzapine versus placebo in the treatment of borderline personality disorder. *Journal of Clinical Psychiatry, 65,* 104-109.

Bond, W., Mandos, L., & Kurtz, M. (1989). Midazolam for aggressivity and violence in three mentally retarded patients. *American Journal of Psychiatry, 14,* 925–926.

Breese, G. R., Criswell, H. E., & Duncan, G. E. (1989). Dopamine deficiency in self-injurious behaviour. *Psychopharmacological Bulletin, 2,* 353–357.

Brent, D. A. (2004). Antidepressants and pediatric depression: The risk of doing nothing. *New England Journal of Medicine, 351,* 1598–1601.

Bridge, J. A., Iyengar, S., Salary, C. B., Barbe, R. P., Birmaher, B., Pincus, H. A., et al. (2007). Clinical response and risk for reported suicidal ideation and suicide attempts in paediatric antidepressant treatment. A meta-analysis of randomized controlled trials. *Journal of the American Medical Association, 297,* 1683–1696.

Burgess, S., Geddes, J., Hawton, K., Townsend, E., Jamison, K., & Goodwin, G. (2001). Lithium for maintenance treatment of mood disorders. *Cochrane Database System Review, 3,* CD003013.

Cardish, R. J. (2007). Psychopharmacologic management of suicidality in personality disorders. *Canadian Journal of Psychiatry, 52*(Suppl. 1), 115S–127S.

Cassano, P., Lattanzi, L., Pini, S., Dell'Osso, L., Battistini, G., & Cassano, G. B. (2001). Topiramate for self-mutilation in a patient with borderline personality disorder. *Bipolar Disorders, 3,* 161.

Chengappa, K. N. R., Ebeling, T., Kang, J. S., Levine, J., & Parepally, H. (1999). Clozapine reduces severe self-mutilation and aggression in psychotic patients with borderline personality disorder. *Journal of Clinical Psychiatry, 60,* 477-484.

Cipriani, A., Pretty, H., Hawton, K., & Geddes, J. R. (2005). Lithium in the prevention of suicidal behaviour and all-cause mortality in patients with mood disorders: A systematic review of randomized trials. *American Journal of Psychiatry, 162,* 1805–1819.

Coccaro, E. F., & Kavoussi, R. J. (1997). Fluoxetine and impulsive agressive behavior in personality disordered subjects. *Archives of Gen Psychiatry, 54,* 1081-1088.

Cordás, T. A., Tavares, H., Calderoni, D. M., Stump, G. V., & Ribeiro, R. B. (2006). Oxcarbazepine for self-mutilating bulimic patients. *International Journal of Neuropsychopharmacology, 9,* 769-771.

Cornelius, J. R., Soloff, P. H., Perel, J. M., & Ulrich, R. F. (1993). Continuation Pharmacotherapy of Borderline Personality Disorder with Haloperidol and Phenelzine. *American Journal of Psychiatry, 150,* 1843-1848.

Cornell, C. U. (2007). Weight gain and metabolic effects of mood stabilizers and antipsychotics in pediatric bipolar disorder: A systematic review and pooled analysis of short term trials. *Journal of the American Academy of Child and Adolescent Psychiatry, 46,* 687–700.

Cowdry, R. W., & Gardner, D. L. (1988). Pharmacotherapy for borderline personality disorder. *Archives of General Psychiatry, 45,* 111–119.

Criswell, H. E., Mueller, R. A., & Breese, G. R. (1989). Clozapine antagonism of D-1 and D-2 dopamine receptor-mediated behaviour. *European Journal of Pharmacology, 159,* 141–147.

de la Fuente, J. M., & Lotstra, F. (1994) A trial of carbamazepine in borderline personality disorder. *European Neuropsychopharmacology, 4,* 479-486.

Donovan, S., Clayton, A., Beeharry, M., Jones, S., Kirk, C., Waters, K., et al. (2000). Deliberate self-harm following antidepressant drugs. *British Journal of Psychiatry, 177,* 551–556.

Frankenburg, F. R., & Zanarini, M. C. (2002). Divalproex sodium treatment of women with borderline personality disorder and bipolar II disorder: a double-blind placebo-controlled pilot study. *Journal of Clinical Psychiatry, 63,* 442-446

Goldstein, M., Kuga, S., & Kusano, N. (1986). Dopamine agonist induced self mutilative biting behaviour in monkeys with unilateral ventromedial tegmental lesions of the brainstem: Possible pharmacological model for Lesch-Nyhan syndrome. *Brain Research Bulletin, 367,* 114–119.

Good, C. R. (2006). Adjunctive Quetiapine targets self-harm behaviors in adolescent females with major depressive disorder. *Journal of Child and Adolescent Psychopharmacology, 3,* 235-6

Goodyer, I., Dubicka, B., Wilkinson, P., Kelvin, R., Roberts, C., Byford, S., et al., (2007). Selective serotonin reuptake inhibitors (SSRIs) and routine specialist care with and without cognitive behaviour therapy in adolescents with major depression: Randomised controlled trial. *British Medical Journal, 335,* 142–150.

Griengl, H., Sendera, A., & Dantendorfer, K. (2001). Naltrexone as a treatment of self-injurious behaviour: A case report. *Acta Psychiatrica Scandinavica, 103,* 234–236.

Hallahan, B., Hibbeln, J. R., Davis, J. M., & Garland, M. R. (2007). Omega-3 fatty acid supplementation in patients with recurrent self-harm. *British Journal of Psychiatry, 190,* 118–122.

Hammad, T. A., Laughren, T., & Racoosin, J. (2006). Suicidality in paediatric patients treated with antidepressant drugs. *Archives of General Psychiatry, 63,* 332–339.

Harbour, R., & Miller, J. (2001). A new system for grading recommendations in evidence based guidelines. *British Medical Journal, 323,* 334–336.

Harper, G. (2006). Psychopharmacological treatment. In B. W. Walsh (Ed.), *Treating self-injury: A practical guide* (pp. 212–220). New York: Guilford Press.

Hawton, K., Arensman, E., Townsend, E., Bremner, S., Feldman, E., Goldney, R., et al., (1998). Deliberate self harm: Systematic review of efficacy of psychosocial and pharmacological treatments in preventing repetition. *British Medical Journal, 317,* 441–447.

Hawton, K., Townsend, E., Arensman, E., Gunnel, D., Hazell, P., House, A., et al., (2006). Psychosocial and pharmacological treatments for deliberate self harm. *Cochrane Library, 3,* 1–61.

Herpertz-Dahlmann, B., & Fegert, J. M. (2004). Zur Problematik der Gabe von selektiven Serotoninwiederaufnahmehemmern (SSRI) bei depressiven Kindern und Jugendlichen. *Nervenarzt, 9,* 908–910.

Hollander, E., Swann, A. C., Coccaro, E. F., Jiang, P., & Smith T. B. (2005). Impact of trait impulsivity and state aggression on divalproex versus placebo response in borderline personality disorder. *American Journal of Psychiatry, 162,* 621-624.

Hough, D. W. (2001). Low-dose olanzapine for self-mutilation behavior in patients with borderline personality disorder. *Journal of Clinical Psychiatry, 62,* 296-297.

Isacsson, J., Holmgren, P., & Ahlner, J. (2005). Selective serotonin reuptake inhibitor antidepressants and the risk of suicide: A controlled forensic database study of 14 857 suicides. *Acta Psychiatrica Scandinavica, 111,* 286–290.

Jacobson, C. M., & Gould, M. (2007). The epidemiology and phenomenology of non-suicidal self-injurious behaviour among adolescents: A critical review of the literature. *Archives of Suicide Research, 11,* 129–147.

Kapfhammer, H. P. (2003). Pharmakotherapie bei Persönlichkeitsstörungen. In S. C. Herpertz & H. Saß (Eds.), *Persönlichkeitsstörungen.* Stuttgart: Georg Thieme

Karwautz, A., Resch, F., Wöber-Bingöl, C., & Schuch, B. (1996). Self-mutilation in adolescence as addictive behaviour. *Wien Klinische Wochenschrift, 108,* 82–84.

Katz, L. Y., & Fotti, S. (2005). The role of behaviour analysis in the pharmacotherapy of emotionally-dysregulated problem behaviour. *Child and Adolescent Psychopharmacology News, 10,* 1–5.

King, R. A., Riddle, M. A., Chappell, P. B., Hardin, M. T., Anderson, G. M., Lombroso, P., et al. (1991). Emergence of self-destructive phenomena in children and adolescents during fluoxetine treatment. *Journal of the American Academy of Child and Adolescent Psychiatry, 30,* 179–186.

Klonsky, E. D. (2007). The functions of deliberate self-injury: A review of the evidence. *Clinical Psychology Review, 27,* 226–239.

Konicki, P. E., & Schulz, S. C. (1989). Rationale for clinical trials of opiate antagonists in treating patients with personality disorders and self-injurious behaviour. *Psychopharmacology Bulletin, 25,* 556–563.

Kumra, S., Oberstar, J. V., Sikich, L., Findling, R. L., McClellan, J. M., Vinogradov, S., et al., (2008). Efficacy and tolerability of second-generation antipsychotics in children and adolescents with schizophrenia. *Schizophrenic Bulletin, 34,* 60–71.

Kutcher, S., Papatheodorou, G., Reiter, S., & Gardner, D. (1995). The successful pharmacological treatment of adolescents and young adults with Borderline Personality Disorder: a preliminary open trial of flupenthixol. *Journal of Psychiatric Neuroscience, 20,* 113-118.

Libal, G., & Plener, P. L. (2007). Pharmakotherapie selbstverletzenden Verhaltens im Jugendalter. In R. Brunner & F. Resch (Eds.), *Borderline-Störungen und selbstverletzendes Verhalten bei Jugendlichen.*. Göttingen: Vandenhoeck & Ruprecht

Libal, G., Plener, P. L., Ludolph, A. G., & Fegert J. M. (2005). Ziprasidone as a weight-neutral treatment alternative in the treatment of self-injurious behavior in adolescent females. *Child & Adolescent Psychopharmacology News, 10,* 1-6.

Linehan, M. M. (1993). *Cognitive-behavioral treatment of borderline personality disorder.* New York: Guilford Press.

Lloyd, K. G., Hornykiewicz, O., & Davidson, L. (1981). Biochemical evidence of dysfunction of brain neurotransmitters in the Lesch-Nyhan syndrome. *New England Journal of Medicine, 305,* 1106–1111.

Loew, T. H., Nickel, M. K., Muehlbacher, M., Kaplan, P., Nickel, C., Kettler, C., et al. (2006). Topiramate treatment for women with borderline personality disorder: A double-blind, placebo-controlled study. *Journal of Clinical Psychopharmacology, 26,* 61–66.

Markovitz, P. J., Calabrese, J. R., Schulz, C., & Meltzer, H. Y. (1991). Fluoxetine in the treatment of borderline and schizotypal personality disorders. *American Journal of Psychiatry, 148,* 1064-1067.

Mitchell, J. E., deZwaan, M., & Roerig, J. L. (2003). Drug therapy for patients with eating disorders. *Current Drug Targets CNS Neurological Disorders, 2,* 17–29.

Montgomery, S. A., & Montgomery, D. (1982). Pharmacological prevention of suicidal behaviour. *Journal of Affective Disorders, 4,* 291-298.

Montgomery, S. A., Roy, D., & Montgomery, D. B. (1983). The prevention of recurrent suicidal acts. *British Journal of Clinical Pharmacology, 15* (Suppl 2), 183-188.

Mueller, K., & Khan, W. (1982). Pharmacologic control of pemoline-induced self-injurious behaviour in rats. *Pharmacology, Biochemistry, and Behavior, 16,* 957–963.

Mueller, K., Saboda, S., Palmour, R., & Nyhan, W. L. (1982). Self-injurious behaviour produced in rats by daily caffeine and continuous amphetamine. *Pharmacology, Biochemistry, and Behavior, 17,* 613–617.

Newman, T. B. (2004). A Black-box warning for antidepressants in children. *New England Journal of Medicine, 35,* 1595–1598.

Nickel, M. K., Loew, T. H., & Pedrosa Gil, F. (2007). Aripiprazole in treatment of borderline patients, part II: an 18-month follow-up. *Psychopharmacology (Berl), 191,* 1023-1026.

Nickel, M. K., Nickel, C., Kaplan, P., Lahmann, C., Muhlbacher, M., Tritt, K., et al. (2005). Treatment of aggression with topiramate in male borderline personality disorder: A double-blind, placebo-controlled study. *Biological Psychiatry, 57,* 495–499.

Nickel, M. K., Nickel, C., Mitterlehner, F. O., Tritt, K., Lahmann, C., Leiberich, P. K., et al. (2004). Topiramate treatment of aggression in female borderline personality disorder patients: A double-blind, placebo-controlled study. *Journal of Clinical Psychiatry, 65,* 1515–1519.

Nickel, M. K., Muehlbacher, M., Nickel, C., Kettler, C., Pedrosa Gil, F., Bachler, E., Buschmann, W., Rother, N., Fartacek, R., Egger, C., Anvar, J., Rother, W. K., Loew, T.H., & Kaplan P. (2006). Aripiprazole in the treatment of patients with borderline personality disorder: a double-blind, placebo-controlled study. *American Journal of Psychiatry, 163*, 833–838

Nixon, M. K., Cloutier, P. F., & Aggarwal, S. (2002). Affect regulation and addictive aspects of repetitive self-injury in hospitalized adolescents. *Journal of the American Academy of Child and Adolescent Psychiatry, 41*, 1333–1341.

Nose, M., Cipriani, A., Biancosino, B., Grassi, L., & Barbui, C. (2006). Efficacy of pharmacotherapy against core traits of borderline personality disorder: Meta-analysis of randomized controlled trials. *International Clinical Psychopharmacology, 21*, 345–353.

Perrella, C., Carrus, D., Costa, E., & Schifano F. (2007). Quetiapine for the treatment of borderline personality disorder: an open-label study. *Prog Neuropsychopharmacological and Biological Psychiatry, 31*, 158–163

Philipsen, A., Richter, H., Schmahl, C., Peters, J., Rusch, N., Bohus, M., et al., (2004). Clonidine in acute aversive inner tension and self-injurious behaviour in female patients with borderline personality disorder. *Journal of Clinical Psychiatry, 65*, 1414–1419.

Pies, R. W., & Popli, A. P. (1995). Self-injurious behaviour: Pathophysiology and implications for treatment. *Journal of Clinical Psychiatry, 56*, 580–588

Pinto, O. C., & Akiskal, H. S. (1998). Lamotrigine as a promising approach to borderline personality: An open case series without concurrent DSM-IV major mood disorder. *Journal of Affect Disorder, 51*, 333–343.

Plener, P. L., Fegert, J. M., & Libal, G. (2005). SSRIs bei jugendlichen Mädchen mit selbstverletzendem Verhalten.Gibt es Auswirkungen auf die Suizidalität ? In *Die Sprache in der Kinder-und Jugendpsychiatrie. XXIX. Kongreß der DGKJPPP- die Abstracts* (p. 312). Göttingen: Vandenhoeck & Ruprecht.

Primeau, F., & Fontaine, R. (1987). Obsessive disorder with self-mutilation: A subgroup responsive to pharmacotherapy. *Canadian Journal of Psychiatry, 32*, 699–701.

Rinne, T., van den Brink, W., Wouters, L., & van Dyck, R. (2002) SSRI treatment of borderline personality disorder: a randomized, placebo-controlled clinical trial for female patients with borderline personality disorder. *American Journal of Psychiatry, 159*, 2048–2054.

Roberts, N. (2003). Adolescent self-mutilatory behavior: Psychopharmacological treatment. *Child and Adolescent Psychopharmacology News, 8*, 10–12.

Roth, A. S., Ostroff, R. B., & Hoffman, E. R. (1996). Naltrexone as a treatment for repetitive self-injurious behaviour: An open–label trial. *Journal of Clinical Psychiatry, 57*, 233–237.

Salzman, C., Wolfson, A. N., Schatzberg, A., Looper, J., Henke, R., Albanese, M., Schwartz, J., & Miyawaki, E. (1995). Effect of fluoxetine on anger in symptomatic volunteers with borderline personality disorder. *Journal of Clinical Psychopharmacology, 15*, 23–29.

Sandman, C. A., Barron, J. L., Crinella, F. M., & Donnely, J. F. (1988). Influence of naloxone on brain and behaviour of a self-injurious woman. *Biological Psychiatry, 22*, 899–906.

Sandman, C. A., Hetrick, W., Taylor, D. V., Marion, S. D., Touchette, P., Barron, J. L., et al. (2000). Long-term effects of naltrexone on self-injurious behaviour. *American Journal of Mental Retardation, 105,* 103–117.

Sandyk, R. (1985). Naloxone abolishes self-injuring in a mentally retarded child. *Annals of Neurology, 17,* 520.

Simon, G. E. (2006). The antidepressant quandary: Considering suicide risk when treating adolescent depression. *New England Journal of Medicine, 355,* 2772–2773.

Simpson, E. B., Yen, S., Costello, E., Rosen, K., Begin, A., Pistorello, J., & Pearlstein, T. (2004). Combined dialectical behavior therapy and fluoxetine in the treatment of borderline personality disorder. *Journal of Clinical Psychiatry, 65,* 379-385

Soler, J., Pascual, J. C., Campins, J, Barrachina, J., Puigdemont, D., Alvarez, E., & Pérez V. (2005). Double-blind, placebo-controlled study of dialectical behavior therapy plus olanzapine for borderline persoanlity disorder. *American Journal of Psychiatry, 162,* 1221-1224.

Soloff, P. H., Cornelius, J., George, A., Nathan, S., Perel, J. M., & Ulrich, R. F. (1993). Efficacy of phenelzine and haloperidol in borderline personality disorder. *Archives of General Psychiatry, 50,* 377–385.

Swedo, S. E., Leonhar, H. L., & Rapoport, J. L. (1989). A double-blind comparison of clomipramine and desipramine in the treatment of trichotillomania (hair pulling). *New England Journal of Medicine, 321,* 497-501.

Teicher, M. H., Glod, C. A., & Cole, J. O. (1993). Antidepressant drugs and the emergence of suicidal tendencies. *Drug Safety, 8,* 186–212.

Tritt, K., Nickel, C., Lahmann, C., Leibereich, P. K., Rother, W. K., Loew, T. H., et al. (2005). Lamotrigine treatment of aggression in female borderline-patients: A randomized, double-blind, placebo-controlled study. *Journal of Psychopharmacology, 19,* 287–291.

Verkes, R. J., Van der Mast, R. C., Hengeveld, M. W., Tuyl, J. P., Zwinderman, A. H., & Van Kempen, G. M. (1998). Reduction by paroxetine of suicidal behavior in patients with repeated suicide attempts but not major depression. *American Journal of Psychiatry, 155,* 543-547.

Villalba, R., & Harrington, C. J. (2000). Repetitive self-injurious behavior: A neuropsychiatric perspective and review of pharmacologic treatments. *Seminars in Clinical Neuropsychiatry, 5,* 215–226.

Villeneuve, E., & Lemelin, S. (2005). Open-label study of atypical neuroleptic quetiapine for treatment of borderline personality disorder: impulsivity as main target. *Journal of Clinical Psychiatry, 66,* 1298-1303.

Wagner, G. C., Avena, N., Kita, T., Nakashima, T., Fisher, H., & Halladay, A. K. (2003). Risperidone reduction of amphetamine-induced self-injurious behaviour in mice. *Neuropharmacology, 46,* 700–708.

White, T., & Schultz, S. K. (2000). Naltrexone treatment for a 3-year-old boy with self-injurious behaviour. *American Journal of Psychiatry, 157,* 574–582.

Whittington, C. J., Kendall, T., Fonagy, P., Cottrell, D., Cotgrove, A., & Boddington, E. (2004). Selective serotonin reuptake inhibitors in childhood depression: Systematic review of published versus unpublished data. *Lancet, 36,* 1341–1345.

Yaryura-Tobias, J. A., & Nezirogly, F. (1978). Compulsions, aggressions and self-mutilation. *American Journal of Orthopsychiatry, 7,* 114–117.

Zahl, D. L., & Hawton, K. (2004). Repetition of deliberate self-harm and subsequent suicide risk: Long-term follow-up study of 11,583 patients. *British Journal of Psychiatry, 185,* 70–75.

Zanarini, M. C., & Frankenburg, F. R. (2003). Omega-3 fatty acid treatment of women with borderline personality disorder: A double-blind, placebo-controlled pilot study. *American Journal of Psychiatry, 160,* 167–169.

Zanarini, M. C., & Frankenburg, F. R. (2001). Olanzapine treatment of female Borderline Personality Disorder patients: a double-blind, placebo-controlled pilot study. *Journal of Clinical Psychiatry, 62,* 849-854.

Zanarini, M. C., Frankenburg, F. R., & Parachini, E. A. (2004). A preliminary, randomized trial of fluoxetine, olanzapine, and the olanzapine-fluoxetine combination in women with borderline personality disorder. *Journal of Clinical Psychiatry, 65,* 903-907.

15

Resource Guide for Working with Youth

JESSICA R. TOSTE, SHAREEN HOLLY,
AND KRISTIN SCHAUB

> Hi all, I've been here a few times but left because I haven't found a lot of support here. This board has actually kinda confused me because sometimes people give each other support and other times people ask for suggestions on how to hide or continue their self-injury. So I guess I'm just wondering why people came to this board? Were you looking for support in recovering from self-injury or were you looking for ideas on how to continue it?
>
> ~little_candle"

This chapter presents a variety of text- and web-based resources for practitioners working with youth who engage in nonsuicidal self-injury (NSSI), as well as for parents of youth who are self-injuring. When practitioners or parents are beginning to learn about NSSI, critical resources can be obtained through text, media, and the Internet. A multitude of resources are available, and it is often unclear which represent best practice in the field of NSSI. The purpose of this chapter is to detail resources that describe the behavior that has been discussed within this book, self-inflicted destruction of body tissue without suicidal intent and for purposes not socially sanctioned, and have a similar approach to the understanding of NSSI.

In addition to consulting these resources, practitioners are encouraged to establish connections with other professionals, in their community or via the Internet, to create a network for sharing information and discussing issues that arise during their work with youth. This network can serve as an important way to share new resources in this growing field of research.

The following pages are divided into three sections: print materials, electronic resources, and books. The listed resources are those found to be consistent with best practice with NSSI and most helpful for practitioners working with parents and youth who engage in this behavior. Each resource includes a brief description of the content and intended audience. All references are ordered alphabetically.

SECTION I: PRINT MATERIALS

Articles for Practitioners

Heath, N. L., Toste, J. R., & Beettam, E. (2006). "I am not well-equipped": High school teachers' perceptions of self-injury. *Canadian Journal of School Psychology, 21,* 73–92.

This article described an empirical study exploring high school teachers' perceptions of NSSI among adolescents, including their experiences, knowledge of NSSI, and attitudes toward youth who engage in this behavior. The findings can be helpful for school-based professionals, allowing them to have a better sense of current understanding in the schools and to target the information they share as they begin to educate other personnel about NSSI.

Lieberman, R. (2004). Understanding and responding to students who self-mutilate. *Principal Leadership (High School ed.), 4,* 10–13.

This brief report provides an overview of issues related to NSSI in the schools, including appropriate prevention and intervention strategies. The emphasis in this report is on preparing schools in advance to improve the response to students who engage in NSSI and thus create opportunities for more successful outcomes for these students. This information is targeted toward school mental health professionals, but is also useful for administrators and teachers.

White Kress, V. E., Gibson, D. M., & Reynolds, C. A. (2004). Adolescents who self-injure: Implications and strategies for school counselors. *Professional School Counseling, 7,* 195–201.

This article focuses on strategies for school counselors working with youth who engage in NSSI (on both individual and school-wide levels), including the school counselor's role in prevention, intervention, referral, education, and advocacy. This information is targeted specifically at school counselors and other mental health professionals working in the schools.

White, V. E., McCormick, L. J., & Kelly, B. L. (2003). Counseling clients who self-injure: Ethical considerations. *Counseling and Values, 47,* 220–229.

This article provides an overview of ethical concerns for counselors working with clients who engage in NSSI (consistent with the American Counseling Association's code of ethics and standards of practice). Various ethical issues are discussed in relation to client welfare, counselor competencies, counter-transference, referral and consultation, informed consent, and duty to protect. Emphasis is placed on the counselor's understanding of NSSI prior to working with clients who engage in this behavior. The intended audience for this work is primarily counselors working in community or school settings.

Whitlock, J. L., Powers, J. L., & Eckenrode, J. (2006). The virtual cutting edge: The Internet and adolescent self-injury. *Developmental Psychopathology, 42,* 1–11.

The purpose of this article is to document the use of message boards in the exchange of information, promotion, and discussion of NSSI among adolescents. The Internet is widely used among adolescents, and this is one of few studies that has examined the potential role of websites and message boards in encouraging this behavior. Although message boards may provide support and a network for adolescents who may otherwise be isolated, it is important to note that it is a public domain and only somewhat censored. This article is targeted toward researchers in the field, as well as all practitioners working with youth to give them a better understanding of the limitations of Internet use.

Fact Sheets

Purington, A., & Whitlock, J. (2004). Self-injury fact sheet. ACT for Youth Upstate Center for Excellence. *Research Facts and Findings,* 001–04.

This brief fact sheet was developed to provide essential information about NSSI to researchers, practitioners, parents, and youth. It highlights current research in the field and is written for a general audience.

SECTION II: ELECTRONIC RESOURCES

The Internet provides many opportunities for youth to share experiences and connect with peers from around the world. Youth, as well as practitioners and parents, can access websites that provide essential information on NSSI to help them better understand the behavior, its function, and ways to seek help. When searching online, one should look for sites created by reputable organizations or that cite work that has been published within the field. Many websites provide inaccurate information. Below are several examples of websites that provide excellent information and resources.

Another resource available within many websites is message boards. Many youth who experience difficulties have a feeling of disconnect from their peers or communities. It is important for them to connect with other youth who share similar concerns, and message boards provide opportunities for this type of connectedness, especially for youth who may live in a community with few resources to support someone engaging in NSSI. A couple of message boards are available on the websites listed below, but numerous others can be found through an online search. When deciding what message boards will be helpful to share with youth engaging in NSSI, consider that the healthiest boards are monitored, have rules that govern posts and comments, and do not allow the posting of images or photos that could potentially trigger NSSI in other visitors. Some examples of rules you will find on message boards that are healthy and monitored include:

- Be respectful of others if you post on a sensitive subject. Notify other users of the topic in the subject line of your post and be careful about posting graphic details about sexual situations, abuse, or violence.
- Do not post asking for methods of self-injury or describing them in detail. It's okay to say "I cut" but not to describe when, where, and how you cut.
- Suicide notes and threats are not permitted.
- If you're asking for help here, be willing to listen to what's said. If you're asking for help with an immediate self-harm situation, put down your tools before you log on to the board.
- Do not link to or post pictures of self-inflicted wounds.

American Self-Harm Clearing House (http://www.selfinjury.org): This website was created by Deb Martinson and hosts the "Self-Injurers Bill of Rights." This document is meant to inform self-injurers of their rights and is endorsed by Dr. Armando Favazza. This site is intended for individuals who engage in NSSI. It provides information about understanding the behavior in addition to ways to seek help.

Life SIGNS: Self-Injury Guidance and Network Support (http://www.lifesigns.org.uk): The main purpose of this website is to raise awareness and provide information about NSSI. It is intended for self-injurers, practitioners, as well as family and friends of those who engage in NSSI. It is clearly laid out, easy to navigate, and provides current evidence-based information. Suggestions and contacts are available for those seeking help to stop self-injuring. The directors of this site are individuals who have personal experiences with NSSI. This site contains message boards for self-injurers, as well as one specifically geared toward family and friends of individuals engaging in NSSI. The boards are moderated and users must be registered to post messages.

S.A.F.E. Alternatives (http://www.selfinjury.com): This website is maintained by S.A.F.E. Alternatives, cofounded by Karen Conterio and Dr. Wendy Lader, authors of the book *Bodily Harm: The Breakthrough Healing Program for Self-Injurers* (Hyperion, 1998). This website provides extensive information about NSSI, as well as information on treatment programs. The site is meant to be used by self-injurers, family members, and practitioners working with individuals who engage in NSSI. This website also hosts a blog (http://www.safe-alternatives.com/blog). You must register to post to the blog or comment on previous posts. The CEO and clinical director of S.A.F.E. Alternatives both post and respond to the blog. It is an excellent resource for those seeking help or interested in learning more about treatment programs. A new feature on the site is a listing of research centers studying NSSI across Canada and the United States that allow graduate students or new researchers to connect with those working in this area.

Secret Shame (http://www.selfharm.net): This website was also created by Deb Martinson, as above. Her description of the site is, "The information here comes from the five years I've spent listening to, talking with, and skills-coaching people who self-injure; peer-reviewed journals; books; internet surveys; and other sources." This website contains many resources geared toward helping individuals who engage in NSSI to understand and stop this behavior.

SIARI (Self-Injury and Related Issues) (http://www.siari.co.uk): This website provides extensive information for family, friends, and supporters of individuals who engage in NSSI. It is maintained by Jan Sutton, who has extensive counseling training and has conducted research in the area of self-injury, written several articles, and presented numerous papers on the topic to practitioners working with individuals who engage in NSSI. Downloadable PDF files are available on the site to ensure easy access to this information, which can be printed and shared.

Teen Health (http://www.kidshealth.org): This website is maintained by the Nemours Foundation's Center for Children's Health Media and has won several awards for best website in the area of parent, kid, and teen information. The site provides a searchable database with information on health-related topics (search term: cutting) for parents, kids, and teens. The content is up-to-date, jargon-free, and is presented in a question and answer format for easy reading.

SECTION III: BOOKS

Researchers and Clinicians

Bowman, S., & Randall, K. (2004). *See my pain: Creative strategies and activities for helping young people who self-injure.* Chapin, SC: YouthLight.

This manual provides practitioners with strategies and activities designed to help adolescents who engage in NSSI. It was created for use by mental health professionals working with self-injurers in a private practice or school settings.

Connors, R. E. (2000). *Self-injury: Psychotherapy with people who engage in self-inflicted violence.* Northvale: NJ: Jason Aronson.

This book provides information about therapeutic interventions with individuals who engage in NSSI. The author presents guidelines for clinicians that will improve their ability to respond appropriately and respectfully to individuals who self-injure. The target audience is clinicians interested in a more psychotherapeutic orientation.

Conterio, K., & Lader, W. (1998). *Bodily harm: The breakthrough healing program for self-injurers.* New York: Hyperion.

The purpose of this book is to give detailed information about NSSI, as well as a thorough description of the S.A.F.E. (Self-Abuse Finally Ends) Alternatives treatment program, along with case studies, diaries, and success stories from patients. This book is targeted toward self-injurers, practitioners, and anyone who knows an individual who engages in NSSI.

D'Onofrio, A. A. (2007). *Adolescent self-injury: A comprehensive guide for counselors and health care professionals.* New York: Springer.

The book provides an overview of NSSI and practical guidelines for school counselors and other health care professionals working with youth who engage in this behavior, including identification, assessment, and a discussion of working with teachers, administrators, and parents. This is a good resource for any clinician working with youth who engage in NSSI.

Favazza, A. R. (1996). *Bodies under siege: Self-mutilation and body modification in culture and psychiatry.* London: John Hopkins University Press.

This book provides a history and background of early research in the field of self-injury. It is an essential read for any researchers or practitioners working in the field of NSSI. This is the first book to examine the full scope of this behavior.

Selekman, M. (2002). *Living on the razor's edge: Solution-oriented brief family therapy with self-harming adolescents.* New York: W. W. Norton.

This book, geared towards family therapists, presents an integrative and flexible solution-oriented family therapy model for working with adolescents who engage in self-harming behaviors. This model integrates elements of solution-focused, narrative, postmodern, strategic, cognitive, and expressive therapy approaches. This book provides many case examples and transcripts of client interviews.

Simeon, E., & Hollander, E. (2001). *Self-injurious behavior: Assessment and treatment*. Washington DC: American Psychiatric Publishing.

This edited book presents a comprehensive review of information related to self-injurious behaviors. The contributors to this book allow for both theoretical and practical insight as they discuss etiology and occurrence, biological and psychological theories and varied treatment approaches for individuals who engage in self-injury.

Walsh, B. W. (2006). *Treating self-injury: A practical guide*. New York: Guilford Press.

This book provides an overview of information on NSSI, including assessment and treatment of the behavior within a biopsychosocial model, issues surrounding contagions, and school protocols. Although it is written as a guide for clinicians, it is also a good resource for those who are looking for a concise overview of current thinking within the field of NSSI.

Parents and Families

McVey-Noble, M. E., Khemlani-Patel, S., & Neziroglu, F. (2006). *When your child is cutting: A parent's guide to helping children overcome self-injury*. Oakland, CA: New Harbinger.

This book is a guide for parents of children and adolescents who engage in NSSI. It describes how to understand this behavior, cope with it, and help the child. This is one of the only books directed specifically to parents. It attempts to normalize parents' fears and worries about this behavior and offers advice for parents in communicating with their children and supporting them through treatment.

Strong, M. (1999). *A bright red scream: Self-mutilation and the language of pain*. New York: Penguin Books.

The main purpose of this book is to understand NSSI from the perspective of the self-injurer. It is targeted at individuals who engage in NSSI, as well as their families and friends. This book was written in consultation with Armando Favazza, Karen Conterio, and Wendy Lader (from S.A.F.E. Alternatives), and other clinicians working in the field.

CONCLUDING COMMENTS

Listed above are resources that we have examined and endorse, but youth who engage in NSSI will likely have sought out other resources that may not be as reliable or healthy. It would be helpful to inquire of youth what resources online and otherwise they are accessing regarding NSSI. Practitioners need to be aware that many online forums are very counterproductive to the therapeutic process, and collecting information concerning online activities around NSSI is important.

16

Concluding Comments from the Editors

NANCY L. HEATH AND MARY K. NIXON

Self-injury took seven years of my life; it was seven years of hell. It was a crutch, a burden, an excuse, a drug. I slowly became addicted, moving from injuring once in a while to everyday to more. I was punishing myself. I was hospitalized for a suicide attempt and it was then I realized how addicted, dependent, and desolate I really was. But what I didn't realize was that self-injury was a *choice*. No one forces you to self-injure; other's actions or words might lead you to self-injuring but you alone control your actions. Self-injury is nothing more than a dangerous bandaid, covering emotions with physical pain. Physical pain is more concrete than emotional pain and that's what's so appealing. Self-injury is nothing to live with: you deserve so much better. Remember, life is what you make of it. I'm not saying you won't have impulses because you will. But, people are there to help, yet it won't do any good unless you're ready. Ready to change, to be free, to live. Ready to ask for help. (Written by K.A., age 17)

Despite the growth in research on nonsuicidal self-injury (NSSI), only a handful of books are available to help the practitioner in working with youth who engage in this behavior. This book is the first to bring together a wealth of expertise from psychiatry, psychology, counseling, and community health to create an edited text wherein leaders in each field share their knowledge directly with practitioners to improve practice in working with adolescents who engage in NSSI. The reader has had the opportunity to cross disciplinary boundaries to learn about current best practice for working with youth who engage in NSSI in inpatient, outpatient, and community settings.

The first section of the book focused on background information about the prevalence of NSSI and possible underlying functions of the behavior for youth. The second section explored possible etiology of NSSI using a biopsychosocial model. The next section centered on effective practice, first assessment, and then prevention, intervention and treatment across disciplines and settings. In closing, Chapter 15 provided a background and context to selecting best resources for use in working with youth who engage in NSSI. Throughout, the book has aimed to offer the practitioner user-friendly access to a burgeoning area of research that can inform best practice. Most importantly, this book acknowledges that youth who self-injure are attempting to cope the best they can at that moment. They are not just "cutters" or "self-injurers." Although working with these youth and their families may pose many challenges, the support, guidance, and interventions that they receive, provided in a nonjudgemental and informed manner, offer the opportunity for them to begin a journey of change.

My scars are my own
So I do not ask
I try to hide them
But some just show

From falling or falling in love
From broken bones and broken hearts
My scars are my own
I don't like to tell
Where they all came from
A tree, a rock, a knife
My scars are my secrets
My untold likes

My scars are mine to hide
So if you see
Then do not ask
For though they are scars
They still hurt inside

—Anonymous

Index

Note: locators for figures are in italics and for tables in bold

A

A Bright Red Scream: Self-Mutilation and the Language of Pain, 269
acute dystonia, 281
acute inpatient services, 258
addiction, 83
 endogenous reward system of the brain, 97
adolescence, 174–175
 decision making in, 175
 developmental issues in, 175
 developmental tasks, 247
 risk-taking in, 175
adolescent behavior
 marital conflict and, 248
adolescent NSSI, 1–6, 5, 29, 32, 62, 63, 115, 125, 130, 174, 176, 254, 270
 African-Americans, 17
 African-Canadians, 17
 anxiety, 75, 197
 assessment of, 116, 143–170, 166–169, 270
 automatic-negative reinforcement, 33, 35, 37
 Axis I disorders and, 61
 Axis II disorders and, 61
 borderline personality disorder (BPD) and, 61, 65, 258
 community-level prevention and intervention, 65
 co-morbidity, 260
 confidentiality and, 211
 contagion and, 196, 207, 209, 211, 270
 contingency management approach, 219
 co-occurrence and, 60, 62, 64, 73, 75, 263, 276
 as a coping mechanism, 207
 creative work and, 202
 dangers of offering peer support groups, 207
 depression, 75
 distress tolerance, 197
 eating disorders and, 65
 evidence-based practices (EBP), 116–117
 expression of emotions, 197
 family environment and, 238, 239
 functions of, 29–42, 116
 gender and, 260
 in "Goth" groups in the UK, 179
 group therapy and, 229, 231
 help-seeking skills and, 198
 high-school teachers perceptions of, 310
 hostility and anger, 75
 increasing prevalence of, 178
 internet discussions of, 37–38
 Internet-based survey, 217
 key beliefs about, 209
 longitudinal studies of, 61
 in nonclinical settings, 178
 numbers of, 196
 outcomes with multiple disorders, 61
 parent contact and, 206–207, 211
 peers and, 37, 202
 personality disorders and, 61
 pharmacotherapy and, 275, 275–308, 276
 prevalence among inpatients, 258–259
 psychoeducation and, 242
 psychopharmacological interventions, 283
 psychosocial interventions, 217–236
 repetitive, 276
 research and, 75, 116
 risk factors for, 183
 school personnel and, 195
 school policies and, 195, 203–204
 school response protocol, 195, 197, 202
 in school settings, 197, 213
 school-based approaches to intervention, 195
 self-derogation, 197
 signed "contracts" and, 219

social negative reinforcement and, 37
spread of, 179, 181
studies of, 73
substance use, 65, 75
suicide and, 61, 74, 205, 263, 296
teacher training and, 199
treatment of, 116, *294*
warning signs for, 202
adolescent NSSI, assessment of, 143–170,
    166–169
  first contact and initial response,
    144–148
  level 1 assessment: screening and
    triage, 148–157
  level 2: basic assessment for
    determining interventions,
    158–162
  level 3: complex assessment for
    determining interventions,
    162–166
adolescent NSSI, inpatient, 257–274,
    257–275, 258, 271
  assessment, 264–267
  clinical treatment guidelines for,
    268–271
  empirically supported treatment,
    267–268
  prevalence of, 258–259
  reasons to study, 259–260
  recent trends in inpatient services for
    children and adolescents, 258
  research limitations and future
    directions, 264
  research on, 260–263, 263–264
adolescent NSSI, measurement of, 115,
    115–142, 115–143, 116
  clinical assessment, 116
  evidence-based practice, 116–117
  measurement selection for adolescent
    self-injury, 133–138
  research, 116
  review of existing measures, 117–118
  self-report measures, 118–131
  structured interviews, 130–133
  summary and future direction,
    138–139
  through structured interviews,
    130–133
  treatment planning and monitoring,
    116

adolescent NSSI, self-report measures
    of, 118–131
  deliberate self-harm inventory
    (DSHI), 128–129
  functional assessment of self-
    mutilation (FASM), 124–125
  Ottawa Self-Injury Inventory (OSI),
    129–130
  self-harm behavior questionnaire
    (SHBQ), 128
  self-harm inventory, 125–126
  self-harm survey and motivations
    underlying self-harm
    questionnaire, 130–131
  self-injury motivation scale-II,
    126–127
  self-injury questionnaire (SIQ),
    127–128
adolescent self-injury and
  interventions for, 241
adolescents, 75
  cognitively intact, 176
adult NSSI, 63, 239
  functions and, 35
adult patient groups
  Self-Injury Motivation Scale II (SIMS-
    II), 126
adulthood, 175
affect regulation model, 32
agonist, 109
alcohol and substance abuse problems,
    263
alexithymia, 102
  nonsuicidal self-injury (NSSI), 100
alliance building, 208
American Academy of Child and
    Adolescent Psychiatry, 74, 246
American Psychiatric Association
    (APA), 60, 61, 280
American Self-Harm Clearing House,
    312
amygdala, 91, 97
  extended, 97
andrenocorticotropic Hormone (ACTH),
    109
anhedonia, 35
animal models of self-injury
  6-Hydroxydopamine Neonate model
    of SIB, 86–87
  calcium channel agonists and, 86

calcium channel agonists and SIB, 87–88
dopamine models (6-hydroxydopamine and pemoline), 86
limitations of, 88
neuroscience and, 86–88
pemoline-induced SIB, 87
primate model of self-injury, 86, 88
animals
neglect in, 99
anorexia nervosa, 296
nonsuicidal self-injury (NSSI) and, 50
spread of in the 1980s, 180
anterior cingulated cortex, 91
anticonvulsants (mood stabilizers), 282–283
antidepressants
tetracyclic, 280
antidissociation, 31
antipsychotics, first generation, 295
antipsychotics, second generation (SGAs), 281, 295, 296, 301
treatment of NSSI, 293
weight gain and, 296
weight neutral, 296
antisuicide, 31
anxiety, 220, 263
Anxiety BC, 233
anxiety disorders, 45, 100, 102, 260, 301
increase in, 176
nonsuicidal self-injury (NSSI) and, 50
anxious-avoidant problems
adolescents and, 75
aripiprazole, 281, 296
assessment, 75, 117–118, 162–166
basic assessment for intervention, 143
clinical, 36–38, 38, 38–39
clinical assessment, 38
detailed mental health, 183
evidence-based, 264
first contact and initial response, 144, 146–148
hierarchical step approach to, *145*
level 1: screening and triage, 148–157
level 2: basic assessment for determining interventions, 149, 158–162

level 3: complex assessment for determining interventions, 144, 162
levels of, 144
nonsuicidal self-injury (NSSI), 143
in schools, 206
treatment planning, 38–39
triage, 143
assessment, comprehensive, 143
assessment, comprehensive baseline, 137
OSI, 137
SASII, 137
SIQ, 137
SITBI, 137
associative learning
nonsuicidal self-injury (NSSI), 96
attention-hyperactivity problems
adolescents and, 75
Australia, 17, 18, 22
autism, 99, 117
auto-aggression, 83
automatic functions, 33
automatic negative reinforcement, 37, 125
hopelessness and, 262
automatic positive reinforcement, 125, 262
major depressive disorder (MDD), 262
autonomy
as basic needs, 246
avoiding doctor when ill, 127
Axis I disorders, 61, 74, 291, 293, 295
bulemia, 227
major depression, 226
obsessive-compulsive behavior, 226
posttraumatic stress disorder, 226
schizophrenia, 226–227
selective serotonin reuptake inhibitors (SSRIs) and, 296
separation anxiety, 226
social anxiety, 226
Axis II disorders, 61, 74
Aztecs, ancient religion of, 2

B

Bacon, Sir Francis, 269
basic needs, 246

"basins of attraction," 100
behavior
    influence of social environments
        and, 179
behavior therapy, 33
behavioral analysis, 32
behavioral approaches, 92
behavioral chain analyses, 265, 271
behavioral reinforcement or exogenous
        reward, 94–98
benzodiazepines, 282, 295
    addictive potential of, 282
    paradoxical reactions an, 282
Bible, references to self-injury and, 2
biopsychological model, 143
    self-injury and, 144
bipolar disorder, 293
    adolescent, 242, 260
    family history of, 296
    selective serotonin reuptake
        inhibitors (SSRIs) and, 296
blood poisoning, 270
*Bodies Under Siege: Self Mutilation and
        Body Modification in Culture and
        Psychiatry*, 2–3
*Bodily Harm: The Breakthrough Healing
        Program for Self-Injurers*
        (Conterio and Lader), 313
body modification rituals
    ancient religions and, 2
body modification rituals, ancient
        religions and, 2
body piercing, 4
body scarification
    tribal cultures and, 3
bones, breaking, 80
books, 314–315
    parents and families, 315
    researchers and clinicians, 314–315
    for researchers and clinicians,
        314–315
borderline personality disorder (BPD),
        32, 35, 47, 61, 80, 91, 126, 129,
        130, 228, 239, 280, 282
    antipsychotics and, 293
    Deliberate Self-Harm Inventory
        (DSHI) and, 129
    emotion dysregulation and, 50
    etiological studies of, 91
    mood stabilizers and, 283

nonsuicidal self-injury (NSSI) and,
        32–33, 50, 90, 91, 92, 94, 98, 177
    risk for NSSI, 50
    Self-Harm Inventory (SHI) and, 126
    self-injury and, 90
    symptoms of, 183
boundary definition, 31
brain
    chemistry of, 81
    functioning of, 102
brain chemistry
    genetic, 83
brain opiate activity
    self-injurious behavior (SIB) and, 85
brain physiology
    behaviors and, 100
brain signals
    actions and, 83
bulemia, 295
    nonsuicidal self-injury (NSSI), 51
burning, 4, 11, 52, 127

C

calcium (Ca) channel agonists, 87, 88
    self-injurious behavior (SIB) and,
        87–88
Canada, 278
    hospitalization and, 258
carbamezepine, 282, 283
carving, 4
case conceptualization, adolescents and,
        74
case studies, 30–31, 195, 211
    assessment for medication and,
        277–278
    Axis I disorders, 291
    bipolar disorder, adolescent, 291
    family factors associated with
        nonsuicidal self-injury, 249
    psychotherapeutive intervention and
        assessment, 162
    reduction of mental illness in a
        college population, 187–188
    suicide prevention in the U.S. Air
        Force, 186
    suicide risk, 153, 156
Caucasian samples, 64
caudal group, neuron clusters, 83
celebration, as basic need, 246

cerebrospinal fluid (CSF) levels of 5-HIAA
  self-aggressive behaviors and, 84
Child and Adolescent Mental Health Division, Hawaii State Department of Health, 75
Child and Adolescent Self-harm in Europe (CASE) group, 10, 17, 22
Child and Adolescent Therapy: Science and Art (Shapiro, Friedberg, & Bardenstein), 74
childhood abuse, 47, 91
  neglect, 99
  nonsuicidal self-injury (NSSI) and, 80
childhood abuse, sexual, 99
  nonsuicidal self-injury (NSSI) and, 92
childhood trauma, 47
Children's Interview for Psychiatric Syndromes-Child and Parent Forms, 74
Chorpita, Bruce, 75
cigarette smoking, 97
clonidine, 282
clozapine, 281
cluster symptoms, 295
cocaine, 97
  endogenous reward system of the brain, 97
cognitive behavior modification, 226
cognitive behavioral therapy (CBT), 219, 220, 222, 226–228, 270, 296
  families and, 244
  principles of, 227
  relationships between thoughts, feelings, and behavior in, **228**
  Socratic method of questioning and, 227
cognitive deficits, 102
cognitive restructuring, 209–210
colleges, 174
Columbia University, TeenScreen Program, 198
Columbine High School, 176
communication
  skill-building, 208–209
community, 182
  definition of, 174
  intervention and, 174
  role in initiation and maintenance of NSSI, 178–180
  virtual, 174
community samples, 173
  co-occurrence and, 64
  suicidal acts and, 65
  suicidal ideation, 65
co-morbidity, 59, 60, 62, 92, 178
  apparent, 59
  research on, 75
  true, 59
compulsions, 295
concluding comments from the editors, 317–318
conduct disorder, 221
contagion
  hospitalized youth and, 257
  minimizing risk of, 211
  in the schools, 210–211
Conterio, Karen, 313, 315
co-occurrence, 60, 168
  adolescent NSSI, 60–62
Cornelia de Lange syndrome, 281
cortisol, 90
covariance, 60
  research on, 75
crisis intervention
  approach for parents and families, **244**
  with families, 242
  problem solving therapy and, 222
  services, 149
crisis team preparedness, 198–199
cutting/carving, 4, 11, 52, 127, 260
cyclothymia, selective serotonin reuptake inhibitors (SSRIs) and, 296

D

D1 receptor, 85, 87
D2 receptor, 85, 87
DARE program, negative outcomes of, 187
Dealing With Depression, 233
decarboxylaxe, 109
decosahexaenoic acid, 283
definitions and self-injury, 3–5
delayed gratification, 94
deliberate self-harm (DSH), 4, 30, 221
Deliberate Self-Harm Inventory (DSHI), 128–129

borderline personality disorder (BPD) and, 129

denervate, 109

Depp, Johnny, public admission of NSSI, 180

depression, 35, 100, 102, 219, 220, 260, 263, 295
  nonsuicidal self-injury (NSSI), 50
  screening for, 198

depression, adolescent
  family therapy and, 240

depressive-withdrawn problems adolescents and, 75

developmental delays, 64, 84

developmental disabilities and, 80

Diagnostic and Statistical Manual, fourth edition (DSM-IV), 60, 61, 259, 264, 280
  Axis I disorders, 149, 263, 266
  Axis I symptoms and, 74, 75
  Axis II disorder, 149, 266
  Axis II symptoms and, 74, 75

diagnostic interview, 163

Diagnostic Interview for Borderlines [DIB], 126

Diagnostic Interview for *DSM-IV* Personality Disorders, 74, 266

Diagnostic Interview Schedule for CHildren Version 2.3 (Shaffer et al., 1996), 266

dialectical behavior therapy (DBT), 53, 92, 185, 219, 228–229, 241, 245, 252, 254, 268, 270–271
  adolescent inpatients and, 265
  family therapy sessions, 229
  individual (outpatient and inpatient), 229
  in-group skills training, 229
  modes of delivery, 229
  phone consultation, 229
  stages of treatment, 229
  therapist consultation meetings, 229
  vs. treatment-as-usual (TAU), 267
  Zen Buddhist ideas of acceptance and tolerance, 228

diazepam, 295

Difficulties in Emotion Regulation Scale (DERS), 49

"Digital Natives," 180

disordered eating prevention, 183

disruptive behavior disorders, 220

disruptive-oppositional problems, adolescents and, 75

dissociation, 32, 183
  self-injury and, 99

divalproex, 282
  polysistic ovarian cyndrome and, 283

D'Onofrio, 144

dopa, 84, 109

dopa decarboxylase, 84

dopamine, 83, 84, 84–85, 88, 102
  animal studies and, 84
  neuronal projections to areas of the brain, *82*
  reward system of the brain, 97
  self-injurious behavior (SIB) and, 84

dopamine agonists, 85, 87

dopamine neurons, 97

dopamine pathways, pemoline (2-amino-5-phenyl-4-oxazolidinone) and, 87

dopamine receptors, 281
  D1, 84, 85
  D1-D5, 84
  D2, 84, 85

dopamine systems, 85
  nonsuicidal self-injury (NSSI) and, 92

dopaminergic neurons, 84

dopaminergic neurotransmission, self-injurious behavior (SIB) and, 87

dopaminergic projections, 84

dopaminergic system, 281
  medications targeting, 281

Dorset Mental Health Services, 233

dorsolateral prefrontal cortex, 91

drug overdose, 10

DSM-IV-TR (American Psychiatric Association), 163

dynorphins, 85, 109

dysphoric state of anxiety, 100

E

early help-seeking, 186

eating disorders, 37, 176, 181, 187, 263
  assessment tools and, 117
  media and, 181

electronic diaries
  adolescent self-injury and, 133

emotional connectedness, increasing,
246–247
emotional dysregulation, 49, 53, 55, 228,
291
emotional state regulation, 83
emotions, management of, 53
endogenous opiods, 85
reward system of the brain, 97
endorphins, 85, 92
μ receptors and, 85
enkephalins, 85, 109
epinephrine, 90
Epps, Kevin, clinical guidelines of, 270
ethical and legal considerations, 212–213
ethical framework, 301
ethyl-eicosapentaenoic (E-EPA), 283
European Medicines Agency (EMEA),
276
Evidence Based Services webpage
Child and Adolescent Mental Health
Division of the Hawaii State
Department of Health, 75
evidence-based practices (EBP), 74, 75
*Evidence-Based Psycho-therapies for
Children and Adolescents*
(Kazdin & Weisz), 74
Evidence-Based Services Committee, 75
existing measures, review of, 117
exocytosis, 110
exogenous opiods
self-injury and, 100
exogenous reward, 102
training and, 94
eye enucleation, 80

F

fact sheets, 311
families, 179
cognitive behavioral therapy (CBT)
and, 244
families of adolescents with NSSI,
working with, 160, 162, 163,
237–256, 250, 253–254
assessment, 242–249, 246
case study, 249
crisis intervention, 242
enabling adolescent developmental
tasks, 247
evidence for, 240–241

evidence for family interventions,
240–241
family risk and protective factors,
238–239
group model, 250
improving communication, 246–247
improving interactions, 246–247
increasing emotional connectedness,
246–247
individually based family therapy,
251–253
parent group for parents of self-
injuring youth, 252–253
parental functioning and parental
factors, 247–248
parents as effective advocates,
249–250
promoting predictability of
environment, 246
psychoeducation, 242
reviewing basic needs, 246–249
suicidality with remarriages, 239
two models of working with
families, 250–253
Family Adaptability and Cohesion
Evaluation Scale, 238
family and social support
as protective factor, 51
Family Assessment Device (Epstein,
1983), 245
Family Inventory of Life Events, 238
family resilience and protective factors,
244
belief systems, 244
communication processes, 244
organizational patterns, 244
family risk and protective factors,
238–239
family therapy, 231, 241
self-injury and, 52
family therapy, individually based,
251–253
phase four: ending therapy, 251
phase one: family assessment, 251
phase three: improving
family interactions and
communication, 251
phase two: psychoeducation, 251
family-school connectedness, 197
fasting, 127

Favazza, Armando, 2, 312, 315
    anthropological study of NSSI, 189
Favazza and Rosenthal, 4
Favazza and Simeon, 4
Federal Drug Administration (FDA), 276
fenfluramine, 84
Finland
    hospitalization and, 258
first contact and initial response,
    144–148
flashbacks, 295
fluoxetine, 296
functional analysis, 32
functional assessment of self-injury, **161**
functional assessment of self-mutilation
    (FASM), 124–125, 265
functional assessment questionnaires,
    271

G

gangrene, 270
gender, 181
German adolescent community sample
    suicidal ideation in, 65
glass, eating, 80
Great Britain, 278
    self-injury studies in, 174
Greek texts, ancient, references to self-
    injury and, 2
Grey's Anatomy
    nonsuicidal self-injury (NSSI) themes
        and scenes in, 180
group therapies, 229
    combined, 229, 231

H

haloperidol, 281
    borderline personality disorder
        (BPD) and, 281
Health and Psychosocial Instruments
    (HaPI), 117
Health Canada, 276
"helpful" vs. "non-helpful" responses,
    147
high school counselors, 144
    ethical concerns for, 311
    strategies for, 310
hippocampus, 97

"How I Deal With Stress" (HIDS)
    survey, 117, 148, *150–151*
humanistic therapy principles, 222
hypomania
    selective serotonin reuptake
        inhibitors (SSRIs) and, 296
hypothalamic-pituitary-adrenal (HPA)
    axis, 110
    nonsuicidal self-injury (NSSI) and, 92

I

impaired prolactin response
    increased self-aggression and, 84
    suicide attempts and, 84
impulsivity, 83, 263, 301
infection, 270
inpatient samples
    co-occurrence and, 64
    suicidal acts and, 65
    suicidal ideation, 65
inpatient services for children and
        adolescents, recent trends in,
        258
inpatient treatment of NSSI
    empirically supported, 267–268
inpatient treatment, reduction of
        coverage for by managed
        health care organizations, 258
instantaneous physiological state,
        behavior and, 89
Institute of Medicine
    nomenclature for intervention and
        prevention, 182
Institute of Medicine nomenclature
    application to NSSI, **184**
integrity, as basic need, 246
intent of NSSI
    to alleviate emotional distress, 63
    to die, 65
    suicide attempts and, 63
interdependence, as basic needs, 246
internal states, regulation of, 33
International Classification of DIseases
        (World Heath Organization),
        280
Internet, 180, 181
    communities, 173
    knowledge of NSSI, 186
    psychosocial treatment and, 233

interpersonal effectiveness, 53
intervention
  pharmacotherapeutic, 265
  psychotherapeutic interventions, 265
intervention, behavioral, 209
intervention, community-based,
        173–194, 182, 182–183
intervention, Internet-based, 174
intervention, school-based, 204–212,
        207–210
  alliance building, 208
  assessment in schools, 206
  behavioral interventions, 209
  cognitive restructuring, 209–210
  communication skill-building,
        208–209
  contagion, 210–211, 211–212
  no-harm agreements, 210
  parent contact, 206–207
  referral, 205–206
  response to student disclosure, 205

J

Japan, 17
Japanese texts, ancient, references to
        self-injury in, 2
Jolie, Angelina, public admission of
        NSSI, 180
jumping from heights, 10

K

Kaiser Permanente Center for Health
        Research, 233

L

Lader, Wendy, 313, 315
lamotrigine, 282
  borderline personality disorder
        (BPD) and, 283
L-dopa
  self-injurious behavior (SIB) in
        monkeys, 85
learning and behavioral reinforcement
  nonsuicidal self-injury (NSSI), 94
learning and memory
  NSSI in humans and, 89
learning mechanisms, 96
learning theory, 33
Lesch-Nyhan syndrome LNS, 84, 87, 281

dopamine dysregulation, 86
lethal weapons, access to, 197
Life SIGNS: Self-Injury Guidance and
        Network Support, 312–313
limbic-cortical-striatal-thalamic circuit,
        97
Linehan, Marsha, 228, 241
lithium, 282, 295
Living on the Razor's Edge by Selekman,
        242
long-term potentiation, 96
lorazepam, 295
L-type calcium channel activation, self-
        injurious behavior (SIB) and, 88
L-type voltage-gated Ca channel, brain
        and, 87

M

major depressive disorder (MDD), 240,
        253, 293, 296
  adolescent, 242
  family therapy and, 241
mammals, 90
mania, selective serotonin reuptake
        inhibitors (SSRIs) and, 296
Martinson, Deb, 312
Mayans, ancient religion of, 2
media
  nonsuicidal self-injury (NSSI) in, 180
medication, dosing for children and
        adolescents and side effect
        profiles, **297–300**
medication in the treatment of
        self-injury and associated
        disorders, review of evidence
        for, **284–290**
medication in treatment of adolescent
        NSSI, 275–308
  case study, 277–278
  conclusion, 301
  ethical framework, 301
  key points in considering the role of
        medication in youth with NSSI,
        274–278
  levels of evidence for, **279**
  a proposed algorithm for the
        pharmacological treatment of
        adolescent NSSI, 292–301

a review of the evidence for the
        treatment of NSSI, 278–291
medications
    anticonvulsants (mood stabilizers),
        282–283
    benzodiazepines, 282
    clonidine, 282
    monitoring, 296
    "off label," 276
    Omega-3 fatty acids, 283
    overview of psychopharmacological
        trials with NSSI, 283, 291
    side effects, 301
MEDLINE®, 64, 117, 260
mental health agencies, 116
Mental Health Issues Checklist, **157**
mental health services
    access to, 197
    Canadian youth and, 218
Mental Measurements Yearbook
        (MMYB), 117
mental retardation, 64
mesolimbic pathway, 97
message boards, 312
    contagion and, 312
    rules for, 312
met-enkephalin
    self-injurious behavior (SIB), 86
Middle Ages, 3
Modified and combined DBT and
        therapeutic support groups,
        232
modular "common-elements" approach,
        74
monkeys
    nigrostriatral dopamine neurons
        and, 85
    self-injurious behavior (SIB), 85
mood dysregulations, 83
mood instability, 301
mood stabilizers, 295
morphine, 97
motivational interviewing (MI), 222,
        226, 233
    avoiding argumentation, 226
    core principles of, 222
    developing discrepancy, 226
    expressing empathy, 226
    rolling with resistance, 226

Motivations Underlying Self-Harm
        Questionnaire, 130–131
Musafar, Fakir, 3
music, endogenous reward system of
        the brain, 97

N

naltrexone, 98, 281, 295
National Institute of Mental Health
        (NIMH), 117
    guidelines for treatment planning
        and outcomes assessment,
        117–118
National Registry of Evidence-Based
        Programs and Practices, 197
National Self-Harm Network, 269
negative emotions, alleviation of, 53
negative emotions, effective
        management of
    as protective factor, 51
neighborhoods, 174
Nemours Foundations's Center for
        Children's Health Media, 313
neurobiological schema for
        understanding the etiology of
        NSSI, 93, 93–94
    behavioral reinforcement or
        exogenous reward, 94–98
    disordered sensory experiences,
        98–100
    state regulation, 100–102
neurobiology, 90
    nonsuicidal self-injury (NSSI),
        repetitive, 80
    of NSSI and associated assumptions,
        schemata for investigating, **94**
neurodynamics
    emotional state regulation, 80
    NSSI in humans and, 89–90
neurons, 81, 83, 110
    plasticity of and learning, 96
    schemata of neurotransmission, *81*
neuroscience
    habit formation, 80
    of learning, 80
neurotransmitters, 83, 86, 89, 110
    addiction, 81
    impulsivity and, 81
    mood symptoms, 81

psychiatric conditions and, 80
(self-) aggression, 81
neurotransmitters and self-injury, 80,
    81–86, 102, 102–103
    dopamine, 84–85
    opiate, 85–86
    serotonin, 83–84
New York State, survey of secondary
    school nurses and counselors,
    180
N-lipotropin, 86
no-harm agreements, 210
nonspecific vulnerability-stressor model
    (NSVS), 183, 183–185
    teaching of life skills, 183
nonsuicidal self-injury (NSSI), 4, 118,
    264, 295, 317
    abuse and, 96
    addictive features of, 97, 295
    in adolescents, *see* adolescent NSSI
    affect regulation and, 89
    alexithymia and, 101
    algorithm for treatment of, 293–295
    alteration of state and, 101
    among pop icons, 180
    among prison inmates, 37
    anger and, 64
    animal studies and, 80, 88
    anorexia and, 52
    antecedents of, 181
    antidepressants, 92
    antipsychotics, second generation
        (SGAs), 92, 281
    antisuicide function and, 32
    anxiety disorders and, 50, 64
    anxiolytics, 92
    autism and, 117
    automatic negative reinforcement, 35
    automatic positive reinforcement, 35
    automatic reinforcement functions,
        35, 262
    avoiding emotional arousal and, 94
    background, 7–42
    behavioral approaches to decreasing,
        93
    behavioral reinforcement and
        learning, 96
    behavioral reinforcement or
        exogenous reward, 94
    benzodiazepines, 281, 282

beta-blockers and, 92
biopsychological factors and, 74
blood phobia and, 55
borderline personality disorder
    (BPD) and, *see* borderline
    personality disorder (BDP) and
    nonsuicidal self-injury (NSSI)
boundary definition function, 32
bulemia and, 52
childhood abuse and, 80, 91
childhood sexual abuse and, 54–55,
    90–91, 91
childhood traumatic exposure and,
    90
clinical populations and, 80
clinical variables, 52
clinical vs. non-clinical samples, 178
in cognitively intact population, 94,
    102
college students and, 47
in community settings, 47, 173,
    177–178, 180
community-level risk reduction
    strategies, 186
contagion and, 179
co-occurrence and, 50, 59–78, 259
as coping behavior, 180
as a coping mechanism, 174, 175, 269
decreased insurance coverage and,
    259
depression and, 50, 64, 262
developmental context and, 174
developmental disabilities and, 33,
    94, 98, 117
diagnostic populations at risk for, 80
Difficulties in Emotion Regulation
    Scale (DERS) and, 49
difficulty of stopping, 98
disordered sensory experiences, 98
dissociation and, 49
drug treatments for, 92
dysregulation of the endogenous
    opioid system, 175
eating disorders and, 50, 52
emergency room populations, 177
emotion dysregulation and, 49
emotional and personality disorders,
    181
as endogenously rewarding or
    addictive process and, 98

epidemiological studies of, 177
etiological studies of, 90–91
evidence based functional analysis
    of, 160
exogenous rewards and, 94
experiential avoidance model, 32, 33
feelings of abandonment and, 96
functional approach to assessment
    of, 262
functional brain imaging scanner, 98
functional model of, 31–38, 33
functions of, 32, 36–38, 93, 158, 160,
    176
gender and, 23, 52
haloperidol, 281
hostility and, 64
human populations and, 80
impulsivity and, 99
incest and, 238
inpatient assessment of, 264–267
institutional settings and, 179
intellectual disabilities and, 117
intent and, 62, 62–64, 63
Internet and, 181
internet and, 181
Internet and, 311
intervention and prevention issues,
    171–318
intrapsychic constructs and, 93
issues in schools, 310
lack of baseline data, 177
learning and memory, 88
location and, 52
manifestation and, 52
as manipulative behavior in BPD, 94
measurement of, 118
media and, 180, 181
medications and, 283
message boards and, 312
methods and, 52
models for understanding NSSI in
    humans, 88
mood stabilizers, 92
motivations for, 79
multiple methods of self-injury, 262
negatively reinforcing properties of,
    30, 33
neurobiology of, 79, 80, 81, 92, 98, 102,
    276
neurocognitive defects, 99

neurotransmitters and, 83, 86
numbness and, 35
obsessive-compulsive behavior and,
    101
opioid antagonists, 92
as overdetermined behavior, 31
overwhelming sensory stimuli and, 99
pain perception, 55, 98, 101
pharmacological approaches, 93
physical abuse and, 47, 90–91
prevention, 186
promoting knowledge and
    awareness of, 186
protective factors and, 53
psychiatric patients and, 47, 52
psychiatric status and, 50
psychodynamic constructs, 93
psychopharmacological treatment
    for, 278, 280, 283, 292
psychosis and, 177
public health perspective, 176
reasons for, 127
recurrence following discharge, 270
reducing, 54
reinforcement and, 33
relief from overwhelming negative
    emotions, 49
religious affiliation and, 52
repetition compulsion, 96
resources for, 309
risk factors and, 53, 189
screening and, 138–139
self-derogation and, 50
self-report measures, 163
sensory input and, 99
sensory stimulation, 98
severity, 52, 54
sexual abuse and, 47
sexual orientation and, 17
social positive reinforcement (SPR), 35
social reinforcement and, 262
social-negative reinforcement, 35
squeamishness, 55
state regulation and, 99
stimulants, 92
stressful or traumatic situations and,
    99
substance use and, 51, 64
suicide and, 62, **63**, 63–65, 73, 75, 90,
    126, 128, 186, 221, 264, 269, 291

symptom clusters and, 301
symptom-oriented approach for
    treatment, 293–295
tissue damage and, 62
tools used for, 179
trauma (most often sexual abuse), 181
treatment of, 291
U.S. Air Force (USAF) suicide
    prevention program and, 187
verbal expression and, 101
violence of, 176
virtual communities and, 174
warning signs for, **200**
way to quickly alter state, 100
women and, 33
nonsuicidal self-injury (NSSI),
    assessment of, 113–170, 138–139,
    143, 253, 264
Level 2, **160**
nonsuicidal self-injury (NSSI),
    characteristics associated with,
    188
association with friends who self-
    injure, 188
bisexual or questioning sexual
    orientation, 188
disordered eating or other self-
    harming behaviors, 188
history of emotional or personality
    disorders, 188
history of trauma and family
    difficulties, 188
poor coping mechanisms, 188
risk factors and, 188
self-deprecating cognitive appraisal
    style, 188
sleep disorders, 188
strongly negative emotionality, 188
tendency to somatize stress, 188
nonsuicidal self-injury (NSSI), college
    students
eating disorders and, 52
scratching, 52
nonsuicidal self-injury (NSSI), co-
    occurrence and, 75
clinical recommendations, 73
research limitations and future
    directions, 73
research on, 64–65, **66–72**
suicidality among adolescents, 65–73

nonsuicidal self-injury (NSSI), etiology
    of
neurobiological schema for
    understanding, 93
nonsuicidal self-injury (NSSI), functions
    of, 35
four-factor model of, 125
nonsuicidal self-injury (NSSI) in the
    schools
prevention and intervention, 195–215,
    195–216
nonsuicidal self-injury (NSSI),
    neuroscientific investigation
    of, 102
behavioral reinforcement or
    exogenous reward, 102
disordered sensory experiences, 102
endogenous reward-addiction, 102
state regulation and, 102
nonsuicidal self-injury (NSSI)
    prevention efforts
community level, 174
nonsuicidal self-injury (NSSI),
    repetitive, 80, 92
neurobiological underpinnings of, 81
as risk factor for suicide attempts, 91
suicidal behavior and, 65
nonsuicidal self-injury (NSSI), theories
    of, 32
affect regulation model, 32
boundaries model, 32
dissociation model, 32
North America, 64
NSSI, selective prevention approach,
    188, 296
emotion regulation training, 183
individuals considered high risk due
    to biological psychological and
    socio-cultural factors, 183
nonsymptomatic individuals, 183
reducing help-seeking stigmas, 183
target risk factors believed to
    predispose individuals to the
    disorder, 183
NSSI in humans, models for
    understanding, 89–90
learning and memory, 89
neurodynamics, 89–90
numbness, 35

O

obsessive-compulsive behavior, 102, 219, 220
  dysphoric state of anxiety and, 101
  nonsuicidal self-injury (NSSI), 100
obsessive-compulsive behavior (OCD)
  in children, 280
obsessive-compulsive disorder (OCD), 296
olanzapine, 281
Olmecas, ancient religion of, 2
Omega-3 fatty acids, 283, 291
  ethyl-eicosapentaenoic (E-EPA), 283
  randomized controlled trials (RCTs), 283
one allelic variant of the G protein beta 3
  nonsuicidal self-injury (NSSI) and, 92
opiate, 85–86, 88
"opiate tone"
  decreased pain perception, 86
opiate-agonists, 295
opiates
  endogenous reward system of the brain, 97
  neuronal projections to areas of the brain, *82*
opiods, 83
opioid agonist, 281
opioid antagonism
  naltrexone, 86
opioid receptor subtypes (κ, μ, and δ), 85
opioid signaling pathway, 85
  developmentally delayed SIB population, 85
  self-injurious behavior (SIB) and, 86
opioid system, 281–282
oppositional defiant disorder, 221
orbital and medial front l cortices, 97
Ottawa Self-Injury Inventory (OSI), 129–130, 163
  functions (OSI-F), 163, *164–166*
outpatient samples
  co-occurrence and, 64
  suicidal acts and, 65
  suicidal ideation, 65
oxacarbazepine, 282

P

pain perception
  decreased, 100
  tolerance for, 85
pain perception, alteration of
  opioid signaling pathway, 85–86
pain perception system
  nonsuicidal self-injury (NSSI) and, 92
pain sensitivity, diminished
  differences in brain activity and, 91
pain threshold
  high, 91
parasuicide, 4
parent contact, 206–207
Parent-Adolescent Communication Scale, 238
parental difficulties
  impact on adolescent well-being, 248
parental factors, 247–248
parental functioning, 247–248
parent-child incest, 238
parents as effective advocates, 249–250
parents of self-injuring youth, group for, 252–253
  session five: parental modeling, 253
  session four: effect of family history, 253
  session one: introduction, 252
  session six: where to go from here, 253
  session three: family interactions, 252–253
  session two: basic needs and self-care, 252
pathological gambling, 97
Pattison and Kahan, 3
peer support groups
  issues of contagion and, 207
pemoline, 110
pemoline (2-amino-5-phenyl-4-oxazolidinone), 87
  opioid activity and, 87
  serotonin activity and, 87
pemoline-induced SIB, 87
  dopamine and, 87
  in rats, 87
  serotonin and, 87
Personality Diagnostic Questionnaire Revised [PDQ-R], 126
personality disorders, 61

fenfluramine challenges and, 84
pharmacological treatment of
adolescent NSSI, proposed
algorithm for
second generation antipsychotics,
296, 301
selective serotonin reuptake
inhibitors, 296
pharmacotherapeutic, 271
physical injury
evaluation of, 148–149
Physical Injury Assessment, **154–155**
physical nurturance
as basic needs, 246
piercing, 127
pin-scratching, 4
plasma levels of β-endorphin
Adrenocorticotropic Hormone
(ACTH), 86
self-injurious behavior (SIB), 86
play
as basic needs, 246
playing a game for monetary reward
endogenous reward system of the
brain, 97
posterior parietal cortex, 91
posttraumatic stress disorder, 35
Practice Parameters of the AACAP, 295
Prader-Willi syndrome
decreased pain perception and, 98
prevention
approach, 182
culture and, 189–190
development and, 189–190
issues in, 189–190
objective, 182
target, 182
unintended consequences and,
189–190
universal approaches for NSSI,
183–188
universal strategies, 197
prevention, community-based, 173–194,
182, 182–183
prevention, Internet-based, 174
prevention, school-based, 197–202
crisis team preparedness, 198–199
school-based prevention strategies,
197–198
strategies, 197–198

teacher training, 199–202
universal prevention strategies, 197
prevention, targetted approach
focus on individuals with precursors
to behavior of interest, 183
prevention, universal approaches, 187, 189
change group norms and practices, 182
founded on credible evidence or
theory, 182–183
groups and, 182
teaching media literacy, 182–183
unintended consequences and, 187
prevention of HIV/AIDs
approaches used in, 189
previous learning, 83
primate models
sub-aggression, 85
Princess Diana, public admission of
NSSI, 180
print materials
articles for practitioners, 310–311
fact sheets, 311
"pro re nata" PRN medication, 295
problem solving therapy, 222
prolactin, 110
protective factors, 45, 46, 51–52, 54, 92
effective management of negative
emotions, 51–52
resilience and, 46
psychiatric disorders, 162
hospitalization and, 258
increase in, 176
referral for, 163
PsychInfo, 260
psychoeducation about NSSI, 221–222,
241, 244, 268–269, 270
for parents and caregivers, **243**
psychoeducation programs, evidence-
based, 269
Psychometric Theory (Nunnally and
Bernstein), 118
psychopharmacological treatment for
NSSI, 276, 280
algorithm for, 292
model for integrating, 291
psychopharmacological trials with
NSSI, 291
overview of, 283
psychosocial interventions for
adolescents, 217–236, 231

current evidence for psychotherapies
  in children and adolescents
  with axis I disorders, 220–221
points for consideration prior to
  initiating treatment, 218–220
psychosocial risk, 92
  protective factors and, 45–58
psychosocial treatments
  internet sites and, 233
*Psychosocial Treatments for Child and
  Adolescent Disorders: Empirically
  Based Strategies for Clinical
  Practice* (Hibbs & Jensen), 74
psychosocial variables
  clinical applications of, 52
psychotherapeutic approaches, 92
psychotherapies in children and
  adolescents with axis I
  disorders
  cognitive behavioral therapy (CBT),
    226–228
  combined group therapies, 229, 231
  crisis intervention and problem
    solving therapy, 222
  current evidence for, 220–221
  dialectical behavior therapy, 228–229
  family therapy, 231
  motivational interviewing, 222, 226
  psychoeducation, 221–222
psychotic disorder, 293
psychotic individuals
  nonsuicidal self-injury (NSSI), 99
psychotic symptoms, 163
PsycINFO®, 64, 117
PubMed, 280

Q

Queen's University
  Department of Child and Adolescent
    Psychiatry, 129
Queens/Ottawa Self-Injury
  questionnaire, (OSI), 265
quetiapine, 281

R

randomized controlled trials (RCTs), 282
raphe nuclei, 83
rational emotive therapy (Ellis), 226
receptors, 81, 110

referral, 149, 160, 162, 205–206
  family therapy and, 163
reflective listening, 226
reinforcement, automatic negative, 33,
  35
reinforcement, automatic positive, 35
relaxation, 220
reliability, 118
resilience, 46
  factors in, 197
resource guide for working with youth,
  309–316
  articles for practitioners, 310, 310–311
  books, 314–315
  books for parents and families, 315
  concluding comments, 316
  electronic resources, 311–313
  print materials, 310
resources, electronic, 311–313
  American Self-Harm Clearing
    House, 312
  Life SIGNS: Self-Injury Guidance and
    Network Support, 312–313
  S.A.F.E. Alternatives, 313
  Secret Shame, 313
  SIARI (Self-Injury and Related
    Issues), 313
Ricci, Christina, public admission of
  NSSI, 180
risk and protective factors for NSSI,
  52–53, **53**
  clinical implications, 53–55
risk factors, 45–46, 47–51, 54, 54–55
  childhood environment and
    adversities, 47–50
  psychiatric status, 50–51
risperidone, 281
rodent models, sub-aggression, 85
Rogers, Carl, 226
Roman texts, ancient
  references to self-injury and, 2
rostral group
  neuron clusters, 83

S

S.A.F.E. Alternatives, 313
schizophrenia, 64
school-based professionals, 197
  referrals and, 199

schools
 crisis teams, 199
 response protocol, 198, 202–204, **203**
schools, secondary, 174
SCOPUS®, 117
scraping skin, 11
scratching, 52
screening measures, brief, 133
secondary school nurses and
   counselors, survey of, 179
Secret Shame, 313
selective (or targeted) prevention
   approaches for NSSI, 188–189
selective serotonin reuptake inhibitors
   (SSRIs), 280, 295
 cognitive behavioral therapy (CBT)
   and, 296
 fluoxetine, 296
 major depressive disorder (MDD),
   296
 non-OCD anxiety disorder, 296
 obsessive-compulsive disorder
   (OCD) and, 296
 suicide and, 293, 295, 296
 treatment of NSSI, 280, 293
 warnings from EMEA and, 296
 warnings from FDA and, 296
Self Mutilation (Ross and McKay), 3
Self-Abuse Finally Ends (S.A.F.E.), 314
self-aggression, 83
 cerebrospinal fluid (CSF) levels of
   5-HIAA, 84
Self-Assessment Sheet (SAS), 158, *159*
self-biting behavior, 85
self-carving, 4
self-castration, 80
self-cutting, 4
self-derogation, 50
self-destructive behaviors, 179, 228
self-directed anger, 50
self-flagellation, 3
self-harm
 definition of, 10
 deliberate, 4
Self-Harm Behavior Questionnaire
   (SHBQ), 128
Self-Harm Inventory (SHI), 125, 125–126
 borderline personality disorder
   (BPD) and, 126
Self-Harm Survey, 130

motivations and, 130–131
self-harming adolescents
 working with families of, 242
self-harming behavior, 280
*Self-Help Books on Deliberate Self-Harm
   (article)*, 269
self-hitting, 4, 52
self-injurers
 eating disorders and, 51
self-injuring adolescents
 family therapy for, 241
self-injurious behavior (SIB), 4, 24, 30, 59,
   80, 86, 90, 102, 130, 158, 317
 addictive nature of, 85
 adolescents and, 137
 adults and, 61, 137
 age and, 11, 22
 alexithymia and, 49
 alterations in cerebral dopamine and,
   84
 in animals, 86, 88, 102
 assessment of, 73
 β-endorphin and, 86
 biopsychosocial model for, **146**
 borderline personality disorder
   (BPD) and, 61
 calcium (Ca) channel agonists, 87, 88
 Caucasian youth and, 23
 clinical vignettes, 30–31
 community sample studies, 17
 contagion and, 137
 continuum of severity, 52
 definitions and measurement issues,
   10–12
 determining reason for, 137–138
 in a developmental context, 174–177
 developmental psychopathology of,
   238
 dopamine and, 84, 87
 dopaminergic signaling pathway
   and, 85, 280
 early separation from parents and, 47
 effect on physiology, 100
 emotional neglect and, 47, 238
 etiology of, 43–110
 family and, 47
 family environment and, 47
 family violence and, 47
 gay and lesbian youth and, 23
 gender and, 11, 13, 17

genetics in animal studies, 88
historical and social-cultural
    considerations of, 2–3
implications for practitioners, 23–24
intervention and prevention in the
    community, 173–195
in Japan, 17
kinds of, 80
low self-esteem and, 50
in macaque monkeys, 88
measures of (overview), **119–123**
neglect and, 47
neurobiological perspectives, 79–110
N-lipotropin, 86
in nondevelopmentally delayed
    human beings, 91
nonsocially sanctioned, 3
opioid signaling pathway and, 85
in patient population and, 86
pemoline model of, 87
personality disorders and, 17
physical abuse and, 238
physiology and, 100
prevalence studies: the findings,
    12–22, 22, 23
primate model of, 88
reducing, 219
repetitive, 11
rodent studies and, 87–88
sample selection, 12
setting issues, 12
sexual abuse and, 238
shared, 209
socially sanctioned, 3
suicide and, 118
tissue damage and, 52
types of, 92
Self-Injurious Thoughts and Behaviors
    Interview (SITBI), 132
    nonsuicidal self-injury (NSSI),
        132–133
    suicide, 132, 133
self-injury, adolescent
    brief screening measures, 133
    comprehensive baseline assessment,
        137
    determining reason for self-injury,
        137–138
    measure selection for, 133
self-injury, animal studies of, 88

rodent studies and, 88
rodents and, 87
self-injury, functions of
    measures to identify, 137
self-injury, information about
    Internet and, 249
    libraries and, 249
self-injury, measures to identity
        functions of, 137–138
self-injury, types of, 127
    body alteration, 127
    failure to care for self, 127
    indirect self-harm, 127
    overt self-injury, 127
Self-Injury and Related Issues (Web
        site), 269
self-injury checklists, 11
Self-Injury Implicit Association Test, 139
self-injury in humans, etiological
        studies of, 91–92
    borderline personality disorder, 91
    childhood abuse, 91
self-injury in humans, treatment
        studies, 92–93
    neurobiological schema for
        understanding the etiology of
        NSSI, 93–94
self-injury in youth
    effective practice, 111–318
Self-Injury Inventory (SII), 124
self-injury message board, 176
Self-Injury Motivation Scale II (SIMS-II),
        126–127
self-injury norms, opportunities,
        reinforcement, and antecedents
    in community settings, 180–181
Self-Injury Questionnaire (SIQ), 127–128
    adult clinical sample and, 127
self-injury subscale, 124
self-injury today
    psychosocial risk and protective
        factors, 45–58
    review of population and clinical
        studies in adolescents, 9–28
Self-injury: You are NOT the only one
        (formerly Secret Shame) web
        site, 269
"Self-Insurers Bill of Rights," 312
self-mutilation, 30
    practices, 2

subscale, 124
self-poisoning, 10
"self-protection contract," 219
self-punishment, 31, 50
self-report measures, 115, 118
   Deliberate Self-Harm Inventory
      (DSHI), 128–129
   Motivations Underlying Self-Harm
      Questionnaire, 130–131
   Ottawa Self-Injury Inventory (OSI),
      129–130
   Self-Harm Behavior Questionnaire
      (SHBQ), 128
   Self-Harm Inventory (SHI), 125–126
   Self-Harm Survey, 130
   Self-Injury Inventory (SII), 124
   Self-Injury Motivation Scale II (SIMS-
      II), 126–127
   Self-Injury Questionnaire (SIQ),
      127–128
   treatment plans and, 130
self-tattooing, 11
sense perception, abnormal
   borderline personality disorder, 91
   nonsuicidal self-injury (NSSI), 91
sensory deprivation, 98
sensory experiences, disordered,
      98–100, 99
   nonsuicidal self-injury (NSSI), 98
seratonin systems, 85
serotonergic neurons, 83
serotonergic system, 280–281
serotonic-norepinephrine, 280
serotonin
   neuronal projections to areas of the
      brain, *82*
serotonin (5-hydroxytryptamine [5-
      HT]), 83, 83–84, 87–88, 88, 102
serotonin hypothesis
   increased self-aggression and, 84
Seventh Heaven
   nonsuicidal self-injury (NSSI) themes
      and scenes in, 180
sexual conflict, 31
sexual orientation, 181
SGAs, 281
"shared care"
   medication management and, 276
skin, erasing, 11
skin-cutting, 51, 80

smoking marijuana, 127
"Snoezelen room," 99
social anxiety disorder, 219
social deprivation, 99
social environments, influence on
      behavior, 179
   facilitating or inhibiting the
      antecedents of the behavior,
      179
   providing or limiting opportunities
      to engage in the behavior, 179
   shaping of norms, 179
   social (re)enforcement of behaviors,
      179
social epidemiology, 179
   framework, 181
social isolation, 181
social negative reinforcement, 35
social norms, 186
social positive reinforcement (SPR), 35
Socratic method of questioning and, 227
SOS (Signs of Suicide) program, 198
   middle schools and, 198
spiritual communication
   as basic needs, 246
state changes
   neurodynamics of, 90
state regulation and, 100
   affect regulation and, 100
stress hormones
   self-injury and, 100
structured clinical interviews, 263, 271
structured interviews, 74, 130
   Self-Injurious Thoughts and
      Behaviors Interview (SITBI),
      132, 132–133
   Suicide Attempt Self-Injury
      Interview (SASII), 131–132
student disclosure, response to, 205
substance abuse, 37
substance disorders
   nonsuicidal self-injury (NSSI), 51
   self-injury and, 51
substance P, 110
   nonsuicidal self-injury (NSSI) and, 92
suggestions for reducing contagion of
      NSSI, **212**
suggestions for teachers: helping youth
      who self-injure, **201**
suicidal behavior

interventions and, 74
suicidal ideation, 63
suicidal self-injury, 64
    nonsuicidal self-injury (NSSI) and
        co-occurrence, 62
suicidality, 181, 186, 264
    family intactness and, 239
    history of, 74
    treatment of, 74
suicide, 62, 92
Suicide Attempt Self-Injury Interview
    (SASII), 131–132
suicide attempts, 4, 45, 65, 74, 83
suicide ideation and attempts
    past, 263
suicide prevention programs, 183
suicide risk assessment, 148, 149,
    152–153
"summary key," 163
Summary Key for the Ottawa Self-
    Injury Inventory Functions
    (OSI-F), **167–168**
Summary of DBT Skill Modules, **230**
summary of grades of
    recommendations, **279**
synapse, 110
synaptic cleft, 81, 110
synaptic plasticity
    learning and, 96

T

T allele of the G protein beta-3
    childhood sexual abuse and, 92
    nonsuicidal self-injury (NSSI) and
        co-occurrence, 92
tardive dyskinesia, 281
tattooing, 4, 127
TeenScreen Program, 198
tension, 301
*The Scarred Soul: Understanding and
    Ending Self-Inflicted Violence*, 269
Therapies for Self-Injury or Self-Harm:
    Main Goals and Components
    of Interventions, **223–225**
therapists, 54
therapy, interpersonal, 220
thyroid disease, 293
topiramate, 282

borderline personality disorder
    (BPD) and, 283
transactional individual-environment
    relationship, 228
Treatment of Childhood Disorders (Mash &
    Barkley), 74
treatment of NSSI
    dopaminergic system, 281
    evidence for, 278–291
    opioid system, 281–282
    other medications, 282, 291
    planning, 38, 38–39
    serotonergic system, 280–281
triage, 143
"trigger log," 209
tryptophan, 83
Turkey
    self-injury in, 17

U

United Kingdom
    National Institute for Health and
        Clinical Excellence guidelines,
        295
    self-harm inventory, 22
United States, 278
    hospitalization and, 258
    New Freedom Commission on
        Mental Health, 258
unprotected sex, 127
U.S. Air Force (USAF)
    community gatekeepers, 185
    Eleven Initiatives, 186
    Suicide Prevention Program, 185,
        186, 187
U.S. managed health care cuts, 268
U.S. Substance Abuse Mental Health
    Services Administration
    (SAMHSA), 197

V

viewing attractive faces
    endogenous reward system of the
        brain, 97
violence
    media and, 181
violent offenders
    cerebrospinal fluid (CSF) levels of
        5-HIAA, 84

virtual communities
  influence in off-line behavior, 181

W

Walsh, Barent, 144
  dissertation on nonsuicidal self-injury (NSSI), 177
  Treating Self-Injury, 219
"Werther" effect
  increased incidence of suicide and, 187
Will and Grace
  nonsuicidal self-injury (NSSI) themes and scenes in, 180

World Health Organization, 280
"wrist-cutter syndrome," 3

Y

youth programs, 174
YouTube, 180

Z

Zen Buddhist ideas, 228
ziprasidone, 281, 296